THE END OF DIALOGUE IN ANTIQUITY

'Dialogue' was invented as a written form in democratic Athens and made a celebrated and popular literary and philosophical style by Plato. Yet it almost completely disappeared in the Christian empire of late antiquity. This book, the first general and systematic study of the genre in antiquity, asks: who wrote dialogues and why? Why did dialogue no longer attract writers in the later period in the same way? Investigating dialogue goes to the heart of the central issues of power, authority, openness and playfulness in changing cultural contexts. This book analyses the relationship between literary form and cultural authority in a new and exciting way, and encourages closer reflection about the purpose of dialogue in its wider social, cultural and religious contexts in today's world.

SIMON GOLDHILL is Professor of Greek at the University of Cambridge and a Fellow of King's College. He has published widely on many aspects of Greek literature, including *Reading Greek Tragedy* (1986), *Foucault's Virginity* (1995), *Who Needs Greek?* (2002) and *How to Stage Greek Tragedy Today* (2007). He is in demand as a lecturer all over the world and is a regular broadcaster on radio and television.

THE END OF DIALOGUE
IN ANTIQUITY

EDITED BY
SIMON GOLDHILL

CAMBRIDGE UNIVERSITY PRESS
Cambridge, New York, Melbourne, Madrid, Cape Town, Singapore, São Paulo, Delhi

Cambridge University Press
The Edinburgh Building, Cambridge CB2 8RU, UK

Published in the United States of America by Cambridge University Press, New York

www.cambridge.org
Information on this title: www.cambridge.org/9780521887748

First published 2008

Printed in the United Kingdom at the University Press, Cambridge

A catalogue record for this publication is available from the British Library

Library of Congress Cataloguing in Publication data
The end of dialogue in antiquity / ed. Simon Goldhill.
p.   cm.
Includes bibliographical references and index.
ISBN 978-0-521-88774-8
1. Dialectic.   2. Dialogue.   3. Philosophy, Ancient.   4. Church history.   5. Dialogue – Religious
aspects.   I. Goldhill, Simon.   II. Title.
B105.D48E53   2008
809′.926–dc22
2008040781

ISBN 978-0-521-88774-8 hardback

Contents

Notes on Contributors   *page* vii

Introduction: Why don't Christians do dialogue?
Simon Goldhill   1

PART I   CLASSICAL MODELS   13

1   Fictions of dialogue in Thucydides
    Emily Greenwood   15

2   The beginnings of dialogue: Socratic discourses
    and fourth-century prose
    Andrew Ford   29

3   Plato's dialogues and a common rationale
    for dialogue form
    Alex Long   45

PART II   EMPIRE MODELS   61

4   Ciceronian dialogue
    Malcolm Schofield   63

5   Sympotic dialogue in the first to fifth centuries CE
    Jason König   85

PART III   CHRISTIANITY AND THE THEOLOGICAL
            IMPERATIVE   115

6   Can we talk? Augustine and the possibility of dialogue
    Gillian Clark   117

v

7 'Let's (not) talk about it': Augustine and the control
   of epistolary dialogue
   Richard Miles   135

PART IV CHRISTIANITY AND THE SOCIAL IMPERATIVE   149

8 Christians, dialogues and patterns of sociability
   in late antiquity
   Richard Lim   151

9 Boethius, Gregory the Great and the Christian 'afterlife'
   of classical dialogue
   Kate Cooper and Matthew Dal Santo   173

PART V JUDAISM AND THE LIMITS OF DIALOGUE   191

10 No dialogue at the symposium? Conviviality in Ben Sira
    and the Palestinian Talmud
    Seth Schwartz   193

11 Dialectic and divination in the Talmud
    Daniel Boyarin   217

Bibliography   242
Index   263

Notes on Contributors

DANIEL BOYARIN is Professor of Rabbinics at Berkeley, California, is one of the best-known figures in Jewish studies, particularly for his use of modern theory with ancient texts. His numerous books include *Midrash and Intertextuality* (1990); *Carnal Israel* (1993); *Paul: a Radical Jew* (1997); *Border Lines* (2004), which have become standards of the modern academy.

GILLIAN CLARK is Professor of Ancient History at Bristol and a renowned scholar of the philosophy and history of late antiquity and of Augustine in particular: she published *Augustine: The Confessions* (1993) and a commentary on the first four books of the *Confessions* (1995). *Women in Late Antiquity: Pagan and Christian Life Styles* and *Christianity and Roman Society* were both published in 2004.

KATE COOPER is Lecturer in Theology at Manchester. Her first book, *The Virgin and The Bride* (1996), was on interrelations between classical and Christian literature around the topic of virginity. Her most recent book, *The Fall of the Roman Household*, was published in 2007.

MATTHEW DAL SANTO is a Junior Research Fellow in History at Trinity College, Cambridge.

ANDREW FORD is Professor of Greek at Princeton, and an expert on the development of Greek genres and literary culture in archaic and classical Greece. His book *The Origins of Criticism: Literary Culture and Poetic Theory in Classical Greece* on the invention of criticism in the classical city was one of *Choice*'s outstanding academic books of 2003.

SIMON GOLDHILL is Professor of Greek at Cambridge University and has published very widely on Greek literature. His most recent books are *Who Needs Greece?* (2002); *The Temple of Jerusalem* (2004); *Love, Sex and Tragedy* (2004); *How to Stage Greek Tragedy Today* (2007); and *Jerusalem, City of Longing* (2008).

EMILY GREENWOOD is Lecturer in Classics at St Andrews. Her first book, *Thucydides and the Shaping of History*, was published in 2006. She has also co-edited two volumes of essays, one on Herodotus, *Reading Herodotus* (2007), and one on the modern reception of Homer, *Homer in the Twentieth Century* (2007).

JASON KÖNIG is Lecturer in Classics at St Andrews. His first book, *Athletics and Literature in the Roman Empire*, was published in 2005. His second book will be on the symposium and its literature in Empire culture.

RICHARD LIM is Professor of History at Smith College. His book *Public Disputation, Power, and Social Order in Late Antiquity* (1995) has become a standard work on the history of late antiquity.

ALEX LONG is now a Lecturer in Classics at St Andrews. His PhD thesis discusses Plato's conception of dialectic and uses of dialogue form.

RICHARD MILES is a fellow of Trinity Hall, Cambridge. He is an expert on late antique culture who is currently writing a book for Penguin on Carthage, following on from his major excavations there. He is the editor of *Constructing Identities in Late Antiquity* (1999).

MALCOLM SCHOFIELD is Professor of Ancient Philosophy at Cambridge. He has worked in many fields of ancient philosophy, and is author of a series of major articles on Cicero's philosophical writings, as well as the seminal *The Presocratic Philosophers* (with G. Kirk and J. Raven) and *The Stoic Idea of the City*. His most recent book is *Plato: Political Philosophy* (2006).

SETH SCHWARTZ is currently Professor of History at the Jewish Theological Seminary in New York. His prize-winning book, *Imperialism and Jewish Society* (2001), is on the cultural interaction of Jews and Empire culture, and he is now finishing a book on ideas of reciprocity in Jewish culture.

Introduction
Why don't Christians do dialogue?

Simon Goldhill

Dialogue is a banner word of contemporary politics, religion and culture.

Politicians claim that they wish to have a dialogue and to listen, and demand that opposed parties open dialogue; interfaith dialogue is held up as the answer to the racial and religious tensions that scar modern urban living; art forms are said to enter into dialogue (with society, with their audience, with artistic principles). At one level, it is no surprise that communities that privilege the term democracy will also demand dialogue. From the invention of democracy in fifth-century Athens, dialogue has been central to the political theory and practice of democracy: it is only after hearing both sides of the question and allowing different views to be expressed, that a vote can properly be held. Dialogue is endemic to democracy, though, as we will see, this is not simply a blithely benign claim: with dialogue comes also a recognition of the necessity of dissent, persuasion (spin) and the repression of minority views. The privileging of dialogue spreads to broader cultural issues, so that it would be extremely hard for any serious religious figure in the West to reject dialogue as a form of doing business. It would be to open oneself to the charge of totalitarianism (or worse). In the intellectual arena, Bakhtin has also made 'the dialogic' a buzz word. It is associated with anti-authoritarian exploration, playfulness and challenge. The dialogic has consequently been taken up as a positive term in a range of disciplines.

All of this makes dialogue a key term in the modern West. But it does not make it an understood term, nor is it an idea that has been treated to an adequate history. This book aims to look seriously at the development of the idea of dialogue in the ancient world, as a way of exploring the deep background of the term and as a way of exploring what the main issues and implications of it are for modern thinking. *The End of Dialogue in Antiquity* looks at the genre of the written dialogue and its relation to social forms of exchange. This enquiry is conducted within the polemical context of suggesting that, with the coming of Christianity as the religion of the Roman Empire, a sea-change occurred in the use of dialogue, and this establishes a crucial template for understanding why dialogue matters so much. The opening term of the book's title, 'The End', is designed to invoke both the *purpose* and the *demise* of ancient dialogue as a literary form and a social privilege. The title of this introduction, 'Why Don't Christians Do Dialogue?', is to put most provocatively one possible history of the genre and practice of dialogue. And the task both of the introduction and of the essays in this volume is to provide the nuance – or the argued disagreement – to make such provocation productive.

There are three crucial frames for the following chapters. The first concerns the history of the literary genre of dialogue. There is a prima facie plausibility to the claim that dialogue as a literary form is integrally related to its genesis in the fifth- and fourth-century BCE culture of democratic Athens. The exchange of staged debate as a form of discourse is privileged in any version of democratic theory. The assembly as the key political institution of the state is predicated on the assumption that different views must be laid open to public scrutiny if the best decision about action is to be reached. This is matched by the law court – and equality before the law is a principle of democracy – where opposed positions are articulated before a jury of citizens. The theatre, another invention of democracy, stages dialogue as a form of civic practical reasoning. When the historian Thucydides writes what is known as the Melian Dialogue – where the speeches of the ambassadors from Melos and the Athenian negotiators are represented as if they are a drama script, without comment or analysis from the historian – he appears to be representing the political exchanges of a specific moment in a specific institution of democracy. History writing cannot ever fully hide its mediation, but here, more vividly than in even the most dramatic historical narrative, the historian seems to hide behind the appearance of the unmediated report of an actual dialogue, dialogue as the motive force of democratic negotiation, dialogue placed at the centre of democratic power.

What is more, the connection between dialogue and democracy has been set at the forefront of some of the most exciting contemporary work on Athenian culture. Geoffrey Lloyd famously made democratic dialogue one of the conditions of possibility for the Greek enlightenment in his *Revolutions of Wisdom*.[1] For Lloyd, the historical, political conditions of democratic dialogue encouraged the development of self-conscious reflection – second-order questions, a metadiscursive expectation – which took medicine (which every society knows) towards the theory of medicine, and politics (which

---

[1] Lloyd (1987).

every society knows) towards political theory. And it is the drive towards theory above all that distinguishes, for Lloyd, the Greek enlightenment. Similarly, Josiah Ober's investigation of the political rhetoric of the classical city, one of the great bodies of evidence for democratic ideology, repeatedly emphasises the importance of the dialogue between the elite and the masses in the institutions of the city, where speech-making and speech-evaluating were basic to democratic practice.[2] In a similar light, contemporary attempts to understand the social role of Athenian theatre, which have followed on from the ground-breaking work of Jean-Pierre Vernant and Pierre Vidal-Naquet, have stressed not merely that drama stages dialogue, but also that theatre is a medium for introducing dialogue into social values: to open cherished values to the questioning of multiple understandings, multiple opinions.[3] From all these points of view, not only do dialogue and democracy have an absolutely integral link, but the literary forms prevalent in democracy reflect this powerfully.

Because of this critical understanding of the inherent link between democracy and dialogue, it is immediately fascinating that the single figure most evidently associated with the invention of the literary form of the dialogue, Plato, should be someone deeply opposed to democracy as a political system, and that Plato's teacher and star of so many of his dialogues, Socrates, should be someone executed by democracy, executed indeed at least partly because of how he did dialogue. At one level, it would be easy to say that Plato's dialogues reflect the dialogues Socrates held around the city: chatting in the gym, the symposium, the market-place. But Plato also develops the most extended theoretical expression of how discursive forms affect the nature of argument; develops the most extended critique of democracy, not least for allowing the wrong people a determinative voice; and develops the most thorough-going analysis of the role of public speech as a political force in the state. The genre of dialogue comes into being fully formed with a self-reflective, highly sophisticated, brilliantly articulated and performed consideration of its own nature as genre and as practice. A good deal of modern philosophical debate on Plato is motivated precisely by the tension in Platonic writing between the drive towards ideal, normative, authoritative knowledge and the slipperiness and playfulness of dialogue as a means of expression.[4]

---

[2] Ober (1989). See also Hesk (2000).
[3] Vernant and Vidal-Naquet (1988); see also, for example, Goldhill (1986); Halperin, Winkler and Zeitlin (1990).
[4] See Griswold (1988); Morgan (2000); Nightingale (1995); Vlastos (1991); and Long in this volume (with further bibliography).

The first three essays in this volume look at the genesis of the literary form of the dialogue in the classical city of Athens, and each is concerned to move away from over-simplified models which assert that dialogue is by definition democratic, open and easily explained as a historical phenomenon. Together, they interrogate the relationship between Plato's writing and other contemporary writing, and show both how many different explanations of the dialogue form there are already in Plato himself, and how complex the recognition of dialogue as a form can be. This provides a necessary hesitation at the start of the project. It is regrettably common in comparative endeavours to assume that there is a clear and simple beginning from which complexity and sophistication is derived. ('In Greece/ Homer/archaic period … but in modern days/now/ in Rome/Britain things are much more complex …') There is no uncomplicated origin for the dialogue as genre; it is always already a conflicted, self-conscious and multiple form.

The history of the genre goes on, of course. Hellenistic culture continued to develop the dialogue form. It was associated not only with philosophy, from its privileged Platonic beginnings, but also with the symposium (and the importance of Plato's *Symposium* creates a philosophical and intellectual genealogy to complement the social role of sympotic performance).[5] The symposium was a fundamental aspect of Greek self-definition, a cultural ritual through which the values of the group were enacted, displayed, discussed. Sympotic dialogues, as a literary form, asked questions about how to behave at a symposium, about the knowledge of the group, about cultural identity. Reading (and writing) sympotic dialogues offers a reflective version of the construction of this cultural identity, as attending the symposium was a performance of a citizen's cultural identity. Sympotic literature, especially when the Roman Empire becomes the dominant political force in the Mediterranean, is heavily invested in projecting and promoting a sense of the long past of Greek culture as formative for the contemporary citizen. The dialogue, despite any expectations of spontaneity or casualness, is profoundly aware of its own history. From Plutarch to Athenaeus to Macrobius, however, this literature has rarely attracted modern critical attention or praise. This dismissiveness is now changing, as the significance of the genre for understanding Greek culture in the Roman Empire is being re-evaluated.[6]

---

[5] See Henderson (2000); Hunter (2004).
[6] See Konig in this volume, with bibliography; Braund and Wilkins (2000) is paradigmatic of the attempt to recoup an undervalued sympotic text; see also Preston (2001).

Roman culture for its part adopted the dialogue form especially after it had conquered Greece itself. Just as Roman comedy closely translates and adapts Greek dramatic models, particularly Menander, so Cicero rewrites Greek philosophy in a Roman form in his dialogues. What we see in Roman dialogue is a doubled vision: dialogue is also a way of negotiating a space between cultures and traditions, a way of expressing Roman intellectual life in and against Greek models. Cicero has often been denigrated as failing to live up to the great model of Plato – heavy-handed, literal, formal, undramatic, as opposed to elegant, ironic, vivid. The essays in Part II of this book look at the role of the sympotic and Ciceronian philosophical dialogue in later Greek and Latin, and finds not only an important and underappreciated intellectual openness in Cicero, but also a significant cultural and intellectual role for sympotic dialogues within the normative structures of society. This interest in the connection between the literary dialogue and cultural forms of exchange will be picked up later in this book.

Early Christianity, however, appears to have little time for dialogue. Augustine, although he did write some short dialogues early in his career, explicitly rejects the form for serious theological thinking, and all his major works are in treatise form, even when there are obvious antecedents in Platonic or Ciceronian prose.[7] The dialogue is only very rarely evidenced as a form for normative Christian writing, despite the strategic place of conversion and theological discussion in Christian communities. The catechism and other question-and-answer structures are not in any significant sense a dialogue: they are forms of exchange to aid controlled learning and to produce certain, fixed responses. (Nor, in general, is there Christian drama, until at least much later.) The exceptions to this general case tend to support it rather than to construct a counter-case. The second-century Syrian Christian Methodius writes a *Symposium*, where a group of virgins 'discuss' the benefits of virginity: it is clearly modelled on Plato as well as the sympotic tradition and aims to replace the Platonic image of desire with a Christian repression of desire. But in the piece, each virgin gives a set speech, and they end by singing hymns together: it is a dialogue without conversation. It inevitably – and proudly – lacks the dangerous thrill of a drunken Alcibiades crashing into the party, flute girl on each arm, to relate his failed attempt to seduce Socrates.

Many a saint's life ends with a martyrdom, where the saint gets to deliver a brilliant rejoinder to his/her torturer. This looks back to the long tradition of philosophical *chreiai* (the *bon mots* of the wise): it is a conversation in that

---

[7] See Clark in this volume.

the saint delivers a put-down to a pagan. But there is never space for an extended dialogue in the martyr text. When there is a longer dialogue between a Christian and an opponent, as in Justin Martyr's 'Dialogue with Trypho', the opponent is canon fodder for the Christian's rhetoric: as Paula Fredriksen puts it, 'talking *at* Trypho' would be a more apt title.[8] The dialogue between competing forces within a soul (*Psychomachia*) allows for mutually exclusive and opposing positions to be expressed; but they are within one person's inner life, and rarely allow evil the attractive threat it is likely to pose in less controlled social circumstances. It is telling to compare, say, Prudentius' *Psychomachia*, from the very end of the fourth century, with the internal debate staged by the character Callirhoe in Chariton's first-century novel *Chaireas and Callirhoe*. Callirhoe imagines a debate between herself, her absent husband and her unborn baby about whether she should allow the baby to live: each gets to make a rhetorical speech, and each gets a vote (II. 11). The husband and child vote for life – so by a majority vote Callirhoe decides to let her baby live. This is internal debate modelled as political institution – a witty, sophisticated and yet moving image of a young woman's doubts and fears in which competing claims create a dialogue in her mind. Prudentius writes a long, narrative poem, which centres on an imagined battle between virtues and vices, where each virtue gets to deliver a speech, like a Homeric warrior on the battlefield, upholding Christian values, before vanquishing the enemy. On the rare occasions when any vice gets a word in, it is only to lament impending and inevitable defeat. It is more like an extended model of the martyr's put-down to his enemies than an exchange. There is no uncertainty, the only questions are rhetorical, and the dominant model is the battlefield boast – where good can only defeat evil, not exchange views.

Mark the Hermit, writing from within the fifth-century monastic community, is paradigmatic of this view of Christian resistance to dialogue. His *Against the Lawyer* does dramatise a dialogue between a monk and a lawyer, which justifies the monk's rounds of prayer and fasting over and against a more worldly existence. 'If you were a philosopher', says the lawyer, 'I would have no qualms; but as it is . . .' (The philosopher might be expected to hold extreme views on deprivation, and, in a dialogue, the turn towards philosophy, however sniffy, is generically motivated as well as marking the agonistic competition between different authoritative discourses for control over a man's soul.) The intense and powerfully argumentative monk duly forces the lawyer to beat a retreat. But the manuscript at this

[8] See Fredriksen (1999).

point falls into question-and-answer format, like a catechistic text. A young monk, worried by his senior's rhetorical flair and by his perhaps precarious hold on the truth and nothing but the truth, asks a sharp question. He is described, fascinatingly, as 'thinking of himself as suffering unjustly, like a martyr'. Being like a martyr is clearly not what is wanted in the monastic community: after his brilliant rhetorical display, the senior monk rubs home a point about humility and lowliness. He demands that the junior monk lie prone on the floor and ask his question from there. Mark the Hermit certainly draws on the forms of dialogue: exchange of view, debate, multiple positions. But it is a text aimed at reinforcing and indeed demanding a strict hierarchical world picture, a single truth, and the physical suppression of any sign of the uppity. This is a dialogue where answering back is not a real possibility.

The dialogue in this way seems to lose much of its generic force. An ideal democracy (if such an imaginary being is not inimical to democracy in itself) would still demand difference of opinion. Would an ideal Christian community find difference of opinion unwelcome or even dangerous? Although Socrates provides one model for Christian asceticism and commitment to belief, the Trappist monk (say) is as far from Socrates chatting on the street as you can get.

This image of Christianity moving towards hierarchy, with a commitment to certainty and the repression of difference ('heresy') as it increases its power as the religion of Empire, is not attractive to most modern Christians. The third and fourth parts of this book take a close look at it. The third part looks in detail at Augustine, as a major and exemplary figure of the fourth- and fifth-century Church. While recognising Augustine's resistance to certain types of dialogue, and to certain assumptions that modern supporters of the value of dialogue would care to make, this part aims to provide a more sensitive account of Augustine's position as a bishop in the Church's power structures and a recognition of the role of letters in the scattered Christian communities. It still leaves us with an image of an authoritarian Augustine, but it sets his authority in a context that makes it more comprehensible. The fourth part looks at the social place of dialogue and dialogue forms in Christian communities. It finds that there are more demonstrations of genuine exchange, and more possibilities of debate, than the strong model outlined above would seem to allow. One answer to the question of why Christians didn't do dialogue is to note that actually they did: in some later texts, and in different institutional structures, debate and the generous, sincere and engaged exchange of views could also be found. Whether this is enough to dislodge the model of increasing resistance to dialogue in the name of orthodoxy's resistance to heresy remains to be seen.

The Talmud, however, which develops orally and is written down in around the sixth century CE, is full of dialogues – every Mishnaic pronouncement is followed by discussion, often between named rabbis, of the questions, problems and implications raised by it. For some modern critics, the Talmud demonstrates a truly dialogic spirit – a polyvalence and playfulness to set against the drive towards orthodoxy's certainties.[9] Like all monotheistic religions, Judaism certainly has its extreme statements of principle and its acts of violent exclusion. Yet, it has been argued, the Jewish texts are always qualified by the regularly vertiginous dialogue of conflicting opinion in the Talmud. Should the Talmud be set against Christianity's orthodoxy as a counter-model of interpretative practice? The final section of the book considers the role of Jewish thinking on reciprocal exchange, and the normative force of the Talmud as a dialogic text. The Talmud and Christian normative theological writings develop alongside one another, with different strategies of recognition and mis-recognition of each other. It is important to consider what the differences are between Jewish and Christian writing in terms of dialogue, and, most importantly, how these differences may affect the structures of power, authority and normative value. Is dialogue only possible for the marginal? Can dialogue change the authoritarian commitments of monotheistic religion?

What this brief account of dialogue as a genre reveals immediately is that there is always more involved than discrete issues of literary history. We are also repeatedly taken up with how such literary history relates to structures of authority, power, and institutionalised religion and politics. This is the first book, we believe, to have explored this long history of dialogue, and to have looked in particular at its relative absence in Christianity. What is it about the expression of conversation in the form of dialogue that makes it integral to democracy and difficult for early Christianity? The first aim of this project is to provide a foundation to explore these questions – and we hope to stimulate further work in these and later periods.

This relation between a history of a genre and the political and social history of the ancient world provides, then, the first frame for the essays that follow. The second and third frames emerge from what has already been said, and each can be expressed more briefly. Bakhtin, despite the obscurity in which he lived his life, now that his writings have been translated (first into French and then English), has become a major intellectual figure in the

---

[9] Instrumental in this view was Handelman (1982); see also Boyarin (1990).

West; and it would be impossible to write about dialogue in an informed way without engaging with his thought. This is not the place for a full exposition of Bakhtin's work, which has been very well treated by modern scholarship – including its relation to ancient texts, which play such an important role for his view of the past.[10] For classicists, Bakhtin's use of terms such as 'novel' and 'epic' can be frustrating, since they rarely relate closely to contemporary understanding of the ancient use of the terms as generic markers or as literary form. The same is true of dialogue. Bakhtin rarely writes with any detailed attention on ancient dialogues, for all that he privileges ancient history and the term dialogue. Plato is barely discussed in *The Dialogic Imagination*, and the history of dialogue as a form passes unmentioned. From Bakhtin, 'the dialogic' has entered contemporary discourse as a term to encapsulate the subversive, anti-authoritarian potential of language to undercut the claim to univocality typical of totalitarian government and of orthodoxy as a principle. 'The dialogic' expresses the ludic power that is released when multiple viewpoints inter-react. Yet it is quite unclear how dialogic Bakhtin found ancient dialogue.

It was Karl Popper who most influentially outed Plato as a theorist for the great totalitarian systems of Hitler's Germany and Stalin's Soviet Union.[11] For Popper, Plato's political thought emerges as an enemy of the open society, as he termed it, and as an enemy of Socrates himself, his teacher. For Popper, Plato constantly fights against what Bakhtin would recognise as the dialogic. Yet Plato's texts remain a more vexing test-case for Bakhtin and for the politics of reading than Popper allows. The *Republic* and the *Laws* can appear as handbooks for the closed society, and have been taken as such by governments in practice as well as by political theorists. But Socrates' irony, subversiveness and challenge to normative authority are known primarily through Plato's representation. How can the representation of the ironic and subversive Socrates, the playfulness or instability of dialogue form, and the idealist and authoritarian views of Plato all be brought together? How do ancient dialogues relate to Bakhtin's idea of the dialogic? Or to put the question in its most general form: To what degree can dialogues escape their own dialogic potential?

Each essay in this volume is concerned with issues of openness of meaning, of authority and playfulness, of the relation between texts and social forms. As such the volume makes a contribution to thinking through the relationship between Bakhtin's notion of the dialogic and the genre of

---

[10] From a huge bibliography, see especially Holquist (1990); Emerson (1997); Möllendorf (1995).
[11] See Popper (1945); also Lane (2001).

ancient dialogue, and the broadest questions about authority and writing
that such a problematic evokes.

This leads on to the third frame of reference. We intend that this book
will contribute energetically to an ongoing debate about authority and
difference, and, more specifically, about religious authority and dissent.
The historiography in this book is not teleological (despite the title of the
volume). Its hazard is that one of the best ways to understand the religious
discourse of early Christianity and Judaism is to approach it through the
form and practice of dialogue, and, in turn, one of the best ways to understand what is at stake in the ancient tradition of dialogue is to approach it
from the perspective of how religious writers later appropriated, resisted and
manipulated the form. Its historiography is in this sense comparativist (and
the range of topics covered, along with the structure of the book, is designed
to help this comparative strategy). The sense of historical change in the
treatment of dialogue is necessarily framed by evident intellectual continuities between the classical city and the Christian Empire – the role of
Neo-Platonism in Christianity, and, more generally, the dual resistance to
and adoption of ancient philosophical methods and questions in Jewish and
Christian writings; the role of rhetoric; the role of education through
Homer and other classical sources. And also by the equally evident social
continuities – both Christian and Jewish communities are formed within
Greco-Roman culture, and the deep influences of these dominant social
structures are strongly marked in ritual, liturgy and in patterns and expectations of behaviour. (Christians and Jews were not always as different from
pagans as all sides colluded in believing.) But the problems that dialogue
raises for the Church and for the Rabbis – about authority, about the place
of certainty and doubt, about control and freedom of expression – have not
gone away, and indeed may seem as pressing in the twenty-first century as
ever before. A naive if potent image contrasts the freedom of expression and
the value of dialogue in the democratic, Christian West to the fundamen-
talist control of expression, demand for conformity and aggressive suppression of dissent in the Islamic, dictatorial East. There is a palpable need to
find a more sophisticated, engaging and participatory way to talk about
religious authority, the political process and consent. In a small way, we
hope that this book may show some paths forward towards at least having a
more thorough historical understanding of one of the central terms in any
such discussion, namely, dialogue.

The essays in this volume are each new and were commissioned for it.
A colloquium was held in Cambridge, England, in 2006 where first drafts of
the chapters by Ford, Long, Lim, Boyarin, Schwartz, Konig and Clark were

pre-circulated to seventeen other invited academics. Each paper was then submitted to an hour and a half of discussion by the participants, and each session was led by a respondent. The chapters of Greenwood, Schofield, Cooper and Dal Santo, and Miles grew out of their original brief responses. The book is thus itself the product of three days of intense, committed and sharp dialogue, and each essay has benefited from the criticisms of the participants. I wish to take the opportunity here to thank all those who contributed, and especially Christopher Kelly and James Carleton-Paget, respondents who in the end did not contribute essays to the volume. The colloquium was sponsored by the Cambridge Centre for Arts, Social Sciences and Humanities, under the excellent direction of Mary Jacobus, and by the Classics Faculty of the University of Cambridge, and by King's College Cambridge. They are all thanked warmly for their sponsorship and hospitality.

PART I

Classical models

CHAPTER I

Fictions of dialogue in Thucydides

Emily Greenwood

This chapter arises out of a realisation that was articulated by many at the original colloquium: namely the realisation that the subject of dialogue in the ancient world is richly over-determined and prone to manifold inter-ference. As a test case for thinking 'dialogue' in Greek prose before Plato, I take as my example one of the most famous dialogues in Greek literature: Thucydides' 'Melian dialogue' (*History* 5.85–113). In offering yet another reading of the Melian dialogue,[1] I will suggest that both the dialogue and critical literature on the dialogue illustrate the pitfalls inherent in 'doing dialogue' as a comparative project in the modern academy.

INTERFERING IN DIALOGUE

The first source of interference is a lexical one: in invoking dialogue we invoke a term with a broad semantic range. The *OED* gives two meanings for dialogue: the primary meaning is 'a conversation carried on between two or more persons; a colloquy, talk together' (1a), with the additional shades of meaning 'a verbal interchange of thought … a conversation' (1b) and, in politics, 'discussion or diplomatic contact between the representatives of two nations, groups or the like' (1c).[2] This latter usage yields the general use of dialogue to denote 'valuable or constructive discussion or communica-tion'. This cluster of meanings is further complicated by the secondary meaning of dialogue: (2a) 'a literary work in the form of a conversation between two or more persons', and (2b) 'literary composition of this nature'. These divergent meanings pose challenges for the study of 'dialogue' as a coherent project. Take the widespread, popular usage of 'dialogue' (1c above)

---

[1] The bibliography is extensive: important discussions include Wassermann (1947); Hudson-Williams (1950); Liebeschuetz (1968); Macleod (1983) 52–7; Connor (1984) 147–57; Bosworth (1993); Orwin (1994) 97–117; Morrison (2000); and Price (2001) 195–204.

[2] All definitions taken from the second edition of the *OED* (1989).

as 'valuable or constructive discussion or communication'; in contemporary speech this usage tends to lie dormant in the term 'dialogue', whether consciously intended or not, and this dormant meaning colours the topic of 'dialogue' with a liberal humanitarian ideology. Or take the lexical distinction between 'dialogue' as conversation and as literary form: often these two forms are mutually entailing. Here it is helpful to draw on Mikhail Bakhtin's work on the variety of speech genres.[3] In literature it is obvious that the dialogue form (a 'secondary' or 'complex' speech genre in Bakhtin's typology) is dependent on dialogue as spoken conversation (a 'primary' or 'simple' speech genre). However, Bakhtin argued against a simplistic flow of influence from primary to secondary speech genre, and insisted on the interrelationship between the two.[4] Primary speech genres are precisely that: genres. They presuppose the creative use of discourses, semiotics and stylistic registers. Hence the study of dialogue as literary form can cast light on the phenomenon of dialogue in everyday speech.

The second source of interference is the Platonic dialogues, which include not just the dialogue form, but Platonic dialectic.[5] In terms of generic invention, Thucydides is in some sense 'pre-dialogue', in that he pre-dates the Platonic dialogues, which have shaped our understanding of the literary genre known as the dialogue form. But insofar as Thucydides' *History* features dialogues, as they were later named, and other rhetorical speech genres (e.g. brachylogies, antilogies) that inform the representation of speech in the Platonic corpus, he can be said to be a precursor to Plato. In addition, scholars have observed that Thucydides' treatment of speeches and the abstraction of Thucydidean language are an important model, both positive and negative, for the Platonic dialogues.[6]

The third source of interference will already be apparent in the reference to Bakhtin above. In the humanities, and especially in the study of literature, the study of dialogue cannot escape echoes of Bakhtin's theories of dialogism ('double-voicedness'), according to which both literary language and language in general are characterised by the presence of different and distinct voices in each individual utterance.[7] This double-voicedness is at once a property of all language usage, which necessarily involves the

---

[3] I refer to Bakhtin's essay 'The Problem of Speech Genres' (Bakhtin (2006a) 60–102), written in 1952–3 and first published, in Russian, in 1979. See Bakhtin (2006a) xv.

[4] Bakhtin (2006a) 61–2.

[5] For discussion of the interdependency of dialogue and dialectic, see the discussion of Alex Long, pp. 45–59 below.

[6] Crane (1996) 23; Allison (1997) xiv and 22–3; Price (2001) 198.

[7] I use the plural 'theories' in recognition of the ambiguity that critics have discerned in Bakhtin's writings both about literary dialogism and dialogue as spoken language.

'dialogic orientation of a word among other words' (Bakhtin (2006b) 275), and a property of literary texts, where the dialogue between different words, whether as used in everyday speech or in previous texts, creates potential for the creation of new meanings and explorations of language and experience. In Bakhtin's thought, dialogism helps to explain the relationship between languages that exist in the larger phenomenon of heteroglossia ('differentiated speech') – Bakhtin's term for the diversity of languages that is present in both literary and non-literary language.

In fact, Bakhtin's concepts of dialogism and heteroglossia, or dialogised heteroglossia, pose a useful metaphor for the sources of interference that I have been trying to describe. In discussing the lexical meanings of 'dialogue' in contemporary English, I suggested that the idea of 'political, diplomatic discussion' is often dormant in the popular usage of the noun 'dialogue', even when it is used to connote something quite different (p. 16 above). Here the adjective 'dormant' evokes Michael Holquist's description of the challenge involved in Bakhtin's basic scenario of the diversity of meaning in a conversation between two people, where the interlocutors attempt to use discourses to convey their intentions, rather than '[the intentions] which sleep in the words before they use them'.[8] These dormant intentions or meanings are part and parcel of Bakhtinian heteroglossia. If the scope for interference from dormant and inferred meanings is great in a conversation between two people, how much more so will it be in a colloquium convened on the subject of 'dialogue', and the subsequent proceedings? Although the scope of the colloquium was constrained or disciplined by the specific subject of dialogue in antiquity, the academic context in which our discussion took place repeatedly impinged on the object of discussion: was our discussion dialogue and is what has emerged in this volume dialogue?[9] At several points in the colloquium, voices around the table cautioned against blurring different meanings of 'dialogue', with salutary reminders that 'dialogue is not necessarily dialogic', or the need to distinguish, fundamentally, between dialogue as literary form and dialogue as spoken conversation.

These observations themselves reveal interference between different historical instantiations of dialogue. In the phrase 'dialogue isn't necessarily

---

[8] Holquist in Bakhtin (2006b) xx.

[9] A good example of putting dialogue as intellectual methodology at the heart of an edited volume is the volume of essays on Athenian democracy edited by Josiah Ober and Charles Hedrick, subtitled 'A Conversation on Democracies Ancient and Modern' (Ober and Hedrick (1996) 1–6). In their Introduction the editors express a multi-way conversation that is characterised by interdisciplinarity, comparativism, a conversational community between contributors and readers, and the dialogue between historicist and contemporary readings. For the difficulties of preserving the dialogue of a colloquium in edited volumes, see the remarks in Irwin and Greenwood (2007) 2–5.

dialogic', the adjective 'dialogic' would seem to evoke Bakhtinian dialogism. In which case the claim is arguable, as Bakhtin seems to have held that all speech, both in everyday life and in literature, is subject to dialogic hetero-glossia – multiple meanings are present and possible. Construed differently, with a loose, non-theoretical use of 'dialogic', the statement that 'dialogue isn't necessarily dialogic' might mean that not all exchanges between two or more people are interested in dialogue, in the evaluative sense of 'dialogue' as 'valuable or constructive discussion or communication' (see the *OED* definition on p. 15 above).[10] Alternatively, it might be interpreted as an allusion to the fact that dialogues in literature are essentially in some sense monologues, insofar as they are authored by a single author.[11] Here again, there is evidence of yet more scope for interference: this time between different etymologies of the English word 'dialogue'. The OED's etymo-logical note explains the derivation of 'dialogue' from the Greek noun διάλογος but suggests that many users infer the prefix '*di-*' ('two'), rather than the true prefix '*dia-*' (Grk. διά- 'through').[12]

In the following discussion of Thucydides' Melian dialogue, I will argue that this interference between different discourses and historical contexts is a productive one, and that it reflects the Thucydidean legacy of dialogue as a politico-literary compound form that cross-examines an Athenian ideal of political dialogue in the midst of an attempt to impose his own historical account on competing *logoi* about the truth. Critical interventions in Thucydides' *History* are voices in this dialogue, shifting between different discourses, and worrying about questions of knowledge, power and ideal speech.[13] We should no more impose our understanding of dialogue on Thucydides than we should exclude voices from the contemporary academy from our discussion. As Tim Whitmarsh has commented, 'the study of an ancient culture is not a monologue but a dialogue, between – at least – two full and equal partners'.[14]

---

[10] I will suggest below that this humanitarian inflection influences discussions of dialogism and Thucydides' historiography, leading to an ethics of the dialogue form; see Dewald's phrase 'respon-sible dialogism' quoted on p. 27 below.

[11] This is a topos of the debate about the openness of the dialogue form in the Platonic dialogues. See, e.g., Barber (1996) 363 'the mood of the dialogues is monophony masquerading as polyphony'.

[12] *OED ad loc.*, 'The tendency is to confine it [sc. dialogue] to two persons, perhaps through associating dia- with di-: cf. monologue.' For discussion of the etymology of the noun διάλογος from the verb διαλέγεσθαι in Plato and Greek literature of the fourth century BCE, see Ford, p. 35 below.

[13] For a project that links Thucydides' historiographical commitment to truthful representation to Habermas' theory of Ideal Speech (speech committed to the truth and free from coercive power) see Williams (2002) 151–71 (on Thucydides) and 225–6 (on Habermas).

[14] Whitmarsh (2006) 107.

In the first part of my discussion ('Forms of power') I review the historico-political context of the Melian dialogue as a dialogue that is circumscribed by power and yet informed by a recognisable ideal of democratic debate. I suggest that one of the major preoccupations of the dialogue is the conflation of listening and submission in the verb ὑπακούειν. In the second part ('The power of the form'), I examine how the political issues of fairness and equality of speech raised by the dialogue pose challenges for the critical interpretation of Thucydides' historiographical project and the attempt to identify dialogism in Thucydides' narrative.

THE MELIAN DIALOGUE AND FORMS OF POWER

In his introduction to the Melian dialogue, Thucydides sets out the hard, imperial backdrop against which the dialogue takes place. In Thucydides' account, the dialogue over the fate of Melos is framed by significant military activity. Before the dialogue commences, Thucydides' reader is reminded of Athenian intervention in the geopolitics of other territories in spite of the notional Six Years' Peace between Athens and Sparta (agreed in 422/1 BCE). At 5.84.1 the Athenian general Alcibiades takes three hundred Argive oligarchs captive on suspicion of pro-Spartan sympathies and resettles them in territories of Athens' island empire. Meanwhile (also 5.84.1), the Athenian generals Cleomedes, son of Lycomedes, and Tisias, son of Tisimachus, have amassed forces on Melos – in the wings of the dialogue, as it were. These forces comprise 38 ships, carrying 1,200 Athenian hoplites, 300 archers, 20 archers on horseback, and a further 1,500 hoplites from Athens' allies and island subjects. Not only do these combined forces loom over the dialogue, intimidating the Melians with annihilation, but their constituency also reminds the reader of other islands, which have already ceded to Athens' empire. As Bosworth has observed, critical literature on the dialogue frequently overlooks this aggressive context and the constraints that it places on the dialogue: the Athenian forces are already in position with a mandate from the Athenian demos to subdue Melos.[15]

The off-stage military forces undermine the spirit of the discussion, which cannot be a discussion on equal terms because of the unequal balance of power between the two parties. In fact, throughout the dialogue the Athenians confuse force with the force of their arguments. Thucydides illustrates this confusion through the subtle use of the verb ὑπακούειν, which has the primary meaning 'to hear' / 'to listen to' / 'to heed', and the secondary

---

[15] Bosworth (1993) 31–2.

meaning 'to capitulate', 'to submit to'.[16] Indeed, the conventional term for the subject allies of Athens, οἱ ὑπήκοοι (*hoi hupêkooi*, from the adjective ὑπήκοος 'listening to', 'obeying'), derives from this verb. Athens' subject allies are twice referred to as οἱ ὑπήκοοι in the dialogue: in the mouth of the Athenians at 5.91, and in the mouth of the Melians at 5.96.

The tension between listening and submitting, present in the verb ὑπακούειν, is examined throughout the dialogue. Indeed, the dialogue is framed by ring composition involving this verb: from the description of the Melians as an independent state that refuses to capitulate to Athens (τῶν δὲ Ἀθηναίων οὐκ ἤθελον ὑπακούειν, 5.84.2), to the conclusion of the dialogue at 5.114.1, where the Athenian ambassadors retreat to their camp to report the outcome, and their generals subsequently turn to war with immediate effect, on the grounds that 'the Melians were not capitulating / listening at all' (ὡς οὐδὲν ὑπήκουον οἱ Μήλιοι). Although at 5.84.2 ὑπακούω means 'to submit', the echo of the secondary meaning 'to listen' does not bode well in the introduction to a dialogue, which is supposedly premised on mutual 'hearing' of each other's views (5.85–6). The Melians who are introduced as refusing to capitulate to the Athenians will also refuse to heed their arguments: at 5.114.1 the Melians have both *not listened* to the Athenians' arguments and *not submitted* to the threat of Athenian power. In addition, the references to Athens' subject allies as *hupêkooi* (subjects / listeners) underscore the inescapable logic of this coercive dialogue in which to listen to Athens' arguments is to submit.

At 5.97 the Athenians express the view that the Melians' submission to their empire will enhance their power in the eyes of Athens' imperial subjects. The Melians then change tactic by trying to persuade the Athenians that they have miscalculated their own interests, but the language in which this is couched shows the artificiality of staging a rhetorical discussion at this juncture and under the Athenians' terms (5.98):

Melians: … Then again, just as you urge us to submit to (ὑπακούειν) your interests, restricting our use of just arguments, we must also attempt to persuade you about our interests, in case the two coincide.

MHL. … δεῖ γὰρ αὖ καὶ ἐνταῦθα, ὥσπερ ὑμεῖς τῶν δικαίων λόγων ἡμᾶς ἐκβιβάσαντες τῷ ὑμετέρῳ ξυμφόρῳ ὑπακούειν πείθετε, εἰ τυγχάνει καὶ ὑμῖν τὸ αὐτὸ ξυμβαῖνον, πειρᾶσθαι πείθειν καὶ ἡμᾶς τὸ ἡμῖν χρήσιμον διδάσκοντας.

The use of the verb πείθειν ('to persuade') is striking, as it seems to perpetuate the fiction that this is a genuine discussion in which the speakers can seek

---

[16] This verb occurs at 5.84.2, 5.93, 5.98, and 5.114.1.

to persuade each other to accept their respective arguments. However, as the Melians have already objected at 5.86, this dialogue is no leisurely rhetorical exercise; in this instance the consequence of being persuaded by the Athenians will be enslavement (πεισθεῖσι δὲ δουλείαν).[17] At the heart of this dialogue is an insurmountable tension between the pretext of dialogue, and the underlying reality of coercion. This passage also exposes the ambiguity that surrounds the language of persuasion (*peithô*) in Greek literature, as a process that can be variously sincere and deliberative or manipulative and coercive.[18] As the Melians conceive matters, the Athenians' persuasion does not allow for negotiation, hence the verb πείθετε (referring to the Athenians) takes the infinitive ὑπακούειν as its object, and is translated as 'urge' rather than 'persuade'. For their part, the Melian representatives engage in tentative persuasion (πειρᾶσθαι πείθειν). In fact, the Athenians have already proscribed certain avenues of persuasion, warning the Melians that they will not be swayed by the argument that the Melians have not campaigned with the Spartans or have not wronged them (οὔτε ... οἴεσθαι πείσειν, 5.89).[19] In urging the Melians to submit, the Athenian representatives follow the imperial logic of Pericles' last speech (2.60–4), in which the preservation of empire is premised on not submitting to others,[20] but in the Melian Dialogue this logic is extended to the requirement that others submit to Athens.

There is an obvious contradiction between the niceties of the dialogue as sketched by the Athenian ambassadors, namely that the Melians will be able to respond to and question (ὑπολαμβάνοντες) their proposals point by point (5.85), and the manner in which the dialogue proceeds. For readers approaching the Melian dialogue after Plato, the verb ὑπολαμβάνω is reminiscent of the turn-taking format of the Platonic dialogues in which interlocutors 'talk back' at each other. Wassermann observed that the balance of the dialogue, in terms of speaking time, is weighted in favour of the Athenians. He counted 145 lines of text for the Athenians and 88 lines for the Melians in the Greek text of the Loeb edition (Wassermann

---

[17] As Colin Macleod noted (1983) 56, the alternative also leads to slavery, since resisting the Athenians ultimately leads to the enslavement of the Melian women and children (5.116.4). Compare Bosworth (1993) 34, with n. 24, who argues that 'it [surrender] was slavery only in the most metaphorical sense, whereas resistance could – and did – bring slavery in its fullest form.' Bosworth supports this argument with the claim that 'no Athenian speaker in Thucydides calls submission to empire δουλεία' (*ibid.*). I think that this latter claim is overstated, as there are certainly contexts in which loss of empire is equated with slavery and subjection to others (see 2.62–3, especially 2.63.1). I would argue that the Melians' claim that submission to the Athenian empire would be slavery is not provocative (*pace* Bosworth), but echoes Athenian thinking on this point.

[18] See Hesk (2000) 170–1 with n. 90 on violent forms of persuasion in Greek literature.

[19] The Melians comment on this restriction of persuasion in the following paragraph (5.90).

[20] ὑπακοῦσαι (2.61.1), ἄλλων δὲ ὑπακούσασι (2.62.3).

1947: 34).[21] Further illustrating this imbalance, Morrison notes that the only questions in the dialogue are those posed by the Melians and interprets this as an indication of Athenian reluctance 'to take on the role of learner, they evidently think their purpose is to teach' (2000: 136). The imbalance noticed by Wassermann and Morrison becomes even more pronounced in the polymetric analysis of Alker, which tries to formalise the dialectical play between the Athenians and the Melians in terms of a 'Dialectical Move Sequence' with the Athenians as the 'proponent' of a thesis and the Melians as the responding 'opponent'.[22] Alker concludes, 'Coincident with their major show of force, the Athenians are the proponent, they articulate the major theses of this discussion, and they offer an argument sketch for them. As opponents, the Melians regularly question, or weakly assert their views' (811).[23]

The conflation of listening and submission in ὑπακούειν is symptomatic of the nexus between military force and argumentative compulsion. Several readers have observed that what wins the debate is the Athenians' strength, not the strength of their arguments.[24] The Melians have many valid counterarguments to the Athenians' view, not least the intratextual argument, whereby the Melians hint at the consequences of Athens' hyperimperialism as manifested in the collapse of the Sicilian campaign in Book 7 of the *History*.[25] In the immediacy of the dramatic dialogue, the Athenians win the *agôn*, but in the broader context of Thucydides' narrative their performance in the dialogue reveals weaknesses that will become ever more apparent in the ensuing narrative. As Liebeschuetz saw, the failure of the dialogue results from the fact that the Athenians and Melians occupy

---

[21] In the OCT text the Athenians have 113 lines, compared to the Melians' 73 lines (5.85–112). If we exclude the preamble (5.85–6) and the conclusion (5.112–3), the inequality of speech in the dramatic dialogue (5.87–111) is even greater: the Athenians have 106 lines to the Melians' 58 lines.

[22] Alker (1988) 810–11. Alker's formulation of the dialectical sequence in the Melian dialogue applies Nicholas Rescher's pragmatic model for analysing dialectical inquiry (*ibid.*, 808–10).

[23] See Alker (1988) 809 for the explanation of the 'strong' role of the proponent, versus the 'weak' role of the opponent: 'Every unattacked assertion of the proponent becomes, at least temporarily, a "concession" by the opponent.' Compare Price (2001) 199, 'the Athenian parts of the conversation, if stitched together, create a practically coherent speech in which the Melians' responses and challenges would be hardly felt.'

[24] See Orwin (1994) 100, 'They can well afford to converse on equal terms with the Melians: their superiority to them is irrefutable. It is irrefutable because it is impervious to speech.'

[25] Morrison (2000) 133, 'Although the Athenians win militarily, however, their prohibitions fail to constrain the Melians' words. As "masters of the sea" the Athenians are successful; as "masters of discourse" they cannot control the Melians. In countering and nullifying the Athenian restrictions, the Melians raise an important issue: the long-term consequences of Athenian policy.' I accept Dewald's qualification that the dialogue's critical assessment of excessive imperialism is not restricted to Athens, but extends to the different geopolitical powers who, at this stage in the war, are all trying to calculate strength and weakness, both their own and others' ((2005) 136).

different temporalities.[26] The Melians' counterarguments rely on intra-textual allusions to the long-term consequences of Athens' hyperimperial-ism, but the proofs come too late to save them.

As for the participants in the Melian dialogue, temporality also poses challenges for those seeking to interpret the dialogue; one of the difficulties for the contemporary reader is deciding which voices, historicist and con-temporary, to admit to the dialogue. Once dialogue is introduced as a model, it becomes difficult to ignore the influence of Platonic dialectic, which used the dialogue form, in turn modelled on the spoken conver-sation, as its vehicle for uncovering truth. Indeed, critics have seen in Thucydides' *History* a dialectic on power and justice that is comparable to the search for higher truths in Platonic philosophy. This Thucydidean dialectic on power and justice is interwoven with a pragmatic, interstate dialogue dictated by criteria of expediency, which, at its most pessimistic, hopes that the interest of each side might coincide (5.98, quoted on p. 20 above). Dialogue on this model is more akin to the antilogy, a model that lurks behind the Melian dialogue (5.112.2 – ἀντέλεγον).

There is simultaneous interference from a modern ideal of democratic dialogue according to which dialogue seeks a commitment to debate and the challenging of each other's positions, as well as an accommodation – but not necessarily a resolution – between opposing perspectives.[27] We can point to aspects of Athenian democratic ideology that intersect with mod-ern ideals of democratic dialogue, such as the principle of *isêgoria* 'equality of speech', according to which all citizens were afforded equal opportunity to speak, in principle if not in practice. Conversely, we can also point to the existence of a democratic regime of truth in ancient Athens, in which debate was always capped by a strong ideological consensus, which controlled the limits of argument.

However, the internal audience for the Melian dialogue is not the Athenian demos, and it is not even the Melian demos, since the Melians restrict the Athenian representatives from addressing the citizen body en masse through fear of a pro-Athenian coup on the part of the democratic faction in the state.[28] Instead, the Athenian representatives address the oligarchic faction (οἱ ὀλίγοι, 5.85). In addition, the democratic freedoms that govern debate in Athenian political contexts do not necessarily apply in

---

[26] Liebeschuetz (1968) 76.

[27] For a good example of this debate, see Euben (1996) and the response in Barber (1996). See also Ober (1998) 159 for comment.

[28] The terms used for the citizen body en masse at 5.85 are τὸ πλῆθος and οἱ πολλοί.

the case of interstate diplomacy, particularly in Thucydides' *History* which
depicts the freedom of Athens impinging upon the autonomy of other
states. The depiction of the relationship between the Athenians and their
subject allies in the Melian Dialogue is reminiscent of Pericles' claim that
Athens' empire was akin to a tyranny (ὡς τυραννίδα, 2.63.2). Like the
Athenians in the Melian Dialogue, Pericles dismisses debate about the
justice of this tyrannical position (ἢν λαβεῖν μὲν ἄδικον δοκεῖ εἶναι,
ἀφεῖναι δὲ ἐπικίνδυνον, *ibid.*).

The Melian dialogue is not a 'democratic' dialogue, nor do I accept
Bosworth's argument that it is 'humanitarian'.[29] The dialogue disappoints
the expectations of the modern reader, for whom assumptions about cooperative discussion lie dormant in the word 'dialogue' (see p. 16 above), and it
would also have shocked the expectations of readers familiar with Athenian
democratic ideology. Dionysius of Halicarnassus was right, Thucydides makes
the Athenian representatives sound like Persian kings (*On Thucydides* 39).[30]
The ironies of the dialogue are so pronounced precisely because it evokes
recognisable ideals of democratic dialogue, ancient and modern, even as it
flouts them.

THE MELIAN DIALOGUE AND THE POWER
OF THE FORM

In this section I move from the topic of the forms of power that circum-
scribe the dialogue, to consideration of the power of the dialogue form. If
the Melian dialogue presents the failure of an ideal democratic dialogue,[31]
then is there any justification for turning to dialogue as literary form, as
practised by Thucydides, as the repository of dialogic exchange?

The idea that Thucydides offers us a 'dialogic' narrative has been proposed recently by Carolyn Dewald in the context of her intricate study of
the structure of Thucydides' narrative. Dewald argues that Thucydides'
narrative is structured so as to 'tell its story in a way that allows both the
decisions and actions of people in the past and the historian's own understanding of them to emerge, in tandem with one another, as coherent and
credible for the reading audience.'[32] In turn, this play of voices between
narrator, characters and narratees yields to a 'three-pronged act of dialogic

---

[29] Bosworth (1993).   [30] For comment, see Connor (1984) 155–6.

[31] In this sentence 'democratic' refers to ancient Athenian democracy and its freedoms of speech: an
ideal of equality in speech.

[32] Dewald (2005) 15.

connection' (*ibid.*) between the historical narrator, the historical agents who are the subject of his *History* and audiences across time. Dewald then appeals to Bakhtin's idea of dialogic polyphony to illuminate Thucydides' commitment to a 'dialogic depiction of reality' (2005: 20), arguing that Thucydides attempts to convey the multiple consciousness of historical actors as mediated by his own consciousness and historical voice.

In the case of the Melian dialogue readers have been largely persuaded that the literary dialogue form that Thucydides has chosen corresponds to a real conversation that took place between representatives of Athens and Melos, but there has been deep disagreement about any correspondence between the *content* of the Melian dialogue and any historical debate that may have taken place.[33] However, one can hold this conviction about the historical basis for the Melian dialogue while simultaneously recognising the artificiality of the dialogue and the formal convenience of staging a dramatic dialogue at this point in the narrative, immediately prior to the Sicilian narrative with its tragic outcomes. The dialogue is 'dramatic' both in that it presents an *agôn* between personifications of the Athenian and the Melian positions, as well as being 'dramatic' in its evocations of the debates in extant Greek tragedies, both in terms of structure and language.[34] This second dimension – literary dialogue as intertextual dialogue with other literature – further complicates Dewald's model of Thucydides' dialogic narrative. This expansion of Dewald's model of dialogic polyphony acknowledges that, within individual speeches, different languages speak through the speakers and through the narrator who has composed them, whether these are primary, simple, social languages or secondary, complex, literary languages.[35]

The picture becomes more complicated when we consider how the dialogue is authored. As Dionysius of Halicarnassus observes, at 5.85–6 Thucydides narrates the first exchange of views / arguments in his own person (ἐκ τοῦ ἰδίου προσώπου), using a narrative structure (τὸ διηγηματικὸν σχῆμα)[36] which reports the words of the Athenians and the Melians, before shifting to unmediated direct discourse for 5.87–111 (*On Thucydides* 37). This shift to direct, dramatic discourse is described as

---

[33] Bosworth (1993) 38 (broad acceptance); Hudson-Williams (1950) 167 (dismissal). Hornblower (1994) 52–3 helpfully summarises some of the factors in the debate.

[34] See, e.g., Macleod's comparison of the Melian dialogue with Hecuba's appeal to Odysseus in Euripides' *Hecuba* ((1983) 54–5).

[35] Research into forms of inter-generic dialogue in Thucydides – along the lines suggested by Nightingale (1995) for the Platonic dialogues – is much needed.

[36] οἱ δὲ τῶν Ἀθηναίων πρέσβεις ἔλεγον τοιάδε ... (5.85) ... οἱ δὲ τῶν Μηλίων ξύνεδροι ἀπεκρίναντο (5.86).

putting speeches into the mouths of characters (προσωποποιεῖ τὸν μετὰ ταῦτα διάλογον) and approaching the narrative as drama (δραματίζει).

Andrew Laird's study of discourse in Latin and Greek historical narrative has proposed that 'the historical narrator is as much characterized and constituted by the discourse he reports as those to whom he ascribes it' (1999: 143).[37] Translating this into the language that Dionysius of Halicarnassus used to describe the narrative technique in the Melian dialogue, the shift from the historical narrator speaking in his own character (*prosôpon*) to speaking through the characters of others (*prosôpopoiia*), looks less like polyphony and more like ventriloquism. According to this view, Thucydides' narrative is all his own words; he may enter into a historical dialectic with himself and his readers on subjects such as justice, freedom etc., but the resulting narrative is less dialogic and polyphonic than the speeches would suggest. And yet, a possible compromise is that Thucydides' narrative can, intentionally or not, be dialogic in its effects. Dewald suggests that Thucydides' narrative is 'profoundly dialogic *in its effects*, since the emphasis it puts on the decisions and actions of the actors within the account also links their rational behaviour, as people whose actions are under narration, to the corresponding rationality of the narrating historian'.[38] In Dewald's scenario Thucydides' readers complete the dialogue by adjudicating not just between the different positions of speakers in the *History*, but Thucydides as well, evaluating his authorial judgement and integrity in terms of the representational strategies that he has used as an agent in history.

While admitting, with Laird, that Thucydides' narrative is itself a kind of discourse, we can still agree with Dewald that it admits different discourses – an intention that is signalled very clearly by the inclusion of the speeches, the radical extreme of which is the Melian dialogue in which speakers appear to speak for themselves. This kind of accommodation is envisaged by Gregory Crane, who recommends that we should 'think in terms of Thucydidean voices rather than a single, monolithic authorial voice'.[39] There is an important distinction to be made here between traditional debates about the authenticity of Thucydides' speeches, occasioned by the famous authorial statement at 1.22 (how closely do the speeches conform to the actual words delivered by real historical agents?) and Crane's interest in Thucydidean realism: Thucydides' attempt to represent events

---

[37] Laird's study of historical narrative is chapter 4 of his study of narrative discourse in Latin literature (Laird 1999). See *ibid.* xvi, 'narrative itself is a kind of discourse or speech'.

[38] Dewald (2005) 15; my italics.

[39] Crane (1998) 296. For discussion of Crane on Thucydides' literary realism, see Greenwood (2006) 59, with n. 8 (p. 145).

and speeches realistically and to pay due attention to the consciousness of different characters *qua* historical agents. Many readers of Thucydides, myself included, have argued that Thucydides goes to great lengths to disguise the fact that his own narrative is itself a *logos*, subject to the same constraints and partiality as the *logoi* of others in the *History*.[40] Although I find it hard to accept the concept of Thucydides' narrative being committed to 'responsible dialogism',[41] I am still willing to agree that dialogism may be a byproduct of Thucydides' narrative, not just in the different voices in which he writes, but in the different languages present in the speakers' words (his own included).

CONCLUSION

I have examined forms of power in the Melian dialogue and how power predetermines and constrains the dialogue. Turning to the power of the dialogue form, I have suggested that considerations of power have implications for our opinion of the dialogism of which Thucydides' narrative is capable. In genres with a strong, ideological commitment to truth and historicity, the power of the dialogue form is its veridicality; in the case of historiography, this leads to a definite tension between the fiction of dialogue as a literary form and the realism inherent in the form. Even more so than the speeches with their introductions that 'the Corinthians / Athenians/ Spartans said words to the following effect …', the dialogue purports to be a re-enactment of a conversation. In spoken, primary speech genres, parity in dialogue assumes giving every voice a hearing. In historiography, a secondary speech genre, corresponding parity in dialogue would entail giving each side – the Athenians and the Melians – a hearing, while allowing for the author's voice.[42]

And yet this is for the political definitions of dialogue (*isêgoria* – equality of speech) to intrude upon dialogue as literary form. This kind of interference at the heart of dialogue is already present in Thucydides' Melian dialogue. The Platonic dialogues have long been understood as the retreat of philosophy away from the public space of the city, in part to better study and critique the politics and values of the city. In this context, Sitta von Reden and Simon Goldhill have described the Platonic dialogues as 'a form of performance in exile'.[43] The motif of retreat is also present in the Melian

---

[40] See Greenwood (2006) 63; the classic discussion of this problem is Loraux (1986b).
[41] Dewald (2005) 22.   [42] See 1.22.1: ἕκαστοι … ἕκαστοι.
[43] Von Reden and Goldhill (1998) 265.

dialogue, which is staged in quiet (καθ' ἡσυχίαν, 5.86) and in front of a restricted audience (5.84.3–85).[44] There are similarities with the way in which Thucydides presents his *History* as a product of silent withdrawal (καθ' ἡσυχίαν, 5.26.5).[45] The ideal of dialogue presented in the Melian Dialogue fails, but its failure points to a withdrawal into the written word.[46] In Thucydides' hands the ideal conditions for dialogue are to be found in the quietness of writing, where the dialogue of voices takes place in the mind of the individual. There is an analogy to be drawn here with Harvey Yunis's observations about the shift from oral to written word in Athenian rhetoric, resulting in the phenomenon of orators and prose writers in fourth-century Athens 'using the conventions of literature to avoid the severe encumbrance of actual democratic political discourse'.[47] The paradox is that these written genres presuppose the culture of democratic Athens and enter into dialogue with its ideologies, while simultaneously using writing to sidestep its constraints. This model of closed dialogue presents an ongoing challenge to the modern academy; whatever else, surely we can agree that dialogue *is* interference?

---

[44] See Connor's description of the Dialogue as 'short, blunt thrusts in a closed conference room' ((1984) 148).

[45] See Greenwood (2004) 190.

[46] Compare Price (2001) 197, 'the failure of the historical characters is a triumph for the writer of history'. Morrison has suggested that Thucydides used the controlled environment of the Dialogue to expose the shortcomings of prevailing Athenian speech culture (Morrison (2000) 124, with n. 18).

[47] Yunis (1988) 240.

The beginnings of dialogue
Socratic discourses and fourth-century prose
Andrew Ford

Dialogue is unusual among literary genres in that we can speak quite specifically about where and when it began, and can even point to an historical individual who inspired the form: the first prose dialogues were representations of Socrates, the Athenian philosopher and teacher who was put to death in 399 BCE. One might have supposed dialogue to be far older, given that verbal duelling and antithetical argument feature so prominently throughout Greek literature; but, while a number of antecedents to the genre have been identified, there is no evidence that anyone wrote prose dialogues before these so-called *Sôkratikoi logoi* – Socratic 'dialogues', 'discourses' or 'texts'. Origins, of course, usually turn out to be elusive on close inspection, and there are some cloudy spots in this picture: it is unclear whether Socratic *logoi* began to be written while Socrates was still alive or if it was his execution that provided the impulse for the new form; there is also some question as to whether we should accept Aristotle's testimony that Socratic dialogues were first written by the otherwise unknown figure Alexamenus; it seems unlikely that a person who made such a contribution should be so obscure.[1] What is not in doubt, however, is the sudden and late appearance of prose dialogue in Greek literature, as well as the role that Socrates played in the first specimens of the genre. From these *Sôkratikoi logoi* subsequent prose dialogue in the West – comic as well as philosophic – derives in an unbroken succession.

Dialogue's entry onto the Greek literary scene was not only sudden but massive. Only Plato's and Xenophon's texts survive intact, but Paul Vander Waerdt points out that:

---

[1] Aristotle *On Poets* Fr. 72 Rose (= Athenaeus 505c), cf. Hirzel (1895) I.100 n. 2. Wilamowitz (1920) 28 hypothesised that there was an earlier tradition of prose dialogue pioneered by Alexamenus, while it was Plato who invented Socratic dialogue. But the distinction between dialogue and Socratic dialogue is not supported by our sources (also Diogenes Laertius 3.48 and *POxy.* 45 (1977) no. 3219, on which see Haslam (1972)). This seems wishful thinking intending to make Plato not only the greatest of writers in the form but the first. Diogenes Laertius 3.48 was also moved to credit Plato, against his better judgement, with inventing dialogue.

A remarkable number of [Socrates'] associates became authors of *Sôkratikoi logoi*: of the eighteen Socratics whom Plato mentions as being present or absent on Socrates' last day (cf. *Phd.* 59b–c), nine are attested to have written Socratic dialogues; of the seven associates whom Xenophon names (*Mem.* 1.2.48) as consorting with Socrates for proper motives (in order to become gentlemen, καλοικάγαθοί), three wrote *Sôkratikoi logoi* … while a fourth, Hermogenes, is named as Xenophon's source for his *Apology for Socrates*.[2]

But perhaps the most striking aspect of the rise of dialogue is how intensive it was: Livio Rossetti, one of the most devoted scholars of early Socratic authors, has amassed evidence for every possible Socratic *logos* written during Plato's career; on his construal of the evidence (which some might consider optimistic), around three hundred texts on Socrates may have been composed between 395 and 370 BCE. As a reviewer pointed out, this means that 'a *Logos Sokratikos* would have been published every month, non-stop, over a quarter of a century!'[3]

This literary development will be the focus of the present essay, which will attempt an analysis of how dialogue arose and won a place in the literary culture of late fifth- and early fourth-century Athens. I will be concerned less with the exact origins or sources of the genre than in noting how it defined itself against (and was defined by) other discourses of the time. I refer to this process of differentiation as the beginnings of dialogue, because I believe it took some time for Socratic *logoi* to achieve a firm identity of their own. But I must stress that I do not think these beginnings somehow determine all later versions of the form. Rather, I hold that, as with any genre, the nature and powers of dialogue must always be assessed in relation to whatever other forms of writing were produced and read at the time. The present study is intended to show that early Greek dialogue had more extensive and subtle affinities with rhetorical literature than its practitioners cared to admit, and to expand our sense of the forms the genre could take and the functions it could serve.

I will first argue that explanations of the rise of dialogue along biographical lines (as due to the influence of Socrates) or philosophical ones (as expressing some conception of philosophy) must be imprecise and incomplete. I will then consider some passages in Plato and Xenophon which are held to define the genre in distinction from sophistic display texts (*epideixeis*). I will argue to the contrary that Socratic *logoi* were deeply

---

[2] Vander Waerdt (1994) 3. The remains of the Socratics are collected in Giannantoni (1990). Important discussions are Vander Waerdt (1994), Rutherford (1995) 28–68, Kahn (1996) 1–35, Clay (2000).
[3] See Rossetti (2005). The reviewer is Dufour (2005).

involved with the rhetorical literature of the fourth century, when *logoi* of all kinds were eagerly sought out in Athens. Finally, I will bring out some less obvious literary properties of Socratic *logoi* that helped set them apart from other prose writing of the time.

SOCRATIC *LOGOI* AND SOCRATES

The usual explanation for the rise of dialogue is to say that Socrates' students invented the form to preserve the teaching of the master – who did not himself write.[4] One authoritative account goes from the observation that 'dialogue as a genre was a creation of the first generation of Socrates' pupils' to the inference that 'Undoubtedly, the main motivation for their creation was the visualization of Socrates' personality and his teachings as a holistic entity.'[5] The many comedic portraits of Socrates composed during his lifetime confirm that he had a unique mode of philosophising,[6] but even the most striking personality cannot account, by itself, for the development of a new literary genre. Thinking that dialogue was invented to record Socratic speech runs up against the obvious difficulty that the only two substantial portraits we have of the philosopher differ profoundly.[7] We ought also to question the assumption that contemporaries would have thought the obvious or 'natural' way to capture Socrates' philosophising was to write prose dialogue – a form that as far as we know had never been attempted. Significant literary and textual dynamics would have impinged on the most determinedly 'objective' effort to transcribe Socratic practices, as can be seen in a text which, *prima facie*, may seem to support the 'recording' explanation of dialogue: in that miscellany of Socratic *logoi* known as the *Memorabilia* or 'Memoirs of Socrates', Xenophon tells us that his aim was 'to write down as much as I could remember of how Socrates benefited those who associated with him, partly by the way he comported himself and partly by his conversation [*dialegomenos*]'.[8] The assertion that Socrates benefited his associates makes clear that this alleged

---

[4] E.g. Hermann (1950) 929. More elaborately, Hirzel (1895) I.68–83.
[5] Görgemans (2002) 351–2.
[6] For Socrates' 'prattling', cf. Aristophanes *Frogs* 1492 (*lalein*) and Eupolis Fr. 353 K.-A. This accusation continues at least down to Plutarch's *Life of Cato*. The excellent article by Clay (1994) 25 points out that his personality was so distinct that a verb 'Socratizing' was coined by the comic poets, to describe what was evidently a fad of acting like him.
[7] Remarked by Sayre (1995) 1–4, Kahn (1996) 1–35.
[8] *Mem.* 1.3.1: ὡς δὲ δὴ καὶ ὠφελεῖν ἐδόκει μοι τοὺς σύνοντας τὰ μὲν ἔργῳ δεικνύων ἑαυτὸν οἷος ἦν, τὰ δὲ καὶ διαλεγόμενος, τούτων δὴ γράψω ὁπόσα ἂν διαμνημονεύσω. On the quasi-reality of Xenophon's Socratic writings, cf. Chroust (1977) 1–16, Rutherford (1995) 46–56 and Kahn (1996) 29–35.

exercise in memory will in fact be a partisan construction of a figure who was, after all, put to death by the democracy on a charge of corrupting the young.[9] Xenophon soon admits that his recollections are engaged with what others 'have written and said' about Socrates (1.4.1). This particular Socratic is thus partly remembering texts, among which was an influential but equally unreal text of Socratic literature, a fictional *Accusation of Socrates* composed by the rhetorician Polycrates around 393 BCE (cf. *Mem.* 1.2.9). Scholars have long realised that Xenophon is unlikely to have recollected many of the episodes he recounts, so that the declarations of autopsy that recur in the text (e.g. *Mem.* 1.4.2, 2.4.1, 2.5.1, 4.3.2) must be regarded as a pretence not to be taken literally, something like a formula marking a genre.[10]

A degree of literariness and fictionality attends Socratic portraits, however piously they may have been drawn. We will consider more fully below the subtle ahistoricity of Socratic literature that drove Momigliano to call it 'infuriating' three times in a single paragraph.[11] It is enough to remark at present that the evasion of historicity was a feature not just of some writers but of the genre itself. The sheer number of defence speeches of Socrates on offer – from the fourth century alone we can identify *Apologiai Sôkratous* by Plato, Xenophon, Crito, Lysias, Theodectes and Demetrius of Phalerum – ensured that no one would consult an *Apology of Socrates* for a faithful record of what he said in 399.[12] As often, Xenophon is explicit on such points when Plato is implicit, for he begins his *Apology* by acknowledging that he is engaging with what 'others have written' about Socrates' defence (*Apol.* 1). A similar historical elusiveness marks a different Socratic genre or sub-genre, the symposium or 'drinking party' attended by Socrates. Plato's version toys with any hopes of getting an eye-witness account by beginning with a fantastically elaborate chain of witnesses – not all of them reliable – through whom the story has been handed down for his account. Xenophon seems more direct, simply saying at the beginning that he was present at the events described (*Symp.* 1); but he sets the party at a dramatic date (after the Panathenaia of 421) when he happened to be absent from Greece on military campaigns. Devoted readers of Socratic *logoi* could hardly fail to appreciate that they were *imitations* of Socratic speech. Even Polycrates'

---

[9] A good discussion of the political, pamphleteering function of Socratic *logoi* in the fourth century is Magalhães-Vilhena (1952).

[10] The point was well made by Maier (1913) 26–30, esp. 27 n. 1.

[11] Momigliano (1971/1993) 46–7, Kahn (1996) Ch. 1 (on Xenophon).

[12] Cf. Rossetti (1975), Rutherford (1995) 29–35, Danzig (2003), with references on p. 285.

Accusation had what must have been a deliberately anachronistic moment, referring to Conon's repair of the long walls in 393 BC.[13]

The idea of writing dialogues, then, did not simply spring from Socrates' fascinating way of talking.[14] A different way of understanding the form is to consider its philosophical potential. After all, the pioneers in this genre were – setting the mysterious Alexamenus aside – followers of Socrates, and so may have adopted the form as the best expression of his particular philosophy. It is eminently plausible that one attraction of dialogue form was that it encouraged readers to reflect in some way upon the arguments being offered. Such analyses, however, will tend to vary according to what is considered the heart of Socratic philosophy: dialogue thus may be described as the natural vehicle for teaching dialectic or as a way to model philosophy as a cooperative enterprise.[15] Often such explanations contrast the active processes needed to construe meaning from dialogues with passively being indoctrinated through academic treatises, lectures or sophistic orations.[16] A danger in this approach is that, given our limited evidence, it soon devolves into the different (though provocative and fascinating) question of why *Plato* wrote dialogues.[17] Plato's reasons for choosing the form may have been idiosyncratic, and of course may have changed along with the considerable changes in the kinds of dialogue he wrote over a long career.[18] The fact that Plato was neither the first nor only Socratic to write dialogues must make us wary of analyses that tie dialogue to specifically Platonic conceptions. There is also something ahistorical in the tendency of such analyses to contrast dialogue with allegedly more dogmatic forms of exposition dear to sophists: treatises are doubtlessly less polyvocal than dialogues, but no one was publishing lectures at this time (Aristotle, for example, 'published' his dialogues and kept his lecture notes in his school), and the literature of 'treatises' was likely to be far more limited than philosophers imagine; as for *epideixis*, we will see that dialogue was hardly averse to incorporating epideictic passages.

The question of why dialogue arose, then, is not fully illuminated either by biographical or philosophical considerations. One may be tempted to

---

[13] DL 2.39, citing Favorinus (Fr. 34 Barigazzi).   [14] See Greenwood in this volume.

[15] See Long in this volume. Also Gundert (1971); for other perspectives, Klagge and Smith (1992), Frede (1992), Gill and McCabe (1996).

[16] E.g. Görgemans (2002) 352: Dialogue 'opposes the didactic lectures of the sophists and demonstrates that knowledge is not merely transferred but acquired by each individual for himself'.

[17] A number of influential essays on this theme (by Ludwig Edelstein, Paul Plass, Charles Griswold Jr and Michael Frede) are conveniently collected in Smith (1998) Chs. 9–12.

[18] So Kraut (n.d.); Laks (2004) stresses that it is not clear that we can assume that such a varied corpus falls under a single literary formula.

dismiss the matter and say that something like dialogue was bound to surface in this speech-filled literature: after Homer's heroic 'speakers of words', the verbal agons of drama, the antilogies of the sophists and the speech-riddled historians, one might well take the view that it would have been more surprising if Plato had written 'straightforward expository prose' rather than dialogue.[19] Yet the relatively late appearance of the genre in Greek remains remarkable, and the suddenness with which it burst on the scene seems to suggest local influences. I turn then to a closer look at some Socratic texts to bring out certain literary dynamics that, along with personality of the master and the philosophic agendas of its authors, defined the form.

SOCRATIC *LOGOI* AND *DIALOGOI*

Socratic literature is dramatic and normally does not refer to its principles of composition. Some passages of Plato have nevertheless been singled out as programmatic of the genre, but to recognise these in the first place we depend on some definition of dialogue.[20] As a baseline for pursuing possible self-reference in Plato, then, we may consider one of the more popular ancient definitions of dialogue, from a second-century *Introduction* to his works: 'What then is a dialogue? It is a discourse [*logos*] composed of questions and answers on a philosophical or political topic, with the characters of the individuals taking part delineated appropriately, and in an artistically finished style.'[21] Albinus, the author of this text, was a well-trained and orthodox Platonist, and so some elements of the definition he purveys may go far back and illuminate practices of the fourth century BCE. That dialogues ought to exhibit stylistic polish, for example, might not occur to moderns, but was characteristic of the form already for

---

[19] Vlastos (1991) 51–52. On literary predecessors of dialogue, see Hirzel (1895) I.2–67, Laborderie (1978) 13–42, and Rutherford (1995) 10–15.

[20] An undeniably suggestive, but inconclusive text is the opening of *Theaetetus* (143b–c) in which the narrator explains that the book at hand has been written not as Socrates 'narrated' (*diêgeito*) it but as a 'conversation' (*dialegomenon*), dropping the tiresome 'narrative parts [*diêgêseis*] between the speeches', things like 'I said' or 'he replied'. This passage has been taken to imply that 'dramatic' dialogues without frames were a Platonic innovation, but we know far too little about the relative dates of Socratic writings to be sure of this, and the passage in any case does not easily lead to a general theory of dialogic writing; see Long in this volume.

[21] Albinus, *Eisagôgê* (p. 147.15–19 Hermann): τί ποτ' ἔστιν ὁ διάλογος; ἔστι τοίνυν οὐδὲν ἄλλο τι ἢ λόγος ἐξ ἐρωτήσεως καὶ ἀποκρίσεως συγκείμενος περί τινος τῶν πολιτικῶν καὶ φιλοσόφων πραγμάτων, μετὰ τῆς πρεπούσης ἠθοποιίας τῶν παραλαμβανομένων προσώπων καὶ τῆς κατὰ τὴν λέξιν παρασκευῆς. The same definition, abbreviated and lightly glossed, is in Diogenes Laertius' life of Plato (3.48 Marcovich) and underlies that in the anonymous *Prolegomena to Plato* (14 Westerinck). On Albinus, see Witt (1937).

Aristotle.[22] The emphasis on *ēthopoiia* was also essential, for the fact that arguments in Socratic dialogues came with speakers attached was, as we will see, one key feature that distinguished them from other dialogic texts. But the limitation of dialogue to the 'question and answer' format seems less useful. This, of course, can only apply to some Socratic writings with strain. (Does a work so fundamental as Plato's *Apology* really belong 'inside the fold' because of the brief dialectical exchange at 24c–27d? Does the insertion of some perfunctory assenting remarks into long stretches of exposition, as sometimes happens in later Plato, really suffice to make a text a dialogue?) Albinus' identification of dialogue with the exchange of question and answer is logical and etymologically sound, but seems to reflect the philosophy teacher's need to bear down on the arguments in such texts at the expense of their formal variety. The problem here may reduce to whether we conceive the genre under discussion as Socratic *logoi* – apparently a popular designation, and inclusive of more varied kinds of texts – or as Socratic *dialogoi*, emphasising back-and-forth arguing. I suspect that Plato's corpus as it was received in the Academy played a major role (perhaps the role) in subsuming the various Socratic *logoi* under one archetypal notion of philosophical dialogue. Too many works are lost to say more, but one widely cited programmatic passage from Plato at least allows us to see that the question-and-answer format had only a limited role in defining the genre for fourth-century readers.

Aristotle, one of our first sources to refer to the dialogues composed by Plato and others, usually calls them *Sōkratikoi logoi*.[23] In one fragmentary passage, he seems to speak of 'Socratic dialogues' (*dialogoi*), though this isolated usage is possibly an error for *logoi*.[24] The noun *dialogos* and the verb *dialegesthai* are common in Plato's and Xenophon's Socratica to describe what goes on in those texts, but do not appear to be a name for the genre. A few times a stretch of argument is called a *dialogos* (e.g. *Laches* 200e, *Rep.* 354b), but without noticeable generic force; and there is no passage in

---

[22] Aristotle speaks of the grace (*kompson*) and freshness (*kainotomon*) of Socratic *logoi* (*Pol.* 1265a10–12; cf. Fr. 73 Rose praising Plato's style), and Cicero praised their wit: *elegans, ingeniosum, urbanum, facetum* (*Off.* 1.29.104). For the 'golden' fluidity of Aristotle's own dialogues (Cicero, *flumen orationis aureum*), see Düring (1957) 363–4.

[23] *Poetics* Ch. 1 argues that *Sōkratikoi logoi* (1447b11) and mime deserve to be ranked with poetry insofar as they are mimetic arts, producing representations of people in action. The expression is also used in his *Rhetoric* (1417a21), and a variant, 'The *logoi* of Socrates', in *Politics* (1265a11).

[24] *On Poets* Fr. 72 Rose (cited in n. 1 above). The next use of *dialogos* as a genre term of which I am aware is in Dionysius of Halicarnassus. Aristotle's only other use of *dialogos* refers to a form of dialectical disputation (*Posterior Analytics* 78a12); Isocrates uses the word similarly at *Pan.* 26, on which see text below. I examine Aristotle's evidence in a study forthcoming in *Classical Philology*.

which either word need mean anything more formal or technical than 'talking together'. On occasion, each author shows Socrates punning on the active meaning of *dialegein*, 'sort into classes', suggesting that *dialogos* can be in some sense 'dialectical';[25] but usually in these texts the word refers to a social rather than intellectual activity. The language of Socratic 'conversation' in fact seems to owe its currency to the sophists, who deployed it as one of many euphemisms by which they downplayed any suggestion of compulsion or inequality in the teacher–pupil relationship. 'Talking together' (*dialegesthai, homilein*) is part of how sophists in Plato and Xenophon describe their activities, 'associating' or 'spending time together' (*suneinai, diatribein*) with their 'companions' or 'associates' (*hetairoi, sunontes*), not 'pupils' (*mathêtai*). Socratic writers, of course, insisted that his *dialogoi* differed vastly from Sophistic conversations, but on such grounds as the fact that Socrates would talk to people without charging fees.[26] These quarrels to one side, it is clear that the language of 'conversation' belonged to a social vocabulary that represented philosophy or sophistry as a liberal pursuit, an unpressured discussion among men at leisure who were, if not precise social equals, equally free to pass their time this way.[27]

'Conversation' is thus usually the best way to render *dialogos* in Socratic literature, but Albinus' emphasis on question and answer hardly came out of nowhere; he is likely to have found textual support for his definition, as scholars have since, in a suggestive passage from Plato's *Protagoras* 338a: in this passage Socrates insists on a 'form of conversing' (εἶδος τῶν διαλόγων) that proceeds by short question and answer, which has seemed to define his own methods in distinction from those of the great sophist after whom the work is named. This text must be set in context, for the first half of the *Protagoras* is an extended wrangle about how to conduct a profitable discussion. It begins when Protagoras, having been challenged to prove that virtue is teachable, offers (320c) to give an *epideixis* in the form of a *muthos* (i.e. the allegory he gives of Prometheus' distribution of talents among mankind) or of a formal demonstration (*logos*).[28] He ends up doing both, and Socrates congratulates him on his ability to make his 'fine long speeches'. Socrates then asks him to give 'short' answers (*kata brakhu*, 329b)

---

[25] On Plato's evolving conception of dialectic (in the *Republic* and some later dialogues) see Müri (1944). For *dialogos* connected with *dialegein*, cf. Xenophon *Mem.* 4.5.11–2; 4.6.1; Plato *Phaedrus* 265d–266c.

[26] Blank (1988).

[27] Paradigmatic of this attitude is the Platonic Protagoras' opposition between his own tuition and the 'compulsory' education of grammar school (*Prot.* 326a; cf. 318d–e = 80 A 5 DK).

[28] 320c: μῦθον λέγων ἐπιδείξω ἢ λόγῳ διεξελθών. On sophistical *epideixis* (e.g. *Gorg* 448d, 449c, *Rep.* 337a, *Dissoi Logoi* 8.1), Thomas (2000) 252–7.

in his conversation (*dialegesthai*, 334e). Protagoras assents, though cannot suppress the occasional applause-winning outburst until Socrates despairs at 'what shall be our mode of conversing?' (τίς ὁ τρόπος ἔσται τῶν διαλόγων, 336b). Things only get back on track when the host of the event advises Protagoras to trim his rhetorical sails, but he also urges Socrates not to insist on 'this kind of conversation consisting in extremely short answers' (μήτε σε τὸ ἀκριβὲς τοῦτο εἶδος τῶν διαλόγων ζητεῖν τὸ κατὰ βραχὺ λίαν, 338a).

The opposition that is read into this text between Platonic dialogue through short questions and answers and sophistic harangues crumbles away upon a little reflection. There is no doubt Socrates is consistently portrayed – possibly with an historical basis – as favoring brachylogy over *epideixis*.[29] But this passage is far from constituting a programme for Platonic writing, which, as *Protagoras* itself shows, readily incorporated long uninterrupted speeches. Nor are such orations limited to sophistic types: Socrates soon gives an *epideixis* himself in which he fancifully derives the practice of brachylogy from the Laconic utterances of the Seven Sages (342b–343b). Socrates' willingness to fly off into long disquisitions (as in Plato's great myths) is not solely a Platonic device: in the *Memorabilia* Xenophon depicts Socrates 'recalling' at length (2.1.21–34) a composition about Heracles which Prodicus 'displayed' before a great number of people. Socrates poor-mouths his offering as less splendidly adorned than the original, but as a textual practice Xenophon has managed, like Plato, to incorporate his version of a sophist's 'composition' (*sungramma*, 2.1.21) into his own. Conversely, brachylogy was not an exclusively Socratic practice, but one of many modes of speech that versatile performers like sophists controlled. Socrates includes it as among Protagoras' professed skills as a debater: 'you are able, on your own account and as your reputation goes, to practice either makrology or brachylogy in your interactions with people – after all you are a wise man – whereas for my part I am incapable of speaking at length' (335b–c).[30] The sophist Gorgias has the same double competence in the *Gorgias* (447c, 449b–c) and being able both to 'converse in brief replies' (*kata brakhu ... dialegesthai*) and to 'give a public harangue' (*damagorein*) are

---

[29] Clay (1994) 37 points to *Clouds* 482–3, where Socrates proposes to put a few 'short' questions to his pupil (οὔκ, ἀλλὰ βραχέα σου πυθέσθαι βούλομαι, εἰ μνημονικὸς εἶ).

[30] This passage may be part of the basis for the claim in Diogenes Laertius (9.53) that Protagoras 'was the first to develop the Socratic form of discussion [*eidos logôn*]'. On Diogenes' report (3.48) that Zeno first wrote dialogues, see Barigazzi (1966) 204. Aristotle speaks of Zeno's 'question and answer' format at *Soph. El.* 170b19.

among the broad range of competences desiderated of a technically accomplished teacher in the sophistic *Dissoi logoi* (8.1.27).

As in *Protagoras*, Plato's *Gorgias* stages a contrast between declaiming and 'conversing'. It opens with Socrates turning down an offer to hear a reprise of an *epideixis* Gorgias has just performed, preferring instead 'to have a conversation with him, if he would be so kind' (*dialekhthênai*, 447c; cf. 449b). Together, both texts suggest that the significant difference between conversations through questions and answers and long speeches is not Socratism vs. sophistry but between speaking before a mass (and undiscriminating) audience and conducting a private conversation. In *Gorgias* Socrates is very clear that it is impossible to have dialogue with a mass assembly (474a–b, picked up at 475e–476a), and in *Protagoras* when the sophist breaks out into a long speech, Socrates observes acidly, 'I thought there was a difference between conversing together [*dialegomenous*] and making grand public speeches [*dêmêgorein*].'[31] The distinction in *Gorgias* and *Protagoras* between 'conversation' (*dialogos*) and 'demagoguery' defines those texts' audience as much as their methods. Unlike the sophists, Socratics stick to producing texts for private reading; they have no interest in addressing the mass public on its terms.

I infer from these passages that Socratic dialogues did not present themselves in the first instance as manuals for learning dialectic, though they certainly were so used by later students. Viewed without the retrospective agenda of an Albinus, that varied body of works rather resembles a sampler of the different kinds of talk that a Socrates could elicit. Recalling that stylistic polish was one of the hallmarks of the genre, I suggest that part of the appeal of these Attic mimes was in providing scenes of civilised conversation in leisure, forms of discourse distinct from 'the compulsory speeches of the law-courts' (Gorgias *Helen* 13). This is not to deny the moral seriousness and logical rigour of such Socratic authors as Antisthenes and Aeschines of Athens, Euclides of Megara and Phaedo of Elis, all of whom were philosophers in their own right. And it would be going too far to say that Socratic *logoi* functioned merely as conversation manuals, for their agenda always involved working through, with more or less pertinacity and success, 'some philosophical or civic topic'. But the self-presentation of Plato and Xenophon suggests that, over and above preparing readers to undertake philosophy, dialogue was valued for its models for negotiating

---

[31] *Prot.* 336b. Xenophon *Mem.* 3.7.4 also opposes private discussion (*idiai ... dialegesthai*) to 'competing before a multitude' (*en plêthei ... agônizesthai*). Cf. *damagoria* in *Dissoi Logoi* 8.1.27, cited above.

debate and sustaining conversation.[32] After all, in the bustling competition among higher educators in the fourth century, it was not necessary to pack a complete philosophical education into these brief publications. As such the genre would have appealed to those interested in what Aristotle called 'noble leisure' (*Politics* 8.3; cf. 7.13–15), and there is much to be said for Gaiser's suggestion that early Platonic dialogues were indebted to the sophistic genre of protreptic.[33] But it is time to step back to discern other ways by which Socratic *logoi* claimed a place of their own.

SOCRATIC *LOGOI* AND *LOGOI*

Dialogue emerged at a time of unprecedented expansion in the number and kinds of prose texts produced in Athens. It is an obvious fact, but too easily lost sight of, that when cultures acquire convenient means of writing, they do not write everything down all at once, but pick out certain forms of discourse as especially useful to fix in writing and leave the rest to carry on as it had.[34] The early fourth century, when Socratic literature was gaining its feet, was marked by a flood of new prose texts, especially speeches, either orations 'actually' delivered or samples of the kinds of speech suitable for given occasions. In Athens, the publication of rhetorical *logoi* is said to have begun with forensic speeches and exercises circulated by Antiphon (*obit.* 411), followed soon by judicial orations of Lysias and the early texts Isocrates produced as a speechwriter for hire. What we have of Greek literature that was published over the next century, from Antiphon through Demosthenes, is dominated by such speech texts.

Prima facie, Socratic literature was another kind of *logos* – as its name indicated – and so a prime task for Socratics was to distinguish their *logoi* as special and valuable. Having been taught by Plato and Aristotle, we can specify many respects in which Socratics elevated their own truly 'philosophic' texts over rhetorical and sophistic chicanery. But such discrimination was less easy in the early fourth century when the burgeoning *logos* literature made boundaries between genres porous and highly provisional. A look at the genre of funeral orations shows how the constant expansion of the kinds of prose written down and the exponential increase in their numbers made prose forms promiscuous and mobile. This traditional ceremony of lament became a prose affair sometime in the fifth century

---

[32] The rhetorical tradition developed the form called the *Lalia* or 'Talk': see Menander Rhetor 388.17–394.31, with commentary by Russell and Wilson (1981) 294–303.
[33] Gaiser (1959) 21–8. Cf. Rynearson (2006).   [34] More at Ford (2005).

when orators and politicians took over the poets' task of composing dirges (*thrênoi*) for citizens who had died in war.[35] At first, these performances were closely tied to their performative contexts 'at the tomb' (*epitaphios*) and seem not to have been written down, even when they were delivered by such oratorical giants as Pericles. The *epitaphios logos* effectively became a prose genre when sample texts of such speeches began to be circulated. Gorgias produced an *epitaphios* suitable for performance at Athens (82 B 6 DK), presumably as a specimen of his talents since it is doubtful that a Sicilian would have been invited to speak on behalf of the Athenian people. Other rhetoricians competed with their own *epitaphioi*, such as the one ascribed to Lysias purporting to memorialise the fallen in the Corinthian war of the late 390s. A further stage is reached when we find faux-*epitaphioi* introduced into texts of other kinds, such as the splendid impersonation of Pericles' performance in 430 BCE that Thucydides inserted into his history (2.35–46). Socratic writers felt no need to resist a topic so popular (and thus so effective at displaying one's skills): Plato's *Menexenus* is little more than a playful *epitaphios* (236d–249c) nestled in a dialogue (236b may be read as giving, in effect, the 'ground rules' of the game). He hints at the intertextual escapades afoot when his Socrates claims to have learned his speech from Aspasia – who was not only Pericles' mistress but the eponymous figure of a dialogue by the Socratic Antisthenes. The Socratic texts in turn could inspire other writers, and Isocrates took over many epitaphic motifs for his faux-festival speeches, the *Panegyricus* and *Panathenaicus*.

The *epitaphios logos* is far from being the only rhetorical genre involved with the *Sôkratikoi logoi*. Andrea Wilson Nightingale has argued extensively that Plato's dialogues only won their way to the status of 'philosophical' writing by incorporating and parodying a great many genres, poetic and rhetorical.[36] A vivid picture of the process is dramatised in *Phaedrus* when Socrates forces a *logos*-loving companion to disgorge a speech text he has been hiding under his cloak in hopes of studying it: the roll turns out to contain a sample *erôtikos logos* or seduction speech by Lysias, which Socrates duly listens to, travesties and rewrites. A reader of this Socratic *logos* thus is given not only a piece of pseudo-Lysias in a well-tried genre but instructions on how to outdo it as well.[37] In this way the multivocal *Phaedrus* delivers the type of help our poor student had sought from the meagre *logos* text itself.

---

[35] Loraux (1986a).
[36] Nightingale (1995); Goldhill (2002) 80 notes how often Plato's text constitutes itself by 'humiliating' significant civic discourses.
[37] See Lasserre (1944) and Rynearson (2006).

As said above, the exchange between Socratic literature and sophistic rhetoric was not one-sided: a sample erotic speech included in the Demosthenic corpus (*Or.* 61) is set at the house of Epicrates, the very place where Phaedrus claims to have heard Lysias perform (*Phaedrus* 227b). Other discourse genres important to Plato and all teachers of the time include the *protreptikos logos*, exhortations to virtue like Prodicus' text on Heracles at a crossroad, and the encomium or speech in praise of a mortal.[38]

The fecundity of this period in generating new kinds of prose and the evident appetite of the public for such writings are a main reason that Socratic *logoi* are so hospitable to other prose genres and why they range so readily beyond the question-and-answer format. It remained important, however, for Socratic *logoi* to project an identity of their own, especially since they were confusable with the widely practised but discreditable genre of disputation or eristic.[39] The danger emerges clearly in an interesting passage from Isocrates which lists a number of recognisable prose genres (*Antidosis* 45–47). Arguing that prose has as many forms (*tropoi, ideai*) as poetry, Isocrates lists: antiquarian genealogies, scholarly inquiry into poets, history and 'those who have occupied themselves with questioning and answering, which they call "antilogistics"'.[40] The list is incomplete, but clearly the label 'antilogistics' is meant to lump Socratic *logoi* together with the texts teaching disputation. Isocrates has little respect for this kind of writing, which he elsewhere calls 'eristic dialogues' (his sole use of the term *dialogos)* and characterises as a novel element in education in which the young delight overmuch and which older people find intolerable (*Panath.* 26). For such reasons, of course, Plato repeatedly distinguishes *dialegesthai* from *erizein*, 'conversation' from 'disputation'.[41] His anxiety about being assimilated to this class of writer is doubtless projected onto his portrait of Zeno, whom he represents as embarrassed for having published a book of eristic paradoxes; Zeno is made to write off this work (which must have been a pioneer in eristic literature, and probably contained a version of Achilles and the tortoise) as the fruit of his youthful love of contentiousness; he claims quite disingenuously that it was published without his consent.[42]

---

[38] Cf. Nightingale (1993).   [39] On eristic literature and the dialogue, Laborderie (1978) 27–40.

[40] ἄλλοι δέ τινες περὶ τὰς ἐρωτήσεις καὶ τὰς ἀποκρίσεις γεγόνασιν, οὕς ἀντιλογικοὺς καλοῦσιν. On 'antilogies', cf. Thomas (2000) 252–3, 264–7.

[41] E.g. *Euthydemus, passim*; *Phaedo* 90b–91a; *Rep.* 454a, cf. 511c; *Theaet.* 167e; *Sophist* 216b. Isocrates rejects the distinction at *Sophists* 1–3; *Helen* 2, 6; *Antid.* 265.

[42] *Parmenides* 128. Cf. Wilamowitz (1920) 28.

It is clear that the literature of disputation had a following among the young, but was disreputable if pursued too seriously or past the age of youthful contentiousness. 'It would be unseemly', Plato's Socrates says at the beginning of his *Apology*, 'for me to come before you making up speeches like a schoolboy.'[43] And yet Plato says this precisely in a model speech of a kind (defence) that sophists had long cultivated. The need for a shibboleth separating Socratic from dubious sophistic *logoi* was all the more urgent for the difference between them being at times so slight. It is here that the *êthopoiia* of dialogue played a significant role: the fact that Socratic arguments issued from defined personae strongly distinguished them from the usual texts of disputation. Reading an exchange between Socratic characters was fundamentally different from studying the opposed anonymous speeches of the *Dissoi Logoi* or the paired defence and prosecution speeches constituting Antiphon's *Tetralogies*. When, as sometimes happened, the eristic mode entered Socratic *logoi*, personae made a powerful difference. Xenophon reports a 'conversation' (*dialekhthênai*) he heard of between Alcibiades and Pericles about the laws (*Mem.* 1.2.40–47). The substance of the argument is eristic, a captious undermining of a series of definitions of law. The amoral argument is given a certain colour, however, by casting Alcibiades, the future star and bane of Athenian politics, as the indefatigable confuter of every sane statement, while the unworthily abused victim is played by Pericles, Alcibiades' guardian and a revered hero of the Athenian state. Albinus would call it 'fitting' *êthopoiia* that Alcibiades is described as not yet twenty at the time, and that the mature Pericles becomes impatient at this quibbling, saying that he used to enjoy such exercises (*meletê*, 1.2.46) as a lad.

The most important element of Socratic *êthopoiia*, of course, was the persona of Socrates himself. We have already noted that this was not to be the 'real' Socrates of history, but a quasi-historical figure promising a certain kind of text. Wilamowitz noted that the expression *Sôkratikos logos* would have implied a certain ethos, as an Aesopic *logos* promised to be tricky and table-turning and a Simonidean *logos* wise and controversial. We can guess that, amid the forest of rhetorical *logoi*, a 'Socratic' *logos* stood out as a high-minded and elegant discourse; so much is suggested by a phrase from a Lysianic speech that describes Aeschines the Socratic as 'one who had been a pupil of Socrates and who had made so many impressive [*semnous*] speeches about justice and excellence'.[44]

---

[43] *Apology* 17c; cf. *Menex.* 236c.   [44] Lysias *Against Aeschines*, Fr. 1.2 (= Athenaeus 611d–612f).

A final distinctive feature of the Socratic *logoi* emerges if we compare the persona of Socrates with other fictional figures of discourse, for teachers of rhetoric also used a kind of fictionality to give their specimen speeches a less serious appearance. In the fifth century, some sophists produced sample speech texts, but these were presented to 'associates' with a studious casualness, as toys for practice and demonstration, not as valuable prose works in their own right.[45] Especially when recruiting students in democratic societies, it was important not to appear too serious about dominating audiences, and some sophists reinforced their pose of urbane levity by making their speeches about mythical or legendary figures.[46] Such, for example, are Gorgias' defence of Palamedes or of Helen, which he calls 'an encomium of Helen and a plaything of my own' (*Helen* 21; cf. Alcidamas *Against the Soph.* 35).[47] The trend was still ongoing at the time of Plato, to his dismay. Polycrates, for example, wrote an encomium of Clytemnestra in which the matricide was contrasted favourably with Penelope. He also wrote a text praising and defending Busiris, a legendarily bloodthirsty tyrant of Egypt.[48] The implicit logic of the game dictated that the most admirable performance was the one that defended the most impossible case – vindicating Helen's virtue, praising Death or exalting the qualities of mice. Many complained about the cynicism of such exercises.[49] Among these high-minded objectors was Isocrates (*Helen* 8–13; *Panath.* 1), but the popularity of the form put this aspiring rhetorician in a bind: in the end he could not resist the challenge of showing his own talents by discoursing on Busiris, but he preserved his dignity by framing his *Busiris* not as another speech text but as a letter of protest to Polycrates. Rhetoric was the mother of inventive prose.

Socratics also disdained the literature of paradox and myth.[50] But writing speeches for hopeless causes had something in common with Socrates' *Apologiai*, which were, after all, on behalf of the most surprising loser in the history of capital trials. Plato's and Xenophon's versions show that part of the game was in coming up with an explanation of how Socrates, that supreme talker, failed to secure his own acquittal (cf. *Mem.* 4.8.5; 8). There was, however, a saving limit to these similarities in the fact that Socrates was a figure of recent history. Socrates was not Helen, Heracles or Busiris; he

---

[45] See Cole (1991), esp. Chs. 5–7. [46] Cf. Ford (2001).
[47] See Wardy (1996) for the levels of levity here.
[48] For a good recent overview of Polycrates, see Livingstone (2001) 28–40. Polycrates' *Busiris* seems to have been, like Gorgias' *Helen*, a cross between encomium and apology: Livingstone (2001) 39 n. 101.
[49] On the literature of praising small things: O'Sullivan (1992) 84 and Pease (1926).
[50] E.g. Plato *Symposium* 177b; Aristotle *NE* 7 1146a; *Rhetoric* 1366a18–20.

was more like Alcibiades, Pericles or Cyrus, a real figure, bearing, for readers born around the turn of the century, some interest and a certain amount of historical identity, but he was not so well-known as to hem in a writer's themes and style. A fiction but half-real, Socrates' persona helped Socratics produce speech texts without being taken as rhetoricians. They could write ironically without projecting triviality and insincerity; the martyred philosopher allowed them to affect a pose of moral seriousness and careful speech, but without sacrificing the opportunities for novelty and innovation and the appeal that *logos* literature commanded.[51]

CONCLUSION

The ways that Socratics exploited personae could be analysed far more extensively, but it may be fair to sum up by saying that the rhetorical culture of the fourth century shaped early dialogue at least as deeply as previous literature or the activities of Socrates. The connections I have been arguing for between dialogues and speech texts are surprising only if one accepts Plato's position that only his opponents resort to the low tactics of rhetoric. But one great benefit of literary historical studies is that they can unravel such ideological constructs. We can point in conclusion to Antisthenes of Athens as a figure who crossed over between rhetorical and Socratic *logoi*: a follower of Socrates some twenty years Plato's senior, Antisthenes wrote not only Socratic *logoi* but a defence speech for the matricide Orestes and a pair of speeches by which Odysseus and Ajax ought to have contended for the arms of Achilles.[52] The line between Socratic and rhetorical *logoi* is also straddled by a figure like Alcibiades, whose notorious career furnished material for dialogues and faux-prosecution speeches in equal measure.[53] Plato would not approve of this proximity, but he would be hard pressed to deny that, when he first took up his pen, Socratic dialogue was inseparable from its rhetorical 'other'. In other words, dialogue began life as a genre of Greek prose.

---

[51] Cf. Joël (1894–1895) 476: 'Man schämt sich in eigenem Namen zu schreiben und scheut sich vor der toten Schrift, darum versteckt man sich hinter einen andern und fingiert ihn als lebendig redend – das ist die μίμησις im λόγος Σωκρατικὸς.'

[52] Wilamowitz (1920) II.26–7 questions whether Antisthenes can be credited with *Socratic* dialogues.

[53] Dialogues on Alcibiades include Plato's *Alcibiades* I (and Alcibiades' speech in Plato's *Symposium*), pseudo-Plato *Alcibiades* II, and works of that name by Aeschines of Sphettus and Antisthenes (the latter of whom claimed to have been an eye-witness, *autoptês genomenos*, of Alcibiades' beauty: Fr. 30 Caizzi). These are matched by forensic speeches about him (sometimes focalised through his son, Alcibiades the younger) including [Lysias] 6, Andocides 4, and polemical passages in Isocrates 16 and Lysias 14. On these, see Goldstein (1968) 122–5.

CHAPTER 3

Plato's dialogues and a common rationale for dialogue form

Alex Long

INTRODUCTION: EXPLAINING DIALOGUE FORM

The project of this volume is to explain why the dialogue genre was put to minimal or no use by early Christian authors, despite the previous prominence of the genre in antiquity. One might approach our task in the following manner: first determine what attracts authors to dialogue form, and then use that determination to explain the genre's absence or rarity in early Christianity. For when we have unearthed the rationale for writing in dialogue form – a rationale common to all writers of dialogues – explaining the preference for *other* media will become a straightforward business; once we have found the desiderata secured by dialogue form, we can infer that early Christians thought that other genres would achieve the same ends more effectively, or alternatively that such desiderata simply ceased to be desiderata in the Christian era.

At the risk of caricature, let me give an intuitive example of the sort of account which this approach would yield. An author writes dialogues because of what she values in dialogue. Now dialogue allows for disagreement and candid exchange, and is thus an inherently non-authoritarian medium. All writers who choose dialogue form do so because they value this feature of dialogue, and so the natural home of dialogue form is democracy, where open debate is valued; little wonder, then, that the dialogue form first flowered in classical Athens. But early Christians stopped using dialogue form (at least to the same extent), showing thereby that open debate was no longer valued (at least to the same extent). We could of course make further refinements to this account. Perhaps there was something newly doctrinaire in early Christianity, or maybe an authoritarian malaise was already endemic.

This example and the kind of approach it illustrates assume that dialogue form is the hallmark of a certain outlook. On this assumption there is a universal rationale for writing in dialogue form, and, more generally, an author's choice of genre betrays his attitude and values. Indeed, on a particularly strong version there is little choice for the author himself to make; his outlook and way of thinking choose his genre for him.[1] On any version of the assumption, however, an author broadcasts his sympathies – inadvertently or not – simply by writing in a certain mode.

This view of genre has obvious promise and application: if it were true, the rise and fall of genres would allow the historian to track the rise and fall of certain kinds of value or ideal.[2] But should we trust it? In this paper I argue that we should not. More precisely, I argue that we cannot find a rationale for writing in dialogue form that is both common to every writer of dialogues and yet also substantial enough to reveal something significant about authors who did not write dialogues. I do so by arguing for a stronger (and equally controversial) claim. We cannot find such a rationale – common and substantial – even if we confine our attention to the dialogues of one author: Plato.

Plato's commitment to writing in dialogue form was – with the exception of the *Apology* – exclusive. So surely *Plato*'s dialogues, if any, would show a consistent and substantial rationale for writing in dialogue form, and there is a considerable scholarly industry devoted precisely to explaining what this rationale was. And yet several scholars dissent, arguing instead that our ingenuity is better spent explaining why an *individual* dialogue was written in dialogue form, for Plato's varied uses of dialogue form require varied explanations, rather than a monochrome account.[3]

I side with these dissenters. But rather than attempt to challenge every account of Plato's rationale on the market, I shall instead challenge what seems to me the most promising candidate: the view that Plato wrote dialogues because of a particular conception of the importance of dialogue for philosophy. Put at its most bland and general – 'Plato wrote dialogues because of his interest in philosophical dialogue' – this explanation is surely true and applicable to all Plato's dialogues. But, as we shall see, once we develop and amplify the explanation we can no longer generalise across all Platonic works. And develop it we must, if we are to have a suitably

---

[1] 'Might it be that a work of a certain shape is the only one possible for certain thoughts?', Jordan (1981) 202.

[2] This sort of enterprise is of course associated above all with Bakhtin. See, for example, his account of the characteristics of the novel and the Socratic dialogue at (2006b) 7 and 25.

[3] Andrew Ford's paper in this volume notes as much. In addition to the scholarship he cites (p. 33, n. 18), see Kraut (1988), Rossetti (1997) and Nehamas (1999) xvii–xix. McCabe also notes that Plato's dialogue form was not 'uniform' and its purposes were not 'singular', (2006) 40 and 52. Compare Cox's prudent refusal to work with a unitary notion of the dialogue's function in her study of Renaissance dialogues at (1992) 4.

substantial explanation of dialogue form to inform our understanding of other authors (or our understanding of Plato himself, for that matter). So the dissenters are right to warn us away from unitary accounts of the Platonic dialogue; even the most promising explanation must be colourless if it is to be true to the entire corpus.

Before turning to Plato's appraisals of dialogue I shall briefly illustrate the way in which other attempts to explain dialogue form would be beset by similar problems of substance and generality. Take first the influence of Socrates. Socrates and his interpersonal mode of philosophising undeniably coloured Plato's way of writing; like other Socratic authors, Plato resorted to dialogue form when reflecting on Socrates' life, method and convictions. In granting Socrates this influence one need take no line on Plato's evaluation of Socrates, for dialogue form allows for criticism as well as celebration of Socratic dialogue. Indeed, some scholars have read the first book of the *Republic* as an implicit *attack* on Socrates' practice of elenchus and conception of virtue,[4] but the book is no less a Socratic dialogue in form for that. Socratic influence cannot, however, explain the form of every Platonic dialogue, for Plato of course wrote dialogues in which Socrates is dethroned by a different protagonist (*Sophist*, *Statesman*) or altogether absent (*Laws*). This suggests that Plato had (or came to have) a rationale for dialogue form independent of his ruminations on the historical Socrates.

Let us then make the explanation more open-ended; perhaps Plato's motive was a general interest in *character*, rather than merely in *Socrates* and his character? On this new version, Plato chose dialogue form because of the opportunities for characterisation it offered him; if his interest in the historical Socrates waned, he continued to use Socrates (and others) to illustrate *types* of character. Examples come quickly to mind; turn, say, to the *Cratylus*. Two characters, Hermogenes and Cratylus, have strongly opposed accounts of names and naming, Hermogenes claiming the correctness of a name to be simply convention, Cratylus insisting that things have naturally correct names. But as the dialogue opens the two men have reached an impasse in their discussion; it therefore falls to Socrates to arbitrate between their positions by subjecting their theories to his usual questioning. In so doing he develops one of the dialogue's central claims about expertise. For it is precisely the expert in questions and answers, the dialectician, who is argued to be the expert user and so the appropriate judge of names.[5] Plato's characterisation suggests that a dialectician like Socrates – rather than a theorist of the stamp of Hermogenes or Cratylus – is also

---

[4] See particularly Blondell (2002) Ch.4.   [5] *Cratylus* 390b–d.

best placed to judge *theories* of names and naming. Socrates is of course the exemplar, but Plato's point is a *general* one about dialectic and the dialectician.[6]

Here then we can see how Plato took advantage of the wider possibilities for characterisation in written dialogues, and so we seem to have a plausible explanation of his way of writing: a certain interest in types of character, philosophical or otherwise. But if Socratic influence was too narrow a rationale, this revised version seems altogether too thin to satisfy our curiosity about Plato's intentions (or indeed to explain the decline of dialogue form in later antiquity). And yet once we start to expand this explanation we seem to lose sight of the general question of why Plato chose dialogues. On one plausible account Plato's mode of writing reflects not only an interest in character but a belief that there is an intimate *connection* between philosophical argument and personal character.[7] But this is surely to explain why Plato wrote dialogues of a certain sort, rather than why he chose dialogues at all. And so when trying to account for the entire corpus – at least when speaking about character – we seem doomed to buying generality at the price of substance, or *vice versa*.

TEACHING AND CONVERTING

In what follows I shall argue that the same is true when we work with a more promising (and widely accepted) explanation: namely, that authors such as Plato choose dialogue form because they value dialogue, or certain distinctive features of dialogue. Many scholars believe that here, at least, we can find an explanation for dialogue form that is both sufficiently general and suitably substantial: Plato wrote dialogues because he saw dialogue with others as the only appropriate medium for philosophy.[8] But I shall suggest that here too the picture is not as unitary as these scholars would have us believe.

We should first ask precisely what activity it is that dialogue is supposed to facilitate. Let me distinguish between three processes which a philosopher like Plato might have thought best served by dialogue: intellectual discoveries, *teaching* such discoveries to others and *converting* others to the life of philosophy. Of course, two or maybe even three of these could take

---

[6] For an alternative account of the form of the *Cratylus* see n.25 below.
[7] 'By their artful characterization of the dramatic context of the arguments the dialogues show in an unsurpassable way how philosophy is tied to real life, to forms of life, to character and behaviour', Frede (1992) 216.
[8] See, for example, Rowe (1993) 4; Rutherford (1995) 9; Gill (2002).

place within a single conversation, but it seems prudent to distinguish them at the outset, as a philosopher could easily regard dialogue as essential for proper teaching but inessential for rigorous discovery. Or he could view dialogue as essential for both activities, but believe that discovery and teaching profit from different characteristics of dialogue.

And some caution about the nature of the activities involved proves advisable when we turn to the most famous celebration of dialogue in Plato's works. Near the end of the *Phaedrus* Socrates offers a critique of written texts and praises living dialogue as a superior and 'nobler' (276e5) alternative for intellectual pursuits; we might be tempted to highlight this passage as *the* Platonic statement of dialogue's merits. It is important, however, to be clear about the nature of the pursuits which Socrates has in mind. Texts are faulted on the grounds that they cannot preserve one's native memory, cannot defend their content from assault or misrepresentation and cannot '*teach* the truth adequately' (276c9). As such, they should not be used in earnest; earnest interaction with a 'learner' (276a5) should rather take place in living, dialectical exchange. Socrates' point here is about the communication and record of intellectual finds, rather than about the process of discovery itself; indeed, in his account the philosopher who chooses between texts and dialogue *already has* knowledge (ἐπιστήμας ἔχοντα 276c3–4).[9] So Socrates is not prescribing how the serious philosopher is to make discoveries, but claiming that when one attempts to share or memorialise previous discoveries the best vehicle is a human soul. And when sharing these insights with other souls dialectic is required (276e5–6). In the *Phaedrus*, then, dialogue is praised quite specifically as the best tool for the informed philosopher's *teaching*.

But for Plato the most important insights have a transformative effect, most obviously so in the education of the philosopher in the *Republic*, where increased understanding goes hand-in-hand with a radical change of values and attitude (500b–d). And in the *Phaedrus* dialectical teaching is taken to lead to the greatest happiness for its recipient (277a3–4); if dialogue can improve one's life, then perhaps Plato also views it as the best tool for protreptic and conversion? I suggest that the *Phaedrus* does indeed suggest as much, albeit in a rather subtler way.

Throughout this dialogue Socrates attempts to win Phaedrus over to the life of philosophy and to that end he deploys a dazzling array of devices. At the start of the dialogue Phaedrus is much impressed by a sly speech of

---

[9] Compare the claim that the living statements of dialogue are transmitted 'with knowledge' (276a5, 276e7) and belong to 'one who knows' (276a8).

Lysias, which argues that a boy should grant sexual favours to men *not* in love with him. Socrates first attempts to better Lysias with a similar speech of his own and then offers a fulsome recantation and a glowing celebration of love and the philosophical life. But Phaedrus is not fully swayed by this rhetorical tour-de-force, noting that he will pray, with Socrates, that he may direct his life to philosophy '*if* this is better for us' (257b7–c1). So Socrates changes his tune, inviting Phaedrus to join him in an inquiry about good and poor speech and writing (259e); their interaction now shifts from exchanged speeches to a shared inquiry. At the end Phaedrus seems more convinced, adding his voice to Socrates' prayers with no hesitation (279c). In this abrupt change of register Plato contrasts different instruments of philosophical protreptic, and his moral is that living dialogue is the best medium here as well: to woo someone to philosophy one should engage him directly in its practice. So the drama of the *Phaedrus* illustrates the unique advantages of dialogue not only for teaching but also for recruiting others to philosophy.[10]

I have begun with the *Phaedrus*, as it is often taken to be the classic text for Plato's appraisal of dialogue; if so, a reader seeking to explain Plato's attraction to dialogue form need look no further than this one dialogue. But the *Phaedrus* does not state the value of dialogue for every sort of philosophical enterprise, inquiry included; we see an example, certainly, of collaborative and interpersonal inquiry and are shown that conversation is the best way to win a convert for philosophy. But the work does not suggest that such dialogue is the only setting or even the best setting for discoveries. The philosopher as proselytiser or teacher should resort to dialogue, but as inquirer he may operate in a quite different mode.

It turns out, of course, that he does not; dialogue of *some* kind is routinely taken to be the proper medium for inquiry. But whereas the *Phaedrus* offers a clear and attractive view of the value of dialogue for teaching and conversion,[11] it is far more difficult to uncover a consistent Platonic view of the merits of dialogue for the inquirer. In some works, as I shall show, Plato seems to suggest that one profits from inquiring with people with

---

[10] Note that the philosophical lover benefits his beloved precisely by teaching him and converting him, 'persuading and educating' him to imitate a god (253b5–7).

[11] But it is not clear how well it sits with other Platonic dialogues. The *Phaedrus* critique notes the importance of selecting a *suitable* dialectical partner; in dialogue one can distinguish between those to whom one should speak and those with whom one should be silent (276a) and can choose an 'appropriate soul' (276e). Little is said about what makes a soul 'appropriate' for dialectical teaching, but Socrates seems to have lost the zeal he showed in the *Apology* to question *everyone* he encountered. But perhaps there is no inconsistency or development here, for, unlike Socrates, the dialectician of the critique uses conversation to share his *knowledge* (see n.9).

whom one profoundly disagrees, elsewhere dialogue with like-minded people is favoured and in several passages Plato even envisages someone forming judgements through dialogue with *himself*. There is thus no heuristic analogue to the celebration of didactic dialogue in the *Phaedrus*.

DIALOGUE WITH CRITICS

Let us now turn to Platonic dialogues with more to say about the importance of dialogue in inquiry. I begin with the reflections on dialectic in the *Gorgias* and *Protagoras*.[12] Both these works suggest that conversation with a certain sort of interlocutor can help an inquirer to confirm his suppositions or theories. In both dialogues Socrates claims to be glad to have the chance to converse with the specific interlocutors he has encountered, on the grounds that it will further his inquiries. These passages are not without irony, but I suggest that they contain a serious point of method: dialogue with those who radically *disagree* with Socrates offers the best test for his moral theory.

In the *Gorgias* Socrates defends his ethical tenets and pursuit of philosophy in the face of fierce opposition from Callicles, his interlocutor in the final part of the dialogue. Socrates states that he counts himself lucky to have met Callicles (486e2–3); as one can test gold against a touchstone, he says, so he can test his soul against Callicles. For if Callicles turns out to agree with one of Socrates' convictions, this conviction will be confirmed as true (486e–487a) and sufficiently tested (487e). So conversation with a certain sort of interlocutor provides a unique opportunity to confirm the truth of the philosopher's beliefs.

But why is *Callicles* a suitable touchstone? Because he is wise, well disposed and frank, Socrates explains (487a). This smacks of irony, but Irwin has made the persuasive suggestion that another feature of Callicles does indeed qualify him as a suitable touchstone: the fact that he is a 'radical critic' of Socrates' views.[13] The context supports this interpretation, for Socrates hails Callicles as an ideal touchstone directly after Callicles' heated criticism of Socrates' arguments and scathing attack on the philosophical life (482c–486d).

---

[12] I do not of course mean to suggest that these works are *exclusively* interested in dialogue as a means to philosophical discoveries; in the *Gorgias*, for example, Socrates not only inquires but also tries to win Callicles round to the pursuit of virtue.

[13] Irwin (1979) 183.

We find a similar scenario in the *Protagoras*; here as well Socrates suggests that dialogue allows for *confirmation* of one's discoveries or conjectures. Socrates cites with approval the Homeric maxim of 'when two go together, one notices ahead of the other' (348d1; Hom. *Il.* 10.224). Collaboration makes people more resourceful, he explains, adding that even if one has an idea by oneself, one immediately finds someone to whom it can be shown and with whom it can be 'confirmed' (348d2–5). And it seems that there are certain interlocutors better suited to this sort of confirmation. For Socrates states his happiness at having encountered Protagoras in conversation and his belief that he would inquire best in collaboration with the sophist (348d–349a).

Now Socrates explains his claim that Protagoras is an ideal interlocutor by noting that the sophist not only claims to be noble but can make other people virtuous – and charges a fee for it to boot. Irony, once again, but we may suspect that in another respect Protagoras is indeed a promising interlocutor. For his disagreement with Socrates (and his ability to defend his own account) suggests that consensus between *him* and Socrates is likely to signal objective success. And in the *Protagoras* Socrates undertakes a more ambitious project than his attempt to convince Callicles. For a host of renowned and independent sophists have flocked to the setting (Callias' house) and Socrates extracts consensus not only from Protagoras but from other intellectuals, questioning Hippias and Prodicus together with Protagoras (358a–359a).

We might contrast Socrates' conversation with Hippocrates near the start of the *Protagoras* (311–4). Hippocrates seems to be a close member of Socrates' circle, and so Socrates' ability to unsettle and convince this young man might seem a rather trifling achievement. Not so when the scene shifts to Callias' house, where Socrates can win round an array of foreign intellectuals. These are significantly harder test cases for Socrates, and his ability to devise consensus with *them* provides powerful confirmation for his views.[14]

So these two dialogues tell a rather nuanced story about the place of consensus and dissent in dialectic. The philosopher aims to secure agreement and concord by close argument; this is how his suppositions are tested and (should he succeed) confirmed. But initial *dissent* is not only allowed but thoroughly welcome, and it had better be sincere and genuine dissent. For independent and dissenting interlocutors make for the strongest confirmation, should the philosopher be able to drive them too to consensus.

This process of course requires dialogue with others. We therefore have one Platonic account of the heuristic value of interpersonal exchange, one

---

[14] For a fuller account see Long (2005).

which puts a premium on open disagreement and a range of views. Might this not form the basis for the sort of account outlined above?[15] The exchange should certainly be open, in the sense that interlocutors should be open and candid with any disagreement or qualms. But they must also offer open and candid *agreement*, should Socrates show them compelling reasons to toe the Socratic line; compare the dialogue between Socrates, Agathon and Aristophanes at the end of Plato's *Symposium*, where Socrates is said to 'compel them to agree' that an expert tragedian is also a comedian (223d). Of course, we may sympathise when assent is wrung from Protagoras at the end of his conversation with Socrates (360d–e) and, like Callicles, we might feel that this sort of dialogue is rather 'coercive' (505d). But the dialectician of course coerces on the strength of the interlocutor's own admitted beliefs and their entailments, rather than from personal prestige or authority.

DIALOGUE WITH ALLIES; DIALOGUE WITH ONESELF

This is not, however, Plato's last word on the use of dialogue for intellectual discovery. The *Protagoras* and *Gorgias* suggest that we can confirm tenets through dialogue with unsympathetic respondents, but this seems a risky strategy. Is there not a danger that such interlocutors might prove too recalcitrant for proper exchange? Already in the *Gorgias* we see Callicles giving insincere answers (499b) and refusing to answer Socrates (505d–507a). And in the *Protagoras* Socrates is able to pursue the inquiry on his own terms largely thanks to the protests of the assembled company, by whom Protagoras is 'compelled' to persevere (338e). But what if the interlocutor proves intransigent and the dialectician has no eager crowd to whom he can appeal for help?

These worries are raised and addressed in the *Republic*. Thrasymachus profoundly disagrees with Socrates' conception of justice and political rule, and so is eminently qualified as a 'hard case' for the dialectical testing portrayed in the *Gorgias* and *Protagoras*. But in the event he proves over-qualified, flatly refusing to give sincere replies to Socrates' questions (351c6, 351d7, 352b3–4). So Plato seems to be raising the very dangers sketched in the previous paragraph. How can Socrates proceed?

I suggest that the *Republic* offers two solutions, both of which revise the model of dialectic in the *Protagoras* and *Gorgias*. The first has already been acknowledged in the scholarship – replace Thrasymachus with more

---

[15]　See p. 45 above.

sympathetic interlocutors.[16] From the second book of the *Republic* Thrasymachus falls silent and Glaucon and Adeimantus renew his challenge, claiming themselves to be in sympathy with Socrates but unable to defend his assertions. They begin by setting out the best case they can for Thrasymachus' position, and during the remainder of the *Republic* they frequently call on Socrates to develop or defend his proposals.[17] And their challenges are fundamental to the course of the dialogue. Socrates' central proposal that philosophers must rule and his description of philosophers' nature and education are his response to a challenge by Glaucon to show that the ideal city is possible (471c–e); if the city is to be established, Socrates replies, philosophical rule is the best recipe for success.

In this view of dialectic a critical voice remains and the goal is still consensus; Socrates completes his inquiry by convincing his interlocutors and answering their challenges. But actual dissent is no longer required in the same way as in the *Protagoras* or *Gorgias*. The respondent must be willing to raise objections, certainly, and must be given the chance to voice his doubts. But there is no longer a suggestion that a rigorous dialectical inquiry moves from existing opposed conviction to consensus; interlocutors must still be sincere, engaged and prompt to voice qualms, but they need not disagree at the outset. For at the start of the inquiry Socrates' interlocutors, Glaucon and Adeimantus, are hesitant about, rather than opposed to, Socrates' claims. In this sort of dialogue the *opportunity* for opposition is essential; opposition itself is not.

This revised dialectic will enjoy a long career in Plato's dialogues, and in subsequent works sympathetic and pliable interlocutors are openly preferred.[18] But philosophical inquiry still seems to call for an interlocutor of a certain moral and intellectual stamp, one who is willing to take part in a (possibly extensive) intellectual search and capable of providing relevant and appropriate challenges. Of course, in the *Republic* Socrates is able to call on Adeimantus and Glaucon, but what if no suitable collaborator is available? Here Plato gives a second, more radical solution; the philosopher will still proceed by testing accounts and asking questions, but this sort of dialogue can be conducted within himself.[19]

This solution is sketched very lightly within the *Republic*. In his account of the dialectician, the expert in questions and answers (534d–e), Socrates

---

[16] See Scott (1999).   [17] 372c–e, 419a, 422a, 449c, 457d–e, 487b–d and 519d.

[18] See *Parmenides* 137b–c and *Sophist* 217d.

[19] Compare Epictetus' claim that solitude need not bring inactivity, as we have the ability to converse with ourselves (*Diss.* 3.13.6–8).

notes that someone only understands a subject if he can give an account of it 'to *himself* and to someone else' (534b4–6). So it would seem that in dialectic one can offer an account to oneself as well as to others for scrutiny and testing; it is possible to internalise the sort of criticism and scrutiny that Socrates receives from Glaucon and Adeimantus. Socrates also gives an example of how this internal dialogue might get started. He notes that when we are faced with contradictory appearances we are provoked to ask ourselves questions to resolve the confusion, describing the soul as 'stirring up thought in itself' (524e–525a). So Plato may believe not only that this sort of internal dialectic could be cultivated, but also that it is the natural and inevitable response to perplexity.

One passage of dialogue within the *Republic* may also allude to this solution. At the end of book 5 Socrates attempts to devise an argument that would convince a non-philosopher, a lover of sights and sounds, that he possesses no knowledge. He asks Glaucon to represent the sight-lover in their exchange (476e), and so it seems to be Glaucon's role to voice the objections that the sight-lover would have given. But Glaucon raises no such objection, and so it falls to Socrates himself to bring the argument to a halt where necessary (477b10–12) – before they reach the conclusion, he interjects, they must set out a general account of faculties. Here the dialogue of course remains spoken and interpersonal, but by putting the hesitation into *Socrates'* mouth Plato suggests that in devising an argument we can act as our own critic.

So the *Republic* gives two quite different solutions to the problem of an interlocutor's intransigence. Plato may still believe that interpersonal dialogue has its distinctive merits; in the first solution, cooperative and engaged interlocutors are enlisted in the expectation that they will point out oversights and criticise unduly swift reasoning. But the second solution, internal reflection, suggests that dialogue with others is not essential after all for the philosopher. And in neither solution does Plato put a premium on opening an inquiry with opposed commitments. Already, then, it seems difficult to trace a single Platonic view on the nature and value of philosophical dialogue.

INTERNAL DIALOGUE

I now turn to the fate of the second solution in a later dialogue. The *Republic* is sketchy at best about the nature of internal reflection, and so it is unclear to what extent this reflection resembles *conversation*. This is vital for understanding Plato's evaluation of dialogue. If Plato believes that

solitary thought can take the place of conversation with others, to what
extent is he abandoning the models of conversational inquiry in the *Gorgias*
and *Protagoras* (and in the *Republic* itself)?

So I turn to the description of thought as internal dialogue in the
Theaetetus (189e4–190a8):[20]

ΣΩ. τὸ δὲ διανοεῖσθαι ἆρ᾽ ὅπερ ἐγὼ καλεῖς;
ΘΕΑΙ. τί καλῶν;
ΣΩ. λόγον ὃν αὐτὴ πρὸς αὑτὴν ἡ ψυχὴ διεξέρχεται περὶ ὧν ἂν σκοπῇ.
     ὥς γε μὴ εἰδώς σοι ἀποφαίνομαι. τοῦτο γάρ μοι ἰνδάλλεται
     διανοουμένη οὐκ ἄλλο τι ἢ διαλέγεσθαι, αὐτὴ ἑαυτὴν ἐρωτῶσα
     καὶ ἀποκρινομήνη, καὶ φάσκουσα καὶ οὐ φάσκουσα. ὅταν δὲ
     ὁρίσασα, εἴτε βραδύτερον εἴτε καὶ ὀξύτερον ἐπᾴξασα, τὸ αὐτὸ
     ἤδη φῇ καὶ μὴ διστάζῃ, δόξαν ταύτην τίθεμεν αὐτῆς. ὥστ᾽ ἔγωγε
     τὸ δοξάζειν λέγειν καλῶ καὶ τὴν δόξαν λόγον εἰρημένον, οὐ
     μέντοι πρὸς ἄλλον οὐδὲ φωνῇ, ἀλλὰ σιγῇ πρὸς αὐτόν· σὺ δὲ τί;
ΘΕΑΙ. κἀγώ.

Soc. And do you describe thinking as I do?
Tht. How do you describe it?
Soc. As the talk which the soul goes through with itself about any subjects
      which it investigates. Now I don't claim to know what I'm declaring to
      you. But the soul, as I picture it, when thinking is merely conversing,
      asking itself questions and answering, both affirming and denying. When
      it has arrived at a decision, whether slowly or with a sudden bound, and
      now says one and the same thing and is not in doubt, we call that its
      judgement; and so I describe judging as talking and judgement as talk
      held, not with someone else, nor aloud, but in silence with oneself. How
      do you describe it?
Tht. In the same way.

The importance of this passage is often noted, but not its relevance to the
problem posed by an interlocutor who refuses to take part in dialectic. But
the *Theaetetus* is no less aware of this problem than the *Republic* was. The
first part of the dialogue is an attempt to engage with Protagoras' relativism
and Heraclitus' theory of flux in the *absence* of a Protagorean or Heraclitean
interlocutor. And this is no accident, for it is suggested that neither party
would get involved in dialectic. Were Protagoras' relativism true, Socrates
says, the attempt to criticise one another's opinions and the practice of
dialectic would be merely a waste of time, as everyone's opinions would be
correct (161e–162a). As for the Heracliteans, it is claimed that they never

---

[20] Compare *Sophist* 263e3–5, 264a8–b1.

offer a firm account or remain engaged in conversation (179e–180c), so comprehensive is their opposition to stability. The *Theaetetus* thus offers fresh reasons to suppose that dialogue with some parties may be impossible; not only are there those who, like Thrasymachus, lack the moral qualities required of an engaged and cooperative interlocutor, but some parties have a doctrinal or partisan aversion to dialectic itself. So it is natural to suppose that Plato sees the notion of internal dialogue as (at least in part) a solution to this difficulty.

Let us now see what exactly is claimed in the passage quoted above. First of all, is Plato claiming that *everything* we might call 'thinking' takes the form of an internal conversation? As Burnyeat objects, various mental events simply do not conform to this description.[21] But happily Plato is not making so extravagant a claim. For Socrates is quite specific about the *sort* of thinking which does take this form – that undertaken when a soul investigates something about which it has not yet reached a 'judgement' or 'verdict' (δόξα). He thus has in mind deliberative inquiry in an undecided soul. So while διανοεῖσθαι here is commonly translated as 'thinking', a more accurate translation might be 'thinking something through' – note the play on διανοεῖσθαι, διεξέρχεται and (of course) διαλέγεσθαι.

This is merely to say that there must be something deliberative in the thinking described here. But Socrates grants that deliberations vary greatly in their depth and rigour. Elsewhere (*Philebus* 38c–d) he imagines someone questioning himself on a quite mundane matter – 'what is that object in the distance?' – and reaching a simple answer: 'a man' or 'a statue'. Nonetheless, this is deliberation, a case of the soul attempting to 'judge' (κρίνειν) what it sees. The *Theaetetus* provides similar examples, such as the simple (though failed) attempt to identify an animal (190c). So internal deliberation can be of an altogether humdrum kind.

But in the *Theaetetus* Socrates also allows for reflection of a more philosophical nature, for he speaks of the soul reaching its decision 'whether slowly or with a sudden bound'. A reader versed in Plato's dialogues should not miss this nudge. For the proper or necessary *length* of an inquiry is one of Plato's most frequent concerns in discussions of philosophical method and practice.[22] The suggestion that a soul can conduct a slow and elaborate process of questioning thus seems to allow an individual to traverse the

---

[21] Burnyeat offers as counterexamples the thoughts with which a child reads a story or an artist paints at (1990) 84.

[22] See *Republic* 435c–d, 504a–d; *Theaetetus* 172c–d, 187d–e; *Sophist* 261a–c; *Statesman* 277a–c, 283a–d, 286b–287a.

'longer roads' of proper philosophical conversation. So Plato uses the notion of internal dialogue to capture philosophical as well as mundane reflections.[23] Indeed, he may wish to stress that there is a fundamental *kinship* between the two; just as διαλέγεσθαι [*dialegesthai*] can mean both 'to have a conversation' and 'to philosophise', so internal dialogue can be either commonplace or expert reflection.

The internal dialogue of the *Theaetetus* thus gives an individual scope for solitary philosophising. Let us finally consider the nature of this internal conversation. As we might expect, there remains the suggestion of an exchange – the soul raises a question ('what is that object in the distance?') and either gives an answer directly ('it's a statue') or works more 'slowly' in a sequence of questions and answers as it puzzles through the question. But think back to the distinction I drew between heuristic dialogue as portrayed in the *Protagoras* and *Gorgias* and its representation in the *Republic*. In its internal dialogue does the soul move from opposed convictions to inner agreement, or is the dialogue more akin to the collaborative conversation of the *Republic*?

I suggest that Plato envisages both sorts of dialogue being internalised. He gives examples of cases where there need be no initial divergent beliefs. To take the case of the *Philebus*, the soul *could* of course be torn between conflicting impressions of the object or consider alternative interpretations of what has been seen. But that is not how Socrates presents the case – in his account the soul simply opts for one view or the other. In this example of internal dialogue the soul moves from hesitancy to conviction, rather than from two conflicting convictions to one. If we are to believe that a soul could conduct a similar *philosophical* inquiry, we might imagine it reflecting at length on a topic where it has as yet reached no verdict. Of course, in so doing it could *consider* opposed beliefs and choose between them; it could raise objections and alternatives in the manner of Glaucon and Adeimantus. But on this model the soul contains competing considerations, not competing convictions.

However, the *Theaetetus* passage also suggests that a more adversarial sort of dialogue could take place. It speaks of the soul not only failing to say 'one and the same thing' but 'both affirming and denying' during the dialogue; on this model, the dialogue concludes when the soul resolves *conflict* rather

---

[23] Ryle supposed that Plato had in mind philosophy in particular when he describes thought in the *Sophist* (and presumably in the *Theaetetus* too): 'doubtless when Plato said, in his *Sophist*, that in thinking the soul is conversing with herself, or – I surmise rather – that she is debating with herself, he was considering what he himself did and had to do, when tackling philosophical problems in particular', (1979) 33.

than mere doubt or ignorance. So whereas the examples of thinking and judgement do not refer to conflicting views, the analysis of 'thinking through' as dialogue seems far more interested in adversarial exchange.[24] If so, then we can also practise internally the sort of dialogue depicted in the *Protagoras* and *Gorgias*, putting contending beliefs to the test.[25]

CONCLUSION

These examples show the difficulty of giving a synoptic overview of Plato's attitude to dialogue and its merits; his works contain a wide range of views on the very nature of the dialogue from which the philosopher is to benefit. As soon as we flesh out the skeletal claim that Plato's dialogues reflect his interest in philosophical dialogue, we no longer have a unitary account to explain his use of dialogue form. Instead we find that in two works he suggests that the philosopher should seek to engage his opponents in dialogue, in another dialogue that the philosopher should collaborate with sympathetic interlocutors, and elsewhere that the philosopher can question himself and indeed *always* questions himself when thinking a problem through. On the strength of this evidence, at least, it seems unlikely that we shall find a sufficiently rich account of dialogue form that also accounts for Plato's entire *oeuvre*. It thus seems unlikely – a fortiori – that we shall find a significant rationale for dialogue form common to *all* writers of dialogues. And so the use or neglect of a genre, in and of itself, may perhaps tell us little about an author's ideals and outlook. There would then be no reliable short cut from the history of genres to the history of ideas.[26]

---

[24] It is beyond the scope of this paper to explain why. A suggestion: the interpersonal dialogue practised in the *Theaetetus* is of a broadly adversarial character, with Socrates as midwife attempting to refute the suggestions of his interlocutor. Plato's intention in stressing the adversarial nature of internal dialogue may be to suggest that we can internalise *midwifery*, practising this sort of test on our own beliefs.

[25] McCabe emphasises this feature of internal dialogue, reflection on opposed (or at least *different*) points of view at (2000) 275 and (2006) 49 and 51. See also Sedley (2003) 2. Sedley draws on Plato's descriptions of thought as internal dialogue to suggest an intriguing account of the dialogue form: in Plato's dialogues the author is 'thinking aloud', (2003) 1. But it is difficult to read *every* Platonic dialogue as a transcript of Plato's own thinking. In the *Cratylus*, as Sedley notes, two of the speakers (Cratylus and Socrates – though presumably not Hermogenes) represent ingredients of Plato's own 'intellectual make-up', (2003) 3. So far so good. But surely the assorted speakers of, say, the *Protagoras* and *Symposium* cannot *all* represent elements of Plato's own thinking.

[26] I wish to thank the participants at the CRASSH colloquium and all those with whom I have discussed Plato and dialogue form, particularly Simon Goldhill, M. M. McCabe, Malcolm Schofield, David Sedley and James Warren.

PART II

Empire models

CHAPTER 4

Ciceronian dialogue

Malcolm Schofield

THE ACADEMIC DIALOGUE

Cicero is often perceived as a much inferior composer of dialogues when judged against the Platonic gold standard.[1] No mesmerising Socrates fascinates the reader. There are no dramatic *coups de théâtre*. We miss the erotic complexities of the gymnasium and the symposium, and even more the nagging of Socratic dialectic. Above all, Plato writes philosophy of a power and originality beyond Cicero's capacity. In this paper I attempt to do something to redress the balance. I am going to argue that Cicero does things with the dialogue that Plato doesn't – and that Hume (another standard of comparison) doesn't either.

There are two particular dimensions in which Ciceronian dialogue achieves something all its own. First, in its final Academic form (as represented by the major works of 45 and 44 BCE) Ciceronian dialogue is more genuinely open-ended than Platonic. In dialogues such as *Academica*, *De Finibus*, *De Natura Deorum* and *De Diuinatione* Cicero gives properly argued alternatives a real run for their money, and adopts a variety of literary strategies for indicating that further reflection on their merits and choice between them is left to the reader. If the point of dialogue is to explore and to invite to exploration through debate, the form of the Academic dialogue looks better constructed to achieve this than the Platonic. Contrast, for example, the treatment of Thrasymachus' position in Plato's *Republic*. Thrasymachus is represented as a *rhêtor* who has no sympathy with philosophical investigation and no wish to define himself in terms of an argued theoretical position. When in a sequence at the beginning of Book 2 of the dialogue running to ten Stephanus pages Glaucon restates what he takes

---

[1] 'These courteous, formal discussions in the libraries and gardens of the great villas belonging to Roman nobles differ greatly from Plato's more casual and incomparably vivid encounters in the streets and shops of Athens, in which everyday conversation glides insensibly into philosophic argument': Rawson (1975) 233. Others less sympathetic to Cicero than Rawson might have put the point more trenchantly.

to be an improved version of Thrasymachus' views in just such theoretical terms, with Adeimantus bringing further arguments in support, the response Plato attributes to Socrates occupies the whole of the rest of the work (around 250 Stephanus pages), and ends with moral exhortation. Conversion to the Socratic viewpoint is the objective, not balanced consideration of alternatives.

Cicero's second claim on our consideration rests on his highly original exploitation of authorial presence. Here he shows to advantage by comparison with Hume as well as Plato. Hume's *Dialogues concerning Natural Religion* do preserve a Ciceronian open-endedness. But like Plato, Hume is careful to avoid participating in the conversation himself, or even appearing as narrator. Cicero's dialogues, particularly the Academic dialogues, take more of a risk in this regard. Cicero puts *himself* into his dialogues, and thereby gives dialogue an existential dimension of engagement and self-exposure that anonymity and the urbanities of Platonic or Humean anonymity can't reach. Philosophical dialogue is converted into exploration of what it is for a Roman statesman forced from the political arena to grapple with disjunctions between politics and philosophy, and to try to bridge the gulf between public and private, acting and writing, concealment and disclosure.

In these two dimensions, at least, Ciceronian dialogue may claim to be more truly dialogic than either Plato or Hume. The trouble is that other features of Cicero's writing may make it look much less so. Chief among them is something Pamphilus may be getting at when on the first page of Hume's *Dialogues* he says: 'To deliver a SYSTEM in conversation scarcely appears natural.' Aren't Cicero's dialogues really treatises, not dialogues at all? This is a difficulty it may be advisable to address before I elaborate on the two distinctive strengths I have identified in Ciceronian dialogue. I shall approach this issue slightly crabwise.

THE CICERONIAN DIALOGUE-TREATISE

In a selection of Hume's writings published in 1963, the editor – Richard Wollheim – had this to say about the *Dialogues*. He has been talking of what he calls the chronically sceptical disposition of Hume's mind, 'which no sooner adopted one intellectual position than it tried to see the best in all the arguments that would refute it'.[2] He goes on: 'It is significant that Hume made a far more genuinely dramatic use of the form [i.e. dialogue] than

[2] Wollheim (1963) 18.

either of his two great predecessors in the *genre*, Plato and Berkeley, whose sympathies as between the various participants are immediately and unambiguously declared.' Two things are striking about this remark. First, Wollheim makes no reference to Cicero as a predecessor of Hume, even though he must have known perfectly well that the literary model of the *Dialogues* was Cicero's *De Natura Deorum* (something he never actually tells the reader).[3] Hume himself would no doubt have been mildly astonished, living as he did in an age in which 'the fame of Cicero flourishes'.[4] Second, the main grounds on which Hume is preferred to Plato and Berkeley are oddly stated. Pamphilus' preface identifies Demea with 'rigid inflexible orthodoxy' and Philo with 'careless scepticism', whereas Cleanthes – his mentor, we subsequently discover – is credited with an 'accurate philosophical turn'. His sympathies are made crystal clear. Of course the careful reader subsequently discovers that Hume makes Philo's contributions to discussion so weighty as to call these relative valuations into question. But Cicero would have been a better choice to exemplify the claim about declaration of sympathies that Wollheim actually makes.

If we think of the dialogues included in the philosophical encyclopedia of 46–44 BCE, what Wollheim adds about Hume could be said of Cicero also: 'The dialogue form … not merely reflected, it also reinforced, the ambiguities in Hume's position.' Cicero could see all too clearly the attractions of both Stoic providentialism and Academic scepticism in theology, or in ethics both of the heroic Stoic stance on virtue and of Aristotelian recognition of the badness of pain and the power of fortune for good or ill. Working through the arguments on either side not only suited his tastes and skills as an advocate, but gave him the opportunity to enact and perfect the judiciousness and hesitation of the Academic method that were second nature to him.

Of course, there is one epithet Wollheim applies to Hume that will not work for Ciceronian dialogue: 'dramatic'.[5] That presumably helps to explain Wollheim's silence about Cicero. Cicero is usually rather more impressive than Hume at stage-setting and in introducing his interlocutors, as for example in *De Legibus* or in the evocative walk through Athens that launches the discussion of Book 5 of *De Finibus*. He can convey the flavour of witty and combative philosophical conversation when he wants to, as in

---

[3] The point had been made by Norman Kemp Smith, in the classic edition of the *Dialogues* on which Wollheim was heavily reliant. See Kemp Smith (1935) 77–8.
[4] *An Enquiry concerning Human Understanding* 1.4.   [5] However, see below, p. 79.

De Legibus (again),[6] or in the closing section of *De Finibus* 5. In fact the sparring of Hume's gentlemanly protagonists in *Dialogues concerning Natural Religion* strikes me as itself very Ciceronian. But though Cicero commands these dramatic resources, he doesn't exploit them dramatically. Often enough their use is incidental to uninterrupted exposition of the Stoic or Epicurean or Aristotelian theory of the subject at issue, followed by similarly uninterrupted development of an Antiochean or Academic critique of the theory: *in utramque partem perpetua oratio*, as he puts it at the beginning of *De Fato* (*Fat.* 1).

Cicero is well capable of seeing the philosophical limitations of this procedure. He has this to say before the start of his critique of Torquatus' exposition of Epicurean ethics (*Fin.* 2.3):

> Much as I enjoyed hearing him [i.e. Torquatus] speaking uninterrupted, it is none the less more manageable if one stops after each individual point and ascertains what each of the listeners is happy to concede, and what they would reject. One can then draw the inferences one wishes from the points conceded and reach one's conclusions. When, on the other hand, the speech races on like a torrent, carrying with it all manner of material, then there is nothing the listener can grasp at or get hold of. There is no way to check the raging flood. (Trans. Raphael Woolf)[7]

And the first few moves in the critique itself are indeed couched in the form of a Socratic conversation. But then Cicero reverts to the oratorical mode (with one interruption from the young Gaius Triarius) for the rest of the book. I suppose he might have wanted to explain that he only adopts it to draw inferences and reach conclusions, and only after it has become clear by dialectical questioning just how muddled the Epicureans are about what is meant by 'pleasure'.[8]

Negation of the dramatic in the interests of exposition of systems is no doubt what has made it pretty standard for scholars to talk in the first

---

[6] As James Zetzel rightly says, while 'much of the dialogue is composed of long speeches by Cicero himself, it is a far more vivid and realistic conversation than those of *On the Orator* and *On the Commonwealth*', with Cicero's brother Quintus particularly stroppy in places: see Zetzel (1999) xxi.

[7] See Annas (2001) 27.

[8] Cicero's procedure here anticipates the method he follows in the five books of the *Tusculans*, where after the interlocutor has stated a thesis, there follows Socratic questioning until both parties are ready for more or less uninterrupted exposition of a contrary argument from Cicero. The Socratic pedigree of the method is flagged at the outset (1.8). A later example is the fragmentary *De Fato* (although Hirtius' statement of the thesis Cicero will seek to refute is one of the missing sections), where Hirtius refers to its employment in the *Tusculans* as Academic practice (*Fat.* 4). Elsewhere Cicero attributes its use to Arcesilaus and Carneades, e.g. at *De Oratore* 3.80 (quoted below): in fact Arcesilaus 'revived' (*revocavit*) Socratic method (*Fin.* 2.2). When he is being careful (as at *Fat.* 1–4), Cicero clearly distinguishes this method from the *argumentum in utramque partem* of the main Academic dialogues, in which continuous speeches are given successively on both sides of the case.

instance not of dialogues but of *treatises* when referring to Cicero's philosophical corpus.[9] To take one recent example, this is the mode of reference preferred throughout Catherine Steel's *Reading Cicero*. Typical is her chapter on 'Genre', which after 'speeches' and 'poetry' turns to 'treatises', and manages to present a preliminary discussion of the philosophical works without once using or mentioning the word 'dialogue'.[10] Later sections of the book make it clear that Steel is not insensitive to the status of many of these works *as* dialogues. On the contrary, she has illuminating things to say particularly about Cicero's interlocutors and his predilection for locating the philosophical conversations he constructs in the republican past.[11] Nonetheless the frequent preference in the scholarly literature for 'treatise' over 'dialogue' is liable to reinforce assumptions or perceptions that (leaving quality and ambition of philosophical vision aside) Cicero opts for a *form* of writing that is less challenging than the Platonic dialogue.

It might be better to follow Paul MacKendrick's lead and speak of the 'dialogue-treatise', which at once sounds more intriguing, especially if one registers MacKendrick's claim that this is a form of writing actually pioneered by Cicero.[12] It doesn't appear that anyone before Cicero had thought to use the dialogue form to write a treatise, that is to say a work which deliberately sets out to give a systematic exposition of a particular philosophical topic.[13] If you prefer Hume's *Dialogues* to Cicero, a chief reason may be that they do *not* constitute a 'dialogue-treatise', but the representation of free-flowing conversation twisting and turning as it will – naturally, as Pamphilus might have put it. Hume must have seen a problem to be negotiated here. When Pamphilus is made to remark in the preface that his report will allow him to 'enter into a more exact detail of their reasonings [i.e. the interlocutors'], and display those various systems, which they advanced with regard to so delicate a subject as that of Natural Religion', the choice of vocabulary is surely significant. It is as though Hume is saying: Cicero was right to want to explain and debate philosophical *systems* (see e.g. *ND* 1.9), and to choose dialogue as his medium. But good conversation requires one to 'display' rather than 'deliver' (or as we might say 'expound') system.

---

[9] A pleasing exception is Rawson (1975) Chs. 9 and 13.
[10] See Steel (2005) 33–43. The word does start getting used in later sections, as soon as she gets down to more specific consideration of individual dialogues.
[11] See Steel (2005) 106–14, 131–40.   [12] See MacKendrick (1989) 25.
[13] I suppose that in surviving Greek material Plato's *Timaeus* comes closest to doing that – interestingly the Platonic dialogue Cicero translated *in extenso*, although not so far as we can tell the opening conversation which marks *Timaeus as* a dialogue.

To Cicero that would be to attach more weight in philosophical dialogue to conversation than by the time of the encyclopedia of 46–44 BCE he seems to have come to think it deserved. He has another ideal: the thoroughly rhetorical conception of what he calls *perfecta philosophia*. Cicero aspires to be like Aristotle in combining *prudentia* with *eloquentia*. 'I have always judged philosophy in its perfect form', he says at the beginning of the *Tusculan Disputations* (1.7), 'to be philosophy which on the most important questions can speak fully (*copiose*) and with embellishments (*ornateque*).' In the preface to Book 2 he elaborates further on this. Instead of Greek libraries we need liberally educated people who can apply elegance of expression to rational and methodical philosophising. He castigates those who fail on both counts simultaneously. They cannot make the right distinctions nor organise their arguments, and they cannot write elegantly or with the embellishments of good style (*TD* 2.6–7).[14] The perfect philosopher, in short, is the perfect orator Cicero had had Crassus delineate in Book 3 of *De Oratore* (3.71–2) ten years before. Rhetorically compelling exposition of a system is precisely the performance that will best express this combination of powers.[15]

Or rather, systematic expositions of opposing viewpoints, as *De Oratore* goes on to explain (3.80):

If there has at some time existed a person who in Aristotelian fashion can speak on both sides about all subjects, and in every case can develop two opposing speeches through knowledge of his rules;[16] or in the manner of Arcesilaus and Carneades can argue against every position put forward; and who combines with that method the experience and practice in speaking we have been discussing: that person would be the true and perfect and indeed only orator.

In the *Tusculans* Cicero explains why the Aristotelian model is appropriate for philosophy too (*TD* 2.9):

The custom of the Peripatetics and the Academy – of arguing on opposite sides about all subjects – always commended itself to me, not only for the reason that approximation to truth on each subject could not be discovered in any other way, but also because it afforded maximal practice in speaking. Aristotle was the first to follow this custom, then those who followed him.

---

[14] Cicero seems to have in mind chiefly the writings on Epicureanism of C. Amafinius and his imitators: *TD* 4.6–7; cf. 1.6, *Ac.* 1.5.

[15] For more discussion of *perfecta philosophia* see Gildenhard (2007) 148–56; and on the characteristics of Cicero's philosophical rhetoric as actually practised in the Academic dialogues, see Smith (1995).

[16] The rules (*praecepta*) in question are presumably the rules for invention supplied by the Aristotelian topics (cf. *Or.* 46): see Long (1995) 52–8; Reinhardt (2000) 542–4.

Here in a nutshell is the rationale for the Academic dialogue-treatise. For a philosophical position to be presented properly, it must be developed logically and systematically, *and* also with an elegant and full persuasiveness that will appeal to the liberally educated person. But it needs to be balanced with an equally compelling counterargument. Challenging a position in dialogue is the only or at any rate the easiest way to discover what it is that approximates to truth (approximation, not Stoic certainty, is the best that Academics think can be hoped for). In Book 1 of the *Tusculans* Cicero represents this ingredient of his method as his Socratic inheritance (1.8).

At this point we encounter a complication. A Socratic challenge, as Cicero was well aware, took the form not of a continuous piece of oratory *Aristotelio more*, but of question and answer: *brachylogia*, not *makrologia*, to use the terminology of the *Gorgias* and *Protagoras*.[17] Indeed in the immediate sequel to the reference to the Socratic method, he conducts a sustained examination of his interlocutor's opinion that death is an evil precisely by Socratic questioning (*TD* 1.9–16). It is indicative, however, that after a few pages of this a point is reached at which the respondent is represented as wanting something fuller (*uberius*): what Cicero has just argued is rather thorny (*spinosiora*), forcing him (*cogunt*) to say 'Yes' before he's really in a position to assent (*TD* 1.16).[18] He wants to hear a continuous speech (*continentem orationem*): which is what he gets (after a further bout of question and answer: 1.23–5) for the rest of Book 1 of the *Tusculans*.[19] Elsewhere Cicero represents the superior richness and flow of continuous speech as less open to criticism than confined and narrow argumentation in the Stoic manner – just as a flowing river is less easily polluted than an enclosed body of water (*ND* 2.20; cf. *Parad.* Praef. 1–3). I suppose the point may be that someone who speaks at length is in a better position to express his meaning with all the precision and due qualification (and so to avoid misapprehension by his readers or hearers), than in short exchanges is feasible.

So for the most part dialogue embodying the challenge of counterargument will be constructed in Cicero more on the Aristotelian than the Socratic model. This does not prevent him from conceiving of *continens oratio* as a thoroughly Academic practice (in fact he suggests that the Socratic method had actually been abandoned in the Academy of his own day: *Fin.* 2.2). It was evidently something for which the great second-century scholarch

---

[17] See the discussions of Long and Ford above, Chapters 2 and 3.
[18] On questions to do with the 'coerciveness' of Socratic dialectic, see Irwin (1986).
[19] This stretch of Book 1 of the *Tusculans* is well analysed in Gildenhard (2007) 207–27.

Carneades was particularly notable. Carneades' speeches during the Athenian embassy to Rome of 155 BCE for and against the idea of natural justice, delivered on successive days,[20] must presumably lie somewhere behind Cicero's presentation of him as someone who like Aristotle married philosophy with oratory (*De Or.* 3.68). And by Cicero's time it is clear that the construction of speeches on either side of the case was seen as the hallmark of rhetoric as taught in the Academy as much as by Peripatetics (*De Or.* 3.107).[21] But there is no evidence that the *literary* form of the *philosophical* dialogue-treatise pairing speeches *in contrarias partes* was the invention of anyone but Cicero himself.

The complaint that the Ciceronian dialogue is really a treatise, not anything dialogic at all, has led us inexorably to the old dispute between philosophy and rhetoric. As his history of that dispute in Book 3 of *De Oratore* makes crystal clear, Cicero knows perfectly well that the attempt to achieve a marriage between the two is an enterprise which contradicts most of the tendencies in both rhetoric and philosophy that have developed from the point when (as he represents it) Socrates effected a divorce between them. His creation of the philosophical dialogue-treatise is self-consciously designed to demonstrate that philosophy by oratory is better philosophy – and more not less dialogic. Oratory's expansiveness permits presentation that is more complete and carefully expressed than sequences of question and answer are well adapted to provide. Its rules of construction make for resourcefulness in finding and organising material. It is geared to persuasiveness, rather than the coercion the respondent in the *Tusculans* complains about when coping with Cicero's Socratic questioning, or the nit-picking and bone-stripping characteristic of Stoic dialectic (*Fin.* 4.6). Above all, the practice of *argumentum in contrarias partes* gives readers the opportunity to exercise their own judgement after reflecting on systematically articulated positions ideally set out fully and elegantly, yet with requisite precision and complexity.

THE JUDGEMENT OF THE READER

The point of writing Academic dialogues is not to advise us of what *Cicero* thinks on a question at issue – he follows, he says, the Socratic practice of

---

[20] See Lact. *Inst.* 5.14.3–5 [= Cic. *Rep.* 3.9 Ziegler; cf. Cic. *Rep.* 3.7 Powell], with discussion by Ferrary (1988) 349–63.

[21] There is a case for thinking that Cicero's Academic teacher Philo of Larissa taught a version of Aristotelian topics, and that Cicero's knowledge of the theory and evaluation of Aristotelian argumentative practice derives principally from this indirect source. See Long (1995) 52–8; Brittain (2001) 338–42; Reinhardt (2003) 9–17.

concealing his own view (*TD* 5.11) – but to relieve the reader of error and investigate (*quaerere*) what approximates to the truth. The method and the objective are nowhere stated more clearly than on the final page of *De Diuinatione* (2.150):

> But since it is characteristic of the Academy not to introduce any judgement of its own, but to approve what seems most like the truth; to compare cases and to express what can be said against each view; and (without bringing in play any of its own authority) to leave the judgement of the audience free and all their own – we shall hold to this practice, which was inherited from Socrates, and use it as often as we can, brother Quintus, if you are agreeable.

I have shown elsewhere how the two books of *De Diuinatione* themselves constitute an exemplary demonstration of the method put to work: with Book 1 a weighty appeal to historical experience, particularly Roman experience, as evidence for the efficacy of divination, and Book 2 a brilliant deployment of the weapons of sceptical reason against it. Even in that case, where Cicero the Academic sceptic develops the sceptical case himself, the choice is explicitly left with the reader.[22]

Perhaps it is significant that the manifesto for Academic dialogue just quoted is to be found in the last of Cicero's major exercises in the genre.[23] One gets the impression that his desire to emphasise that it is down to the reader to judge, and that the Academy will not try to exercise any authority to push the judgement in one direction or another, grew stronger as he composed more dialogues in the form of *argumentum in utramque partem*. From the outset it was his practice to end a dialogue by representing the interlocutors as locked in continuing disagreement (in the case of Stoics or Epicureans or Antiocheans from the standpoint of entrenched positions), and acknowledging the need for further argument. Things start to get more complicated in Book 5 of *De Finibus*. No Book 6, putting a contrary case, follows Book 5's exposition of Antiochus' version of Peripatetic ethics. That might suggest the theory is one to which the author himself inclines.[24] But if we are meant to register such a thought, we are also clearly intended to understand something else of rather greater importance.

Cicero communicates this more important message by splitting the Ciceronian response to Piso's Antiochean *oratio* into four. First, he has his young cousin Lucius assert without more ado that so far as he is concerned,

---

[22] See further Schofield (1986).
[23] That *De Divinatione* is a work dealing with the politically sensitive topic of religion may also, of course, have something to do with it.
[24] See further p. 82 below.

the Antiochean case meets his 'strong approval' (*Fin.* 5.76). Second, he makes it clear that as an Academic he too *could* give it his approval if it appeared to him probable (while at the same time indicating that so far as he is concerned, certainty as the Stoics and Antiocheans conceive it is not an option). Third, from the vantage point of Stoic ethics he then (from 5.77) launches into a sharp critique of some of the major theses of the Antiochean system – to which Piso responds, ostensibly addressing his remarks to Lucius (5.86) rather than Cicero himself (who by 5.90, however, has become the addressee). Fourth comes a more conventional conclusion, with Quintus Cicero contented that his own Aristotelianism has been confirmed, Atticus complimentary while indicating his unchanged Epicurean allegiance, and Cicero suggesting that Piso has more work to do – he himself, as well as Lucius, could be convinced if Piso could succeed in holding his position against attack (5.95–6).

Julia Annas says in her note on this final passage: 'Piso has won the rhetorical battle' – but 'Cicero leaves it to the reader to judge the importance of the philosophical argument against the elegantly presented theory'.[25] But it's not a matter of rhetoric against philosophy. What Piso has been made to offer is something which approximates to Ciceronian *perfecta philosophia*. And the absence of a full-scale response that might have occupied a further book is presumably not unimportant. Cicero's critical remarks flag up his dissatisfaction with just one aspect of Piso's Aristotelianism: his Antiochean distinction between a happy life and the *most* happy life – he argues that that's effectively Stoicism without the clarity and consistency of Stoic conviction. Nonetheless the main burden of Annas's comment is exactly right. Piso has certainly convinced a callow Lucius, who has not 'compared cases' nor even heard any argument against when he expresses his approval. We the readers are by contrast prodded by Cicero's criticisms and the divergent reactions of the participants, as they decide that is enough debate for the moment, into wondering and probing further, in the effort to make our own minds up. Indeed all that follows Lucius' premature acceptance of Piso's case is designed as an object lesson in the need to 'compare cases'.

The conclusion of *De Natura Deorum* is much briefer: a beautifully crafted cameo, even more highly nuanced. After Cotta has completed his sceptical demolition of Balbus' exposition of Stoic theology, Balbus requests a subsequent opportunity to reply (*ND* 3.94), and Cotta (like Cicero at the end of *De Finibus* 5) declares that he is ready to be convinced by him (indeed

---

[25] Annas (2001) 150 n.70.

is confident that he will be) – to the disgust of Velleius, the Epicurean spokesman (3.95). Then follows the celebrated final sentence:

When these remarks had been made, we parted with the following thoughts: to Velleius Cotta's argument appeared truer, to me Balbus' seemed to be more weighted towards approximation to the truth.

Cicero has already distanced himself from the Carneadean arguments against Stoic theology by making Cotta the voice of the Academy on this issue. Now he indicates that a sceptic is free to find the non-sceptical position more convincing (in the qualified terms of *veritatis similitudo* which the Academic is always careful to employ)[26] than the sceptical arguments levelled against it. But once again the main message is conveyed by the representation of divided opinion: Cicero cannot determine the issue – the reader must judge.[27]

Contrast the ending of (for example) Plato's *Phaedo*. However much the dialogue may harbour expressions of lack of conviction (*apistia*) on the part of Socrates' interlocutors (see especially *Phd.* 107a–b: Simmias' response to the final argument for the soul's immortality),[28] its last few pages – the eschatological myth followed by the powerfully affecting death scene – are designed not to invite cool examination of alternative philosophical positions, but to persuade the reader of the validity of the Socratic conception of philosophy, and of the need for Socratic care for the soul (see especially 114d–115a). Ciceronian dialogue, not Platonic, articulates the voice of dispassionate reason.

Contrast, too, the last page of Minucius Felix's *Octavius*, a 'Ciceronian' dialogue written under the high empire probably in north Africa, which presents arguments first for traditional Roman religion against Christianity, and then (at much greater length) for Christianity and against Roman religion.[29] When Octavius, advocate for Christianity, brings his speech to a close, the other two interlocutors are lost for a while in silent admiration (*Oct.* 39). Then Caecilius, the spokesman for Roman religion, announces

---

[26] On the vocabulary see Glucker (1995).

[27] It has often been supposed that Cicero in truth endorses the sceptical argument, and writes here as he does to protect himself from any popular charge of irreligion. This was presumably Hume's view (e.g. *The Natural History of Religion* Section XII), and recurs in modern scholarship (e.g. Momigliano (1984) 208–9). See Schofield (1986) 57–8 for counterargument, which notes *inter alia* that at *Div.* 2.148–9 Cicero reaffirms his Stoic inclinations in theology and associates this stance with the propagation of religion, sharply distinguished from the superstition of divination.

[28] See Sedley (1995) 14–21 for argument that the reader is meant to be less than impressed by Simmias' reservations.

[29] See the useful Budé edition: Beaujeu (1964).

his capitulation – except that Octavius' victory is a victory for him too: a victory over error (40.1). As in Cicero there will be a need for further discussion – but to clear up minor issues that require settling if Caecilius' instruction is to be perfected (40.2). Minucius himself was to have been arbiter or judge (4.6, 15.1),[30] but now is exempt from the duty. He can simply praise Octavius and thank God (40.3). 'After this', he says (40.4), 'we parted [Minucius echoes the *discessimus* of *ND* 3.95] joyful and light of heart: Caecilius because he had found belief, Octavius because he had won, and I because the one had found belief and the other had won.'

Consider, finally, the last paragraph of Hume's *Dialogues*:

CLEANTHES and PHILO pursued not this conversation much further; and as nothing ever made greater impression on me, than all the reasonings of that day; so I confess, that, upon a serious review of the whole, I cannot but think, that PHILO's principles are more probable than DEMEA's; but that those of CLEANTHES approach still nearer the truth.

The similarities to Hume's Ciceronian model scarcely need comment. As in Cicero, so in Hume the talk is of probability and approximation to truth; and the speaker again inclines more to rational natural theology than to scepticism. But no less significant are the differences. Cicero's final sentence is basically narrative, describing a parting of the ways, mirroring the divergent reflections of those who had listened to the debate just terminated: provisional reflections, for there will always be room for further consideration of the issues – as is symbolised by Balbus' request for a rematch. Hume's sentence is more final, not just because there is no talk of another subsequent conversation, but because the speaker gives us his summing up. What is offered is basically not narrative, but first person reflection – 'I', not 'we'. And whereas 'we' in Cicero parted differing, the 'I' in Hume has reached a conclusion conforming to the requirements of piety.

CICERONIAN PRESENCE

Cicero's 'I' is him, Cicero, doubling as character and author. In Hume the words are those of Pamphilus, his narrator. The author is off stage throughout, concealing his own sympathies (Hume scholars continue seemingly endless debate on what they were, or indeed whether there can be any

---

[30] Perhaps an idea Minucius took from *De Finibus* 2.119, where a similar role is briefly proposed for Gaius Triarius, although there is no striking verbal echo of the passage in the *Octavius* references to arbitration (such echoes as there are recall other writings of Cicero and Sallust: see Beaujeu (1964) ad locc.)

answer to that question).[31] Cicero is quite literally in all his dialogues – in one way or another. A letter of June 45 (*ad Att.* 13.19.3–5) documents a shift in his authorial practice in this matter:

I had made a resolution not to put living persons in my dialogues, but because you wrote that it was Varro's wish and that he set much store by it, I have composed these and finished off the whole Academic question in four books – how well I cannot say, but with supreme conscientiousness. In them I have given Varro the arguments Antiochus had put together brilliantly against *akatalêpsia*. To these I reply myself. You are the third party to the conversation. If I had made Cotta and Varro discuss the topic between them, as you advise in your last letter, I should have had a silent walk-on part. This is something I find agreeable where the characters are historical (*in antiquis personis*), like those Heraclides created in many works and I did myself in my six books *On the Commonwealth*. And there are my three *On the Orator*, which I definitely consider a good job of work. In them too the characters are such that my own role had to be a silent one. The speakers are Crassus, Antonius, the elder Catulus, Gaius Julius (his brother), Cotta, Sulpicius. The conversation is represented as occurring when I was a boy. So there could be no role for me.

But the dialogues I have written recently follow the Aristotelian pattern, where the speeches made by others are so conceived as to ensure that the lead role is with the author. In composing the five books *On Moral Ends* I gave the Epicurean material to L. Torquatus, the Stoic to M. Cato, and the Peripatetic to M. Piso. I thought that would excite no jealousy, because they were all deceased. The material to do with the Academy I had given, as you know, to Catulus, Lucullus and Hortensius. To be sure, it did not fit the characters. The arguments were more technical than anybody could ever suppose they dreamed of. So when I read your letter about Varro, I seized upon it as my lucky break. Nothing could have been better suited to that brand of philosophy – he seems to me to take particular pleasure in it. And his role is such that I haven't succeeded in making my own case appear the stronger. (Adapted from D. R. Shackleton Bailey)

The division Cicero makes here between dialogues set quite a while back in the past, and dialogues in the Aristotelian style, requires some nuancing. In the two dialogues he mentions from the 50s BCE, Cicero is in fact not wholly absent nor wholly silent. In both *De Oratore* and *De Republica*, and both times addressing his brother Quintus, he speaks in his own voice in prefaces to each of the books.[32] With their large and ingeniously orchestrated casts, and their themes of politics and rhetoric, both dialogues strike scholars as Platonic in their dramaturgical style and ambitions. When in a

---

[31] A recent discussion is Dancy (1995).

[32] In the case of the heavily fragmentary *De Republica* the existence of prefaces to each book addressed to Quintus (cf. *Rep.* 1.13: a reference to *mihi tibique … adulescento*) remains a hypothesis.

letter of the period (*ad Fam.* 1.9.23, dated September 54) Cicero describes *De Oratore* as written 'in the Aristotelian manner', that is presumably because he is present in its prefaces, even though the main conversations he can report only as retailed to him (as also in *De Republica*) by one of the minor participants. What he doesn't mention in *ad Att.* 13.19 is that in what was in all probability the third dialogue of the 50s – the *De Legibus*, never published in his lifetime – he does already take the main role in the substantive conversation (with Quintus and Atticus as the other interlocutors), probably in delayed response to his friend Sallustius, who had urged him to abandon the use of *antiquae personae* in *De Republica*, and say what he had to say in his own authoritative statesman's voice (*ad Q.Fr.* 3.5.1–2).[33]

But when Cicero gives himself a leading role in dialogues of the later cycle, it's in a very different mode from the one he takes in the *De Legibus*. *De Legibus* is still a conversational Platonic dialogue, the only philosophical dialogue by Cicero written throughout as script not report, and in other ways too designed to evoke specific Platonic memories. Cicero's own part is roughly comparable with the Athenian Stranger's role in the *Laws*. The dialogues of the later sequence are typically not Platonic but (as we have been seeing) Academic in one way or another. Here *perpetua oratio* has largely displaced conversation. And Cicero invariably appears either as critic (developing the sceptical case in the second limb of an *argumentum in utramque partem*), or as proponent developing a sustained case contrary to a thesis that has been briefly stated by an interlocutor (as in the *Tusculans* and *De Fato*). The one major formal element of continuity with *De Oratore* and *De Republica* is the Ciceronian preface (absent in *De Legibus* as in Book 5 of *De Finibus*). I shall offer some brief observations first on Cicero in his prefaces, then on his persona as controversialist.

Cicero ends a letter to Atticus written in July 44 sounding distinctly foolish (*ad Att.* 16.6.4):

Now I must come clean about some carelessness on my part. I have sent my book *On Glory* to you, and in it the preface to Book 3 of the *Academica*. This came about because I keep a volume consisting of prefaces. From it I am in the habit of selecting when I have started on some *sungramma*. So back at my place in Tusculum, not remembering that I'd used up that preface, I inserted it into the book I've sent you. But when I was reading the *Academica* on the boat, I noticed my mistake. So

---

[33] Cicero there tells his brother that he will revise *De Republica* to make the two of them the interlocutors, but is about to send the unrevised draft to Quintus – who will appreciate how upset he is at abandoning it. Whether or not Quintus took the hint and protested, the *De Republica* we have is plainly the unrevised version (contrary to the view of Zetzel (1995) 3–4 with n.11).

straight away I bashed out a new preface and sent that off to you. You are to cut out the other one and glue on this one.

This confession tells us quite a lot about Cicero's attitude to his prefaces.

First, it is to confirm what the prefaces themselves suggest, that they were for him a separate art form, and might have little intimate or specific connection with the works to which they would eventually serve as introductions. Their importance to him was such that he composed them in numbers, apparently sometimes well ahead of dialogues not yet written on topics perhaps not even conceived of. It is also clear that those in the preface collection must have played variations on a number of stock themes – themes Cicero presumably wanted to present to his readers with tireless and urgent insistence. Without a high degree of interchangeability he could never have made the mistake he owns up to in the first place. This makes it possible to form quite a decent guess about which of the surviving prefaces belonged to the collection. Not, interestingly, that to *De Natura Deorum* (except perhaps for some of the material in the central sections: *ND* 1.6–12) or to Book 1 of *De Diuinatione*, where Cicero evidently felt that the politically sensitive subject matter required something more tailor-made. Nor those in works like *De Senectute*, *De Amicitia* or *De Fato*, nor again the first book of the *Academica*. The likeliest candidates must be the prefaces to Book 1 of *De Finibus* (where Cicero modulates to the specific topic of ethics only in sections 11 and 12) and several books of the *Tusculan Disputations* (only that to Book 3 could not have been readily adapted to other purposes), with many commonalities between those to *Fin.* 1 and *TD* 1 and 2, and again between those to *TD* 4 and 5 (both texts which explore the nature of philosophy itself, and particularly of Pythagoras' role in promoting it).[34] Finally, as Catherine Steel has pointed out, Cicero's blunder 'underlines that works composed on either side of Caesar's death are, to at least some extent, part of the same project'.[35]

That project can be described in different ways. But one common and overarching preoccupation of Cicero's dialogue writing in general, and of his prefaces in particular, from *De Oratore* and *De Republica* on, is the assertion of Rome against Greece. In *De Republica*, for example, despite the respect for Plato that Cicero expresses here as elsewhere (in this work by

---

[34] A contrary view is put in Gildenhard (2007) 89–90. If these particular prefaces were originally written for the *volumen*, it need not follow that those used in the *Tusculans* (for example) were not also conceived of as suitable for the purposes of the work – as Gildenhard argues them to have been in his sustained and powerful treatment of this sequence of dialogues.

[35] Steel (2005) 138.

the very writing of a dialogue with that title and with the main themes it pursues), a key claim is that the theory of the *optimus status rei publicae* he puts in the mouth of Scipio is *superior* to Plato's (*Rep.* 2.21–2), because it is not utopian and because it reflects the historical experience of the Romans as they worked out their own compromise between monarchy, aristocracy and popular rule. Aspects of the form of the dialogue, too, are designed to assert the superiority of Roman ways over Greek. The ideas developed and debated in *De Republica* are discussed by leading Roman political figures, above all the great Scipio. The choice of the political life over the philosophical is insisted on in the preface to Book 1 before he even takes the stage. And Cicero clearly thought the way he ended the whole work a distinct improvement on Plato. Instead of the improbable tale of a visit to the underworld recounted by an obscure Pamphylian miraculously resurrected from the dead, Scipio recounts a dream in which the final conversation of the dialogue occurs – between him and his adoptive grandfather Africanus, conqueror of Hannibal – confirming all over again recognition of service to the *res publica* as the highest of callings.

In the preface (which must have been 'far longer' than in any other of his dialogues),[36] Cicero finds occasion to list the injuries inflicted by their own fellow citizens on distinguished statesmen who have served their country well, and characteristically refers at some length to his own experience in this regard (*Rep.* 1.6–7).[37] His own exclusion from public life under Caesar's dictatorship becomes a major theme in the prefaces to the later cycle of dialogues, and with it a transformation of the conception of public service he continues to make central to his agenda. Here notoriously Cicero claims that even in enforced retirement from political life he himself continues to promote the interests of the *res publica*: by writing philosophy in Latin for Romans. And by the time we reach the composition of *De Finibus* and the *Tusculans* – i.e. dialogues making use of the prefaces that had probably become the discrete special project of his *volumen prohoemiorum* – we find him suggesting that philosophy as written by him in Latin will or could surpass anything the Greeks have done, not least because of the greater riches of Latin vocabulary and his own skill and experience in rhetoric (e.g. *Fin.* 1.6, 10; *TD* 1.1, 2.6). Over and over again he explores tensions between the political and the philosophical life, between philosophy and rhetoric,

---

[36] Zetzel (1995) 95.
[37] In the 50s, as Gildenhard (2007) 51 well argues (cf. Steel (2005) 80–2), he writes as someone for whom literary production was squeezed into 'an *otium* in very short supply, on account of his continued involvement in the government of the *res publica*'.

between Greek and Roman culture and the resources of Greek and Latin, and the possibilities for resolving them – all with reference to his own situation, his own history and his own contribution and capacities.

Cicero, in short, explains *himself* in the prefaces – formally speaking to Brutus, addressee of many of the writings of 46 and 45 BCE, including *De Finibus*, the *Tusculans* and *De Natura Deorum*, but beyond him to a broader Roman readership (he is read, he tells us at *Div.* 2.5, by quite a number among the older generation, and even a few of the young, the target audience). In the process he creates an authorial voice engaged in a more explicit and sustained exercise in self-definition and self-presentation, as well as in comparative cultural analysis, than can ever have been attempted within the framework of the philosophical dialogue before. The prefaces aren't themselves dialogues. But in the introduction to *De Finibus*, in particular, Cicero argues with a range of critics, real and imagined, who do or might question the value of the project – doing philosophy, writing in Latin, writing philosophy in Latin. This is debate, if not dialogue, in the familiar combative mode of the supple and resourceful orator. Like the forensic rhetoric, it's a high-risk performance. As always, Cicero's own self-promoting estimation of his contribution to Roman political life is and was contentious at best. His claims about the intrinsic superiority of Latin over Greek as an instrument for philosophy cut no ice with us, however much we might admire his achievement in creating a Latin philosophical vocabulary almost single-handed. And his grand ambition – to create in Latin a philosophical corpus that would improve on what the Greeks had done and shape Roman education – could scarcely succeed, although of course over the long haul the legacy to Rome and to Western civilisation was immense.

The prefaces are not without an element of the dramatic and the self-dramatising. The second book of *De Diuinatione* opens unexpectedly with a review of his literary production in philosophy to date, introduced as usual in the later cycle of dialogues as 'advice to the *res publica*' (*Div.* 2.1). But now there is an interruption (2.4):

So much to date. I was pressing on to the rest, so fired with passion for the project that – had not some more weightier motor of events intervened – I would be permitting there to be no topic in philosophy that would not be elucidated in Latin and made accessible. For what greater or better service could I perform for the *res publica* than to teach and shape our young people, especially with morals and the times as they are?

And so he goes on for another page or two, before referring to the circumstances which drove him from public life, and then – but only by implication[38] – to the *causa gravior* which is reversing all that: Caesar's assassination and the ensuing political turmoil. Cicero is beginning to be asked to 'advise the *res publica*' in the more usual sense once more. But more of that, he says, another time. Now to resume the philosophical discussion (2.7).

It has sometimes been suggested that Cicero had finished Book 1 of *De Diuinatione* and perhaps much of Book 2 when news of Caesar's murder reached him. The introduction to Book 2 could then be read as instant reaction. Whether we should believe that or not, announcing half way through *De Diuinatione* that the current political crisis is threatening to disrupt the work of Cicero the author by necessitating the reappearance on the public stage of Cicero the statesman is a brilliant stroke – the perfect literary self-exemplification of the disruption.[39] Cicero had done something similar ten years or so before. The preface to the third and last book of *De Oratore* disturbs the even temper of the discussion with an arresting account of the premature death after a sudden illness of L. Licinius Crassus, the dominant speaker in the dialogue, and then the violent ends met by others among the participants, with Cotta (Cicero's alleged informant) driven into exile. At least Crassus did not live to see Italy ablaze, politics at home in disarray, his daughter's grief and her husband's exile, the savage massacre that followed Marius' return to power, and the ruin of the once prospering state in which he had outshone everybody (*De Or.* 3.1–12).

Philosophy is remote from all that. It is impersonal. Its discussions have no other object than to chisel out the truth or what approaches closest to it (*Luc.* 7). Curiosity about what view Cicero himself holds on a given topic is therefore out of place (*ND* 1.10). He seeks to conceal his own view (*TD* 5.11). So we are to take it that there is the starkest of contrasts between the highly opinionated author of the prefaces and the reticent author of the dialogues they introduce.

There's something not quite convincing about this. Recall that Cicero chooses to make *himself* the leading speaker in many of the later cycle of dialogues. If philosophy is impersonal, why should it matter how much or how little Cicero himself is on stage? Of course, there's the point he makes in the letter to Atticus (*ad Att.* 13.9.5) quoted above (p. 75): by virtue of

[38] But the reader doesn't have to progress much further before reading an explicit and mildly satiric account of the scene: *Div.* 2.23. And portents of Caesar's death were produced as clinching evidence for the efficacy of augury in the concluding section of Book 1 (1.119).

[39] So Steel (2005) 138.

their knowledge and philosophical capacity, he and Varro would be more convincingly portrayed as debating difficult questions in epistemology than the speakers he had lined up in the first version of the *Academica* (i.e. *Catulus* and *Lucullus*). But Varro is written into the script as someone who really did adhere to Antiochean views in epistemology; and Cicero plainly gives himself the role of Academic sceptic in the dialogue because an Academic is epistemologically what he was. It is hard to splice author and Academic interlocutor apart in this case.

Moreover Cicero's own references to the *Academica* in subsequent works represent it as a partisan piece of writing. According to his own account, this is how it was received by his contemporary readers (*ND* 1.6), and they were clearly correct to take it that way (*ND* 1.11). In Book 2 of the *Tusculans* he speaks of the work as having 'explained with sufficient precision what could be said on behalf of the Academy' (*TD* 2.4), while in the catalogue in the preface to Book 2 of *De Diuinatione* he says he expounded 'that brand of philosophising which I think least arrogant and at the same time most consistent and elegant' (*Div.* 2.1).[40] The *Academica* has of course articulated the Antiochean point of view too, which in Cicero's opinion as expressed in the letter came out very well argued; and presumably there will have been no final authorial verdict, leaving that with the reader, as was to become standard in the Academic dialogues.[41] But to judge from Cicero's retrospective descriptions of the work, the reader will also have been left in little doubt that 'Cicero's' position is indeed Cicero's.

The *Academica* may well be something of a special case. It tackles a second-order question, about the epistemological status of any first-order views we might have about any subject, whether philosophical or otherwise. As Cicero frequently reminds us, the Academic is defined as such by his stance on the second-order question and on that alone (e.g. *ND* 1.11–12). He may adopt whatever first-order views may seem to him to approximate most closely to the truth (e.g. *Off.* 3.20). So in Academic dialogues devoted to first-order issues we can't expect anything similar to the partisanship of the *Academica*. On such questions there is no Academic position to be partisan

---

[40] See further Griffin (1997) 7–8, with the further suggestion that the main function of the first version of *Academica* – the lost *Catulus* and the still surviving *Lucullus* – 'would be to answer the obvious question which would occur to readers of the *Hortensius*: which school did Cicero himself favour?' When in the preliminaries before his speech in the *Lucullus* 'Cicero' describes himself as particularly engaged with this philosophy, and goes on to say that if it weren't inept in a discussion to do so, he would swear by Jupiter that he holds the views he states (*Luc.* 65), he clearly speaks for Cicero the author.

[41] Only a fragment of Book 1 of the revised version of *Academica* survives, so this supposition is necessarily conjectural.

for. And the catalogue in *De Diuinatione* 2 describes these dialogues in very different terms – mostly focusing on their encyclopedic purpose. Our antecedent expectation must be that Cicero the interlocutor won't necessarily be committed to positions he argues (the important thing is to present both sides of every case); and that whether he is or not in some particular instance, we won't necessarily be able to infer anything about the view Cicero the author might take.

Nonetheless it's surely significant that in *De Natura Deorum* Cicero abandons his Aristotelian *principatus* in the debate, and turns himself once again into a bit-part player. As we noticed above (p. 73 and n. 27), the sceptical case against Stoic (as against Epicurean) theology is given instead to Cotta, leaving Cicero free in his minor role to indicate at the end of the dialogue his own inclination to the Stoic position (reiterated at *Div.* 2.148). We cannot of course be confident that he is here expressing the *views* of Cicero the author. And this is after all the very work in which we are warned against being curious about those (*ND* 1.10). It does however seem a reasonable inference that Cicero the author writes Cicero the interlocutor this way because for reasons political or personal or both *he* does not wish to be associated with the sceptical case. In *De Diuinatione*, by contrast, he resumes *principatus* and *does* himself develop the sceptical case against divination, without any disclaimer like the one Quintus is allowed at *Div.* 2.100, dissociating himself from the Stoic arguments he put in Book 1. Here it seems reasonable to infer that the author shares the interlocutor's scepticism – even though the dialogue is not written to tell us that, and if Cicero hopes and expects the scepticism to be highly persuasive, all the more reason for the author to emphasise more strongly and explicitly than ever before that the judgement is ours to make when we have considered both sides of the case.[42]

Again, in the treatment of Stoic ethics in Books 3 and 4 of *De Finibus*, we don't doubt that Cato, Stoic spokesman in Book 3, really held Stoic views. We might have more of a question as to how far Cicero either as interlocutor or author is committed to the critique of the Stoic position developed in Book 4. Here a fascinating passage from the fifth book of the *Tusculans* becomes pertinent. Cicero has there been arguing that nobody who like a Peripatetic or an Antiochean recognises other good things besides virtue (or bad things other than vice) can claim that virtue will always secure

---

[42] See again the treatment in Schofield (1986). *De Natura Deorum* may perhaps still be best approached through the introductions to two older works: Mayor (1880–5); Pease (1955).

happiness – as the Stoics can by reason of their contrary insistence that virtue *is* the only good. His interlocutor now charges him with inconsistency. Does this square with 'your Book 4 in *De Finibus*'? There, he points out, Cicero had argued that the only difference between Stoic and Peripatetic positions in this area is terminological. If terminology is all that is at issue, why shouldn't the Peripatetics too be able to claim that 'in virtue there is great power to secure happiness in life' (*TD* 5.32)?

Cicero *doesn't* reply: I was in *De Finibus* 4 only arguing a case – to which I didn't necessarily subscribe – and the same is true of the different case I am arguing now. In effect he says (5.33): I am an Academic – one day it can be that one thing strikes my mind as probable, the next day it might be something else. In short, he brushes the objection off with a joke that evokes thoughts of the 'careless scepticism of PHILO'. He then suggests more seriously (if not very convincingly) that his interlocutor is missing the point of the present argument. What he doesn't deny is that he was advancing his own views in *De Finibus* 4. He wouldn't have been well placed to do so, given his statement in the preface to Book 1 of the work that in it – as well as being encyclopedic in coverage – he has worked right through 'the views I accept' (*Fin.* 1.12), which must presumably be found in his arguments in Books 2 and 4 if anywhere. Moreover in neither the objection nor the reply at *TD* 5.33 is any attempt made to distinguish author from interlocutor. Cicero accuses the objector of treating 'what I *said or wrote* on some occasion' as set in aspic. There is no talk whatever here of concealing his own opinion (as there had been in the preface, at 5.11).[43]

CONCLUSION

I conclude that Cicero is no less present in his first person contributions to dialogue than in his prefaces. In the Academic dialogues which take the form of *argumentum in utramque partem* that presence is mostly critical. His performance elsewhere in the later cycle – notably in the *Tusculans* and *De Fato* (not forgetting that non-dialogue *De Officiis*) – would have to be material for discussion on another occasion. What will I hope already be clear is that Ciceronian presence is an exercise in authorial performance of considerable ambition and complexity, requiring of the reader varying

---

[43] Debate about Cicero's stance in ethics is endless. A useful starting point for exploration is the introductory material in Annas (2001). She rightly comments (xii): 'Cicero appears to have gone back and forth on the arguments for and against the Stoic view all his life.'

registers of intellectual engagement. If we add to this the task Cicero sets us of following the conflicting and often intricate trains of argument he presents to us and making our own response to them, we find ourselves faced – I submit – with a uniquely challenging form of philosophical dialogue.[44]

---

[44] In commenting on Alex Long's paper at the March 2006 colloquium, I offered some remarks that were the germ for this paper. Early versions were read to gatherings in Cambridge and Oxford in May 2007. I am grateful to Roberto Polito and Jean-Louis Labarrière respectively for invitations to speak, and my audiences for their comments. I would also like to thank Simon Goldhill for the opportunity of contributing to this volume, and for a number of kindnesses.

CHAPTER 5

Sympotic dialogue in the first to fifth centuries CE

Jason König

SYMPOTIC QUESTIONS

Many of the essays in this volume, the introduction included, interrogate the idea that Christian writers felt uncomfortable with the dialogue form, and so either neglected it completely or else used it very differently from their Greco-Roman or Jewish counterparts. There are reasons for expressing reservations about those formulations. Most strikingly, it is easy enough to amass a long series of counterexamples: many Christian writers did write dialogues.[1] However, one area where dialogue form does come to a very conspicuous halt is in the area of sympotic writing.[2] The Greek literature of the Roman Empire is saturated with descriptions of sympotic commensality and philosophical conversation. For whatever reason, literary representation of the symposium seems to have been an attractive vehicle for writing which explores and dramatises the relations between Greek past and Greek present (more on that below). But it is hard to find anything in Christian literature which resembles Plato's *Symposium* or Xenophon's, or even the more loosely structured, miscellanistic composition of Plutarch's *Sympotic Questions*, with their vivid sketches of social context and their conversational style, or of Athenaeus' more chaotic compilation of quotations and erudite sympotic discussions, the *Deipnosophists*. Methodius' *Symposium* is one exception. But there is little to match it within the landscape of surviving Christian writing throughout the long period of

---

[1] See Hoffmann (1966); Voss (1970).

[2] Martin (1931) assumes a clearly defined sympotic genre, and usefully outlines some of the recurring sympotic motifs which helped to signal membership of it; while I agree that there are many texts (including the four main texts discussed here, by Plutarch, Athenaeus, Methodius and Macrobius) which represented themselves as part of a sympotic tradition descended from Plato's *Symposium* – and I will sometimes use the phrase 'sympotic genre' as a shorthand for that tradition – it also seems to me important to go beyond Martin's excessively rigid model, and to recognise that many texts which contained sympotic motifs had a more marginal or hybrid relation with that Platonic tradition, though without being clearly separable from it.

the first to fifth centuries CE. Similarly within classicising pagan literature of late antiquity, there are relatively few examples. Keith Hopkins, in his imaginative reconstruction of early Christian culture, invents a 'recently discovered' work by an author he names Macarius which draws on many of the apologetic motifs familiar from the works of Justin and others.[3] The work is set, however, at a symposium, where Macarius debates with non-Christian interlocutors. In that sense it is starkly unlike any other Christian apologetic writing. One might imagine that the symposium would be a promising space for Christian writers to explore their own cultural self-positioning in relation to other communities, in the light of traditions of the symposium as a place for cosmopolitan dialogue, as well as being a promising place to appropriate the familiar images of Greco-Roman culture for new Christian uses, given its relevance to Christian metaphors of feasting with Christ. Certainly Hopkins' Macarius exploits that potential. However, Justin and his fellow apologists seem uninterested in following the same path. Whether Hopkins was aware of that disjunction between imaginative reconstruction and surviving material is not immediately clear from his text, but either way his chapter usefully poses for us the question of why there is so little in surviving Christian literature whose setting even faintly resembles that of Macarius' *Symposium*.

This chapter outlines some of the key texts which might lie at the heart of an account of this later history of the literature of sympotic dialogue.[4] It also attempts to answer a number of questions. How do we account for the

---

[3] Hopkins (1999) 210–21.
[4] Histories of the ancient world's sympotic literature have generally taken an unflattering view of the Roman Empire's sympotic accumulations of erudition, seeing them as degenerate imitators of their inspired and more lifelike Platonic predecessor, in line with a tendency to denigrate the Greek literature of the Imperial period more generally for its derivativeness; the bulk of symposium scholarship has accordingly been directed towards the Archaic and Classical periods. It is only recently that we have begun to appreciate some of the attractions these Imperial texts must have held: important examples include Romeri (2002) on the symposia of Plutarch, Athenaeus and Lucian; Braund and Wilkins (2000) on Athenaeus; Jeanneret (1991). There is also discussion of late sympotic texts in works by Relihan (1992) and Martin (1931), both of whom survey the sympotic genre across its whole history; even these studies, however, tend to take little interest in late-antique and Christian symposium texts. Other important discussions of pre-Imperial sympotic literature include Ullrich (1908–9); Dupont (1977) 19–89; *RE* 4a 1273–82; Hunter (2004) on Plato; Cameron (1995) 95–7, with reference to Slater (1982) 346–9, for literary symposia in Hellenistic Alexandria. For major works on the symposium as an institution, see (amongst very many others) Murray (1990a) including comprehensive bibliographies in major areas of symposium scholarship, with updated bibliographical addenda for the later paperback edition; also Murray (1983) and (2003); Lissarague (1990); Slater (1991); Murray and Tecuşan (1995). Recent works on Christian institutions of eating and drinking and Christian attitudes to consumption include Smith (2003) and Grimm (1996), but neither gives any great attention to narrative representation of consumption, or to the sympotic form. On the massive renaissance tradition of sympotic dialogue, see Jeanneret (1991).

obsession with sympotic writing within Imperial Greek works? How do we account for the loss of sympotic forms within Christian writing, and within late-antique literature more broadly? How reliable is that model? How do Christian writers and their late-antique classicising counterparts give expression to their own relationship with sympotic traditions even as they shy away from them? In the process, and picking up on that last issue in particular, I aim to move beyond my original formulation – why Christian/late-antique disinterest in sympotic form? The more revealing question, as I aim to show, is about how Christian and late-antique literature, when they do it, do sympotic dialogue differently, engaging with their classical and Roman precedents while also reshaping them subtly and self-consciously.

REACTIVATING THE PAST

First, some claims about the development of the symposium genre. Why does sympotic dialogue matter for Greek writers under Roman rule? One answer is simply that the symposium could be envisaged as a key space for displaying elite, Hellenic identity, and so offered a natural home for the obsession with explorations and assertions of elite identity in the writing of the Imperial period. Those connotations of elite display were not new. In the Archaic and Classical period the symposium was a venue for the politically charged elite performance culture which we glimpse in lyric poetry. In the post-classical world we see an extension of the Platonic/Xenophontic philosophical symposium as a venue for socially empowering performance of knowledge, for bringing to light the accumulated wealth of the Greek archive. That latter project was one that sympotic writing held in common with many of the Roman Empire's many other miscellanistic, scientific or encyclopedic texts;[5] but few other compilatory genres showed so vividly how this kind of knowledge could be mobilised for the purposes of displaying social status.[6] That sense of the symposium – and particularly dialogue in the symposium – as a space for performing Greekness, for displaying a particularly Hellenic form of philosophical identity and traditional knowledge within conversation, is one reason for its attraction for Plutarch and Athenaeus, and similarly for satirical authors like Lucian: his misbehaving philosophers in the *Symposium or Lapiths*, with their preference for Homeric one-to-one conflict at the expense of any kind of dialogic

---

[5] See König and Whitmarsh (2007) on compilatory styles of writing in the Roman Empire.
[6] Cf. Schmitz (1997) 127–33 on competitions in wisdom at the symposium as socially prestigious.

interaction whatsoever, are an extension of Lucian's characteristic interest in undermining inherited convention.[7]

More specifically, the sympotic form in Imperial Greek writing is concerned with *active* treatment of inherited knowledge, which enacts continuity with and inheritance of the past while also reshaping it for its new context.[8] Plutarch and Athenaeus, far from being faceless reorganisers of inherited erudition, dramatise obsessively the *processes* of performing knowledge, inviting us to admire the inventiveness of sympotic speech as we read. Christian Jacob has demonstrated that claim at length for Athenaeus.[9] Display of knowledge for the deipnosophists, at least under Jacob's guidance, becomes a masterful performance of improvisation for an audience acute to the smallest innovation, akin to the mastery of sophistic oratory.[10] Similarly, the style of dialogue Plutarch puts on show is one which relies both on intricate knowledge of the writing of the past, and at the same time on ingenious improvisation, drawing on long-standing traditions of competitive speech and spontaneous invention in the symposium,[11] and based in particular around the technique of offering a range of different answers to each question discussed.[12] Often successive speakers contradict each other, as if on the assumption that dialogue between opposed viewpoints can help them to reach the truth. At other times, however, ingenuity and conviviality seems to be just as important as getting the right answer. Plutarch often

---

[7] See Branham (1989) 108–20; Frazier (1994); Männlein (2000); for other pictures of sympotic philosophy done wrongly, cf. Lucian *Nigrinus* 25; *Pisc.* 34; *Timon* 54–5; *Lexiphanes passim*; see also Philostratus, *VS* 627 for the sophist Aspasios declaiming in wine shops; Dio Chrysostom 27.1–4 for examples of sympotic speech done badly, but also for the claim that the symposium is a venue for display of moral character through fitting conversation; cf. 30.28–44 and 32.53 for a similar contrast. All of these passages as well as other examples of engagement with the symposium in sophistic writing are discussed by Amato (2005); what all of them have in common, regardless of whether their aims are satirical or protreptic, is an emphasis on interactive philosophical speech as the pinnacle of good behaviour, and an awareness of how this ideal falls down when the symposiast becomes self-absorbed. It is relatively rare to find examples of dialogue form in Imperial Greek literature which do not have philosophical overtones; however, see Lucian's *Dialogues of Courtesans, Dialogues of the Dead, Dialogues of the Gods* (on the last of those see Branham (1989) 139–63) for one set of exceptions.

[8] Cf. Martin (1998) on the way in which the seven sages in Archaic Greek literature are used to illustrate an active, performative concept of wisdom.

[9] See Jacob (2001).

[10] See Anderson (1997) on Athenaeus' links with his sophistic contemporaries, and more generally Amato (2005) on links between sympotic and sophistic writing.

[11] See esp. Frazier and Sirinelli (1996) 177–207; the *Sympotic Questions* has often had a bad press, denigrated for the implausibility of its arguments by scholars who have not recognised the prestige of these argumentative styles: e.g., see Fuhrmann (1972) xxiv; Flacelière and Irigoin (1987) lxxxiii; Teixeira (1992) 221. Romeri (2002) 109–89 is an important exception. On traditions of agonistic discussion and performance at the symposium, see esp. Collins (2005).

[12] See Hardie (1992) for discussion of some of the many precedents and connotations of this kind of alternative explanation; and further discussion and bibliography in König (2007).

stresses, for example, the way in which his contributions are improvised, made whether or not he is confident of having a reliable answer. In 3.5 (652b), for example, he tells us that he is reusing an argument he had come up with a few days before, when he had been forced to extemporise (αὐτοσχεδιάσαι). In 2.2 (635c), similarly, Plutarch speaks 'in order to avoid the impression of joining in the conversation without making a contribution'. The image of the festival often provides a metaphor for that kind of active, engaged treatment of tradition. Plato and Xenophon both set their symposia on festival occasions, at dinners celebrating victories in agonistic competition. It is striking that festival settings become standard features of the sympotic genre throughout the following centuries.[13] One effect, I suggest, is to portray philosophical debate and elite conviviality as a more elevated equivalent of the active citizen involvement in spectatorship and sacrificial ritual which was central to festival culture. Plutarch sets many of the conversations in his *Sympotic Questions* at festivals, offering us in the process a sustained vision of philosophical conversation as an elevated equivalent of sacrificial banqueting and agonistic competition. Performing knowledge in the symposium becomes, by that metaphor, an active process of publicly celebrating Hellenic tradition within a specific local context.[14]

Moreover, the dialogue form is crucial not only to the agonistic experience of the symposium guests, but also to our own involvement as readers in the process of reactivating the past. The recurring emphasis on the requirement for young men to learn from their fellow symposiasts offers, I suggest, a model for the reader's engagement with the text.[15] The text's scenes of learning contain both explicit and implicit instruction on the styles of speech and interpretation one should aim for, lessons offered both to the young symposiasts themselves and to us. For example, Plutarch's teacher Ammonius plays a prominent role, both in Book 9 and elsewhere, as if to remind us of the way in which Plutarch's own interpretative virtuosity has itself been learnt, painstakingly and gradually, in the course of a long process

---

[13] That said, there were models available for almost entirely non-contextualised portrayal of erudite sympotic conversation, perhaps most famously in the sympotic writing of Epicurus, which seems to have conspicuously neglected any detailed attention to dramatic setting: see Usener (1887) 115, with reference to several passages of Athenaeus (177b, 182a, 186e, 187b). On Plato's appropriation for philosophy of the civic settings of festival and gymnasium, see Blondell (2002) 63–4.

[14] See König (2007) for longer discussion; cf. Schmitt-Pantel (1992) 471–82 for comparison of *Sympotic Questions* 2.10 with the picture of sacrificial feasting we gain from the epigraphical evidence, emphasising both Plutarch's engagement with civic life and also his tendency to distance himself from it; see also Dio, *Or.* 27 for comparison between festival and symposium.

[15] See König (2007) on the didactic atmosphere of Plutarch's text; and cf. Jacob (2001) xcvii on the way in which Athenaeus' text offers its readers models and resources for their own scholarly activity.

of development from pupil to expert. For both Plutarch and Athenaeus, moreover, there are right and wrong ways of speaking: Plutarch often shows his characters correcting or criticising each other.[16] But combined with that prescriptive atmosphere, as we have seen already, is an equally strong, sympotic ideal of equal dialogue, where each contributor has an equal right to speak, where no single answer to a question is ever validated as the correct and only response. The point of the work's ingenuity seems to be the way in which it encourages each listener to think actively for him- or herself, on the principle that curiosity is the first step on the road to learning and philosophical reflection, a claim Plutarch makes at length in his work *On Listening*. Each listener, if he or she is listening well, must be ready with his or her own addition to the string of alternative explanations on offer. And crucially we too, as readers, are drawn into contributing. The work's structures of dialogue and its atmosphere of unfinalisability – which is conspicuous within sympotic speech perhaps more than anywhere, with its balance between *spoudaion* and *geloion* (the symposium is always at least in part about play) and with its traditions of equal contribution from all guests in turn – draw us in as we read, prompting us to make our own interventions, and our own reactivations of our Greek heritage.

CONVERSATION AND DIALOGISM

There is a further question of why the symposium should be seen at all as such a promising place for replaying tradition and collecting knowledge: where might that assumption have come from in the first place? One answer, I suggest, is that the central role of conversation with one's peers in the symposium allows the further fantasy of entering into conversation with the writings of the past.[17] Plutarch uses that metaphor.[18] For Athenaeus

[16] E.g., see *Sympotic Questions* 8.4 (723f–724a) for an example of a character criticised for excessive ingenuity.

[17] That technique of introducing authors of the past into dialogue occurs outside sympotic writing too, and stretches back at least to Plato (e.g. the ventriloquising of Simonides at Pl. *Prt.* 339a–347b); for other good examples, see Vitr. *De arch.* 9, preface, 17; and Lucian *VH* Book 2, where the narrator dines regularly with the inhabitants of the Isles of the Blessed (2.14–16, 2.24, 2.25), and questions Homer about his work (2.20).

[18] E.g., see *Sympotic Questions* 8.2 (718c), where Plato is brought into conversation. For similar examples of the processes of reading described with overtones of personal interaction, see (amongst many others), the opening of 3.5 (651f) where Plutarch describes himself having 'come across', or alternatively 'met with' or even 'talked with' (ἐντυχών) a text of Aristotle; or the opening of 3.6 (653b), where he describes a group of young men who have only recently begun to 'spend time with' ancient texts (προσπεφοιτηκότες — the word also can mean, more specifically, to spend time with a teacher: LSJ 1530).

it is even more deeply ingrained. In his work the voices of the deipnosophists, who spend so much of their time quoting, repeatedly blend with the voices of their source texts. Athenaeus orchestrates that effect carefully, showing his characters losing sight of the distance between past and present, between written and spoken, allowing the voices of the past to speak through them.[19]

This technique makes Athenaeus' work, I suggest, profoundly dialogic in a Bakhtinian sense. For Bakhtin all human expression is to a certain degree dialogical, in the sense that it is in dialogue with the multi-faceted linguistic and social background from which it emerges and to which it is in turn directed. All utterances are inescapably ingrained with the many different meanings and connotations imposed on them by previous users of language. Moreover, all utterances are directed towards addressees whose positioning makes a difference to the utterances themselves: the making of meaning comes from the always provisional process of sorting through an enormous variety of competing possible meanings, and that process is always a social act, undertaken with a particular audience in mind. Some types of literary writing, according to Bakhtin, do their best to shut out that multi-faceted, polyphonous character of language, attempting to stress their own singleness and consistency of voice; others, however – which often receive the label 'dialogic' or 'heteroglossic' in modern scholarship on Bakhtin – do the opposite, revelling in the richness of the competing voices and tones which are woven into them: 'for the prose writer, the object is a focal point for heteroglot voices among which his own voice must also sound; these voices create the background necessary for his own voice, outside of which his artistic prose nuances cannot be perceived, and without which they "do not sound."'[20]

The relevance of those formulations for Athenaeus' fictional world, where the voices of the library speak through his characters, should be fairly clear. But how far do these effects depend on the work's dialogue form in particular? Bakhtin himself hinted, albeit rather vaguely, at connections between dialogue form and dialogic character, for example in viewing the Socratic dialogue – along with a number of other ancient sympotic and more

---

[19] See König (forthcoming) for longer discussion; and cf. Jacob (2001) l–li and Too (2000) on the way in which the deipnosophists come to embody the texts of the library, allowing those texts to speak through them.

[20] Bakhtin (2006b) 278, with good discussion by Bialostosky (1992) 55–6. Bakhtin (1984) is also particularly relevant here; for a good introductory discussion of Bakhtin's concepts of dialogue, see (amongst many others) Holquist (1990); cf. Lodge (1990) for an attempt to apply these concepts to criticism of the modern novel in English; for application of this and other Bakhtinian concepts to Classical texts, see Branham (2002), and Greenwood and Long in this volume.

broadly seriocomic texts – as a precursor of the dialogic novel.[21] Andrea
Wilson Nightingale has recently built on that claim in discussing Plato's
dialogues as texts which aim at incorporating and reshaping/parodying a
great range of other genres.[22] Bakhtin also named the *Deipnosophists* – albeit
without any lengthy justification, and without particular discussion of its
dialogue form – within that selection of seriocomic texts.[23] Perhaps more
importantly, it is clear that the idea of communication between present and
past is central to Bakhtin's concept, and that the image of dialogue between
sympotic interlocutors in the present has the potential to act as a model for
that other kind of communication. For example, in characterising the ancient
'seriocomic' genres Bakhtin stressed not only their 'deliberate multi-styled
and multi-voiced nature', but also their tendency to bring past and present
into contact, in ways which are strikingly appropriate to the sympotic enterprise: 'In these genres the heroes of myth and the historical figures of the past
are deliberately and emphatically contemporised; they act and speak in a zone
of familiar contact with the open-ended present'.[24] That image again seems
strikingly appropriate to Athenaeus and to the other sympotic writings of this
chapter and the next. It seems odd that Bakhtin's work has to my knowledge
had almost no attention in modern scholarship on Athenaeus, or indeed on
other ancient sympotic miscellanies.[25]

Moreover, this sense that dialogue between the work's interlocutors is
both a model and a vehicle for dialogue with the voices of the library is
enhanced, as I have already suggested, by the work's carefully managed
techniques of blurring between the voices of speakers and their source
texts. One of the difficulties of Bakhtin's theory is to distinguish in practice
between dialogic and non-dialogic texts,[26] and to work out exactly what it is
that makes the difference. If language is always inherently dialogic, how
can we say that some texts are dialogic or heteroglossic when some texts
are not? What exactly is it in the novel, as Bakhtin defines it, which makes it
inherently heteroglossic? If we accept that not all novels are heteroglossic,
and that some non-novelistic texts are, how do we distinguish in practice?
Would we not be better off seeing a continuum between these two poles;
or else seeing all works oscillating between the two poles, or offering the

---

[21] Bakhtin (2006b) 21–2 and 24–6.   [22] See Nightingale (1995), esp. 6 on Bakhtin and Todorov.
[23] Bakhtin (2006b), esp. 53.   [24] Bakhtin (1984) 108.
[25] The obvious exception is Jeanneret (1991), whose whole approach to the classical and Renaissance
symposium genre is informed by Bakhtinian concepts of polyphony, although he does not at any
point discuss their significance for Athenaeus in particular; see also Whitmarsh (2000) 572, n. 28 for
brief acknowledgement of Bakhtin's interest in Athenaeus.
[26] E.g., see Lodge (1990) 90–99.

potential to be read from either of these two perspectives at different moments?[27] There is, however, one particular technique which for Bakhtin sets the novel genre apart from others, enhancing its dialogic potential in particularly novelistic ways, and that is its capacity to produce utterances which seem to blend the voices of author and character through what he refers to as 'doubly oriented speech'. This happens in particular when the narrator records the words or thoughts of a character outside direct quotation marks, in such a way as to leave it unclear what degree of authorial paraphrase has crept in, or to make us suspect that the character's thoughts have been overlaid by the narrator with styles of speech drawn from other genres, which cast the character momentarily in terms alien to his or her conscious self-perception.[28] That confusion of boundaries is a staple effect of much novelistic fiction. My suggestion here is that we see a similar though not identical effect within the dialogue form as Athenaeus presents it. Athenaeus presents us in the work with an elaborate series of frames: the outside frame of the conversation between himself and Timocrates, which contains the conversation of the deipnosophists, which in turn contains the source texts they quote, some of which themselves contain inserted speech or quotation.[29] Because the text moves quite readily, sometimes abruptly, backwards and forwards between these framing levels (unlike, for example, Platonic dialogue, where such movements are for the most part clearly signalled), and because Athenaeus' own quotation-obsessed style of speech, in his role as narrator, is so similar to that of his characters and in some cases to that of the quoted texts – for those reasons it often becomes easy to lose track at least momentarily of which level we are in at any one moment. Athenaeus' own voice merges with those of his deipnosophists; their voices merge with their source texts; and we slip between these different levels as we read, lured into missing the points of transition from one level to the next, so that the boundaries between library and life become broken down.[30] That technique is obviously not available for dialogues which are presented in play-script form, but it is an opportunity which the ancient technique of framing philosophical dialogue within one or more outside layers of narrative opens up powerfully, although to my knowledge no other ancient author pursues it so intricately as Athenaeus.

---

[27] Cf. Lodge (1990) 98: 'One could develop a typology of genres or modes of writing according to whether they exploit and celebrate the inherently dialogic nature of language in living speech or suppress and limit it for specific literary effects.'

[28] See Lodge (1990) 25–44, with good examples, and 90–93.

[29] Cf. Ceccarelli (2000), drawing on but adjusting Letrouit (1991).

[30] For discussion of that effect, see Ceccarelli (2000); Romeri (2002) 268–78.

For Athenaeus' deipnosophists, then, as for Bakhtin, there is no voice which is not simultaneously a compound of previous utterances and associations, and the dialogue framing makes a central contribution to that effect. It is easy enough to see how we might fit the late-fourth- or early-fifth-century work of Macrobius into the same template, as a late reactivation of some of those same dialogic characteristics. He too shares a sense that sympotic conversation – or in his case, in Latin, convivial conversation – is the proper place for display of identity. His work is set in Rome at the festival of the Saturnalia; it is fundamentally concerned with displaying knowledge of the Roman heritage, centred in particular on the writing of Virgil, and delving into the most intricate corners of Roman religious tradition and Latin etymology. And despite the surface appearance of derivativeness it dramatises an active style of speaking, and a fundamentally dialogic one (in a Bakhtinian sense). He shows a fascination, for example, with the many different layers which lie behind the words of his text, the way in which his own text and whatever his readers will themselves make of it in the future is both derived from the existing material of the past and also reshaped seamlessly and organically to fit the voice of the speaker:

We ought in a sense to imitate bees, which go from place to place and gather the flower blossoms, and then distribute the harvest among their honeycombs, transforming the varied juices into a single flavour by a process of mingling and by imbuing them with their own distinctive qualities. (*Saturnalia* i.pr. 5)

That metaphor is itself borrowed from Seneca who in turn borrows from Virgil, as Sabine MacCormack notes: 'Language, for Macrobius, was what the present user made of it, even though the thoughts and expressions of the present were inseparable from what had been thought and written earlier by others'.[31] And for Macrobius, too, as I will argue in more detail later (see pp. 107–113), the conversation between his guests becomes an important metaphor for their dialogue with the writings of the past.

TWO FORMS OF DIALOGUE?

Where does Christian writing fit into that equation? Is Macrobius reactivating a kind of sympotic speech and a kind of dialogue which is largely absent within Christian literature? If it is the case that sympotic dialogue fails to feature within Christian writing, why is that? Is it because the particular kind of dialogue which the symposium attracts, with its emphasis on

---

[31] MacCormack (1998) 82.

convivial openness and ingenuity, the sympotic dislike of authoritative statement – of the kind I have outlined for Plutarch – is not a comfortable one for Christian writers? The dialogue form in itself may not require that kind of openness, but in the symposium, one might suspect, it is hard to escape from. Is it, too, because the sympotic fascination with setting dialogue in specific social contexts is something Christian writing tends to feel uncomfortable with? In other dialogue forms it is much easier to skate over setting, to skate over the awkward realities of real speech and the distorting factors which come with it, but for the symposium, again, are they harder to avoid?

One way of bringing those questions into sharper relief might be through a distinction between open and closed dialogue. M. Prince, writing about the dialogue form in the British Enlightenment, identifies two very different meanings for the word dialogue or dialectic which he suggests stand in uneasy tension with each other as far back as Plato.[32] The first (type a) is a model which sees dialogue as the division of an argument into two parts which eventually come together in the harmony of final resolution, akin to the resolutions of comedy. The second (type b) is a more open form, where verbal interaction may be between two or more voices, and where there is no necessary resolution, as at the end of tragedy. He sees a move from type (b) in the early works of Plato to type (a) in the later works. And he sees type (a) as a form central to Christian writing from its very beginning: 'From the beginning of the Christian era until the middle of the 18th century, dialectic became one of the dominant methods of argument for Christian theology.'[33] The Enlightenment sees a dispute between these two modes of dialogue. We hear, for example, of Floyer Sydenham, an eighteenth-century type-(a) interpreter of Plato, criticising Plato's blunder of allowing the drunken Alicibiades to spoil the carefully crafted metaphysical structure of the *Symposium*: 'we cannot altogether justify and consequently ought not to follow our author [Plato] in introducing to his Banquet the thorowly debauched Alcibiades'.[34] Paradoxically, Prince suggests, that dispute leads both types in the same, increasingly novelistic direction. Proponents of type (a) become increasingly novelistic in their portrayal of characterisation and context 'once confidence in a disembodied criterion of arbitration (reason, logic, common sense) declines'. Proponents of type (b) become increasingly

---

[32] Prince (1996); see also Cox (1992), esp. 2–3 for a similar distinction within Italian Renaissance dialogue.
[33] Prince (1996) 5.   [34] Prince (1996) 173, quoting from Sydenham's *Dialogues of Plato*, pp. 247–8.

novelistic 'in order to show why the contingencies of human desire and self-interest frustrate any move to a forced consensus'.[35]

Some of Prince's scheme looks oversimplified. For example his claim to see a move from open to closed dialogue within Plato's oeuvre looks highly debatable.[36] An alternative model might stress Plato's concern with truth and clarity in all circumstances:

> Plato does not use the possibilities of the genre of drama to produce maximal ambivalence, but as a rule he leads the reader by means of frequently ambivalent steps to a clear final result, and to the equally clear assurance that further substantiation and tracing back to even higher principles is not as yet forthcoming, but is necessary and probable.[37]

Or instead one might prefer to hang on to the view of Plato as a writer who does value openness and ambivalence, and who uses the dialogue form to achieve that aporetic effect, or at least to allow us to experience a tension between certainty and uncertainty. David Halperin, for example, writing of the *Symposium*, views Plato as 'a cunning writer fully alive to the doubleness of his rhetoric ... and who actively courts an effect of undecidability'. Halperin urges a sensitive reading of the 'alternating doctrinal and counter-doctrinal pressures' of the text[38] (although he also notes that the *Symposium* is in some ways highly untypical of Platonic dialogue as a whole). In other words the model of a dichotomy between type (a) and type (b) looks very undernuanced. We might think instead of a continuum between those two poles, with Lucian furthest towards type (b), with his refusal to allow any single perspective in dialogue to predominate,[39] and Plutarch closer towards the centre (hinting as he does at a hierarchy between explanations, with the most plausible usually kept till last, but also constantly undermining any such hierarchy within the frivolous sympotic context of the *Sympotic Questions*).[40] Or we might prefer a more complex picture of texts oscillating self-consciously between the two poles – as Halperin in fact suggests for Plato's *Symposium* – flirting in different ways and to different degrees with the motifs associated with both.

Despite those caveats, however, I want to hang on to that distinction for now, and to test it out as a template for viewing the distinctions between Christian and Greco-Roman sympotica. The dialogues of Augustine are at first sight a promising place to look for a Christian example of the first,

---

[35] Prince (1996) 18–19.   [36] See Long in this volume.   [37] Szlezák (1999) 108.
[38] Halperin (1992) 114.   [39] See Branham (1989).
[40] By contrast some of Plutarch's other dialogues offer a much more clearly signalled progression from less to more plausible explanation: see Hardie (1992) 4755.

transcendental kind of dialogue – type (a) – as something incompatible with the symposium form.[41] His dialogues often seem to be dramatising their own resistance to sympotic tradition, stressing the inappropriateness of mixing rational discussion with prominent features of the symposium tradition. For one thing, Augustine ostentatiously avoids linking conversation with commensality.[42] *De Beata Vita* is set on Augustine's birthday, at lunchtime, in the baths, where he has invited his family to join him – this is a version of post-consumption philosophy, but one that pointedly avoids any hint of drunkenness and discards the model of an evening setting. In several places he leaves gaps in the dialogues for listeners to go off and eat meals and relax, as if suspicious of mixing consumption and serious conversation;[43] and the debates are broken off (rather than begun) at nightfall to allow the scribes who are recording them to work. All of that combines with a more general lack of interest in the benefits of audience response to unresolved dialogic uncertainty: there is a preference for written exchange ahead of oral, and Platonic reminiscence is replaced by reading of transcriptions from previous days' conversation (hence the stenographers). At one point it is suggested that it may be detrimental to the audience to see a public quarrel between the interlocutors.[44] Plutarch's *Sympotic Questions* deprecates excessive disputatiousness, for sure, but for that work disagreement is nevertheless the crucial ingredient which allows the reader's own philosophical response, and he and his fellow guests repeatedly push up against the boundaries of propriety in their disagreements and insults and in the ingenuity and frivolousness of their responses (in line with the classical tradition of the symposium as an institution for sanctioned flirtation with disorder).[45]

Augustine thus seems particularly keen to avoid the kinds of dialogue which are associated most often with the symposium, with its traditions of speculative and playful speech, and it may be that his wariness provides one key to Christian neglect of the sympotic genre more generally.[46] Of course,

---

[41] For Augustine as one of the most important figures for Christian transcendental dialogue, see Prince (1996) 6; cf. Mourant (1970) on Augustine's achievement of overlaying Platonic, metaphysical dialectic with the added certainty of Christian truth.

[42] See Stock (1996), esp. 130–7 for many of the examples here.

[43] That suspicion is actually the topic of the opening sections of *De Beata Vita*, where Augustine's mother draws attention to the way he himself is distracted by food; literal consumption is replaced by metaphor, through a long account of Christian metaphors of nourishment of the soul.

[44] Cf. Mourant (1970) 84–5 on Augustine's preference for dialogue with himself in the *Soliloquies*, on the grounds that it avoids the imperfections of real conversation and the emotional responses which accompany competitive discussion.

[45] E.g. see Relihan (1992) 216; Whitmarsh (2004) 52–67.

[46] Cicero, Augustine's main model for dialogue, similarly prefers to avoid sympotic settings, and one might explain Augustine's anti-sympotic character simply by the fact that there is no sympotic model

there are other reasons too: there must be features of the symposium tradition quite unconnected with the nature of sympotic *dialogue* specifically which similarly contribute to Christian lack of interest. For example, the long-standing association of the symposium with intoxication and seduction, albeit counterbalanced by philosophical overtones, might well have seemed problematic in the context of new Christian attitudes to pleasure and the body, especially to the pleasures of eating and drinking.[47] We might also expect the elitist associations of the symposium to have been at odds with early Christianity's stress on inclusiveness (including the tendency to allow the presence of women, in contrast with the Greek symposium tradition) and its appeal below the elite levels of society.[48] Early Christian feasting consciously broke the mould of hierarchical feasting. It should be no surprise that Christian writing tended to follow suit. It is also striking that our best surviving example of Christian sympotic writing, Methodius' *Symposium*, seems keen to avoid the kinds of locally specific detail we have seen already for Plutarch's work, where philosophical discussion is grounded in the rhythms and institutions of the Greco-Roman city and within the contours of Greco-Roman social status. This too may be an element of sympotic tradition which is out of step with Christian standoffishness from the institutions of the pagan city. Membership of a specific sympotic community is replaced in Methodius' work by attendance at the universal, metaphorical banquet of the Christian church. Despite all those other factors, however, it seems likely that the particular kinds of dialogue which were specific to the symposium were a major factor.

WHAT DOES CLEMENT'S *PAIDAGOGUS* BOOK 2 LOSE OR GAIN BY NOT BEING A DIALOGUE?

I have spent some time already in examining the many-voicedness of Athenaeus' text. How does the *Deipnosophists* measure up against the work of his Christian contemporaries, many of whom were concerned with compiling and inventively reshaping the resources of the past? At the

---

within Cicero's work for him to imitate. That seems like an excessively mechanical explanation, however, especially given Augustine's knowledge of Platonic writing; it might be better to see Cicero's avoidance of the symposium as a symptom of precisely what Augustine finds attractive in his work, that is an interest in shutting out the more frivolous extremes of dialogic playfulness and indeterminacy, rather than something unthinkingly imitated.

[47] See (amongst many others) Grimm (1996).

[48] On the social inclusiveness of the early Christian movement, see (amongst many others) Clark (2004) 27–30; Stegemann and Stegemann (1999) who argue that New Testament communities after 70 CE showed a wide cross-section of social levels, but not the highest and lowest.

risk of oversimplifying, the example I want to examine briefly here is Clement's *Paidagogos* Book 2, which is sympotic in content (containing instructions for how a Christian should behave in dining)[49] and sympotic in language (quoting repeatedly from many of the same sources as Athenaeus, from comic, medical, philosophical writing, but also at the same time from Christian scripture, in an exercise of harmonisation between pagan and Christian tradition),[50] but not sympotic in setting, in the sense that the text presents itself as a prescriptive set of instructions proceeding from a single individual, rather than as a dialogue. It may well be the case, as I will suggest in a moment, that Clement's work is inherently dialogic even though he would prefer it not to be. But I think it is nonetheless a good example of how cutting out the dialogue frame from a subject which is standardly framed within dialogue tends to reduce the impression of polyphony – that is, the sense of a variety of different voices jostling against each other with a degree of independence from any controlling authorial voice. Whether that suppression of polyphony is a distinctively Christian effect is of course highly doubtful, and one might argue that the contrast between Clement and Athenaeus does not stand up to scrutiny, since there are very many examples of similar passages of non-Christian moralising about sympotic conduct, or for that matter non-Christian compilations of quotations which similarly take place outside dialogue form (though none, to my knowledge, which engages with sympotic motifs at quite such length). What sets Clement apart from those Greco-Roman equivalents, however, is the way in which he gives the monovocality of his text an explicitly Christian theorisation: his work has underlying it an assumption that the divine 'Word' (Logos) is the ultimate source of all the utterances he records, and his rationale for quoting from so many pagan authors is that they too were inspired by some spark of divine Logos, albeit without fully understanding its implications.[51]

---

[49] For survey of Clement's attitude to food and feasting, see Grimm (1996) 90–113; on Clement's aims of giving instruction for Christian behaviour, see Brown (1988) 125–6 (with full discussion in 122–39). Cf. Maier (1994); Bradley (1998) 42–5, who sees Clement as representative of typical Greco-Roman concerns with deportment at dinner; Buell (1999) 119–30; Behr (2000) 162–3; Kovacs (2001).

[50] E.g. see Marrou (1960) 49–52 and 71–86 on Clement's position in relation to the range of Greek philosophical doctrines he draws on; also Lilla (1971); Berchman (1984) 55–81; Behr (2000) 131. Marrou also shows (e.g. 77–81) how Clement's erudition is marked by the educated culture which Plutarch and Athenaeus wrote for, and he points out that there are moments when Clement duplicates material presented by those two authors in their sympotic writing: for example (80–81) Clement's list of drinking cups in 2.3 is very close to that of Athenaeus in Book 11, and similarly follows alphabetical order.

[51] See Marrou (1960) 47–8; and for longer discussion, Löhr (2000) 417–25 who shows how this idea is linked with Clement's sophisticated working out of the common Christian claim that Greek

For the first half of Book 2 Clement turns his attention to the question of how to behave at dinner. Comparison with Plutarch brings out vividly Clement's ambivalent relations with sympotic precedent. Here too he draws on Greco-Roman material as well as scriptural instruction: for example, we see here a particularly strong concentration of quotations from comic descriptions of gluttony. Many of the topics duplicate the self-reflexive topics of discussion we find in Plutarch and others, and the chapter headings, where issues of proper behaviour are presented as questions, are very close to the titles of Plutarchan *quaestiones*. For example the topic of *Paidagogos* 2.8 – 'Whether perfume and garlands should be used' (Εἰ μύροις καὶ στεφάνοις χρηστέον) – parallels Plutarch, *Sympotic Questions* 3.1 – 'Whether flower garlands should be used while drinking' (Εἰ χρηστέον ἀνθίνοις στεφάνοις παρὰ πότον). There are other similarities too. For example, the concept of progress in education is crucial for Clement,[52] as it was also for Plutarch. However, Clement's treatment of these topics is also in some ways very different from Plutarch's. In Plutarch's case there is a carefully structured focus on individual initiative and personal response as central features of the process by which individuals make progress in the unsummarisable rules of sympotic philosophy. Clement, by contrast, is much more prescriptive, offering no alternatives to his monovocal instruction, in line with his stress on the importance of uncompromising obedience to the divine Logos.[53] There is nothing here to match Plutarch's scenes of active, convivial debate.[54]

From there Clement launches into a set of moralising instructions on proper attitudes to food, closely paralleling and in places quoting from an eclectic range of both Christian and non-Christian writings – even in just the first few pages of the text we see reference not only to a wide range of New Testament texts, but also in addition Seneca, Philo, Galen, Plato, Epictetus, Semonides, Homer and a whole range of comic writings, some of which also appear in Athenaeus. Sometimes Clement names his sources, and occasionally those named sources are pagan writers (e.g. in 2.1.2.3, we hear that Antiphanes the doctor from Delos condemns varied food), but by far the

---

philosophy had plagiarised from Jewish writing; cf. Ridings (1995) 29–140; Lilla (1971) 9–59, esp. 13–28 on the claim of divine inspiration for Greek philosophy, pointing to his partial dependence on Philo and Justin.

[52] This work is itself the middle part of Clement's trilogy on the topic of progress in Christian life: the *Protrepticus* (*Exhortation*), the *Paidagogos*, and the *Stromateis* (*Miscellany*).

[53] On Clement's concept of authoritative divine voice, which is heavily indebted to Stoic and Platonic conceptions, see Dawson (1992) 183–234.

[54] However, see Behr (2000) 164–6 on tensions in Clement's attitude to meat and wine between disapproval and acknowledgement that Jesus gives his approval to both in the gospels.

most frequent 'interlocutors' are the abstract 'Scripture says', or 'the Apostle says', or, most tellingly 'the Lord says'. In all cases the sources seem to be in agreement with Clement; or rather, in the case of his Christian 'interlocutors', Clement acts as a mouthpiece for their coherent and consistent instruction. Here, then, the text's polyphonic character is pointedly overlaid with mono-logic control.

That is not to say that Clement's control over all these different voices is absolute. There are moments when they threaten to take on a life of their own. Right from the start, he is vehement in his denunciations of improper behaviour; but he goes into another gear straight after his quota-tion from Antiphanes, drawing on the resources of comedy to list some of the disgraceful varieties of food which his gluttonous targets lust after, and it is here that his affinity with Athenaeus' writing starts to become more obvious:

> I feel pity for their sickness; but they are not ashamed to sing the praises of their own devotion to pleasure, and they do everything they can to get hold of sea-eels from the Sicilian straights and Maiandrian eels, kids from Melos and the kinds of mullet that come from Skiathos, Peloridan mussels and Abydean oysters; nor must we pass over the sprats from Lipara and Mantinean turnips... (*Paidagogus* 2.1.3.1)

– and so on, for nearly twenty lines. For a moment we might forget where we are, as we get sucked deeper and deeper into this piscological orgy, which combines vehemence and delight in just as intense a form as any of the texts Athenaeus quotes, as if Clement is enacting the temptations of gluttony even as he denounces them. His list, like the gluttons he is denouncing, doesn't know when to stop. Is he testing us here? Is he setting his own accumulation of material on a more elevated level than the accumulations of the gluttons, or even of his own comic predecessors, flaunting his own ability to turn their comic denunciations to a higher Christian purpose? Or does he risk for a moment associating himself with them? Most strik-ingly, is he able to shut out the self-reflexive connotations of the imagery of variety and overstuffing which are so deeply ingrained in Latin poetry, and in Greek representations of consumption before that?[55] Do his own thun-dering denunciations of variety turn back against himself, at the richness of his own accumulation of literary models and quotations? Athenaeus, too, constantly asks the same question of himself in his obsession with self-reflexive images of excess and intoxication.

---

[55] Gowers (1993).

In many ways, then, the voice of Clement's divine Logos is an arche-typally Bakhtinian, dialogic one, speaking out its own distinctive self through an astonishingly rich and diverse range of ventriloquised others. There also seem to be moments where his text flaunts its own dialogic character almost whether he wants it to or not, in the sense that his *satura* of borrowings has implications which are hard to control. And yet it is also clear that he is trying much harder than Athenaeus to suppress those implications, and that he does so in part through avoidance of the dialogue form. For Athenaeus, by contrast, it is precisely the dialogue form which brings his mixing of so many different speakers and source texts into prominence, allowing him to move between different levels of narrative, in a way which at times make it hard for us to identify whose voice exactly we are hearing.

METHODIUS

This chapter has so far explored the idea that Christian writing (at the risk of vast generalisation) may often be uncomfortable with the kinds of indeterminacy (pp. 94–8) and many-voicedness (pp. 98–102) which are particularly associated with sympotic speech, even more so than other types of dialogue. In this section I want to test those assumptions further by looking at one text – Methodius' *Symposium*, written probably in the second half of the third century, and so several generations after Clement's *Paidagogos*[56] – which I think raises some additional problems and ques-tions, and which might force us into a more nuanced formulation. My main argument here is simply that we should be more ready to see Methodius as a writer who is self-conscious about his own relationship with agonistic or dialogic forms of argument, even as he distances himself from them.

First, a brief summary. The dialogue opens in imitation of Plato's *Symposium*. Two women, Euboulion[57] and Gregorion, are sharing news of a discussion of virginity at a banquet hosted by Arete the daughter of Philosophia. Gregorion recounts the version she heard from one of the participants Theopatra, who tells of a long and difficult journey up a path crawling with terrifying reptiles, and then their arrival in the garden paradise

---

[56] See Musurillo (1958) 4 for dating. For text and commentary, see Musurillo (1963); for English translation, Musurillo (1958).

[57] Others read masculine Euboulios: see Goldhill (1995) 162–3, n. 8 for arguments in favour of feminine identification, with reference to Musurillo (1963) 42–3, n. 1.

of Arete's home. When they have eaten, Arete proposes a discussion of virginity, and her ten guests speak in praise of virginity in turn. The dialogue ends with a hymn performed by Thekla, the companion of St Paul, and a final return to the framing narrative where Euboulion and Gregorion sum up what they have learned. The text is multi-faceted. It is full of practical instruction, influenced in part by Clement, especially in the notion of the 'progressive release of the soul from the domination of the passions'[58] and it had a considerable influence over later ascetic practices.[59] But it also goes beyond day-to-day instruction. Chastity for Methodius is not to be defined narrowly in terms of sexual abstinence only, but instead comes to stand for the whole practice of perfect Christian virtue, by which we can prepare for the final coming of Christ. And the work as a whole stands as an extended refutation of the kind of cosmological dualism which sees embodiment as the origin of sin.[60]

On that basis one might view the text as typically sympotic in the sense that it has compilatory ambitions, ranging over a huge variety of different areas of Christian thought. As Herbert Musurillo puts it:

En un sens, c'est une complète *summula theologiae*, dans laquelle Méthode a incorporé des discussions sur l'encratisme et la christologie, l'astrologie et la détermination, le célibat et la concupiscence.[61]

Effectively, the work stands as a compendium of Christian views on the traditionally sympotic subject of desire, with extensive quotation from a range of Christian authorities (often also with allusions to Greco-Roman authors mixed in, although as for Clement these are rarely named explicitly).[62] Some speakers in Plutarchan fashion use the language of improvisation[63] or contribution[64] to describe their own speeches. There are repeated references to the fact that we are hearing a variety of voices, and to the idea that there are countless numbers of different ways of saying the same thing, although the stress is always on the way in which different contributions

---

[58] See Patterson (1997) 8.   [59] See Musurillo (1958) 3 and 169, n. 2.

[60] On Methodius' theology, see Patterson (1997); and more briefly, Musurillo (1958) 16–23 and (1963) 13–30. Patterson's very clear and comprehensive account nevertheless pays little attention to the narrative form of the work or to Methodius' ambivalent self-positioning in relation to the norms of classical dialogue; those topics are my main interests here.

[61] Musurillo (1963) 13.

[62] Cf. Zorzi (2003) on Methodius' reshaping of Platonic concepts of Eros; Goldhill (1995) 1–4 on the theme of chastity and the work's ambivalence towards its Platonic frame.

[63] E.g. Thallousa in 5.8 (132): ἐκ τοῦ παραχρῆμα.

[64] E.g. Theophila in 2.8 (50): συμβάλλομαι; Thallousa in 5.8 (132): συμβάλλομαι; Agathe in 6.1 (132): εἰσενέγκασθαι.

work by reinforcing rather than undermining each other. In 4.1, for example, Theopatra explains the varied nature of God's inspiration:

If, virgins, the knowledge of the art of argumentation always relied on the same courses of argument and travelled by the same path, there would be no possibility that I could avoid irritating you in attempting subjects which have been fought out already (τοῖς ἤδη προηγωνισμένοις). But if it is right that there are countless starting-points and courses for argument – since God inspires us 'in manifold and varied ways' – what an absurdity it is to hide ourselves and be afraid. (*Symposium* 4.1 (93))

That quotation, taken from Hebrews 1.1, is appropriate for Methodius' theme of unity through diversity, describing as it does the way in which God's early, fragmented communication with the prophets has now been clarified through the words of his Son.[65]

Despite being many-voiced in those senses, it is hard to find the kind of ambivalence and playfulness we might normally view as the defining features of sympotic writing within Greco-Roman tradition. However, that is not to say that Methodius is simply uninterested in the agonistic side of the tradition he is working with. My suggestion here is rather that he is fascinated with the project of actively dramatising his own relationship with the agonistic potential of the dialogue form he is using. Musurillo does not mention that possibility. He notes that there is some disagreement between the first two speakers – a 'faible tentative de conflit dialectique', as he calls it – but characterises the final eight speeches as little more than a string of homiletic instructions, which have only a distant, diluted resemblance to their Platonic ancestors:

En tant qu'exemple de la technique platonicienne, pourtant, le dialogue de Méthode n'est guerre une réussite: car M. a manifestement manqué la profonde habileté dialectique de son maître, qui fait progresser la vérité par l'exposition organique de points de vue opposés.[66]

On closer inspection, however, the picture is rather more complicated. I want to illustrate that claim by focusing in what follows on just one feature of Methodius' engagement with dialogic norms, that is the way in which he saturates his writing with the language of competition – often added into passages where he is otherwise reproducing the language of Plato's

---

[65] See also 7.1 for a similar example, drawing on Eph. 3.10; that passage similarly combines a stress on the varied wisdom of God with the claim that the time is now right for clearer revelation, in this case through Paul's own prophetic voice.

[66] Musurillo (1963) 24.

Symposium very closely – in such a way as to reflect conspicuously on his reshaping of agonistic traditions of sympotic speech.

Competition is immediately prominent in the work. In the opening paragraph, for example, Euboulion describes what she has heard of the banquet: 'they tell me that the women competed so very magnificently and vigorously that they missed out nothing of what needed to be said on the topic (φασὶ γὰρ σφόδρα μεγαλοπρέπως οὕτως αὐτὰς καὶ ἰσχύρως ἠγωνίσθαι ὡς μηδενὸς εἶναι τῶν εἰς τὸ προκείμενον ἀναγκαίων ἐνδεεῖς), (pr. 2). At the end of the framing conversation that agonistic language recurs, as we hear Gregorion complimenting Euboulion: 'You are always brilliant in discussions (δεινὴ ἐν ταῖς ὁμιλίαις) and keen to find the truth, refuting (ἐξελέγχουσα) everyone easily', and then Euboulion's reply: 'do not argue (φιλονεικεῖν) about that subject now',[67] phrases which between them suggest that these two interlocutors share the ten virgins' appetite for debate – although Euboulion's preference for avoiding debate in some ways anticipates the move towards increasing consensus in the later sections of the work. Within the inset narrative of the conversation the language of competition is similarly conspicuous. Arete invites Marcella to speak first, in a sentence which very closely imitates the language of Plato, *Symposium* 177d, but she then rounds her invitation off with an additional sentence – not drawn from Plato – comparing the coming discussion to a contest, offering to crown 'the one who competes successfully (τὴν καλῶς ἀγωνισαμένην)'. Her argument against marriage is then contradicted by Theophila (whose speech begins in almost identical language to the claim of Eryximachus in Plato, *Symposium* 186a that he needs to add to the speech of his predecessor Pausanias, which is incomplete). Not far into Theophila's speech, Marcella interrupts, and we hear again the language of the wrestling ring: Theophila feels dizzy: 'like one who is grasped around the midriff by a formidable opponent (ὥσπερ ὑπὸ γενναίου ληφθεῖσα τῶν μέσων ἀνταγωνιστοῦ)'(2.4). In a sense then, far from downplaying conflict in the opening of the work, Methodius goes out of his way to draw attention to it, although it is a version of competitive dispute that risks violating the Plutarchan friend-making characteristics of the symposium precisely through its vehemence.

Admittedly as we move into the second half, the atmosphere of rivalry drops away: the later speakers tend to become more and more self-deprecating,

---

[67] That expression adapts almost identical phrasing at the end of the framing conversation in Plato, *Symposium* 173e.

more and more keen to stress the fact that their own contributions can only be footnotes to the points already made.[68] For Musurillo this is Methodius running out of steam: after the 'faible tentative de conflit dialectique' in the confrontation between Marcella and Theophila he drifts into lazy sermonising. But I wonder if we should at least be granting Methodius a bit more self-consciousness than that. One of the striking developments, for example, is the way in which the language of agonism tends to be redirected, rather than dropping away entirely.[69] There is an increasing sense that the true struggle is against oneself, rather than against rivals in conversation, with virginity, and the nearness to God it provides, as the prize. That assumption is prominent especially in the speech of Thekla (8) which is saturated with agonistic language; and it culminates in another wrestling image in the work's final lines, where Euboulion suggests that the best wrestler is the one who is being constantly tested against difficult opponents in competition, just as the most valuable type of virginity is one which is constantly being tested against temptation.[70] I suggested earlier that Plutarch in his *Sympotic Questions* appropriates the language of agonistic competition and festival participation as an image for his own competitive philosophical conversations, representing them as elevated forms of common civic activities. Methodius reshapes those same images – in line with widespread Christian fascination with the language of athletics – to rather different purposes.

In that sense Methodius, I suggest, may be consciously crafting his reaction to the agonistic, ambiguous potential of the dialogue form, reshaping it self-consciously, rather than simply passively falling short of it. What matters here, in other words, is not simply the fact that this particular Christian writer may be wary of sympotic dialogue, but also that he explores and signals to us with a great deal of intricacy and ingenuity where the differences of his own approach lie.

---

[68] E.g. 6.1, 9.1, 10.1.

[69] Thekla's speech wins its speaker a special crown at the end of the debate (11, 284), but here we should perhaps see the significance of the agonistic language not so much in its reference to Thekla's victory in conversation, but more in the overtones of the struggles of martyrdom for which she was so famous (see esp. 8.17, where Euboulion and Gregorion, summing up Thekla's contribution, praise her for her triumph in the contests of the martyrs). The details of her speech also stress the importance of contests for virginity: e.g. see 8.2 (175), where we hear of virgins crowned with the blossoms of immortality as the result of their contests; and in 8.13 Thekla talks of the need for contest against the seven-headed beast of Revelation, where the virgin can win the seven crowns of virtue from the seven contests of chastity.

[70] See especially the wrestling imagery in 300, which picks up and rewrites the language of wrestling quoted above from 2.4 (37).

MACROBIUS

This final section jumps ahead by more than a century to roughly 430 CE,[71] asking similar questions of a very different text. How does Macrobius' *Saturnalia* represent dialogue? How self-conscious is Macrobius in his manipulation of traditional uses of the dialogue form? Should we see this as a text which shares Christian wariness of agonistic dialogue communication, and Christian desire to rewrite that inheritance? Or should we see it rather as a text which reactivates Greco-Roman models of agonistic enquiry? Clearly there are some areas, not surprisingly, where Macrobius is much closer than Methodius to his Greco-Roman models.[72] For example, he matches Plutarch and others in his traditionally sympotic fascination with local context and identity, setting the work at the festival of the Saturnalia in Rome, and making it into a celebration of Roman religious and poetic tradition, and of the Latin language. He also matches both Plutarch and Athenaeus, as we have already seen (p. 94 above), in his fascination with the idea that the multiple voices of the past can be made to speak through his characters in the present. There are, however, important differences. What I want to show here is that Macrobius is highly self-conscious about his engagement with and reshaping of sympotic tradition; that he goes out of his way to draw attention to it; and that at least some features of that rewriting are shared with what we have seen for Methodius.

The feature which most obviously aligns Macrobius with Methodius against his Greco-Roman sympotic models is the fact that he seems to value consensus and agreement much more urgently than they do. He stresses not only consensus between guests but also, implicitly connected with that, consensus between past and present, and in the process he tends to suppress the connotations of uncertainty and inventiveness which are a particular feature of the sympotic form within so much of Greco-Roman tradition. One important reference-point here is the work of Robert Kaster.[73] Kaster's primary interest is in examining Macrobius' representation of the grammarian Servius, but in the process he offers an extended reading of the patterning of Macrobius' work. He emphasises, amongst other things, the way in which the guests feel themselves to be part of a clearly defined order, speaking in turn, and with a sense that all are contributing to a common

---

[71] See Cameron (1966) for date; Döpp (1978) for objections.
[72] On Macrobius' use of sympotic traditions, see also Martin (1931) 280–86; Flamant (1968) and (1977) 172–232; Relihan (1992) 238–9.
[73] Esp. Kaster (1980).

enterprise, each from his own different area of expertise. And he points to the way in which that sense of unity is 'facilitated ... by the choice of the dialogue form',[74] which makes a virtue of the fragmentation of special-isation typical (on some accounts) of late-antique society, fitting it in with ideals of sympotic harmony. That cooperative harmony stands as an equiv-alent to the harmony between different ages:

> literary borrowing conceived of as the preservation of and expression of respect for the *societas et rerum communio*, the 'unified community' of the shared culture extending into the past, just as the intellectual 'borrowing' among the participants in the symposium is a means of recognising and affirming the order of the 'unified community' of the present.[75]

The obligation to maintain that harmony is expressed in moral terms. Within that atmosphere there is no place for competition. Nor is there any place for playful humour. Kaster draws a contrast with Cicero's dialogues, 'where the smile is an instrument of amused debate and rejoinder or accompanies ironic banter'; in Macrobius' work, by contrast, the smile (which recurs repeatedly as a motif) is 'a signal that debate is being shut off and is the opposite of bantering ... The only man who smiles in the *Saturnalia* is the expert; and not just the expert ... but the expert who has been challenged precisely in the area of his expertise'.[76] On the rare occasions when conflict does erupt, when one of the guests commits the faux-pas of challenging the atmosphere of consensus, it is suppressed with a brutality which far surpasses the recurrent atmosphere of gentle mockery in Plutarch's *Sympotic Questions* (as Kaster demonstrates through discussion of the quarrel between Disarius and Eustathius in Book 7.13–15, which flares up after Disarius has dared to criticise Plato's explanation of a medical matter). The language of 'brute certainty'[77] which surfaces here, as Kaster points out, is utterly alien to Plutarch.[78]

In what sense, then, does Macrobius draw our attention to this process of reshaping sympotic traditions? There is space here only for three brief examples. My first passage comes in the enormous string of metaphors Macrobius uses to describe his own work in the first preface of the text, which I quoted from briefly above (p. 94). In that passage, he tries out a wide range of different images for giving expression to his principles of creative imitation: like bees, he says, we should sip from many flowers, combining what we gather into a single flavour; like the human body, which

---

[74] Kaster (1980) 230.   [75] Kaster (1980) 233.   [76] Kaster (1980) 239.
[77] Kaster (1980) 241.   [78] For comparison with Plutarch, see Kaster (1980) 241, n. 68.

absorbs and transforms the food it consumes, so we must digest the food of the mind and assimilate it. One of those images seems to have particular self-reflexive significance for the dialogic scenes which follow, and that is the theme of unity within a choir, which is repeated several times in the rest of the work:

You see how many people's voices a choir consists of; and yet it gives out one single voice from all of them. Some of the singers' voices are high, some are low, some are in the middle range; women are combined with men; the sound of the pipe is added; and in such a way the individual voices of the choir are hidden from view but the voices of all are nevertheless heard, and harmony arises from diverse elements. (*Saturnalia* 1.Pr.9)

That image of voices contributing by their polyphony to a single message or a single voice is programmatic for the conversation which follows; and like Methodius' model of unity in diversity it is rather different in emphasis from the Plutarchan obsession with adversariality.

Second, in the third prefatory section of the work, where Macrobius replays the Platonic layering of different levels of narrative (1.2.1–14), we hear a speaker called Decius, asking his friend Postumanius for an account of the banquet in the expectation that Postumanius had been there himself. Postumanius explains that he was not present, but that he heard everything from his friend Eusebius, and will now repeat it to Decius in turn. Decius has already praised Postumanius for his powerful memory:

I have recently spent time with others who are admirers of the strength of your memory, which has often allowed you to recount in order all the things which were said on that occasion. (1.2.2)

The narrative layering – which in Plato raises doubts about the accuracy of the version we are about to hear, in line with the work's interest in the question of how philosophical knowledge is passed on from person to person – is here (quite bluntly) rewritten to fit Macrobius' preoccupations with creative imitation. Presumably we are to imagine that Postumanius' repetition of Eusebius' own repetition of the conversation is an example of precisely the principles of the preface (and precisely the principles of which Virgil is shown to be the supreme practitioner in the bulk of the text which follows) of faithful repetition which is moulded to the idiom of the new speaker but without ever losing its original character. Once again, the Plutarchan practice of debating with the texts of the past is replaced with a very different process of respectful revoicing, a principle which runs right through the text as a guiding aesthetic.

My third point concerns Macrobius' very pointed rewriting of Plutarch's sympotic dialogues. Macrobius reads the *Sympotic Questions* carefully,

especially in imitating it extensively in Book 7. He clearly recognises the
importance of inventive argumentation for Plutarch's work. And yet
Macrobius also ostentatiously signals the difference between his own
'creativeness' and Plutarch's. For one thing, despite the fact that many
passages are translated from Plutarch's version word for word, Macrobius
avoids the typical Plutarchan preference for providing several different
explanations in turn. Repeatedly his guests seem to be more interested in
the performance of a single response to a question, rather than open debate
on the subject; repeatedly we see just one speaker addressing a question,
rather than several. In the *Saturnalia* it is questions, not answers, which
proliferate, as the answer to each enquiry is accepted without challenge and
the next enquiry immediately introduced. Even Macrobius' ingenious
Greeks (some of the guests, as Greek speakers, are characterised by the
other diners as being better suited to inventive argumentation)[79] are relatively happy to let the answers of others go unchallenged; and when they do
lapse into argumentative behaviour they often attract unfavourable comment from their fellow-diners, as if to emphasise the fact that interpretative
flexibility is somehow alien to the Latinate culture the work memorialises.
We have seen already the vicious dispute which erupts between Disarius
and Eustathius in 7.15 – a warning, it seems, of where disagreement can lead
to. Immediately after this dispute, one of the other characters, Evangelus,
mocks them, characterising their argumentativeness as an example of frivolous, Greek addiction to ingenious argumentation (a misleading characterisation, if Kaster is right to point to the alienness of their exchange from the
sympotic ideals of Plutarch and his fellow guests), while at the same time
encouraging them to continue with it:

At this point Evangelus, who was unwilling to allow the Greeks any glory, spoke
mockingly to them, 'That's enough of these subjects; you're discussing them in
order to show off your garrulousness. Instead, if your powers of judgement are of
any use at all, I would much rather know from you whether it was the egg which
came into being first, or the chicken.' (7.16.1)

The doctor Disarius acknowledges that Evangelus is making fun of them,
but launches into a serious answer nevertheless, following the precedent of
Sympotic Questions 2.3, where precisely that question is discussed. The
narrative here offers Eustathius and Disarius another chance to show that
they can behave like Plutarchan symposiasts. However, in their eagerness to
restore harmony, to show that dialogue can be peaceful after all, they go to

---

[79] See 7.5.4 for a good example.

the other extreme, shying away from properly agonistic debate, and treating each other with exaggerated politeness. The work's rewriting of the argumentative structure in *Sympotic Questions* 2.3 makes that departure from Plutarch's agonistic ideals clear: only one speaker, Disarius, replies, summarising both sides of the argument himself, and Eustathius does not even take up the invitation to involve himself, whereas in Plutarch's version many different speakers contribute. In this chapter, then, as elsewhere, and very much unlike Plutarch, Macrobius suppresses divergence of opinion, or at least shows his characters treading very carefully around it. In that sense he enacts his non-Plutarchan attitude to ingenious, creative response precisely through his own allusive engagement with the *Sympotic Questions.*

All of those points may seem fairly straightforward, but they are not necessarily for that reason insignificant, if they remind us that Macrobius, like Methodius, is highly self-conscious and self-aware in his rewriting of dialogue form. Like Methodius, Macrobius tends to avoid sympotic indeterminacy. He does not simply banish or ignore the idea of dialogue entirely, however; rather he redirects it, reshaping the guiding principles of speculative, sympotic speech (ideas of contest and of polyphony) to justify a very different way of understanding the world.

Are the overlaps in this respect between Macrobius and Methodius coincidental? Certainly we should recognise that their attitudes towards authority arise within vastly different social, chronological and theological contexts. Is there really anything to tie them together at all? Or should we stress instead the variety of uses to which the symposium can be put and the danger of generalising? Clearly that last point in particular is crucial. There is, however, one additional feature of Macrobius' text which seems to me to offer a starting-point for thinking about pagan and Christian attitudes to dialogue together, at least within the context of Macrobius' early fifth-century society, and that is the role of the troublemaker, Evangelus. Evangelus is the uninvited guest of the *Saturnalia.* He is argumentative and mocking; we hear several times that the other guests 'shudder' in horror when he intervenes. In that sense he is a figure against whom Macrobius defines the aesthetic of pious harmony to which most of his speakers subscribe. Evangelus is constantly sceptical, constantly keen to catch others out, to encourage his fellow guests to argue with each other. In that sense the passage I quoted above, where he mocks Eustathius and Disarius for their ingenuity, is more complicated than I suggested, given that Evangelus is here criticising the kind of argumentative behaviour he spends most of his time trying to provoke. Evangelus may also be a Christian. That identification (based, for some, simply on his name) was for some time discredited,

especially after Alan Cameron's redating of the text to the 430s CE, half a
century later than originally thought, with the consequent implication that
we should be very cautious about seeing the text as a doctrine of militant
paganism, let alone anti-Christian propaganda. Sabine McCormack
has recently revived that interpretation, however, on a number of different
grounds, with reference (for example) to Evangelus' attack on Virgil, which
she suggests follows the contours of Christian attacks on pagan literature,
and to Evangelus' reference to secret rites of his fellow guests, when he
finds them all assembled together on his arrival (McCormack reads that
reference in the light of legislation against pagan cult).[80] If that is right, what
implications does it have for our understanding of Christian attitudes to
dialogue in the early fifth century? How should we read Evangelus' interventions? At times he seems to be the only dialogic, Plutarchan character in
view, relentlessly dragging his fellow guests away from their consensual
styles of argumentation (despite his typically ungenerous attack on those
who break away from consensual styles of argument in the passage I quoted
in the last paragraph).[81] Or should we read his disruptive, nihilistic style of
argument as something paradoxically and, against first impressions, profoundly unPlutarchan, and in fact not so far removed from that of his pagan
interlocutors, in the sense that it arises from a habit of attacking whatever is
threatening to one's own position, just as Eustathius attacks Disarius,
humourlessly and uncompromisingly, for his criticism of Plato? Kaster
argues that we should not see Evangelus as a Christian,[82] but he hints
nevertheless at a similar conclusion in his final paragraphs:

It may be possible to hear in that passage [Eustathius' attack on Disarius] the idiom
of the fifth century: the language of Macrobius in the heat of controversy is most
closely paralleled by the language used to denounce a contemporary Christian
heresy, as the unrestrained assertion of an idiosyncratic *prudentia* which seeks to
undo the solidarity of the whole.[83]

I have suggested here that Macrobius and Methodius, despite their
enormous differences and despite the gap of more than a century between
them, have a certain amount in common with each other in their cautious,
transformative attitude to traditions of sympotic polyphony and contest.
If Kaster is right, that may be in part because Christian literature and

---

[80] McCormack (1998) 74, 86–7.
[81] On Evangelus' place in a long line of disruptive guests in the symposium genre, see Relihan (1992) 238–9.
[82] Cameron (1966) 35 rejects the idea that Evangelus is Christian, as does Flamant (1977) 74.
[83] Kaster (1980) 262.

Christian thought participated and contributed to wider currents of thought about dialogue and authority which flowed out also into pagan discourse.

CONCLUSION: MORE SYMPOTIC QUESTIONS

This chapter has necessarily skated over many of the nuances and problems which a longer study would need to examine. It also points to many further questions which there is no space to address here. Some of those questions centre around particular works. How, for example, do the many scenes of sympotic discussion in the gospel narratives, especially in Luke, draw on and transform Greco-Roman and Jewish traditions of convivial debate?[84] What should we make of Jerome's claim that there was a *Symposium* among the works of Lactantius?[85] What, if anything, can the emperor Julian's curious Saturnalian work the *Caesares* – a balloon debate held in heaven between the previous emperors of Rome – tell us about changing attitudes to sympotic debate?[86] A longer study of the history of the symposium dialogue might also examine in more detail the impact of the Christian eucharist, Christian asceticism and Christian metaphor as elements which often drown out any interest in the symposium as an institution, but which all nevertheless have the potential, even if rarely, to be overlaid and juxta-posed with sympotic motifs. These questions, however, take us beyond the scope of this volume. What I have tried to do here is to offer a first approach to the question of how and how far sympotic dialogue changes, in the transition from the Greek literature of the Imperial period to the world of early Christianity and late-antique paganism. My argument has been, above all, that we should be wary of generalising too quickly and too simplistically about Christian and late-antique disinterest in dialogue. Even texts like those of Methodius and Macrobius which at first sight have only a very diluted interest in the agonistic potential of the dialogue forms they inherit, nevertheless on closer inspection turn out to be engaging with those tradi-tions intricately, reshaping them for their own new contexts and new uses.

---

[84] E.g. see Braun (1995); Smith (2003) 253–72; see also (amongst many others) Stein (1957); see Smith (2003) 133–72 on the question of how far Jewish convivial literature is influenced by the Greco-Roman symposium form.

[85] Jerome, *De Vir. Ill.* 100.80.

[86] For discussion in relation to other sympotic works, see Relihan (1993) 119–34, with further bibliog-raphy; Relihan (1992) 236–8.

PART III

Christianity and the theological imperative

Can we talk?
Augustine and the possibility of dialogue
Gillian Clark

He said: A man prepared a great dinner, and invited many people, and at the time of the dinner he sent his slave to say to those invited, 'Come, for everything is ready.' And one after another they made excuses. The first said 'I have bought some land and must go and look at it: please excuse me.' Another said 'I have bought five pairs of oxen and am on my way to try them out: please excuse me.' Another said 'I have married a wife, and for that reason I cannot come.' The slave came back and told his master. Then the master of the house was angry, and said to the slave 'Go quickly to the streets and the lanes of the city, and bring here the beggars and the cripples and the blind and the lame.' The slave said 'Master, your order has been carried out, and there is still room.' The master said to the slave 'Go out to the roads and the roadsides and make them come in, so that my house shall be full. I tell you that none of those men who were invited shall taste my dinner.'

(Luke 14: 16–24)

The parables of Jesus have many applications, and this one can be applied in many ways to the relationship of dialogue and Christianity. First, the story: the host and his intended guests belong to the wealthy elite, for whom dinner parties are a normal mode of sociability.[1] The civilised dinner party is a familiar setting for dialogue as a literary form,[2] but here it is the poor who are brought in and fed. Second, the teaching technique: the Gospels are often 'dialogic' or dialectic. Jesus tells stories, like the story quoted here, that work by conversation, and he teaches by question and answer with his

I am indebted especially to Simon Goldhill, who over several years has made me read and think about various peculiar Christian texts; to Richard Lim's path-breaking *Public Disputation, Power and Social Order in Late Antiquity* (1995); to Catherine Conybeare's discussion of Augustine's early dialogues in *The Irrational Augustine* (2006); to Philip Burton for advance sight of *Language in the* Confessions *of Augustine* (2007); and to Christian Tornau for the timely arrival of *Zwischen Rhetorik und Philosophie* (2006).
[1] See Lim in this volume.   [2] See König in this volume.

disciples, with the Pharisees and with people he meets. Augustine made this point when an opponent accused him of being a dialectician:

Did not the Lord himself, the son of God, have conversations about the truth not just with his disciples and with the crowds who believed in him, but with enemies who tested and criticised and questioned and resisted and abused him? Was he reluctant to debate the question of prayer with just one woman, in opposition to the belief or heresy of the Samaritans?[3]

But the gospels became part of a sacred text, and, in a new development of Greco-Roman culture, this text was interpreted by preaching to anyone who came, rather than by discussion within a group of philosophers or initiates.[4] *Sermo* became sermon: conversation became exposition and exhortation. Sermons, *sermones*, were so called because their style was usually conversational. Except on special occasions, they did not use the style of forensic or epideictic oratory, but borrowed techniques for liveliness from philosophic discussions and lectures, including questions to the audience and cross-questioning of imagined opponents.[5] But although they were conversational, they offered a single voice.

Augustine looks like a particularly good example of the move from *sermo* to sermon and a particularly good demonstration of the thesis that early Christianity quashes dialogue. To begin with a rapid survey: here is a man who, on the evidence of his *Confessions*, grew up thinking that discussion with friends was the obvious way to pursue the truth. When he resigned his post, in 386, as the publicly funded professor of rhetoric at Milan, he did what Cicero had taught him was the proper use of *otium*: he withdrew to a country house, discussed philosophy with a group of friends, and wrote philosophical dialogues. He gave them lively scene-setting, characterisation and argument, and he dedicated one (*Contra Academicos*) to his long-term patron Romanianus, another (*De ordine*) to his literary friend Zenobius, and a third (*De beata uita*) to Mallius Theodorus, a philosopher of high social status.[6] After his baptism at Milan in 387, on his way back via Rome to Africa, and in the few years of *otium* with friends at his family home in

---

[3] Augustine, *Contra Cresconium* 1.8.10: *nempe enim Dominus ipse Filius Dei, numquid cum solis discipulis uel turbis qui in eum crediderunt, an non etiam cum inimicis tentantibus, obtrectantibus, interrogantibus, resistentibus, maledicentibus, habuit de ueritate sermonem? Numquid eum etiam cum una muliere de quaestione orationis contra opinionem uel haeresem Samaritanorum piguit disputare?*

[4] See further Clark (2004) 21–6, 85–8.

[5] For *sermocinari* meaning 'engage in dialectic', see Burton (2005) 141–64, at 153–4.

[6] Foley (1999) argues that Augustine wrote the dialogues as a response to Cicero: *Contra Academicos* to Cicero's *Academica*; *De beata uita* to *De finibus* and *Tusc. Disp.*; *De ordine* to the trilogy *De natura deorum, De diuinatione* and *De fato*. For the philosophic lifestyle, see Trout (1988).

Thagaste, he wrote some dialogues, but more treatises. The dialogues he did write moved towards impersonal argument and finally to monologue.[7] From his ordination to the priesthood in 391 until his death in 430, he wrote no more dialogues, and his extraordinary output of work consists of sermons, letters, exegesis, treatises and polemic.[8] In retrospect, a decade after writing his dialogues, he said they were like an athlete still getting his breath back after a contest: they still showed over-confidence in human reason.[9]

Augustine, then, appears to demonstrate a threefold abandonment of dialogue: movement away from dialogue as a literary genre; loss of confidence in dialectic as the way to achieve truth; and failure to engage in dialogue with people who held different views. When he wrote about disagreement with non-Christians, or with Christians who seemed to him to have the wrong idea, Augustine's mode of engagement was not conversation. It was forensic in style and in technique, and when it offered other voices, they were there to make damaging admissions, sometimes quoted from their published work, sometimes invented as the response Augustine claimed they would make. He could have presented a 'brotherly disputation', over a not too frugal meal in the clergy house at Hippo,[10] on the great questions of how people can be good, whether sin comes with conception, and why the grace of God seems not to reach some people. Instead, there are letters and treatises, embassies to Italy and manoeuvres at synods, and all the depressing history of the Pelagian controversy.[11] He could have presented a courteous discussion, over a grander meal in Carthage,[12] on what is really at issue between intelligent Christians and philosophically minded adherents of the traditional religion. Instead, there are the twenty-two books of *City of God*, which from its outset opposes 'their' authors to 'our' scriptures. All this

---

[7] Harrison (2006).

[8] Augustine's *Retractationes* give the contexts of his works. He wrote the dialogues *De ordine, De beata vita, Contra Academicos* and *Soliloquia* between his resignation in autumn 386 and his baptism at Easter 387. At Milan, after his baptism, he wrote the treatise *De immortalitate animae* and began his (unfinished) project to write on each of the liberal arts. Moving to Rome, he wrote the dialogues *De libero arbitrio* and *De animae quantitate* and the short two-book treatise *De moribus ecclesiae Catholicae et de moribus Manichaeorum*. In Africa he wrote a commentary *De Genesi adversus Manichaeos*, the treatise *De uera religione*, and the dialogue *De magistro*. His first work after his ordination was the treatise *De utilitate credendi*.

[9] *Conf.* 9.4.7, discussed below.

[10] There was always wine, and meat when there were visitors: Possidius, *Vita Augustini* 22.

[11] Bonner (1986) 312–93, for the sequence of events and the theological issues; *Augustinian Studies* 33.2 (2002) 201–75 offers a range of papers on whether Augustine invented the Pelagian controversy or whether there really was an important theological debate.

[12] A dinner at Carthage where peacock was served: *DCD* 21.4.

confrontation is worrying for present-day Christian moderates, who think that love of neighbour requires dialogue in the sense that it requires us to talk and listen to our neighbours, to search for understanding even where we cannot agree. In this paper, I shall try to suggest reasons why Augustine stopped using the dialogue form; why this does not mean that early Christianity closed down dialogue; and why it does mean that Christianity prompted newly challenging forms of dialogue.

Augustine's earliest surviving works are dialogues, from the time when he was living a downmarket version of the philosophic life with a small group of friends, students and relations in a borrowed country villa outside Milan.[13] One theme of his later work is already present, in that the members of the group, like the congregations to whom he would preach, have varying levels of education. Augustine reads Virgil and pursues philosophical arguments with his students, but his mother, who has no formal education, also makes important contributions, and the group includes two uneducated male relatives. This is a notable variant on Cicero's elite male participants who discuss philosophy and history as they relax from politics and business.[14] But both the fact that Augustine wrote philosophical dialogues, and the content of those dialogues, have prompted arguments that he had converted to philosophy, not yet to Christianity. He had committed himself to a Platonist understanding of God and the soul: that is, he believed that the One God, immaterial and transcendent, created the world and the immortal souls of human beings. He thought this was compatible with belief in the incarnation of Christ and with the Christian scriptures.[15] 'Your letters will proclaim Christ, Plato, Plotinus', said his friend Nebridius.[16]

A decade later, when Augustine wrote about these early dialogues in *Confessions* (9.4.7), he supplied some arguments that Christianity and dialogue do not mix. His friend Alypius *primo dedignabatur*, 'at first disdained', to have the name of Christ included in such works. Alypius was already sympathetic to Christianity: he was baptised with Augustine a few months later. So this was not an objection to Augustine's beliefs, but a concern about genre and the expectations of fourth-century readers. Alypius, according to Augustine, wanted Augustine's writings 'to be redolent more of the cedars of the *gymnasia*, which the Lord had already laid

---

[13] The exact sequence is debated: for a suggestion, see Cary (1988) especially 161–3.
[14] Conybeare (2006) offers an argument that Augustine used the dialogue form to question the primacy of reason; see 45–9 on the participants.
[15] See Harrison (2000) 15–19 for a summary of this debate; in (2006) she argues that Augustine's philosophy was always Christian.
[16] Aug. *Ep.* 6.1.

low, than of the health-giving herbs used by the church against snakes'.[17]
Cedar-wood and medicinal herbs both smell good and repel pests; but, as so
often in *Confessions*, readers are expected to hear the context in the Psalms
even when Augustine does not quote it:

> *Uox Domini in uirtute,*
> *Uox Domini in magnificentia,*
> *Uox Domini confringentis cedros*
> *Et confringet Dominus cedros Libani.*
> The voice of the Lord in strength,
> The voice of the Lord in grandeur,
> The voice of the Lord breaking the cedars:
> And the Lord will break the cedars of Lebanon.[18]

There were no cedars in the two *gymnasia* on the country estate at
Tusculum, one named for Plato's Academy and one for Aristotle's Lyceum,
where Cicero set several of his dialogues. Augustine equated these places of
high intellectual exercise with the lofty cedars of Lebanon, the greatest trees
then known; he contrasted them with the low-growing plants that give
health; and he evoked the one overwhelming voice that had already laid
low the cedars.[19] He used Scripture to reject Alypius' concerns about overt
Christian commitment. But these concerns were understandable. Alypius
had reacted as readers of this paper would if I cited Luke 11: 23 as a decisive
argument, adding as a clincher that I found it by biblical *sortes*.[20] That would
be to invoke the authority of a text, or set of texts, that many people do not
find authoritative, and it would be to assume that such invocation of an
authoritative text is acceptable in an academic paper. As Cicero said of the
Pythagoreans, *ipse dixit* is not an argument.[21]

Augustine did include the name of Christ in the early dialogues, just as
other Christians had done.[22] He did not often include it, perhaps because he
understood how Alypius and others would react, perhaps because he
thought it obvious that he was advocating a Christian philosophy. A letter
to another friend could be taken to support either of these suggestions.

---

[17] Aug. *Conf.* 9.4.7: *magis enim eas [litteras] uolebat redolere gymnasiorum cedros, quas iam contriuit dominus, quam salubres herbas ecclesiasticas aduersus serpentibus.* On *gymnasia*, see O'Donnell (1992) III.90 (available online at http://www.stoa.org/hippo/).

[18] Ps. 28: 4–5 (Vulgate). Augustine's text had *conteret*, so he could link the fall of the cedars with contrition: *vox Domini contritione cordis humilans superbos. Conteret Dominus cedros Libani (En. Ps.* 28.5). In *Conf.* 8.2.4, the 'cedars of Lebanon which the Lord has not yet laid low' symbolise pagan arrogance.

[19] On Augustine's dismissive use of Greek words such as *gymnasium*, see Burton (2005) 141–64.

[20] 'He who is not with me is against me, and he who does not gather with me scatters.'

[21] Cic. *De nat. deor.* 1.10: *tantum opinio praeiudicata poterat, ut etiam sine ratione ualeret auctoritas.*

[22] *C. Acad.* 3.20.43; *De ord.* 1.8.21, 1.10.29, 1.11.32; see further O'Donnell (1992) III.89.

Hermogenianus had written to say that in *Contra Academicos*, Augustine had won. Augustine was pleased, but asked Hermogenianus to say whether he approved 'what at the end of book 3 I thought should be believed, perhaps more cautiously than confidently, but in my judgement with profit rather than without commitment'.[23] Here Augustine invoked the factors considered by Academic philosophers when choosing which course to follow in a world where nothing is certain and everything can be doubted. What he had said at the end of book 3 was that (unlike the Academics) he did not despair of achieving wisdom, and

it is doubtful for no one that the twin forces driving us to learn are those of authority and reason. So for me it is certain never again to depart from the authority of Christ, for I do not find a stronger. But for that which must be pursued with the most subtle reason (for I am already in the state of mind where I impatiently desire to grasp what is true not only by believing, but by understanding), I am confident that I shall find meanwhile in the Platonists something that is not in conflict with our sacred things.[24]

This is the only explicit naming of Christ in *Contra Academicos*, and Augustine did not name Christ in asking what Hermogenianus himself thought about Christianity and Platonism.

In *Confessions*, Augustine says to God that the early dialogues 'were already in your service, but still breathed the school of pride, like an athlete getting his breath'. The 'school of pride' is Platonism, which Augustine saw as over-confident in human reason.[25] It was 'a man swollen with monstrous conceit', *immanissimo typho turgidum*, who gave Augustine Platonist books. This may have been Manlius Theodorus, to whom Augustine dedicated *De beata vita*, deciding later that he had overestimated him.[26] Even a quarter-century later, writing book 8 of *City of God*, Augustine reiterated how close Platonism was to Christianity, but still saw pride as the obstacle.

---

[23] *Ep.* 1.3: *utrum approbes quod in extremo tertii libri suspiciosius fortasse quam certius, utilius tamen, ut arbitror, quam incredibilius putaui credendum.* My thanks to Phillip Cary for advice on what this means: see further Cary (2000).

[24] *C. Acad.* 3.20.43: *Nulli autem dubium est gemino pondere nos impelli ad discendum, auctoritatis atque rationis. Mihi ergo certum est nusquam prorsus a Christi auctoritate discedere: non enim reperio ualentiorem. Quod autem subtilissima ratione persequendum est; ita enim iam sum affectus, ut quid sit uerum, non credendo solum, sed etiam intellegendo apprehendere impatienter desiderem; apud Platonicos me interim quod sacris nostris non repugnet reperturum esse confido.* The name of Christ also appears at the end of *De ordine* book 1 (1.8.21, 1.10.29, 1.11.32) and the nature of Christ is discussed at the end of *De beata uita* (4.34): Conybeare (2006) 6 n. 20.

[25] *Conf.* 9.4.7; Platonism and pride, *Conf.* 7.20.26. On the connection between pride and willed isolation from community, see the essay '*De civitate Dei*: pride and the common good', in Markus (1994).

[26] *Conf.* 7.9.13; O'Donnell (1992) II.419–20 discusses the identification with Theodorus; see further Hermanowicz (2004) 179. *Retr.* 1.2 thinks the dedication of *De beata vita* was overstated.

Later yet, reviewing his books in *Retractationes* (427), he noted that as a catechumen (that is, when preparing for baptism) he wrote 'still puffed up with worldly literature'.[27] Does it follow from this, not only that Augustine thought his early dialogues were too Platonist, but more generally that Christianity is not compatible with Platonic dialogue? Must the dialogue form be exploratory, open-ended, pluralist and reliant on rational speculation, in a way that is not possible for a committed Christian? Augustine knows that he depends on the grace of God and is subject to the authority of Christ as expressed in the Scriptures, so some lines of argument are already closed, for example that there is no God, or that God does not care about human beings, or that justice is the right of the stronger.

Augustine might counter that everyone has to rely on authority: in *De utilitate credendi*, the first work he wrote after his ordination, he used the example of taking on trust (as every schoolchild did) that Virgil is worth the effort.[28] He might also counter that dialogues are not always exploratory and pluralist and open-ended. Cicero, at the end of *De natura deorum*, comments with suitably Academic caution that Velleius thought Cotta's (Epicurean) argument 'more true' (*verior*), but for him Balbus' (Stoic) argument 'seemed more inclined to verisimilitude'; but the level of uncertainty varies in Cicero's dialogues as it does in Plato's.[29] Moreover, Christian commitment has never yet closed down debate, and Augustine was not among those Christians who wish it would. He did not think that Scripture supplies clear answers to everything, and he did think that other people's interpretations had to be taken seriously. Some interpretations cannot be right, because they conflict with basic Christian principles, but that still leaves many possible interpretations.[30] Augustine could have confidence that he had chosen the best authority and that it teaches the truth, not an approximation, but he would still have to argue that case, and he would still have to discuss the interpretation of his chosen authority, just as Platonists discussed the interpretation of Plato. For this, he could have used the dialogue form, which, as Jerome observed, is a helpful way of setting out a range of arguments. (Jerome said he followed Socratic precedent, but he did not follow the argument where it led: his work is called *Dialogues against the Pelagians*, and he took the further precaution of telling

---

[27] *DCD* 8.9; *adhuc saecularium litterarum inflatus*, *Retr.* Prol. 3. *Inflatus* evokes 1 Cor. 8.1, *scientia inflat, caritas aedificat* ('knowledge puffs up, love builds up').

[28] *De ut. cred.* 13.

[29] Cic. *De nat. deor.* 3.95. On Cicero as Academic, see the Introduction to Powell (1995) 18–23; Schofield (1986); also Schofield in this volume.

[30] *Conf.* 12.31.42; *De doctr. Christ.* 3.38.

his readers at the outset which speaker was right.[31]) But, like the Platonists, Augustine preferred treatises or commentary.

Commentary is an obvious way of doing philosophy when there is a central set of texts, such as the works of Plato, the Bible or even the Chaldaean Oracles, on which the philosopher Porphyry is said to have written a commentary. Recent work on commentary has shown that it can be a productive engagement with the text, a continuing dialogue with the author and with other interpreters, rather than evidence of dependency culture and absence of ideas.[32] But it is not easy to explain why Platonists did not use Plato's own dialogue form to report or to represent the discussions of teachers and students on the central questions of philosophy and the right interpretation of Plato.[33] In the case of Plotinus, the answer is clear: according to Porphyry, Plotinus would not have written anything at all if Porphyry had not made him write notes after his seminars.[34] Sometimes there is a practical reason: for instance, if Porphyry is in Rome and Iamblichus in Syria, their discussion of religion and theurgy is a dialogue only in that Porphyry writes a *Letter to Anebo* and Iamblichus replies, with quotations from Porphyry, in the *Response of the High Priest Abammon* (otherwise known as *De Mysteriis*). But, as Cicero wrote to Varro, dialogues often make their participants say what they did not in fact say: 'I think when you read [the *Academica*] you will be surprised that we said to each other what we have never said, but you know how dialogues are [*nosti morem dialogorum*].'[35] So the absence of Platonist dialogue remains a puzzle.

It is easier to offer a reason why Augustine stopped using the dialogue form. Students of Platonism were highly educated, and for this they had to be rich enough to get the education, travel to the right teacher and spend time studying.[36] But a Christian bishop was responsible for expounding God's word to anyone who cared to come, regardless of age or class or gender or education. Even before his ordination, Augustine recognised the need to include the uneducated, as he had done in the early dialogues, and this need is made explicit in the first work he wrote on returning to Africa.

---

[31] Jerome, *Dialogi aduersus Pelagianos* 1: *hic liber, quem nunc cudere nitimur, Socraticorum consuetudinem seruabit, ut ex utraque parte quid dici possit exponat, et magis perspicua ueritas fiat, cum posuerint unusquisque quod senserit.* He also wrote a dialogue between an orthodox Christian and a follower of Lucifer of Cagliari.

[32] Adamson, Baltussen and Stone (2004).

[33] Christopher Kelly raised this question at the *Dialogue* conference.

[34] Porphyry, *Vita Plotini* 8.

[35] Cic. *Fam.* 9.8.1, explaining that in *Acad.* 1, Varro was Antiochus and Cicero was Philo.

[36] Watts (2006).

De Genesi adversus Manichaeos is his first attempt at exegesis, and it has a programmatic opening statement:

If the Manichaeans chose people to deceive, I too would choose words for replying to them. But they pursue the educated with books and the uneducated with their own error, and try to turn them from the truth while promising the truth; so their futility must be exposed not by elegant style but by evident fact. I have accepted the advice of some truly Christian people, who have had a liberal education, but when they read other books I have published against the Manichaeans, saw that they would be understood with difficulty or not at all by the less educated. They kindly warned me not to abandon the ordinary way of speaking if I was thinking of expelling these lethal errors from the souls even of the uneducated. For educated people also understand simple, ordinary language, but uneducated people do not understand the other kind.[37]

This is a comment on style rather than form. The only book Augustine had (so far) published explicitly against the Manichaeans was a treatise, not a dialogue, contrasting the *mores* of the Catholic church with those of the Manichaeans. But his advisers might also have pointed out that uneducated people would not see how arguments in his other works opposed Manichaean teachings, and that they would find it difficult to follow the dialogue form and still more difficult to take part in discussion. Augustine was used to giving lectures, *tractatio*, on passages of Virgil where his students needed help.[38] He had already shifted the balance from dialogues to treatises, and only one of the works he wrote in Africa was a dialogue. It was a tribute to a brilliant student, his son Adeodatus who died at 18, and it raised questions about the very possibility of dialogue. Can we talk to each other? How do words relate to things? How does the teacher relate to the learner? Is there any traceable connection between what the teacher says and what the student learns, or rather, what he realises that he knows?[39]

After his ordination Augustine wrote sermons, and treatises on theology and exegesis, and letters. Many of these works respond to questions (one of them collects responses to eighty-three questions) and puzzles and challenges,

---

[37] *Gen. Man.* 1.1.1. *Si eligerent Manichaei quos deciperent, eligeremus et nos uerba quibus eis responderemus: cum uero illi et doctos litteris, et indoctos errore suo persequantur, et cum promittunt ueritatem, a ueritate conentur auertere; non ornato politoque sermone, sed rebus manifestis conuincenda est uanitas eorum. Placuit enim mihi quorumdam uere Christianorum sententia, qui cum sint eruditi liberalibus litteris, tamen alios libros nostros, quos aduersus Manichaeos edidimus, cum legissent, uiderunt eos ab imperitioribus, aut non aut difficile intellegi, et me beneuolentissime monuerunt ut communem loquendi consuetudinem non desererem, si errores illos tam perniciosos ab animis etiam imperitorum expellere cogitarem. Hunc enim sermonem usitatum et simplicem etiam docti intellegunt, illum autem indocti non intellegunt.* On Augustine's effort to be inclusive, see Conybeare (2006) 177–8.

[38] *C. Acad.* 2.4.10.   [39] On Adeodatus, see Bonner (1986) 108 n. 6; *De mag.* 45.

so they could be taken as a kind of dialogue, but they do not have the literary form of dialogue. They are lectures and explanations by an authoritative teacher, or display pieces and forensic oratory by an impressive public speaker. Here again there are practical reasons. Augustine the bishop knew that in public dialogue, with Manichaeans or Donatists, he needed to win.[40] He knew that 'much I did not dictate was nevertheless written down as I said it', and that his own secretaries were not the only ones making a shorthand record of his sermons: Donatists made notes for their own bishops.[41] Discussions recorded by shorthand writers were used in court cases about the application of laws on heresy and violence.[42] Sympathetic understanding could be quoted against him; and if he did not convincingly defeat the opposition, his audience might accept beliefs that in his judgement were lethal. He also knew that humankind cannot bear very much uncertainty. In *De utilitate credendi* he challenged people who said they did not need to work at understanding scripture: they knew it was full of absurdities because 'I read it and saw what it means'.[43] At the other end of the range were people in catechism classes who had very little education and were not familiar with different ways of interpreting texts.[44] Even in present-day British society, with much more education on offer, there is still tension between what ordinands discuss in theological college and what they can say in a sermon; and the media routinely blame the Archbishop of Canterbury for making things too complicated, that is, for recognising that there are several possibilities instead of offering a sound-bite.

So the status of a Christian bishop caused problems for dialogue, both as genre and as interchange of views: Augustine experienced the late-antique equivalents of media pressure and media distortion. But even before he had the responsibilities of a priest, Augustine had called into question the possibility of any human dialogue as a way of finding the truth. There is the problem that dialogue so easily becomes debate and competition. Question and answer is the best way of finding the truth, but many people dislike losing an argument because it means losing face.[45] The questions were too important for that. 'I don't want an argument for the sake of argument; that was all very well when we were growing up, but this is about our lives, how

---

[40] On debates with Manichaeans, see Lim (1995) 70–108.   [41] *Retr.* 1 prol. 2; Possidius, *Vita* 7.3, 9.1.
[42] Humfress (2007); cases involving Augustine, Hermanowicz (2008).
[43] *De ut. cred.* 7.17.
[44] *De cat. rud.* 15; see on this text Stock (1996) 181–90, and on catechism Harmless (1995). For different kinds of readers, see also *Doctr. Chr.* pr. 4.
[45] *Sol.* 2.7.14; compare Cic. *Acad.* 2.3.9 on people who hold on to their preferred opinion, and *Tusc. Disp.* 5.4.11 on the advantages of dialogue.

we live, our souls.'[46] Some people talk too much and explain too much: in *Confessions*, the Manichaeans are *loquaces*.[47] Then there are the problems of communication and learning set out in *De magistro*: these were central concerns of Augustine's work.[48] There is also the problem that literary dialogue is not dialogue, because one person writes all the lines.[49] Augustine did not make this point explicitly, but it is made by some of his early experiments in writing. He seems to have invented the term *soliloquia*, which he uses for conversations with Reason 'as if Reason and I were two, though I was alone'. Is this really soliloquy, talking to oneself? Does Augustine also speak for Reason, or does Reason speak to and in Augustine? *Confessions*, which appears to be a monologue, is a one-sided conversation with God, who replies only in the words of Scripture that come to Augustine's mind. But Augustine did not write Scripture: is this, then, a genuine dialogue with God, who speaks through its authors to engage in *elenchus* (examination and refutation) of Augustine?[50]

So together with Christianity came doubts not only about reliance on reason, but about the possibility of dialogue with other people. These doubts are not distinctively Christian, but perhaps they were strengthened by contrast with the experience of talking to God in prayer and finding a response in scripture; according to the prophet Isaiah, God welcomes discussion.[51] Together with a public role in the Christian church came abandonment of dialogue in favour of preaching in various forms: talking to, or talking at, or replying to questions, not talking with. Of course Augustine went on talking with his friends and with the members of his community; as he, or Reason, remarked in *Soliloquia*, depression set in otherwise, especially if he felt ill.[52] But he did not write dialogues, either as a way of exploring Biblical exegesis and its applications, or as a way of engaging with the beliefs of Manichaeans and Donatists and Pelagians and followers of the traditional religion. Instead, he wrote treatises and long polemic refutations, among them the twenty-two books of *City of God*, which occupied, among constant interruptions and more urgent deadlines, thirteen years of his life.

---

[46] *C. Acad.* 2.9.22.   [47] E.g. *Conf.* 3.6.10.   [48] Stock (1996) 190–206.
[49] Neatly raised by Cicero, *De legibus* 3.26, where Marcus (author and speaker) tells Quintus that in this kind of *sermo* it is usual to say 'Absolutely' (*prorsus ita est*) so that the speaker can move on, and Quintus and Atticus say they do not in fact agree.
[50] See also Conybeare (2006) 174 for *Gen. Man.* as a first attempt at dialogue with the Bible rather than with Cicero.
[51] *Uenite, disputemus, dicit dominus* (Isa. 1: 18, cited *Conf.* 13.19.24); for Augustine's changing valuation of *dialectica*, see Burton (2005).
[52] *Sol.* 1.9.16.

In 410/11 Augustine had an exceptional opportunity for interfaith dialogue. Romans of high status, highly educated, came to Carthage to escape from the Goths who had briefly plundered the city of Rome. They circulated pamphlets and open letters arguing that Rome had been invaded because Christian neglect had angered its guardian gods. The practice of traditional religion had been illegal for over a decade, so it was not possible to stage a public debate, even with these confident opponents whose high social status might give them protection.[53] Instead, Augustine was asked (or could claim that he was asked) at the highest level to answer their arguments: the imperial commissioner Marcellinus requested an effective response.[54]

Marcellinus, like Augustine, was in Carthage attempting to deal with the Donatist problem. This was a century-old dispute, sometimes violent, between two groups of Christians who had scripture, sacraments and much theology in common; dialogue in person or by letter repeatedly failed, and the conference that was supposed to resolve the problem was a dire example of dialogue refused and Christian charity forgotten.[55] When Augustine eventually (in 412/3) transferred his attention from resentful fellow-Christians to resentful anti-Christians, he could have chosen to set out the debate in dialogue form. Christians had done this in earlier centuries when it was the traditional religion that was supported by law, and some of them continued to use dialogue or question and answer.[56] Ideally (that is, ideally for present-day Christian moderates), Augustine would have progressed beyond the tendency to use dialogue as a device for presenting the Christian case, and would have engaged with the familiar arguments patiently and courteously, recognising that some arguments return again and again because there are real difficulties.[57] He would have considered what his opponents actually believed, and what they actually did, unobtrusively, to honour their gods.

Instead, Augustine behaved as might be expected from the brilliant student of rhetoric whose abilities had taken him from a small African town to Carthage, then to Rome, then to become professor of rhetoric at the imperial capital of Milan. He chose opponents who were safely dead, and

---

[53] Traditional cult and sacrifice was comprehensively banned in 391 (*C. Th.* 16.10), but nevertheless continued. For Africa, see Lancel (2000) 306–10; in general, Fowden (1998) 538–60.

[54] Aug. *Ep.* 136; McLynn (1999) 29–44.

[55] Lancel (1972). O'Donnell (2005) 217–18 discusses the failure of dialogue, and 234–43 gives a brilliant account of the procedural disputes.

[56] Christian use of dialogue is surveyed by Voss (1970). For 'dialogue' used to present one side of the case, see Lim (1995) 4; Rajak (1999) 59–80. On the varieties of *quaestiones*, see Lunn-Rockliffe (2007).

[57] The opposition material does not survive, but Marcellinus summarised the objections: Aug. *Ep.* 136.

had been dead for much longer than the elder statesmen of Cicero's dialogues. Varro, scholar and philosopher of the later first century BCE, represented traditional religion; Porphyry, scholar and philosopher of the late third century CE, represented Platonist philosophy. Augustine quoted selectively from their writings and added tendentious paraphrase: 'what he is *really* saying is …', 'see, he *admits* …'; he exploited at great length a handful of lines from Virgil, *exempla* from early Roman history, and inconsistencies in the remits of traditional gods. I have tried elsewhere to offer a more sympathetic account of *City of God*, and to show that Augustine did in the course of his work engage with the arguments of his opponents; Christian Tornau has shown how expertly Augustine followed the conventions of forensic rhetoric, addressing both opponents and judges in the way they would expect. But it is hard to blame any reader whose immediate reaction is that Christians don't do dialogue.[58]

The opening chapters of book 6 exemplify the apparent failure of dialogue in *City of God*.[59] This is the point at which Varro, who has already made some brief appearances, takes on a starring role as spokesman for Roman traditional religion. Augustine borrowed critique and examples from Cicero's dialogues on Roman religion, especially from *De natura deorum*, but his most important source and target was the (now lost) *Antiquitates* of Varro, to the point that *City of God* is the major source for fragments of Varro's second subdivision, *res divinae*.[60] It seems extraordinary for Augustine to choose an author whose express purpose was to preserve traditions that were almost lost even in the late first century BCE.[61] But this need not be evasive action. Augustine was seriously, even if polemically, engaging with the Rome that furnished his contemporaries with examples and ideals, language and genre; the classical Rome they wanted their children to learn and imitate as proof of education.[62] They paid good money for this, and he insisted that they think about the values expressed in Roman literature, history and tradition: the nature of its gods, the cost of its empire in wars both foreign and civil, the pride in reputation that motivated its heroes and heroines. They relied on authority for knowledge of this Rome, so he said that he would show, from the authors they took as authorities, that the facts were quite otherwise than

---

[58] See Clark (2007a) 117–38, for an argument that Augustine engages with Rome as his contemporaries understood it; Tornau (2006).

[59] Texts are available at http://www.augustinus.it.   [60] Collected by Cardauns (1976).

[61] Varro's purpose: *DCD* 6.2 (fr. 2a Cardauns). For more on Augustine's use of Varro, see my forthcoming essay 'Augustine's Varro, and pagan monotheism' (in P. van Nuffelen and S. Mitchell (forthcoming)).

[62] Clark (2007a).

they thought. He had Cicero's authority for taking Varro as the authority on Roman religious tradition.[63] In late antiquity Varro was respectfully cited by teachers who provided commentary as, like Augustine in earlier life, they took their students through Virgil.[64] And where else was Augustine to go for an authoritative survey of Roman religion? Present-day books and lectures on this subject often begin by emphasising the differences between Roman practice and Christian expectations: there were many cults, there were no shared sacred texts or statements of belief, and Roman priests did not have a teaching or pastoral role.

The opening of book 6, marked by later editors as a preface, makes it clear that Augustine is entering on a new stage of his argument.[65] As usual, he summarises what he has done so far. His tone is not eirenic and does not suggest any willingness to engage in dialogue with those who have not been persuaded. He has devoted five books to those who think the false gods are to be worshipped for benefits in this life. But 'who does not know that neither those five books, nor any number of others, would suffice for extreme stupidity or stubbornness?'[66] Readers who reflect without prejudice will realise that these stubborn people are ignorant (or pretending not to know), irresponsible and mindlessly hostile. Next (6.1) 'those people are to be refuted and instructed' who think that the gods are to be worshipped for benefits after death. Augustine begins with 'the truthful oracle of the holy psalm', quoting 'blessed is he whose hope is the Lord God, and who does not attend to vanities and lying follies' (Ps. 39: 5). He concedes that, amid these vanities and lying follies, one may listen with greater patience to the philosophers who have unobtrusively noted their objection to popular errors and images and myths. He does not yet name them, but anyone who has read book 4 knows that the plural refers to Varro. He moves to the absurdity of hoping for eternal life from the multiple gods with specialised remits, and thence (6.2) explicitly to Varro, the acknowledged expert on these gods.

Augustine lavishes praise on Varro's erudition, citing Cicero's praise, and suggests that Varro, though committed to Roman tradition and constrained by Roman custom, acknowledged his unease. There follows (6.3) an invaluable contents-list of the *Antiquitates*, which is the basis for an argument

---

[63] *DCD* 4.1, 6.2.   [64] MacCormack (1998).
[65] Book divisions are Augustine's own, and he regularly comments on them. Chapter divisions are a device of later editors: see further O'Daly (1999) 277–8.
[66] Compare the milder formulation of 'some people take a lot of convincing' in Cic. *De nat. deor.* 1.12: 'there has of course been fuller discussion of this question in another place, but, because some people are slow and resistant to teaching, it seems they have to be reminded more often'.

(6.4) that by discussing 'human matters' before 'divine matters', Varro admits that divine matters are human institutions. 'Divine matters', according to Augustine's summary, was concerned with cult. It was divided into four sections, on who did things, where, when and what, with a final section 'for whom', the three books on the gods, who are classed as certain, uncertain and select.[67] Augustine cites (6.4) Varro's explanation that human communities are prior to their institutions as the painter is prior to the picture, and reports Varro's comment that if he were writing about 'all the nature of the gods' (*de omni natura deorum*), he would have discussed gods before humans. Augustine replies that by categorising the gods as certain, uncertain and select, Varro surely has dealt with all aspects; or perhaps, since 'all' can be opposed to 'none' as well as to 'some', Varro intended his readers to understand that he has not written about gods at all. Now Augustine moves closer to dialogue with Varro. In 6.5, challenging Varro's division of theology into mythical, natural and civic, he repeatedly cites Varro ('let us see what he says') and argues with him and with possible objections ('perhaps someone will say'); and at 6.6 he addresses him, *O Marce Varro*, with renewed praise of his learning and objections to his theology.

O Marce Varro does not make a *disputatio* into a dialogue. Augustine behaves like a reviewer who thinks the author should have written a different book, in this instance a work of philosophical theology (*De natura deorum*) not an account of Roman traditional cult; and he combines this with annoying forensic language, claiming 'Varro admits' when his own quotation shows that Varro said it and explained why. But, as in the case of Porphyry, Augustine may be unfair in specific criticisms, and unwilling to present his opponent's argument, but still have a point.[68] Varro is the recognised authority on Roman religion, but if readers consult the recognised authority, they will not find moral teaching, and they will find that Varro gives priority to human custom. Does Roman religion consist of human custom? Moreover, Varro proves to be one of those, mentioned at the opening of book 6, who quietly indicated their disapproval of traditional cult: if he were founding a new community, he would start from different principles (6.4). If he thinks Roman religion is a human construct, why does he give it the authority of his learning? Uneducated people have to rely on the authority of the educated, but the leading authorities on Roman religion were quite prepared to let the people believe falsehoods. Scaevola

---

[67] See further Tarver (1994) 51–2.
[68] I have argued this case in Clark (2007b). Burns (2001) 40–1 argues that Augustine takes Varro more seriously than Tertullian or Arnobius did.

the learned *pontifex maximus* (addressed in book 4 as *O Scaevola pontifex maxime!*), and Varro the leading scholar, even said it was as well that the people should believe falsehoods. The *pontifex* does not suppress the degrading rites and stage-shows, and neither he nor Varro will acknowledge that some popular beliefs are false: dead humans are not gods, statues are misleading images.[69] 'What poor, uneducated man can escape the combination of deceptive statesmen and deceptive demons?'[70] When Augustine's correspondents said, in effect, 'nobody takes all that stuff seriously', he could reasonably reply that nobody took ordinary uneducated people seriously either: there was no one to explain the hidden meanings at the temples and festivals, for the job of the priests was only to carry out the ritual.[71]

It is hard to distinguish personal from rhetorical anger, but a conscientious bishop could well be angered by the attitude of a ruling elite who thought it best to conceal from their people what they knew to be the truth about the gods. In Augustine's own time, educated people knew that Rome had suffered many disasters in the centuries before Christ, but they allowed the uneducated to go on blaming Christianity.[72] In the time of Scaevola and Varro, they knew that some aspects of Roman cult were misleading or corrupting, but they did not say so. Varro explicitly said that philosophical theology was more tolerable within the walls of a lecture-room than in the forum outside.[73] As a social observation, that is quite correct; Cicero remarked that his Epicurean spokesman could not express his beliefs in a public speech, at least not if he wanted to be elected.[74] But it shows why Augustine might come to see philosophical dialogue as a luxury for the few.[75] It is appropriate for a philosopher and his friends and students who can financially afford time out from business, like Augustine and his friends and students in their borrowed country house at Cassiciacum after he had resigned his chair, or back home on his modest family property at Thagaste. It is also appropriate for those who can intellectually afford to set out lines of argument and leave questions unresolved.

In *City of God* Augustine contrasted the inconclusive debates of philosophers with the 'fixed and final canon' of Christian Scripture, which teaches truth.[76] This looks like a clear example of the rejection of dialogue, and seems to support recent arguments that Christianity closed down open-ended

---

[69] *DCD* 4.27; Scaevola may have featured as a character in a dialogue by Varro.
[70] *DCD* 4.32.   [71] Aug. *Ep.* 91.5.   [72] *DCD* 4.1.   [73] *DCD* 6.5.   [74] Cic. *Fin.* 2.76.
[75] Perhaps Sulpicius Severus wrote his *Dialogi* on the life of St Martin as a conscious address to the educated. On Palladius, *Dialogue on the Life of John Chrysostom*, see Katos (2007).
[76] *DCD* 18.41.

discussion among equals of a range of options, and replaced it with exegesis of a central text, agreed statements of belief and hard-line confrontation of orthodoxy and heresy.[77] But there are other factors. Philosophers, according to Augustine, are holed up somewhere with a handful of students who can afford the time. Nobody much is listening, or could understand if they did, and nothing depends on their discussions: that is why no city has bothered to sort out the teachings of philosophers. (Think of Plotinus taking three days to sort out Porphyry's objections on the relationship of body and soul, and Porphyry taking however long it took him to sort Plotinus' writings into the *Enneads*, and philosophers now taking years to interpret the *Enneads*.[78]) Augustine, in contrast, had to explain a text of central importance, week after week, to anyone who cared to come, as well as dealing with his usual workload. He replied to one correspondent, 'It doesn't look right to me when I think of a bishop, distracted by the surrounding clamour of church concerns, suddenly shutting himself off from all this as if he were going deaf, and expounding small points about the dialogues of Cicero to one student.'[79] In fact he went on to answer the questions about Cicero's dialogues, but his comment remained valid. There was no social or educational screening of his congregation, and he felt himself to be responsible for the souls of his hearers, for 'how shall they believe without a preacher'?[80] Philosophers, he said, could use words however they liked, but he had to be wary of prompting misinterpretations.[81] He also had to engage in practical politics. He could acknowledge to Paulinus of Nola that he had no answer to Paulinus' questions about punishment and could not read off answers from Scripture, but he still had to write to the local governor with specific requests for limiting the punishment of slave-traders or Donatists.[82]

Augustine the bishop didn't do dialogue, either in the sense of writing philosophical dialogues or in the sense of serious conversation with opponents.[83] There are various ways of interpreting this. One is to take it as evidence of increasing personal authoritarianism, as in Peter Brown's memorable portrait of 'the elderly bishop' (but there is a *retractatio* in Brown's revised edition), or in James O'Donnell's account of a lonely, frustrated

---

[77] Averil Cameron has advanced this argument in several papers, and discusses it in Cameron (2007). Polymnia Athanassiadi argues that the tendency affected later Platonism: see Athanassiadi (2002) 271–91.

[78] Porphyry, *V. Plot.* 13. [79] Aug. *Ep.* 118. 2. [80] Romans 10:14, used at *Conf.* 1.1.1.

[81] *DCD* 10.23. [82] Aug. *Ep.* 95.3, 108.4, 133.2.

[83] There is more to be discussed about Augustine in relation to dialogue between Jews and Christians. It seems that Paula Fredriksen is right to say 'real Jews have little to do with it': Fredriksen (1999) 26–41. See also Fredriksen (2006); and Unterseher (2002).

man who picks quarrels (but surely that was Jerome?).[84] Another is to take it
as one instance of Christianity closing down options. I have tried to argue
instead that the reason why Augustine doesn't do dialogue is not that he is
a Christian, but that he is a Christian bishop; not that his authoritative
text removes the possibility of debate (it has yet to do so), but that his social
and educational role needs careful handling. His forensic mode of argument
is frankly embarrassing to a present-day moderate, but he was certain that
his opponents were wrong in ways that damaged human souls, and he set
out to defeat them in ways that would carry conviction to an audience who
expected the forensic mode. He might even have argued, as he did about the
Donatists, that he was demonstrating tough love of neighbour. He could
also have argued that personal dialogue with the Scriptures, which are
disconcerting in their language and in their modes of address to God, and
public exegesis of those Scriptures in dialogue with a mixed community of
Christians, was much more challenging than dialogue among people who,
like ourselves, shared a classical education and could enjoy it in comfortable
privacy.

---

[84] Brown (2000) 491–2. O'Donnell (2005): this (to add to his 1970s cultural references) is Augustine the
Lone Haranguer.

CHAPTER 7

'Let's (not) talk about it'
Augustine and the control of epistolary dialogue

Richard Miles

DIALOGUE AND THE DONATIST CONTROVERSY

The growing domination that Augustine of Hippo exerted over all areas of religious debate in North Africa during the early fifth century CE was a key part of Caecilianist success against its rivals.[1] By actively seeking out opportunities for public dialogue with Donatist, Manichaean and Arian opponents then insisting upon the presence of stenographers before organising the distribution and reading out of these transcripts, Augustine effectively seized control of how these debates were presented to the wider Christian community in North Africa.[2] For Augustine this strategy of controlled engagement would be particularly successful in forcing progress on the African church's most long-standing and seemingly intractable dispute: the Donatist controversy. A century of schism had resulted in the development of two quite distinct rival textual communities.[3] Both Donatists and Caecilianists had their own exhaustive archive of legal documents, treatises, council records, sermons and letters which not only proved the rectitude of their respective positions in the controversy but also provided the foundation of the institutional identities which they had established for themselves.[4] Augustine would totally reject this separatist *status quo*. The Donatist dossiers would be subjected to rigorous forensic scrutiny by the bishop of Hippo. By challenging the veracity and in some instances the ownership of key disputed texts, Augustine sought to undermine any notion of a legitimate Donatist community.

---

[1] Monceaux (1901–23); Crepsin (1965); Lancel (1972); Lim (1995) 88–102.
[2] For an invitation to a larger debate see Augustine *Ep.* 88.10 in which Augustine wrote to Ianuarius, the Donatist primate of Numidia requesting a conference of bishops to resolve the differences between them. There were also debates with the Manichaeans (Fortunatus at Hippo Regius in 392 and Felix in either 397 or 398) as well as the Arians (Maximinus in 427 or 428 and Pascentius at an unknown date).
[3] For an account of the origins of the controversy see Frend (2003) 125–92.
[4] For the development of Donatist literature see Tilley (1997a, 1997b).

However, Augustine would increasingly become the victim of his own success as Donatist leaders understandably shied away from face to face public debates with such a formidable and well-organised opponent.[5] Augustine would be reduced to using a number of ingenious but highly dubious ploys to overcome this Donatist *omertà*. When Macrobius, his Donatist counterpart in Hippo Regius, refused to reply to one of his letters, Augustine circumvented the problem by treating the utterances of Macrobius, written down by his own messengers when the letter was read out in front of him, as an official response.[6] In another celebrated episode, a fragmentary pastoral letter written by Petilian, the Donatist bishop of Cirta, fell into Augustine's hands, which he promptly responded to it as if he was the actual addressee.[7] In the second book of his treatise, Augustine actually transformed Petilian's letter, which he now possessed a complete copy of, into a formal dialogue between them with the following self-justification:

I will comply with those who urge me by all means to reply to every point, and that as though we were carrying on a discussion face to face in the form of a dialogue. I will set down the words of his letter under his name, and I will give the answer under my own name, and as if it had all been taken by reporters whilst we were debating.[8]

This provocative gesture bore fruit when Petilian issued a detailed rebuttal to which Augustine responded in the third book of the treatise. At the beginning of this book, Augustine would acknowledge the impact of his staged 'dialogue' on Petilian particularly in relation to the pressure exerted by the wider textual audience amongst whom it had been circulated:

You observed also that the attention of many who had read it was fixed upon you, since they desired to know what you would say, what you would do, how you would escape from the difficulty, how you would make your way out of the bind in which the word of God had encompassed you.[9]

Despite its success, this reorganisation of Petilian's pastoral letter into a dialogue appears to have been extremely controversial. Cresconius, a grammarian, attacked Augustine's use of dialectic against Petilian in a letter which was passed around Donatist circles until it was eventually seen by

---

[5] For such a complaint see Augustine *C. Pet.* 1.1.   [6] *Ep.* 108. 1.   [7] *C. Pet.* 1.1.

[8] *C. Pet.* 2.1: *ita morem geram eis qui me omnino ad singula respondere compellunt, ut quasi alternis sermonibus in praesentia disseramus. uerba ex epistola eius ponam sub eius nomine, et responsionem reddam sub meo nomine, tamquam, cum ageremus, a notariis excepta sint.*

[9] *C. Pet.* 3.1.1: *attendisti etiam multorum qui ea legerant expectationem in te esse conuersam, scire cupientium quid diceres, quid ageres, qua euaderes, quo ex tantis angustiis quibus te dei uerbum circumuallarat erumperes.*

Augustine in 405.[10] Cresconius, citing references from sources as diverse as the Scriptures and Plato, would present a very traditional challenge arguing that dialectic led to deceit.[11] Augustine was portrayed as an ambitious controversialist who was more interested in eloquence than the integrity of his arguments.[12]

The length and prominence of Augustine's rebuttal of the grammarian's attack on his use of dialogue indicates that this was a sensitive issue for the bishop of Hippo.[13] Using the examples of Jesus and Paul, Augustine argued that the use of dialectic was justified if it were employed to proclaim the true Christian message to congregations.[14] Dialogue was only dangerous when there was an intention to deceive.[15] He also pointed out that the Donatists themselves had enthusiastically used dialectic and public debates in their battle to suppress their own dissidents.[16] Then, ignoring the fact that Cresconius had not addressed his letter to him, Augustine asked why the grammarian had involved himself in a dialogue if the Donatist church frowned upon it.[17] Most importantly of all, Augustine claimed, rather optimistically, that this strategy of aggressive engagement had been successful in bringing most of North Africa back into the Catholic fold.[18]

Despite the unapologetic nature of Augustine's response, it is clear that the criticisms that had been levelled against him by Cresconius did have an impact. In a treatise authored in 420 as a response to a letter written by Gaudentius, Donatist bishop of Timgad in 420, Augustine would adopt the impersonal formulae of *verba epistolae* and *ad haec responsio* with the explanation that:

That is the result of having been accused by him (Petilian) of deceit. Never had he debated with me face to face, he said, as if he had never said what he had written, because I had not heard it from his mouth, but read it in his text! Or better that I had never replied because I had not spoken in his presence, but replied to his writings with my own![19]

In fact, the Caecilianist victory at the great council of 411 and the subsequent government repression of the Donatist church meant that there

---

[10] De Veer (1968) 9–24.   [11] *C. Cresc.* 1.1.2 and 1.2.3.   [12] *C. Cresc.* 1.3.5 and 1.4.6.
[13] Much of the first book of the treatise would be devoted to the question of *eloquentia* and dialectic. For the general success of Cresconius' treatise see de Veer (1968) 24–7.
[14] *C. Cresc.* 1.13.16, 1.21–26, 1.7.9, 1.7.10–11, 1.9.12, 1.14.18, 1.16.20, 1.17.21–19.23, 1.20.25.
[15] *C. Cresc.* 1.18.21.   [16] *C. Cresc.* 4.2.2, 4.4.3–4.5.6.   [17] *C. Cresc.* 1.3.4.   [18] *C. Cresc.* 1.4.6; 1.5.7.
[19] *C. Gaud.* 1.1.1: *unde mihi, tamquam mentitus fuerim, calumniatus est, dicens quod numquam mecum comminus disputauerit; quasi propterea non dixerit quod scripsit, quia hoc non in uerbis eius audiui sed in litteris legi, aut ego ideo non responderim, quia non eo praesente locutus sum, sed scriptis eius uicissim scribendo respondi.*

was little debate to be had. In 418 at the cathedral in Caesarea, Emeritus, the Donatist bishop of the city, had been publicly berated by Augustine in front of an audience of civic worthies with the obligatory shorthand writers there to write down every word. Later, in the *Retractions*, Augustine would observe with some bemusement that his opponent had proffered no defence, merely silently listening to his own monologue as 'if he was mute'.[20] In fact Emeritus, a man who Augustine admitted was one of the Donatists' most skilful advocates, might well have been resisting in the only effective way left open to him.[21]

LETTERS AND THE SUPPRESSION OF DOCTRINAL DEBATE

Such formal public meetings would not be the only way in which dialogue played an important role in the Augustinian assault on the Donatist church. On a number of occasions, Augustine was keen to juxtapose the communion that he and the Caecilianists enjoyed with the universal Catholic church against what he deemed to be the self-destructive parochialism of the Donatists:

> The sect of the Donatists, restricted to Africa alone, is an object of scorn to the rest of the world. It does not recognise that by its sterility, which refuses to nurture the fruits of peace and charity, it has been cut off from the root of the eastern churches from which the Gospel came into Africa.[22]

Communion and indeed, doctrinal orthodoxy, he argued, were the product of a process of long-running open dialogue within the ecclesiastical hierarchy of the universal Christian church.

For how could a matter which was involved in such mists of disputation even have been brought to the full illumination and authoritative decision of a plenary Council, had it not first been known to be discussed for some considerable time in the various districts of the world, with many discussions and comparisons of the views of the bishop on every side? But this is one effect of the soundness of peace, that when any doubtful points are long under investigation, and when, on account of the difficulty of arriving at the truth, they produce difference of

---

[20] Augustine *Retract.* 2.51 (78).1. For the very brief exchange between the two men see *Gesta cum Emerito* 3.

[21] Possidius *VA* 14.

[22] *Ep.* 52.2 (*Corpus Scriptorum Ecclesiasticorum Latinorum* 34: 150): *pars autem Donati in solis Afris calumniatur orbi terrarum, et non considerat ea sterilitate, qua fructus pacis et caritatis afferre noluit, ab illa radice Orientalium Ecclesiarum se esse praecisam, unde Evangelium in Africam venit.* For similar arguments used by Augustine against the Donatists see *Epp.* 66.1, 87.5–7, 93.21–25.

opinion in the course of brotherly disputation, until men at last arrive at the unalloyed truth …[23]

If the Donatists were really part of the Catholic community then Augustine demanded that they show him the letters that had passed between themselves and overseas churches. That Augustine should regard letters as prima facie evidence of Christian communion is unsurprising. As Richard Lim suggests in his contribution to this volume letters increasingly acted as a 'surrogate dialogue form' within late-antique Christian communities.[24] It was widely accepted in antiquity that the letter as a literary genre occupied an ambiguous position that straddled the boundaries between text and speech.[25] Christian writers would frequently reassert the long-standing belief that a letter was one half of a private conversation.[26] Yet many of the letters written and received by theologians such as Augustine in Late Antiquity shared another important characteristic with formal dialogue: the acknowledgement of a wider audience than just the participants. These letters were no more private documents than dialogues were private discussions.

In the letters themselves there was often recognition of an open-ended audience which extended beyond the addressee(s). Letters were often dictated to secretaries and then read out for corrections. Furthermore, it was common practice for letters to be passed around by the sender. Augustine and Jerome both sent each other copies of letters that they had written to others. Indeed when Jerome found that a letter written by Augustine to him had been circulating around Rome and Italy, he was angry only because he had not seen the epistle himself and worried that others would think that he was avoiding answering it.[27]

In fact, that would have been a perfectly reasonable deduction to come to, as the wide potential audience of these letters meant that they did not lend themselves very well to unfettered discussion of controversial issues, especially with individuals whom the writer did not personally know. Letter

---

[23] Augustine *De Bapt.* 2.4.5. (*CSEL* 51: 179–80):
  quomodo enim potuit ista res tantis altercationum nebulis inuoluta ad plenarii concilii luculentam inlustrationem confirmationemque perduci, nisi primo diutius per orbis terrarum regiones multis hinc adque hinc disputationibus et conlationibus episcoporum pertractata constaret? hoc autem facit sanitas pacis, ut, cum diutius aliqua obscuriora quaeruntur et propter inueniendi difficultatem diuersas pariunt in fraterna disceptatione sententias, donec ad uerum liquidum perueniatur …
[24] Below, pp. 168–70.
[25] Doty (1973); Stowers (1986); White (1986).
[26] Cicero *Epistulae Ad Familiares* 12.30.1; Seneca *Ep.* 75.1–2; Julius Victor *Ars Orationis* 27; Demetrius *De Elocutione* 223.
[27] Jerome *Ep.* 105.2. For the process of the distribution of letters, see Achard (1991) 138ff.; Llewelyn (1995).

bearers are often portrayed as playing a far more important role than the mere delivery of missives, passing on sensitive information either orally or through additional notes.[28] Instead these letters often served as far more general statements of the wide circle of support that theologians enjoyed. Thus, even the mundane formulaic letters that make up a sizeable proportion of the extant epistolary output of the Church Fathers had an intrinsic value.[29]

In the provincial milieu of North Africa, it was easy for Augustine as a former chief rhetor of Milan to boast of his unimpeachable connections with the wider orthodox community. Within the North African church his episcopal position and the close relationship that existed between himself and Aurelius, primate of Carthage, meant that he was a man to be consulted and deferred to. His correspondence shows a self-confident assertiveness in his dealings with visiting imperial officials, provincial governors, military commanders, bishops and local curial elite.[30] In the narrow sectarian world which he inhabited it was easy for Augustine to separate friend from foe. Staged dialogues were easy to engineer because the relative positions of the two sides were so well known. The Donatist controversy, despite the continual threat of violence, provided a kind of intellectual safety blanket for Augustine. Outside of North Africa, however, the name of Augustine did not inspire the same fear or reverential awe. The Donatist controversy that had dominated his written output for the first two decades of his ecclesiastical career had little relevance or interest for those outside of North Africa. He had, of course, lived overseas but his tenure in Milan had been too brief to really establish the same formidable range of elite contacts that other theologians had. Furthermore, his previous adherence to Manichaeism made Augustine a figure of suspicion to many outside the African church.[31]

The dangers of public theological speculation were not lost on Augustine.[32] The *Retractions* were an accomplished but only partially successful attempt at self-correction in order to deflect some of the barrage of criticism that he

---

[28] Perrin (1992); Conybeare (2000) 33–40.   [29] Brown (1992) 23–124.
[30] Ciccarese (1971); Rebillard (1998).
[31] Paulinus of Nola had to be furnished with a number of treatises including his anti-Manichean works before he would enter into correspondence with him (Paulinus *Epp.* 3.4–6.; 4.1.; Augustine *Ep.* 27.4).
[32] Eno (1981). The theological elite of the late-antique Christian church were trapped by a rhetoric which denied the possibility of change and development of the faith yet at the same time required endless theological speculation to try and arrive at that place of perfect truth. Revelation was fixed and final, a 'deposit of faith' that could not be added to, merely understood in new ways. It was the duty of the orthodox churchman to guard this deposit.

faced in the latter stages of his career.[33] Despite his self-confident espousal of a Christian church sustained by rigorous debate, it is clear that Augustine was often very cautious when it came to discussion of undecided theological issues by letter. Amongst the late antique ecclesiastical community he was certainly not alone in his reticence. In 406 Jerome and Augustine would bat a particularly thorny question on the origin of the soul between them, each extremely unwilling to give a definitive answer themselves.[34] Eventually, after a particularly insistent request from Augustine to set down his views on the subject, Jerome would bring the episode to an end with the warning that 'although in any discussion our joint object is the advancement of learning, our rivals and especially the heretics will ascribe any difference of opinion between us to mutual jealousy.'[35]

Five years later Augustine had still not received an answer.[36]

LET'S (NOT) TALK ABOUT IT: AUGUSTINE
AND THE FRIENDS OF PELAGIUS

The dangers of theological speculation were never more apparent to Augustine than during his two-decade-long dispute with Pelagius. That Augustine faced a difficult task in convincing the wider church of the doctrinal rectitude of his position on Original Sin is clear from the distinctly underwhelming reaction to the barrage of letters and treatises that he sent out across the empire. Even Augustine's most vociferous supporter in the east, Jerome, appears to have had very little understanding of what the Augustinian position on Original Sin actually was.[37] Augustine would claim that the Greek-speaking bishops of Palestine had failed to condemn Pelagius as a heretic because he had bamboozled them with his intricate Latin prose. However, the truth was that he carried very little influence in the eastern provinces and in many parts of the west.[38] In contrast, Pelagius had strong support amongst members of both the ecclesiastical and senatorial establishment in Rome and the east. The endorsement of the former group was a key element in the creation of doctrinal orthodoxy whereas the latter could provide funds and social prestige. Not only did Pelagius' message that each should strive for spiritual excellence resonate with the

---

[33] Burnaby (1954).   [34] Jerome *Epp.* 126, 134; Augustine *Ep.* 166.
[35] Jerome *Ep.* 134.1.   [36] Augustine *Ep.* 202A.1.
[37] Kelly (1975) 315–16. Jerome's motivation for supporting Augustine seems to have been driven by an animosity against Pelagius, whom he viewed as a protégé of his great rival Rufinus (Kelly (1975) 309–11).
[38] Wickham (2002) 202–4; Markus (2002) 215–18.

self-image and aspirations of many elite Christians but as a spiritual mentor he was able to give them the personal attention that they required.[39]

Few such opportunities would arise for Augustine. When they did, as in the case of Albinia, her daughter Melania the younger and her son-in-law, Pinianius, members of the senatorial *über*-elite driven to take refuge from barbarian attacks in Italy, the rough and ready nature of life in small-town North Africa led to grave embarrassment. After Augustine's congregation at Hippo Regius tried to forcibly ordain Pinianius, the golden couple left for the more cosmopolitan Christianity of the Holy Land. Although his relationship with them would remain warm and respectful, it appears to have never been close. In contrast, their attachment to Pelagius was such that Pinianius and Melania sheltered him even when it became clear that he had lost his bitter dispute with Augustine.[40] Indeed, several historians have seen the reticence that Augustine shows in attacking Pelagius by name (he waits until 415 CE) as clear evidence of the influence of his patrons whom the bishop of Hippo did not want to upset.[41]

Augustine could simply not be seen as being at odds with these important individuals. Indeed, it could even be dangerous to attempt to persuade them of the rectitude of his position as such a strategy carried grave risks. A negative response, or even worse, no reply at all might be viewed as an explicit rejection of his position and would do the Augustinian cause great damage. Instead, epistolary dialogue with these prized correspondents would be strictly controlled by Augustine. The bishop of Hippo Regius sent letters to key members of the Christian elite whom he suspected of Pelagian sympathies, that contained an internalised dialogue that mapped out both questions and answers. The letters of Augustine were not one half of a conversation but the whole. In contrast to his public dialogues with the Donatist bishops, the object was not to vanquish and humiliate but to present the illusion of total agreement between close friends. By clearly setting out how he *imagined* that the recipients would respond to his letter, Augustine took total control of the epistolary process. At the same time these letters would function as a powerful coercive force to the much wider audience amongst whom the letters would be circulated. The hidden audience, as witnesses, policed the potential responses of the recipients of Augustine's letters. Recipients were therefore implicated with Augustine in the eyes of the audience. The wider readership not only viewed a conversation which had reached a unanimous conclusion but also Augustine's

[39] Brown (1968, 1970).   [40] Brown (1968) 113.
[41] Brown (1968); Evans (1968) 70–80; Martinetto (1971).

authoritative position as an orthodox thinker was maintained and even strengthened. In this way Augustine not only attempted to control the debate over particular theological issues but also promoted himself as an authoritative figure within that community.

The surviving letters of Augustine show that there were two particular targets amongst Pelagius' friends in the west: the Anicii and Paulinus of Nola. There were clear reasons for this. Firstly, both the Anicii and Paulinus, despite their stronger relations with Pelagius, were still in contact with Augustine throughout the Pelagianist controversy. Secondly, they held an almost iconic status amongst the Christian aristocratic elite. Paulinus has been described in a recent study as 'the emblematic example of Christian aristocratic conversion to ascetic Christianity'.[42] Ambrose of Milan understood well the seismic impact that Paulinus' decision to follow the ascetic life had on his aristocratic Italian contemporaries.

> What will the leading men say when they hear this? That someone from that family, that lineage, that stock, and endowed with such tremendous eloquence has migrated from the senate, and that the line of succession of a noble family has been broken: it cannot be borne.[43]

The relationship that developed between Paulinus and Augustine entirely through letter-writing highlights the limitations of such epistolary friendships. Despite the extravagant pronouncements of Christian fellowship between them and the repeated claims that their respective messengers acted as the physical embodiment of their master, there is no evidence that the two were particularly intimate.

The Anicii were the most celebrated Christian senatorial family in Rome. Sextus Petronius Probus, the recipient of a multitude of imperial honours and offices, had been allowed to build his mausoleum in the apse of St Peter's just behind the altar. Their huge wealth and access to the highest echelons of imperial power had ensured that three generations of Anicii women all played prominent roles in the ecclesiastical politics of the period: Anicia Faltonia Proba, who held the unique distinction of *consulis uxor, consulis filia, consulum mater*; her daughter-in-law, Anicia Juliana; and her granddaughter, Demetrias.[44] Their influence spread far from Italy. Even John Chrysostom, patriarch of Constantinople, lobbied them for support.[45]

---

[42] Conybeare (2000) 1. [43] Ambrose *Ep.* 6.27.

[44] *CIL* vi 1754. See also *PLRE* I, ANICIA FALTONIA PROBA 3, pp. 732–3; *PLRE* I ANICIA JULIANA 2, p. 468; *PLRE* II DEMETRIAS pp. 351–2.

[45] John Chrysostom *Epp.* 167 and 171.

The Anicii had also long been closely associated with Pelagius. They had been important members of his religious circle during his time in Rome and had sheltered him in one of their many houses. Paulinus and the Anicii presented a particular problem for Augustine, not so much because of the active support that they could lend to Pelagius but because of the legitimacy that they gave to his standing as an orthodox teacher. Despite their support for Pelagius, Augustine was careful to keep channels of communication open with the family even whilst the dispute raged. Relations had developed after a meeting in Carthage probably between 411 and 413 CE.[46] In 412 Augustine received and replied to a letter from Proba, the matriarch of the family, requesting advice on how to conduct her life now that she had been widowed.[47] In the same year she wrote to him again asking about the natural state of the human soul.[48] In 414, Augustine dedicated a treatise, *De Bono Viduitatis*, to Juliana. Eric Rebillard has argued that the Anicii letters should be read as a typical exchange between a bishop with a solid reputation as a theologian and two Christian ladies who had consulted him about a matter of faith.[49] However, behind this polite and attentive correspondence a game of political bluff was being carried out.

Despite knowing that the Anicii were part of Pelagius' circle, it is very telling that Augustine made no mention of their relationship. Perhaps the most obvious reason for this is that if their support for Pelagius was made clear in the epistolary record, it would make Augustine's own position look vulnerable. By maintaining a polite façade, Augustine could avoid a potentially problematic Anician public statement of their support for Pelagius. However, in 414 an opportunity arose for Augustine to recast the loyalties of the Anicii in a very public way. Demetrias had decided to take on the ascetic life rather than marry, and her grandmother and mother wrote to Pelagius, Jerome and Augustine inviting them to each send a letter of advice to the girl.[50] That Pelagius was the first choice can be inferred from the fact that both Augustine and Jerome had read Pelagius' letter before composing their own.[51]

All three letters have survived so it is interesting to compare them. Each of the three religious mentors was very aware of what an important task this was. The Anicii were, after all, the best known Christian senatorial family in Italy. These letters would be circulated widely throughout the Christian

---

[46] Perler (1969) 415–16.   [47] Augustine *Ep.* 130.
[48] Augustine *Ep.* 131.   [49] Rebillard (1998) 129–30.
[50] Jerome *Ep.* 130.1, 2; Augustine *Ep.* 150.1; Pelagius *Ep. Ad Demetriam* 1.1.
[51] Augustine *Ep.* 188. For Jerome see Kelly (1975) 313, fn.19.

world. Both Pelagius and Jerome acknowledged the authority that the name of the Anicii would bring to their respective causes. Their language is restrained and referential.

Pelagius started his letter:

Even if I could claim to possess natural talent of a high quality and an equally high standard of artistic skill and believed myself for that reason to be capable of fulfilling with ease the obligation of writing, I would still not be able to enter upon this arduous task without considerable fears of the difficulties involved. It is to Demetrias that I have to write, that virgin of Christ who is both noble and rich.[52]

Jerome, in his opening lines, mirrored similar concerns:

Of all the subjects that I have treated from my youth up until now, either with my own pen or that of my secretaries, I have dealt with none more difficult than that which now occupies me. I am going to write to Demetrias, a virgin of Christ and a lady whose birth and riches make her second to none in the Roman world.[53]

The politely deferential tone of these two letters written in the accepted style of a spiritual advisor to an important patron, stands in sharp contrast to Augustine's own missive. His letter to Demetrias adopted the intimate, authoritative air of a teacher addressing a devoted disciple.

Augustine immediately claimed all the credit for exhorting Demetrias to her new calling:

You have through our ministry received the word of the hearing of God ... and this ministry of ours has borne such fruit in your house by the helping grace and mercy of the Saviour that, although a worldly marriage has been arranged for her, the saintly Demetrias prefers the spiritual embrace of the Spouse.[54]

Later in the letter Augustine requested that Juliana write back with information on how the girl reacted to Pelagius' letter. Pre-empting her written reply, however, Augustine continued to describe in graphic detail how he *imagined* Demetrias to have reacted:

---

[52] Pelagius *Ep. Ad Demetriam* 1.1: *si summo ingenio parique fretus scientia, officium scribendi facile me implere posse crederem; tamen tam arduum hoc opus ingredi, sine magno difficultatis timore non possem. scribendum tamen est ad Demetriadem uirginem Christi, uirginem nobilem, uirginem diuitem.*

[53] Jerome *Ep.* 130.1: *inter omnes materias, quas ab adulescentia usque ad hanc aetatem, uel mea, uel notariorum scripsi manu, nihil praesenti opere difficilius. scripturus enim ad Demetriadem uirginem Christi, quae et nobilitate et diuitiis, prima est in orbe Romano.*

[54] Augustine *Ep.* 188.1: *tamen etiam per ministerium nostrum, cum accepissetis uerbum, auditus Dei ... Cuius ministerii nostri, adiuuante gratia et misericordia Saluatoris, in domo uestra tantus fructus exortus est, ut humanis nuptiis iam paratis sancta Demetrias spiritualem sponsi illius praeferret amplexum.* For further discussion of the letter see Mariani (1982).

Our opinion, however, of the training and the Christian humility of the saintly virgin in which she was nourished and brought up makes us think that when she read these words, if indeed she did read them, she groaned and humbly struck her breast, perhaps wept also, and faithfully prayed to God, to whom she is consecrated and by whom she is sanctified ... inform us about this in your answer and let us know whether we are wrong about her state of mind. For we know one thing very well, that you and all your household are and have been worshippers of the undivided Trinity.[55]

Thus, within this letter, Augustine redrew the theological and physical boundaries of the Pelagianist controversy. The bishop of Hippo was now the trusted spiritual confidante of the orthodox Anicii whereas Pelagius was the opportunistic heretical outsider. By emphasising the orthodoxy of the Anicii on the Trinity, Augustine was careful to side-step the whole divisive issue of Original Sin on which he could not be sure of their agreement with him. By continually emphasising how Demetrias and her mother, as orthodox Christians, *should* have reacted to Pelagius' letter, Augustine was putting the Anicii under intense pressure not to contradict him.

We have no record of an answer from Juliana to Augustine's question on Demetrias' response to the Pelagius letter. In fact, that might have been Augustine's intention. By carefully defining the doctrinal orthodoxy of the Anicii and himself, and the heresy of Pelagius, Augustine was not attempting to convince the Anicii of the rectitude of his cause but rather to implicate them within it in the eyes of the wider Christian church. No reply was needed because Augustine had already supplied his own. Augustine appears to make the assumption that the Anicii might have been sympathetic to Pelagius but, as can be seen by their invitation for both Jerome and Augustine to write to Demetrias, they were far too pragmatic to close down all their options before any definitive decision had been made by the ecclesiastical or imperial authorities.

Three years later, Augustine and his fellow North African bishop would use a similar kind of letter to try to publicly distance Paulinus from his old friend Pelagius.[56] There were no direct accusations, just subtle insinuations.

---

[55] Augustine *Ep.* 188.9–10:

> et nos quidem de sanctae uirginis disciplina et humilitate Christiana, in qua nutrita et educata est, hoc existimamus, quod illa uerba cum legeret, si tamen legit, ingemuit, et pectus humiliter tutudit, ac fortassis et fleuit, Deumque cui dicata et a quo sanctificata est ... de hoc ergo eius affectu utrum non fallamur, inde nos fac potius rescribendo certiores. nam illud optime nouimus, cum omnibus uestris cultores uos esse et fuisse indiuiduae Trinitatis.

[56] For the relationship between Pelagius and Paulinus see Brown (1968) 111–13.

The letter was couched in friendly and familiar terms. The first question that the Africans asked was: 'We know that you loved Pelagius as a servant of God ... but we do not know how you love him now.'[57] The letter had been sent because: 'If what we hear is true, there are some among you, or rather in your city who support that error.'[58]

Throughout the letter Augustine never wavered from the rhetorical assumption that Paulinus had already taken his side in the dispute with Pelagius. The African bishops stated that they had only written to Paulinus because it was something that as orthodox Christians they knew that he would be concerned about. They had no doubt that Paulinus believed in the Grace of God so their letter would strengthen his arguments against the Pelagians. By continually reiterating his belief in Paulinus' orthodoxy, whilst at the same time defining what orthodoxy actually meant (the Augustinian position on the Grace of God), Augustine and his colleagues left Paulinus with very little room to manoeuvre. The purpose of the letter appears to be twofold. Firstly, it is an attempt to warn Paulinus away from Pelagius. Secondly, and perhaps most importantly, to portray to the wider audience amongst whom this letter would be circulated, that Augustine had the undivided support of Paulinus.

CONCLUSION

To conclude: as doctrinal power-play increasingly revolved around reciprocal pressure being placed on those whose opinions were considered to count rather than open dialectical discussion of opposing points of view, so letters became vital tools in the creation and ordering of textual elite communities.[59] Despite his characterisation of a universal church sustained by vigorous debate, Augustine sought to control the epistolary process in much the same way as he did any other form of dialogue. By carefully setting out what his correspondents' reactions to his letters should be, Augustine left little room for dissent or debate. The hidden audience, as witnesses, policed the potential responses of the recipients of Augustine's letters. Crucially their silence could be interpreted as deferral to, rather than a rejection of, Augustine's religious *auctoritas*.

Much like his dialogues with the Donatists, Augustine's letters to the friends of Pelagius were not about an exchange of opinions or debate, but

---

[57] Augustine *Ep.* 186.1: *Pelagium, ... quod ut seruum Dei dilexeris, nouimus: nunc autem quem ad modum diligas, ignoramus.*
[58] Augustine, *Ep.* 186.1.   [59] Lim (1995) 151ff.

the presentation of an Augustinian world view to a much wider readership. By reappropriating and redefining existing networks of support, Augustine was able to construct a powerful 'virtual' community that reinforced his own claims to represent the orthodox majority of the Catholic church. The lessons from those many years of 'dialoguing' in small-town North Africa had been well learnt.

PART IV

Christianity and the social imperative

Christians, dialogues and patterns of sociability in late antiquity

Richard Lim

…Wiederum versank der Dialog in einen Schlummer, an dem nur und wieder Antiquare und Redekünstler vergeblich rüttelten. Er wartete des Tages und der Tag sollte kommen, da neue Geistesstürme ihn zu neuem Leben erweckten.

Hirzel, Der Dialog 2.380

Following a broadly Weberian scheme of reading the history of early Christianity as one in which spiritual charisma was progressively replaced by a deadening ecclesiastical hierarchy, Rudolph Hirzel concludes that the rise of Christianity entailed the virtual demise of the ancient dialogue. Implicit in this stance is an adherence to an influential and long-standing intellectual scheme that regards societies that value open dialogues as categorically better than the ones that do not.[1] Classical Athenian society receives frequent praise for its intellectual openness even as the Greek 'invention' of the ancient dialogue form is itself regarded as one of the signal achievements of western culture that most deserves admiration and emulation. When the turn came for subsequent societies to be judged in accordance with their degree of openness to dialogue, the putative Athens of Socrates and Plato came to be accepted as the benchmark against which all other societies would be measured. Given the prevalence of such an underlying intellectual framework, the question of whether early Christians 'dialogued' in a significant manner entails not only the tasks of identifying sources and analysing them appropriately but also that of undertaking a frank appraisal of our own starting assumptions. Indeed both projects – the discovery of relevant evidence and discussion of how it fits within a broader interpretive scheme – are necessary and consequential. This paper examines several points that will hopefully contribute to such an overall appraisal. I aim first to establish the main social and cultural parameters of the genre of the dialogue as well as the cultural work that it was often made

---

[1] Cf. Popper (1945), esp. Vol I: *The Spell of Plato*.

to perform. Secondly, I will discuss early Christians' use and non-use of the dialogue as a mode of literary production. I will conclude by exploring various alternative modes of communications by which late-antique Christians sought to carry out the social and cultural work that the ancient dialogue performed. Overall, this paper proposes that the use and non-use of the dialogue has to be interpreted against the context of the shape and purposes of textual production of late-antique Christians rather than only as a barometer of their attitudes to authority and the prospect of meaningful dialogue with others.

THE ANCIENT DIALOGUE IN CONTEXT

After its first prominent use by the followers of Socrates to capture the life and teachings of their master, the Greek genre of the dialogue continued to serve as a prime literary vehicle for representing the process of philosophical inquiry.[2] When Plato and Xenophon appropriated the literary form of the dialogue as the means for recording the words and teachings of Socrates, they side-stepped the teacher's own avowed reticence in committing spoken words to writing and created textual embodiments of their master's signature form of philosophising or 'Socratic dialectic'. With this textualisation, the reciprocity of oral conversations came to be presented as a core aspect of philosophical inquiry even while, arguably, it was the literary form of the dialogue itself rather than the inter-subjective exploration of ideas in the texts that served as the primary carrier of cultural meaning in later antiquity.[3] As the scholarly discussion continues as to how Plato's own philosophical agenda shaped the composition of his dialogues, one may discern a broad development from more 'dialogic' early dialogues to more monologic later ones.[4] As philosophers increasingly came to be regarded in the popular tradition as sages, their role in dialogues more and more assumed that of a figure of authority that responds to questions posed by disciples. They were also presented as the objects of the readers' own philosophical pursuit and, indeed, erotic longing.[5] The rise of the philosopher-sage in the postclassical

---

[2] See Goldschmidt (1963); Dieterle (1966); and Meyer (1980). For more recent discussions, see Seeskin (1987) and Henderson (2000).

[3] Plato *Republic* 534ff.; also Ryle (1968). See also Long, Ford, Schofield and for the extended history of dialogue König in this volume.

[4] See the arguments advanced by Kahn (1996), regarding the unity and Socratic character of the early and middle dialogues. The problem for establishing an order of composition remains unresolved as different criteria, including one derived from hypothesised development in Plato's metaphysical ideas, are used to place the dialogues within a temporal sequence, see Poster (1998) 282–98.

[5] Goldhill (2002) 86–7.

period parallels the use of question-and-answer dialogues in which the master's teachings are systematically expounded with only lip service paid to the principle of dialectical exchange. While one may reasonably contend that such texts are not bona fide dialogues in that they feature little 'genuine' intellectual reciprocity or development of ideas, such a dynamic was already present from the beginning of the form in the Platonic dialogues so that the relative absence of the dialectic principle does not in itself constitute a basic violation of genre expectations.

The multiform genre of the dialogue enjoyed a long and varied history.[6] It boasted cognates or generic parallels in even more ancient and prevalent literary forms such as the 'riddle' and 'royal advice' literatures that had roots in the ancient Near East wisdom tradition.[7] The blending together of these forms can be seen in apocryphal tales such as Alexander the Great's reported conversation with Indian gymnosophists and Ptolemy II Philadelphus' banquet dialogue with select Jewish wise men best known as the translators of the Hebrew Bible into Greek (LXX). Nevertheless, it was those dialogues that were set in the sociable and convivial context of the Greek polis that represented the most direct heirs of the Platonic dialogues.

The dialogue was much more than just a literary vehicle for the conveyance of philosophical or literary knowledge. It represents a form of ludic play that unfolds within a carefully delimited cultural space in which interlocutors engage in urbane conversation on the basis of social intimacy as well as cultural homogeneity. In featuring a set of conversations that are dramatised as taking place within a familiar social and cultural milieu, the dialogue inducts its readers into the norms and cultural parameters of the *beau monde*.

While a dialogue could in theory be set in a variety of dramatic contexts, the *symposion* (or similar convivial institutions such as the *deipnion*) became a favoured backdrop.[8] The drinking-party was a noted sociable and cultural occasion in which men of wealth gathered over the ritualised partaking of wine.[9] General merry-making and the singing of drinking-songs constituted the core acts of the symposium while composition and the performance of sympotic poetry also at times played a role.[10] In the postclassical

---

[6] Hirzel (1895).

[7] Such 'question-and-answer' dialogues that combine philosophical, folkloric and antiquarian strands remained popular in the later literary tradition; see Suchier (1910) and Daly and Suchier (1939). Such works can be traced to the ancient near eastern wisdom literature, see Denning-Bolle (1992) and (1987).

[8] As discussed by König in this volume.   [9] Lissarrague (1990).

[10] See Giangrande (1967) and Murray (1985).

period, the symposium symbolically represented 'a microcosm of the city as a whole; the drive to exclude interlopers from the sympotic community also serves to authorize the aristocracy as the true leaders of the community'.[11] As a cultural enclave reserved for aristocratic males, it enabled the elite to enact, on a recurring basis, rituals that validated their superiority and dominance over others in the polis. Not everyone had welcomed the introduction of philosophical conversation to the symposium in the classical period and preferred more sociable themes.[12] Still, although the symposium doubtless remained first and foremost an institution of elite social reproduction, the literary prestige of the Platonic dialogues came to make an imprint on the symposium as a prime institution for the conduct of philosophy and literary conversation as well. In its turn, the privileged context of the symposium enhanced the prestige of those types of conversation one finds represented in dialogues and helped establish that discursive modality as a classical ideal that merits the admiration of posterity. Set in an idealised environment and featuring equally idealised oral exchanges, the dialogue served to conjure up a timeless image of the effortless ease with which a cultivated elite could lay claim to both truth and power in Greco-Roman society.

The social institution of the symposium and the literary and philosophical dialogue offered a discursive space within which men from a common background could indulge in ludic play.[13] The performance of jokes and jibes, even agonistic verbal duels, was premised on this shared culture and the dialogue helped to create the impression that the educated elite was bound together by a common culture as well as bonds of friendship.[14] The conversational style of the dialogue and the literary performance of affective bonds among interlocutors that one finds in even agonistic dialogues could enhance the sense of affective bond between the reader and the work. Certain dialogues, especially literary displays, used the conversational mode to embody the pleasure principle very well indeed. Georg Simmel discusses the ideal sociable conversation in a way that seems applicable to a dialogue in which the journey was more important than the destination:[15] 'in sociability talking is an end in itself; in purely sociable conversation the

---

[11] Whitmarsh (2004) 59. See also Schäfer (1997).   [12] Bowie (1997), esp. 4–5.
[13] See Ausland (1997), esp. 374–5.
[14] Cf. Plutarch, *Sympotic Questions* 612d. The converse of this construction of friendship is the open mockery of 'outsiders', comprising social inferiors and other types of strangers. This is best exemplified by the invocation of the Iliadic figure of Thersites, a common object of mockery within a sympotic context, see Rosen (2003) 121–36.
[15] Simmel (1949) 259–60.

content is merely the indispensable carrier of the stimulation, which the lively exchange of talk as such unfolds … that something is said and accepted is not an end in itself but a mere means to maintain the liveliness of the mutual understanding, the common consciousness of the group'.

The sheer ability to appreciate dialogues as a reader connotes a measure of cultural achievement and social status. First of all, it entails the possession of an advanced level of literacy as well as a committed intellectual seriousness in that dialogues textually provide uncertain internal indicators of the identity of interlocutors, thereby requiring the reader to devote careful attention just in order to follow the developing conversation.[16] For such an elite and dedicated reader, the overlap of the social milieu that forms the backdrop of dialogues and his own experience would have helped create a sense of cultural complicity and an affective bond linking him to a trans-temporal club of the privileged. While the *paideia* of this elite was much less entrenched than the literary and philosophical conversations presented in dialogue suggest, the genre sustains a myth that the type of learned conversation found among sophists and philosophers constituted the operative mode of sociability among the elite as a whole. In this respect, the dialogue helped promote the idea that the Greco-Roman elite constituted a cultural meritocracy of sorts.

In this and similar ways, the dialogue played a dynamic role in the ongoing negotiations over the cultural identity of the disparate social and cultural elite of the Roman world. Among Roman writers, its adoption and use may be seen as one aspect of the cultural assimilation and differentiation among Greek and Roman intellectuals. Latin literary dialogues, including early works such as the compositions of Cicero and the fourth-century *Saturnalia* of Macrobius, were explicitly set by their authors in a festive literary context in order to press home the point that the men engaging in such conversations were making use of the *otium* associated with the observance of particular religious festivals.[17] The aristocratic protagonists unquestionably disposed of leisure in a general sense but it became crucial for them to be represented as only devoting time to intellectual colloquy during periods of *negotium* when Roman religious scruples mandated rest

---

[16] See Andrieu (1954). Indeed, one has to assume that the more technical Platonic dialogues were mostly 'unread' by most, even among those who were notionally counted among the intellectual elite. Thus Dio Chrysostom revealed his own Platonic readings and interests when he cited and alluded to only the most commonly read dialogues that a general learned audience would have read. Also, in his comments and allusions to Plato's ideas, he assumed the role of a grammarian rather than that of a philosopher, see Trapp (2000) 236–7.

[17] For a classic treatment of this theme see André (1966).

from work and official business. Setting Latin dialogues in festival-time thus helped deflect a potential charge against Roman men of affairs for preferring philosophising in the manner of the Greeks to the conduct of serious public business.[18] A not wholly dissimilar use of the dialogue in paralogic negotiations that revolved around the delineation of the cultural identities of those who participated in them appears in the third-century pseudo-Lucianic dialogue of Nero with the philosopher Musonius Rufus and similar works.[19]

EARLY CHRISTIANITY AND THE USE OF THE DIALOGUE: 'DID THE EARLY CHRISTIANS DIALOGUE'?

To respond satisfactorily to this important question requires one to ascertain the operative assumptions that lie behind it. If it means asking whether early Christians composed works that are set in the form of the dialogue, one reasonable answer would be that they did so but rarely.[20] But how rarely? And what normative expectations ought to operate to guide our interpretation of the data and its significance? The likelihood that Christians would compose literary and philosophical dialogues, one supposes, ought to bear some correlation to an author's expectation regarding whether such works would reach an audience that could appreciate them. Recent studies of literacy among the general Roman population and that of the Christians specifically allow us to place the matter in a helpful perspective. By 100 CE, Keith Hopkins has proposed with appropriate disclaimers, there were approximately 140 'highly literate' Christians in the entire Roman world.[21] Such a number is arrived at by taking the figure of 7,000, the estimated total number of Christians at that time, and multiplying it by 2 per cent, which, according to William Harris, constituted the proportion of the Roman population that may be described as highly

---

[18] See Levine (1958) and Schofield in this volume. On Cicero's notion of *otium*, see André (1966) and Laidlaw (1968).

[19] Whitmarsh (1999) 146–7:

The dramatization of spoken language alerts the reader to the presence of the paralogic aspects of communications which inevitably arise in conversation: irony, suggestion, nuance; even (though we must imagine these) gesture, facial expression, tone of voice. Spoken language fundamentally depends upon insinuation and implication. The very incomplete 'openness' of the dialogue both lures the reader in and throws the key questions open: where do we site ourselves in relation to imperial power? What does it mean for any citizen of the Roman empire to style him or herself as 'Greek'?

In any case, this oppositional dialogue is more reminiscent of the venerable royal question-and-answer genre.

[20] See Hirzel (1895); and Voss (1970).   [21] Hopkins (1998).

literate at any given time.[22] Given the geographical dispersal of the Christian population, those 140-plus individuals – and even the proportionately higher numbers during the second and third centuries – would have been spread rather thin on the ground. Proceeding further from these extrapolations, it would thus appear that there would not have been a sufficient critical mass among Christians either of writers or readers for significant production of dialogues even well into the second century.[23]

A further consideration is that early Christian texts were principally addressed to an internal Christian audience even if the works themselves explicitly project a different set of claims. For instance, while Paul is represented in the Acts of the Apostles as having preached publicly before the Athenian citizens on the Areopagus, the historical Paul propounded his teachings mostly within the intimate spaces of the *oikos*.[24] Likewise, when Christian writers such as Athenagoras addressed their works to a reigning emperor, their apologetic works were mainly directed at fellow Christians and were meant to make the point that the new faith to which they belonged was culturally respectable and not what some of its severest critics claimed it was: a fraudster religion. Overall, such acts of Christian persuasion in these early centuries seem to have operated within intimate social settings and were made, generally speaking, without appeal to highly intellectual arguments. Such at least is the impression conveyed by a customary charge made by hostile critics that even Christian retorts do not wholly dispel; thus when the Christian Origen of Alexandria refuted Celsus' accusation that Christianity relied for its dissemination on false representations before 'women, children and old men' rather than debate with educated men, he argued that the religion was superior to philosophy in having the ability to reach down to the lower levels of society.[25]

Another desideratum regarding the parameters of the original question concerns the definition of what should constitute a dialogue. Should a work be self-consciously emulating Platonic dialogues to count? The synoptic gospels and other early Christian texts frequently embed representations

---

[22] See Harris (1989), esp. 222–48.

[23] It is useful to caution that any effort to seek a benchmark rate of production for dialogues in relation to the numbers and cultural levels of Christians risks turning the investigation into a misguided quest for quantifiable social scientific data or 'metrics'.

[24] See, e.g., Stowers (1984).

[25] See Origen, *Contra Celsum* 4.52 (Chadwick (1953) 226–7) on writings such as the *Altercatio Iasonis et Papisci* (a text that is not extant): ' out of all the writings which contain allegories and interpretations written with a literary style, he has chosen one that is worthless, which although it could be of some help to the simple-minded multitude in respect of their faith, certainly could not impress the more intelligent'.

of oral dialogue in the form of direct speech; but this does not in itself constitute the writing of dialogues. Many of the works of Christian apologists in the second century onwards explicitly adopted the literary form of the dialogue, Justin Martyr's *Dialogue with Trypho* being a case in point. Early Jewish-Christian dialogues advance the claims of Christianity as the *verus Israel*, whereby Jews, familiar and familial strangers to Christians, were introduced as interlocutors to showcase the close kinship connection as well as, ultimately, the insurmountable theological gulf that came to separate the two peoples.[26] But should this mean that such Christian dialogues were not 'real' dialogues? They deploy the literary form of the dialogue and, while prosecuting polemical ends, were ultimately written to define the cultural identity of the new ethnos, that of the Christians. In this respect, early Christian dialogues resemble rather than differ from other Greek and Latin dialogues. Yet by and large such texts seem to be accepted by most scholars as constituting evidence that Christians composed dialogues on account of the fact that they are polemical writings expressing a pronounced adversarial tone. Their controversial intent and presentation appear to set many early Christian dialogues apart from the literary and philosophical dialogues that project literary worlds characterised by a degree of social harmony and consensus rather than division.

A number of Christian authors began to compose works in the second century that address a perceived need to present a positive image of Christianity as a philosophical religion.[27] This apologetic effort to fuse Christianity and *paideia* meant appropriating classical literary forms as well as key philosophical terms and ideas. Given the prestige of the dialogue and its association with philosophy, there is no surprise that some Christian authors would adopt the form. Methodius of Olympus was one such author who adapted the philosophical dialogue for the representation of Christian truths. His *Symposium* (which may be more aptly called *Deipnion*) is set in an idealised garden of Virtue or Arete in which ten virgins participated in a banquet.[28] This convivial context became the occasion for them to sing the praises of (Christian) virginity and do so by eroticising of the object of praise in a manner that recalls Plato's own *Symposium*. Methodius clearly aimed to appropriate the cultural capital of the Platonic dialogue of the same name.

---

[26] Simon (1964). On the broader construction of a Christian cultural identity through literary representation, see Lieu (2004).

[27] See Wilken (1986).

[28] Methode d'Olympe, *Banquet*, Sources Chrétiennes 95, Herbert Musurillo and Victor-Henry Debidour, eds. (Paris: du Cerf, 1963). English translation in Musurillo (1958). The text is dated *c.* 260–290.

He also shaped his text upon the motif of literary competition found in the *Symposium* as well as in later sophistic works such as Athenaeus' *Deipnosophistae* where learned men competed in putting forward the best argument to support a set theme. How ought we to read Methodius' work in the context of the broader question of whether Christians dialogued in late antiquity? Methodius seems to have written on the basis of a shared sympotic or convivial context among his Christian readers that was very different from that of the usual readers of literary and philosophical dialogues. Common meals among early Christians were largely conceived of as cultic religious affairs that often included doxological as well as eschatological elements.[29] This context allows us to appreciate why Methodius, a pre-Constantinian writer (d. 311), used his work to showcase his own millenarian leanings through the literary representation of an imagined eschatological scene.[30] It is also important to see this work in the context of his (mostly lost) corpus that includes other works set in the dialogue form, including a treatise 'On Free Will' and another 'On the Resurrection'.[31] Excerpts of these works survived in quotations by Adamantius and Eusebius of Caesarea, neither of whom attributed the passages to Methodius, and these demonstrate an elegant and skilful use of literary Greek that was put in the service of theological refutation, first of gnostic arguments regarding the nature of evil and second, Origen's idea of the resurrection of the spiritual body. In these works, the three main interlocutors comprised an orthodox Christian, a Valentinian Christian and his companion; these protagonists are introduced in the text by their (abbreviated) names.[32] Methodius therefore used the dialogue form to serve didactic and controversial goals within the context of an imminent eschatology. As the author of a work 'Against Porphyry', he was greatly concerned with defending the truth-claims of Christianity against the well-known attacks by the philosopher; but Jerome refers obliquely to other, more 'plebeian' compositions of Methodius that he chose not to name (*De vir. inl.* 83: 'et multa alia quae vulgo lectitantur'), suggesting perhaps that the bishop also produced works in lower literary registers for mass consumption.

---

[29] Many of these themes are well explored in the essays in Quesnel, Blanchard and Tassin (1999).

[30] See the excellent discussion in Buonaiuti (1921); also Patterson (1993) and (1997). Patterson principally addresses Methodius' reception of the ideas of Origen of Alexandria.

[31] Jerome, *De uiris inlustribus* 83: *Methodius, Olympi Lyciae et postea Tyri episcopus, nitidi compositique sermonis aduersus Porphyrium confecit libros et Symposium decem Uirginum, de Resurrectione opus egregium contra Origenem, et aduersus eundem de Pythonissa, et de* αὐτεξουσία *in Genesim quoque et in Cantica Canticorum commentarios, et multa alia quae uulgo lectitantur.*

[32] See Lim (1991). For a comprehensive study of 'paratextual' conventions associated with the dialogue, see Andrieu (1954).

CHRISTIANS AND THE DIALOGUE IN LATE ANTIQUITY

Christian authors whose major concern was to pick an appropriate literary vehicle for bolstering their claim to participate in high literary culture continued to make use of the dialogue. Examples such as the well-attested career of Augustine of Hippo allow us to examine the authorial choice to take up the form of the dialogue in the context of the development of a public Christian persona. Among Augustine's many works, four conform most closely to the ancient literary and philosophical dialogue. His *Contra Academicos*, *De beata vita*, *De ordine* and *Soliloquia*, a quartet that is referred to as the Cassiciacum dialogues, were written at a particularly fraught moment of liminality preceded by momentous personal transitions that he would regard retrospectively as his conversion from Manichaeism to catholic Christianity. Set in a virtually cloistered community that consciously set itself apart from the world of the vulgar, these dialogues re-enact the communal life of the ascetic circles to which Augustine repaired after his early successes in Milan as a rhetor and 'conversion' by Ambrose of Milan to catholic Christianity. Augustine's retreat to Cassiciacum can therefore be cast as an idyllic moment of formation for his new catholic Christian persona. In the company of other cultivated individuals tied to each other by kinship and bonds of sociability, educated men engaged in daily conversations and other spiritual exercises free from pressing mundane cares. When Augustine chose to capture these experiences and use this retreat as the backdrop for making his own literary and philosophical statement regarding his own identity as a highly literate Christian individual, the ancient dialogue form must have seemed to him the perfect vehicle.[33]

Augustine's Cassiciacum dialogues therefore represent the christianisation of the philosophical and literary dialogues. By self-consciously using the ancient dialogue form and making references to the works of Plato, his literary mimesis in part advanced his claim to being a highly cultured Christian who possessed the taste and ability to compose literary and philosophical dialogues. Making such a statement was particularly important for him given his own background and history of upward social mobility. The early Augustine therefore used the dialogue form as a legitimising cultural form to support his own self-fashioning as a learned

---

[33] On Augustine at Cassiciacum, see Brown (2000), 115–17. For an assessment of the historicity of these dialogues, see O'Meara (1951). O'Meara's ultimate judgement that the Cassiciacum dialogues represent 'written compositions of Augustine, and consciously follow closely, in outline and in detail, the form and matter of previous models' (154) highlights how the established dialogue form materially shaped Augustine's presentation.

Christian devoted to the quest for truth and who, moreover, possessed the sort of Roman aristocratic *otium* usually associated with individuals from much more privileged backgrounds.[34]

This early body of work can also be instructively set alongside Augustine's other literary texts that reveal why and under what circumstances individuals might resort to different literary genres broadly associated with the dialogue. The self-consciously classicising philosophical dialogues were later followed by the composition of the *Confessions*, notionally a dialogue between the literary artifice that is Augustine's own 'inner self' (or soul) and God and which in fact amounts to a soliloquy.[35] Overall, Augustine's initial embrace of a platonising dialogue form, as seen in the Cassiciacum dialogues, increasingly gave way to the composition of works that are less and less dialogic in character even if some still subscribe in some respects to the conventions of the dialogue. Augustine's famous writings that showcase disputations with Manichaean teachers, for example, demonstrate a decisive shift away from the private edifying conversations depicted in the Cassiciacum dialogues. The disputations, far from being intimate affairs, were held in public settings and increasingly conformed to a judicial proceeding in which Augustine featured as both disputant and judge.[36] As a priest and later bishop, Augustine regarded his own pastoral care of fellow Christians who, in his view, could not be trusted to hold their own in discussions with heretics, as a primary concern. For this reason, among others, he was to write in ways that demonstrate more authority with a corresponding diminution in the amount of intellectual openness he was willing to grant himself in discussing matters of faith and belief. In this development, the early habit of composing philosophical dialogues that corresponded to his initial need to fashion himself as a catholic Christian intellectual before fellow Christians of learning yielded to the need to prioritise the goal of defining and defending orthodoxy for the sake of a mass Christian audience more highly.

Such a broadening shift in the constitution of Christian society both in realia and in perception also shaped other Christians' choices during this time. While the conversion of the Roman aristocracy to Christianity might reasonably be seen as a development that ought to entail greater potential for elevated intellectual conversations of the sort found in Platonic dialogues, other factors that pull in the opposite direction began to impinge as well.

---

[34] See Trout (1988). On Augustine's efforts to appropriate the Latin literary tradition in these dialogues as part of a broader cultural or religious claim at the time, see Lim (2004).

[35] See Cary (2000).   [36] See Lim (1995), esp. 88–102.

One such factor has to do with the character of aristocratic Christianity in the later fourth century. In subscribing to the prevailing ethos of religious exemplarity based on the virtues of illiterate desert ascetics, aristocratic converts to Christianity were understandably less invested in making urbane philosophical conversations a key element of their spiritual discipline.[37] Rather, reading the life of the martyrs and seeking to model one's own life upon theirs became a prevalent trend. And even within the circles of Manichaean and Pelagian Christians within which one finds a generally higher validation of knowledge and discernment as necessary tools to the religious life, the quest for truth was framed mainly in terms of correct scriptural interpretation. For this reason perhaps, even these more 'elite' religious groups did not make appreciable use of the philosophical dialogue form in their literary production. In any event, religious and philosophical groups that regarded spiritual enlightenment as only pertaining to a privileged few progressively found themselves blacklisted by rivals who advocated a more inclusive 'middle path'. Mass Christianity would come to validate and mobilise a prejudice against 'elite' forms of religiosity that in turn would render the literary vehicle of the dialogue, which ultimately represents a set of closed conversations taking place within an exclusive elite space, not only unpopular but even one touched by the taint of conspiracy or heresy.

The preceding discussion has been premised on the choice of literary forms that the educated Christian elite might have resorted to should the cultural conditions be right. However, when the practices and expectations of the more ordinary Christian population are taken into account, it would appear that the ideal dialogue form would not have been the form of discourse they would necessarily have warmed to, let alone demanded. A cursory exploration here of the various forms of plebeian sociability may serve to illustrate this point. Among the general working population in the cities, the mundane and often menial nature of their occupations tended to produce an inclination, common to work cultures generally, to position themselves within more advantageous frames by constructing a common work identity through particular forms of collective expression. Roman occupational and trade groups were discrete social units that sat together in places of public entertainment and so, both in and out of work, they shared a collective identity that was often celebrated through rituals such as singing songs together. Indeed all Romans sang, at least according to

---

[37] On the figure of the Christian holy man, see Brown (1971) and (1998). On the impact the rise of the holy man has on the ancient rhetorical culture, see Brown (1992).

our sources.[38] Roman subgroups did not so much sing work songs, although these were also known, but songs learned from the theatre, which points again to the important role of the spectacles in promoting city-wide forms of popular sociability.[39] Singing songs together both in the place of work and in public spaces served many functions of sociability and group formation for the common people that dialogues contributed to for the elite.

Still other forms of popular sociability and conversation existed. A selective sampling of these forms unsurprisingly suggests that the patterns and topics of conversation that are represented in literary and philosophical dialogues did not have widespread let alone universal valence. Not only is the ability to access particular topics of conversation in dialogues an overwhelmingly elite possession even in spite of an active ancient literary market and popular appreciation for rhetoric and civic theatre, the sustained nature of the exchanges and the logical development of ideas found in the philosophical dialogues especially marked them as an elite form of discourse that had no homologous parallel in plebeian cultural forms. The very capacity to participate as an informed interlocutor in a literary or philosophical symposium was the preserve of a cultured man who has mastered the elaborate codes necessary for such a performance before a peer group that supposedly shared similar cultural attributes. Conversely, the ideal dialogue could not operate if the interlocutors did not share this common outlook. It was just as difficult to accommodate 'complete strangers' within a dialogue as to find room for an 'outsider' of unknown (social and cultural) origins in a learned banquet. When 'strangers' enter the scene they serve the role of showing or emphasising the overall solidarity of the (other) participants. The dialogue thus relied on as well as helped foster a sense of cultural complicity in those who could follow and appreciate its conventions.

Another consideration that bears on this discussion is the idea that the camaraderie and conversational style of the elite dialogue was fundamentally at odds with common forms of sociability and speech. It is difficult to approach this latter subject except through the refracted lenses of ancient comedies. However, one Pompeian fresco offers a rather interesting glimpse into the kind of verbal exchanges that might obtain between men involved in a dice game.[40] Urban talk about games has been characteristically represented in our sources as being heated and argumentative in tone. Dice games, found universally throughout the city, was part and parcel of this sociable form.[41] The kind of talk that took place at games of *alea* was

---

[38] See, e.g., Macrobius *Sat.* 3.14.10 on Sulla and Roman songs.
[39] Horsfall (2003); Habinek (2005).   [40] CIL IV.3494. See Todd (1943).   [41] Purcell (1995).

one in which one expects to find sharp, staccato exchanges rather than reasoned discursive speech. On the fresco, words have been written above the heads of the players to record either an exchange that had taken place or one that was thought to have been likely in such a setting. The verbal exchange tells of a dispute between two players over a recent roll. One player, much agitated, said: 'Cheater! It's three! I won!' His counterpart sharply disputed the claim: 'No, it's not three, it's a two!' The exchange resembles the proverbially comical 'Yes, it is/No, it's not' type of argument. Such arguments proceed because there is no impartial referee for adjudicating either truth claims or rules that would allow the disputants to resolve their differences aside from repeatedly stating their positions. There exists no relevant hierarchy either of persons or of knowledge that could interpose or mediate in such conflicts. But the stakes were high not in terms of the money wagered but because through the process of argument both sides have invested their own personal honour or reputation in the conflict. In a sense then, through arguments over dice or charioteers, the agonistic culture of the arena and circus was day after day translated into competitive rivalry among discussants not only in the spaces of entertainment but throughout the ancient city. By making claims as to who would win and who would lose in a forthcoming set of games, ordinary individuals appropriated the culture of public spectacles in an active manner to create ludic spaces in which they themselves played key, even starring, roles. Thus talk about the games furnished people with the occasion to create communities of understanding and ephemeral competitive hierarchies based on contingent claims. To outside eyes, this form of solidarity might well appear weak and based on considerations of advantage. But both dicing and arguing about the spectacles also increased the degree of intimacy among members of the group.[42] Such interactions would have accompanied informal conversation about the lives and daily happenings of members, friends and neighbours. Such talk then, which can appear simultaneously agonistic and familial, contributed in decisive respects to the generation of a sense of solidarity among segments of the urban populace – might such arguments then be read as the plebeian version of the dialogue?

The agonistic duelling of words over dice games offers a useful context for appreciating the import of a fourth-century development: the 'technologisation' of Christian theology.[43] On account of a successfully popularised form of Aristotelian dialectic and the deployment of techniques of controversy such as the use of antiphonal songs, argumentation over intricate

---

[42] See Purcell (1995).   [43] See Lim (1995), esp. 109–48.

points of Christian doctrine turned into a popular conversational and sociable pastime for a rising Christian population in the cities. The story regarding this development has already been told in some detail elsewhere. Here it suffices to take note of the fact that the democratisation of Christian knowledge rendered dialogue on obtuse subjects no longer the exclusive preserve of elite men. Instead, it became a daily practice in which even quite ordinary Christians could assume leading roles, much to the consternation of their social betters. In the many theological controversies that divided late-antique Christians from each other, dialogues played no small role. One particularly salient example that highlights such a usage of the dialogue is Theodoret of Cyrus' *Eranistes* (*c.* 447), in which a large cast of characters argues for and against the orthodox Christian theological position.[44] Understandably, most readers would be challenged to keep perfectly clear which statements issued from which speaker and even Theodoret felt obliged to insert external markers (i.e. the speakers' names in initials) outside the main body of the text on the page to help them follow the unfolding discussion. It is interesting that Theodoret chose to employ a dialogue for dramatising the main differences between orthodox and non-orthodox theology despite the perceived need to announce the identity of the speakers at every turn and in such an artless manner. The form of the dialogue showed itself to have been an ungainly vehicle when the goal was catechesis, for which precise and unambiguous representation of an established theological truth was the foremost concern rather than a ludic unfolding of ideas in which a reader need not take particular stands. In this case, Theodoret was eager to help his readers avoid confusing an unorthodox theological formulation with the views of the orthodox speaker, a challenging undertaking that was necessitated in the first place on account of his choice to use the dialogue form. The construction of the *Eranistes* favoured clarity over ludic free play and the spirit of sociable affability. As the various interlocutors basically reiterate already set positions there could be little room for either element to flourish. However, since we have early on established that the presence of a dialogic element is not a *sine qua non* for a dialogue, one cannot claim that the *Eranistes* was therefore not a 'genuine' dialogue. This work offers us a fascinating glimpse into the priorities and constraints that informed whether late-antique Christian writers chose to use the literary/philosophical dialogue. Furthermore, it is instructive to set this text alongside the larger corpus of Theodoret's writings, for instance, his better-known work *History of the Monks in Syria*.

---

[44] Lim (1991); and Wilson (1970).

Theresa Urbaincyzk has offered us a fascinating and convincing reading of this text as Theodoret's attempt to position himself as the intermediary between the urban and urbane Greek-speaking audience of his work and the largely illiterate and non-Greek-speaking ascetics whose lives he saw fit to dramatise and represent.[45] To the extent that Theodoret inserted himself into the frame by highlighting his own personal connectivity in respect to these ascetics, the *Historia religiosa* served many of the same functions of constructing elite solidarity as one finds in a literary/philosophical dialogue. It sets out how, in a christianising society, physical proximity to (largely illiterate) holy men in an idealised sacred landscape that was late antique Syria contributed to the social and cultural formation of a new Christian culture. Rather than socialising with other cultured elite males, Theodoret and other leading Christians took to heart the paradoxical nature of Christianity as a religious ideology that validated as well as subverted the values of traditional culture.[46] The *Historia religiosa* may in many ways be read as a dialogue-less dialogue composed in the humble style to suit the needs of a new Christian elite and culture.

CHRISTIAN 'MASS COMMUNICATIONS' AND
THE *SERMO HUMILIS*

With continuing Christian demographic shifts in the fourth century, not only would one witness a steady rise in the number of converts but also a commensurate increase in the numbers of those who hailed from the ranks of the educated elite. Many of these Christians rose to positions of leadership in Christian communities over the course of the century, a phenomenon often discussed in the scholarship as the rise of curial bishops.[47] What might one expect from this development? First, if one accepts the premise that the literary production of dialogic texts bears some relation to the educational level and cultural horizons of a specific population, the influx of elite Christians into the church ought to augur a rise in the rate of composition of Christian dialogues. Clear evidence exists for a notable rise in Christian textual production from the later fourth century onwards and in terms of sheer volume as measured by the number of lines written, biblical exegesis and commentaries, sermons and doctrinal treatises seem to predominate. In short the dialogue form failed to make a commensurate contribution. Thus with rising Christian textual culture the dialogue

---

[45] Urbaincyzk (2002).   [46] See Cameron (1991a), esp. 155–88.
[47] See Bigelmair (1902); Gilliard (1984). See now Rapp (2005), esp. 183–95.

nevertheless played a minor role. A straightforward correlation between the sheer presence – or absence – of *paideia* among Christians and the writing of dialogues therefore does not hold. The upshot is that we will need to look to the goals of Christian textual production to grasp the more nuanced import of the phenomenon.

One avenue of approach may be found in the idea that Christianity, especially in the post-Constantinian age, aimed to present itself, speaking rather generally and at a certain level of abstraction, as a form of *via universalis* or middle way. This emphasis was manifested by the continuing democratisation of Christian knowledge that had already been a trope from the time when apologists such as Origen of Alexandria represented it as a positive asset in his defence of Christian beliefs against outside critics such as Celsus. In that Origen famously distinguished between three levels of reading and their respective suitability for individuals with corresponding capacities for understanding, one can also see that works such as the Platonic dialogues were seen as principally addressed to an advanced readership that was capable of appreciating spiritual allegories.

The corollary to this is that the dialogue form itself might have seemed incommensurable with the rising demand for a humble style from the fourth century onwards. When the bulk of Christian mass communication came to operate on the level of the *sermo humilis*, that a decidedly elite literary form was not greatly resorted to occasions little surprise. The *sermo humilis* both assumes the presence of and also elides the cultural divide between speaker or writer and audience. It is therefore based on a diametrically opposite premise to the literary or philosophical dialogue that posits a degree of cultural symmetry as well as intimacy among interlocutors (as well as writers and readers) who stemmed from the *pars melior generis humani*.[48]

Thus the rise of curial bishops coincided with the rise in importance of the pastoral role and the *sermo humilis*. The public sermon served as a universal form of address that reifies the hierarchical difference between preacher and audience.[49] This asymmetry that is a cornerstone of the *sermo humilis* stemmed from the pastoral ideology around which episcopal authority developed. To the extent that some preachers actively encouraged (mainly doxological) responses from the audience, there may be said to be a dialogic element in the sermon that bears comparison with some of the later Platonic dialogues where the assent of Socrates' interlocutors comes close to being perfunctory. The element of sociability also operated differently in

---

[48] A classic formulation of this literary mimesis can be found in Auerbach (1965).
[49] See, e.g., MacMullen (1989); Klingshirn (1994); Rousseau (1998) 391–400; and Maxwell (2006).

the two forms: while the dialogue presupposes a private, sociable gathering of like-minded men, the sermon is customarily comported for a public setting before a mixed audience. Did the inherent utopianism of the literary/philosophical dialogue (its inherent agonistic element notwith-standing) and its underlying assumption of cultural and social homogeneity therefore render it less relevant to individuals whose basic function required them to turn to 'mass communications'?

Another consideration is that, regardless of their own personal circum-stances, educated bishops and priests were also not always keen to establish their own elite status independently of their the pastoral role and were indeed often caught in a double bind, needing to find legitimacy among their lay social peers by projecting claims to *paideia* as well as the majority of their more plebeian flocks by other means. In this context, they had both to lay claim to and also to disavow the possession of *paideia*, a difficult challenge that is compounded by the fear of (religious and cultural) elitism. Such an accusation could be made to stick and individuals such as Augustine of Hippo and others were deeply sensitive to their vulnerability on both flanks. Spiritual elitism became particularly suspect and caused many selective groups that believed in their own set-apart status to be tarred as heretics. Thus groups that promoted an intimate and exclusive form of sociability clearly sat ill with the majority Christian population. Is it then reasonable to conjecture that such an aversion to closed groups correspond-ingly led to a suspicion of closed conversations (dialogues) that took place within enclosed social spaces?

EPISTOLARITY AS SURROGATE DIALOGUE FORM?

The ancient dialogue may be described as an elite 'peer-to-peer' literary form both with reference to its normal fictive setting and in its appeal to audience. It enacted functions such as the representation of a shared elite cultural space that in turn helped create solidarity among those who could participate in it as imagined participants or as either writer or reader. The dramatic setting affirms the importance of not only having a shared culture but also a 'common space' for intellectual and sociable interactivity. Thus the Academy, Lyceum and, above all, the symposium (in its various forms) operated as fictive 'cultural spaces' in which intellectual and social peers could, both figuratively and in realia, gather for urbane conversations. In the situation that obtained in the postclassical age, spatial contiguity among groups of educated men could no longer be assumed as readily as had been the case in the putative Athens of the Platonic dialogues.

Such a consideration applied also to Christianity given its character as a diasporic community, at least as some imagined. There was no critical mass of educated Christians to fill a literary or philosophical *salon* even in the larger cities of the empire. Just as importantly, the base logic of Christian culture was such that, while its ranks were increasingly filled with the educated both in terms of their possession of *paideia* and scriptural knowledge, its reliance on the rhetoric of the 'paradoxical' produced a tendency to shun rather than embrace high cultural forms. Instead, by the fourth century, many learned urban bishops or priests maintained daily contact with their mixed local congregations to whom they directed popular sermons cast in the humble style. In contrast, the community of their own peers in social and cultural terms was more diasporic in nature. It was only when communicating with this latter group that educated Christians could set aside the pastoral mode. The main modality of this latter form of communication was, however, not the dialogue but the letter.

As a form of address, the Greco-Roman letter was particularly well suited to a diasporic community that Christianity represented from the start.[50] The practice of letter-writing accordingly became highly developed among Christians and served as a way for the different communities to maintain coherence, culturally, socially and theologically, for it allowed them to see themselves as a Christian people rather than a number of disparate communities. By the fourth century, letter-writing served as a means by which educated Christian figures such as Basil of Caesarea, Augustine of Hippo and others could maintain their own social networks that were neither localised in space nor merely confined to the ranks of Christians. Their surviving letters served a variety of functions that ranged from addressing mundane problems to recommending associates to answering theological questions or *aporiae*. They can therefore be seen as the means by which an active and socially formative dialogue came to be conducted among a (mainly) christianising elite.

The long tradition of Greek and Roman letter-writing speaks to its important role in, among other things, building and sustaining networks especially among the elite. Cicero's well-known corpus of correspondence is instructive in this regard in that it showcases how even the Roman aristocratic elite was not usually found in one place (Rome) due to the peripatetic travels of its members. His letters therefore serve to convey not just

---

[50] See Stowers (1986). See Harris (1989) 229–31 for a concise social historical interpretation of ancient letter-writing. For the role of letters in Christian polemic see in this volume Miles and Clark.

news and information nor represent only his own efforts at persuasion and
self-presentation but indeed helped to enact the affective bond of friendship
that ideally *ought* to bind the Roman elite together.[51] In such practices, one
appreciates how letter-writing was meant to build as well as represent a
tightly knit community of like-minded individuals sharing a common
culture; as such, it often transcended sectarian divides even in late antiquity.
Non-Christian figures such as Libanius of Antioch and Symmachus the
Elder composed numerous letters that spoke to the use of epistolarity as the
means for building a unifying identity for diasporic elite networks that
transcended sectarian identities, in the first case one formed around the
possession of Greek *paideia* and in the latter that of a shared aristocratic
culture. The collection and publication of their letters may in turn be read
not only as efforts to promote the reputations of the authors but also to give
tangible shape to the imagined communities bound by the shared cultural
horizons and practices of epistolary sociability invoked in the letters
themselves.[52]

Might we therefore regard such letters as post-diasporic dialogues? While
letter-writing as a literary form does not appear at first sight to have much in
common with the literary and philosophical dialogue, yet it performed
cultural work similar to that discharged by the latter. It appeared as one
of the principal means whereby a group with common interests and outlook
might cooperate in the creation of a common discursive 'public space' *à la*
Jürgen Habermas and Roger Chartier.[53] This is not to say that the type of
communications contained in letters could be readily compared to those
conveyed in literary or philosophical dialogues nor to suggest that ideas in
letters were debated and developed in a similarly dialectical manner as one
finds in (most) dialogues. At any rate, letters did perform at least some of the
work discharged by the dialogue and advanced a similar set of sociable goals.
By helping to galvanise the collective cultural identity, allowing for a
negotiation of cultural status to take place and representing the connectivity
of a Christian (as well as non-Christian) elite, letters helped mark out an
idealised 'cultural space' in which 'genuine dialogue' and an idealised form
of sociability are made possible for individuals who are able to partake of a
common literary and textual (scriptural) culture.

---

[51] See Hutchinson (1998), esp. 16–17. Cicero's epistles at times incorporate embedded dialogues despite
a prejudice against employing direct speech in literary compositions, see 113–38.

[52] See Altman (1986) on the function of letter collections as spaces for dialogue (as a virtual 'Republic of
Letters') before the founding of formal intellectual institutions such as the Académie Française.

[53] See Habermas (1989); Chartier (1990); and Crossley and Roberts (2004).

CONCLUSION

Despite its cultural pre-eminence and iconic role in the history of philosophy and literature, the dialogue form invokes a modality of social interaction and sociability that had always been confined to a very circumscribed segment of ancient society. Its long-standing importance to the formation of cultural identity for the intellectual elite conferred upon it a weight far beyond what its actual frequency within the overall corpus of ancient literature might suggest. In short then, ancient dialogue was always a boutique literary form and its appeal and prestige stemmed from this fact.

With the rise of Christianity and its demographic expansion in the post-Constantinian age, an alternative cultural logic began to alter the equation. While the christianising elite continued to validate the dialogue form on account of its long-standing stature within literary culture, the overriding need to absorb a minimally christianised population from the later fourth century onwards prompted leading members of that same elite to resort to populist modes of textual and oral communications. The inherent elitism of the dialogue, with its implicit ideal community defined by the common possession of *paideia*, made it less suitable as a tool for Christian 'mass communications' than other, increasingly favoured, vehicles. Furthermore, the status-coded form of speech and elite sociability that informed the deep structure of the dialogue genre were also fundamentally alien to the general Christian population and for these reasons there would have been no groundswell of demand for Christian writers to adopt this literary form in a significant manner.[54]

The resulting lack of investment in the dialogue form among Christians is therefore not difficult to understand. Yet it was still employed in specific instances by individuals and groups as their circumstances permitted and as their needs required. Seen in a broader overall context, it may be said that Christians 'dialogued' in late antiquity as never before, having employed diverse literary genres and techniques that at first sight seem to have as little in common with Plato's *Symposium* as modern internet chat-room conversations resemble an early-modern Humanist dialogue.[55] This shift in emphasis need not, however, be read as a sign of cultural backsliding.

---

[54] If the non-elite appreciated such dialogues at all it would have been when they were expressed in a comic register, that is, through comedic parodies. On Lucian of Samosata as a deliberate subverter or 'moderniser' of the Platonic dialogue, see Branham (1989) 67–8.

[55] See Harran (1970).

With vibrant conversations about things great and small becoming common (or just more visibly represented) and widespread among the populace, dialogue as a social and religious practice now took many forms that are no longer contained within the traditional genre of literary and philosophical dialogue. While, for some, this amounts to a form of decline or even decadence, others can with equal justice see it as simply 'change'.

CHAPTER 9

Boethius, Gregory the Great and the Christian 'afterlife' of classical dialogue

Kate Cooper and Matthew Dal Santo

To ask whether a classical tradition of dialogue ended in late antiquity, it is important to identify what kind of phenomenon ancient dialogue *was*, as our sources reflect it. First and foremost, dialogue, as it has come down to us, was a literary genre. What remains to us, of course, are texts. Dialogic texts involve the reader in a drama. More than one speaker speaks; positions are taken; lines are drawn and dissolve again; the reader has to 'find' himself – herself – among the speakers, among the positions offered.

Secondly, however, the dialogic drama purports to reflect a concrete social formation, a 'happening' in social reality, something that also took place outside of texts. We know less about this, of course, than we do about the literary artefact. But the texts that have come down to us imply that they are reflecting a social ritual, a habit of discourse, a distinctive mode of enquiry, a socially dynamic protocol to which problems were subjected, with a view to finding 'answers' that were more valuable – possibly more 'true' – because of the stake-holder method by which they were derived.[1]

If dialogue is a philosophical tool, it is also a mode of literary representation, and it is a literary medium that is exploding in various directions in late antiquity. How the social ritual changed across time, and how the literary genre changed, are of course very different questions, and it is important to be aware which question we are asking. The present essay, however, will try to find a footing in the field of tension between these two questions. Latin dialogue in the fifth and sixth centuries was a genre undergoing expansion and even explosion. New modes of dialogue were being invented while others were being revised and revitalised. At the same time, new technologies of communication, in particular the church council and the formal public debate, placed new pressures on the representation of literate debate.

In the first part of this essay, we will try to gain an idea of how the literary act of writing and circulating a dialogue could itself serve as a social act, an

---

[1] Lloyd (1987).

intervention into something historians might think of as social reality, by watching two Roman senators, one a consul, the other a *praefectus urbi*, both literary men, as they move through the perilous landscape of sixth-century Rome and Ravenna, firing off texts – many though not all of them dialogues – whether to appease, enchant or intimidate their friends and enemies.

It is certainly significant that our two subjects, Anicius Manlius Severinus Boethius and his kinsman Gregorius, whose other *nomina* are not known, were Christian. But the significance of this fact has to be weighed against the fact that both lived in an age when senators were expected to pay at least lip-service to the rituals of an imperially sponsored Church, even if the only emperor still standing was in Constantinople, not Rome. How their engagement with Christianity influenced their approach to the dialogue genre is a difficult question, made more difficult by a scholarly tradition that projects disparate poses with regard to Christianity onto the two men, seeing Boethius as a reluctant Christian, and Gregory as one of the giants of the early medieval Church.

Of the two men, at least one can be called a serious academic theologian. This was Boethius, whose standing at the head of a splendid and powerful household full of children, rare manuscripts, hangers-on and dinner-guests seems not to have undermined his ability to engage with the mysteries of the Trinity. The other, Gregory, is not known for theological accomplishment. Still, his copious writings on pastoral and ethical subjects (including a sustained critique of the Roman clergy), as well as on biblical criticism in the Alexandrian allegorical tradition, have led to his being remembered as the last of the 'fathers' after whom the patristic period of Christianity is named. In 590, Gregory shouldered a critical role as the bishop of Rome, and this certainly enhanced, but does not account for, his towering status.

The second half of this essay will consider how Christian dialogue evolved during the later sixth century and into the seventh in the context of the formation of a distinctive 'early Byzantine' cultural world which was crucially defined by the interplay between 'Christian' and 'non-Christian' modes of thought. Focusing on Gregory the Great, we will see that his *Dialogues on the miracles of the Italian Fathers*, long dismissed by scholars as a work so meagre in intellectual wherewithal that some scholars believe it could not possibly be by Gregory,[2] could in fact reflect a climate of lively engagement with Aristotle in the Constantinople of the 580s, when Gregory was established in the city as papal *apocrisiarius* (579–84), before his return to Rome and ordination to the diaconate.

---

[2] Clark (1987), (2003).

DIALOGUE AND LATE ROMAN LITERARY CULTURE

Naturally, the Christianisation of the Roman aristocracy during the fourth century changed the landscape of literary expectation dramatically. Different writers proposed different strategies to fuse together biblical tradition with inherited habits of thought and writing. Dialogue was an elite form of discourse, whether we speak of the intellectually charged sociability of the ideal of philosophical friendship – where equality, in the sense of equal standing and equivalent access to a shared cultural patrimony, is considered a *sine qua non*[3] – or whether we speak of the *representation* of this kind of sociability in dialogic form.

One of the most far-reaching and influential developments was that of allegorical dialogue, which took the Western Empire by storm in Prudentius' Latin *Psychomachia* at the turn of the fourth to the fifth century. This strand of development is reflected in a little-known text, the anonymous *Ad Gregoriam in palatio*, produced in Rome probably in the first quarter of the sixth century. This manual of conduct for a senatorial *materfamilias* brings allegorical dialogue home to the reader: it is explicitly the vices and virtues warring in the *domina*'s soul who are given voice.[4] At the same time, Latin writers such as John Cassian were working to appropriate the traditions of the Greek literature of the Desert, which drew heavily on schoolroom traditions of dialogue between master and pupil while at the same time furnishing well-developed Evagrian lore about the soul's wrestling-match with the vices. Monastic rules cast in dialogue form, such as the early sixth-century south Italian *Regula Magistri*, implicitly proposed the claim that monastic Christianity should be understood as the new philosophy. The rise of the 'question and answer' tradition in the East, to which we will return below, was framed explicitly with reference to the traditions of the philosophical schools.[5]

Developing the idea of the soul's struggle with invisible powers was the monk Arnobius the Younger, possibly a native of North Africa, who lived in Rome during the turbulent years between the death of Valentinian in 455 and Ricimer's siege of the city in 471.[6] To understand the imaginary landscape of the Roman church in this period, one can do no better than to turn to his influential *Commentary on the Psalms*. Little is known about Arnobius; the *Commentary* is dedicated to the bishops Leontius (or Laurentius) and

---

[3] White (1992); Konstan (1997).   [4] On this text, see now Cooper (2007).
[5] Averil Cameron (1991b) 91–108; (1992a).   [6] MacGeorge (2002) 247ff.

Rusticus, but their identities are disputed.[7] Yet Arnobius seems also to have been the protagonist of the anonymous *Conflictus Arnobii cum Serapione*, a dialogue on Christ's two natures recorded (or imagined) between two learned monks in Rome, one from Africa and one from Egypt, probably dated to the late 440s, in the run-up to the Council of Chalcedon. This text opens a window onto the public theological disputation, a dialogic genre of later antiquity designed to record, and presumably in many instances to edit, the content of real-life open debates which seem to have been sponsored by various parties, including bishops and some of the barbarian kings.[8] In the 1990s, Richard Lim argued that in late antiquity the content aspect of formal debates held to consider theological issues was suppressed in favour of a 'culture of acclamation', with an ever more important role played by ritual performance of assent, by the *ecclesia*, to a position that had, essentially, been agreed upon ahead of time through the medium of back-room politics.[9]

At the same time, we can see the emergence of a new ideal of persuasive speech in which reason is augmented by the miraculous power of the *logos*: Kate Cooper has argued that the representation of persuasive reasoning in hagiographical texts of the fifth–sixth centuries shifts away from an ideal of dialectic engagement to one of miraculous discourse, 'ventriloquism' of the *logos* by the holy man. Already in the fourth century, this kind of stylised representation of public theological disputes is visible in the Pseudo-Clementine *Recognitions*, and the process seems to culminate in the Latin martyr romances of early medieval Rome, the *gesta martyrum*.[10] This is a point to which we will return below.

DIALOGUE AND THE LATE ROMAN 'CULTURE OF COMMUNICATION'

To address the problem of how writing a dialogue could have 'played' in the sixth-century context, it is useful to consider the evolution of a characteristic late Roman communication medium, the church council. A 1999 study by Doron Mendels, *The Media Revolution of Early Christianity*, offers an approach to this issue from the perspective of contemporary media theory.[11] The church council, Mendels argues, followed implicit rules that have been identified in the context of modern 'media events', among them

---

[7] Von Schubert (1903).
[8] Diepen (1959) 538 thinks the text is the formal *procès-verbal* of an actual debate, similar to the debates held between Arians and Catholics under Thrasamund.
[9] Lim (1995).   [10] Cooper (2000); (2005).   [11] Mendels (1999).

(1) The event itself is perceived as a vehicle for mass communication; its goal is a 'mobilization of new participants' or a new level of commitment by existing participants, with respect to the sponsoring organisation and its goals.

(2) Exposure during the communication event, what we moderns call 'air time', is a commodity that has to be meted out very carefully. If one position in a debate is favoured by the sponsoring authority, it is very important to skew the availability of the communication medium toward exposure of that position. Otherwise, there is the danger that the communicative power of the event may be steered in an unexpected direction by the charisma of low-status players. In other words, 'objective' accounts of non-normative views 'can produce an effect opposite to the one desired, namely, a "mobilization of new participants"' toward the position that is out of favour.[12] Thus 'a concise and derogatory' description of a heresy was more effective in alienating audiences.

To be sure, there is good evidence that at least some councils were 'steered' in this way.[13] But at the same time, frustratingly open-ended 'working sessions' were by no means a thing of the past. It is in this context that we should consider the famous account given by Boethius of a Roman synod, which characterises the confusion of unlearned men in coping with abstract Greek theology. The narrative, which opens Boethius' fifth tractate, *Against Eutyches and Nestorius*, dedicated to the Roman deacon John (possibly the later pope John I), begins by explaining that it arises from the two men's attendance at a church council, along with a number of Roman senators and clergy of high rank, at which a letter from an eastern bishop concerning the two natures of Christ was read and discussed. Here is Chadwick's summary of Boethius' account: 'During the ensuing babble of debate he kept his peace. From his seat he could not see the expression on the face of the man whose opinion most counted ... so that he felt left without trustworthy guidance from authority. Appalled at the ignorance and arrogance manifested by some of the speakers in the debate, he went away to give the matter prolonged consideration.'[14]

In this case, whose opinion 'counted' was not a question of controlling the message to be taken away by the crowd – far from it. Instead, Boethius was looking, unsuccessfully, for guidance in mapping Christological problems across to familiar philosophical terrain. It is this mapping that forms the main task of a number of the tractates of Boethius' *opuscula sacra*. This kind of work may be out of place in the melee of discussion by the

---

[12] Mendels (1999) 155.   [13] Graumann (2007).   [14] Chadwick (1981) 180–81.

uninitiated, but it nonetheless constitutes a contribution to the wider discourse. Again, we may cite Chadwick:

Boethius is confident that the philosopher can help a little, especially by recourse to the classic commentaries on Plato's *Parmenides* for a disentangling of the logical problem of identity and difference. But Boethius begins by taking his stand resolutely within the Catholic tradition of authority. Christians have received a revelation of the word of God, and his concern is solely with the exposition of Catholic orthodoxy.[15]

The tension between revealed truth and dialectic reasoning is central here. The truth has already arrived, via revelation; the job of the interpreter is to perceive the *meaning* of this revelation. While classical Platonic dialogue was deeply committed to a cataphatic ideal of knowledge and how it was to be attained, by the sixth century, Christianity was going down the path of apophaticism: truth was revealed (especially through narrative – biblical, hagiographical, liturgical) and appropriated by the listener through a process of inward encounter. Whereas a cataphatic approach maintained the possibility of positive knowledge of a subject (i.e. the ability to speak truly of a given thing), the apophaticism that developed in patristic tradition was predicated upon the underlying impossibility of complete knowledge, especially of God. The apophatic tradition recognised the limits of speech, often contenting itself with what the subject is not, rather than what it is.[16] This is not actually anti-intellectual, but super-intellectual: not only the mind (as arguably with pure rational dialogue), but the imagination (through the verbal pictures of biblical and hagiographical stories and, later, icons) and the body (above all, the sacraments and the liturgy as a cosmological 'drama' in which a person participates) are the subject of transformation and the locus of epistemological engagement. This was a process reaching back to Philo, the great Jewish allegorist of first-century Alexandria, and forward to Pseudo-Dionysius the Areopagite and St Maximus the Confessor (*c.* 580–662) in the sixth and seventh centuries.

At the same time, if Boethius stands at the end of one tradition in Latin literature, he stands equally at the beginning of another.[17] Ancient historians can possibly learn something from the work of medievalists not only on Boethius himself but more broadly on *disciplina* and the school-room.[18]

---

[15] Chadwick (1981) 213.   [16] Lossky (1957); Meyendorff (1975); Louth (1981).
[17] On Boethius being taken up in the middle ages, see Williams (2007), along with de Carlos (2001). More generally, Leclercq (1982), Reynolds (1996), esp. 8–10.
[18] See Enders (1996) 24–55; Woods (2001) 143–66.

BOETHIUS AND LADY PHILOSOPHY

Does Boethius mean to write the epitaph for Philosophy in his *Consolation*? Almost certainly not, although he may well have been writing his own epitaph.[19] Faced not with the destruction of an entire society – Boethius did not live to see the Gothic Wars which left such a decisive imprint on the contribution of Cassiodorus – but with the narrower if still daunting prospect of his own individual death, Boethius reached instinctively for a Roman tradition cherished by men of his kind since republican times. In the *Consolation*, Boethius draws directly on Cicero, Seneca and Plotinus; it is almost as if Tertullian and Cyprian had not, in the second and third centuries, effected a fusion of the Stoic to the Christian world-view, and Augustine and others had not done the same for Christianity and neo-Platonism in the fourth.[20]

There is an active and playful use, in the *Consolation*, of a layered relationship between the discursive plane of the text and that of the reader. Most important is the triangle of the reader and the two interlocutors within the text. Also present, explicitly and implicitly, are a variety of Boethius' historical 'interlocutors': the friends whom he accuses of having boasted too often of his good fortune,[21] the accusers who saw to his imprisonment and eventual execution.

Two sections of the *Consolation* jump to the eye, when we think about the changing frame of address within the dialogue. The first is in book one (1.4), where Boethius justifies himself to Lady Philosophy, arguing that it was she who urged him to follow Plato and take up public office as the natural consequence of his engagement with her teaching. This section is brazen in its use of Boethius' inner dialogue to set the record straight for posterity about what he did and did not do, and how falsely he has been accused thanks to the pettiness of his enemies in the senate. Intended here is clearly an ironic counterpoint between his conversation with Philosophy and the implied external context known to the reader. An added layer of irony results from the fact that Boethius knows that he is starting a conversation – the evaluation of his own *fama* – whose conclusion he will not be present to judge.

In book five, our second passage, Boethius takes up the question of how the acknowledgement of divine providence alters fundamental questions of

---

[19] See Crabbe (1981); Kirkby (1981); Matthews (1981); Lerer (1985); Barnish (1990) 22.
[20] On Boethius' borrowings, see Crabbe (1981) 238–44, and literature cited there.
[21] *Consolatio* 1, line 21.

human cognition. Here Boethius is interested in how Christian belonging affects human reason and human agency. He is heir to a tradition of grappling by senatorial Christians, known to modern scholarship through the lens of the Pelagian controversy, around the issue of whether human beings can exercise free will if an all-seeing God knows ahead of time how they will choose (think here of a figure such as Julian of Eclanum).[22] Boethius' answers, such as they are, turn on the distance between reason and understanding as discrete levels in a hierarchy of cognition (the scale runs from sensation at the bottom through imagination and reason to understanding at the top). Understanding does not operate within the constraints of what Augustine called the *saeculum*. It exists, but it exists outside the bounds of time. (Thus it is incorrect to class divine knowledge of the future as 'foreknowledge'; on the contrary, divine knowledge exists in a non-sequential frame.) At the conclusion of book five, we find Boethius' acknowledgement that the frame of human interpretation is encompassed by that of divine knowledge (5.6). Just as human knowledge is encompassed and anticipated by divine knowledge, so Philosophy has the last word in the *Consolation*. The irony, of course, is that even as Boethius the interlocutor fails to undermine the unanswerable arguments of Philosophy, it is Boethius the author who sets out the lines of argument.

A different kind of irony governs the anonymous *Ad Gregoriam in palatio*, a conduct manual for a senatorial *domina* who was probably Boethius' contemporary.[23] Here, we see what can only be described as an absurdist attempt to merge the currents of Christian and philosophical dialogue. The treatise contains an extended *Psychomachia*, an allegorical dialogue, in which successive vices attack the Christian soul. Our author's strategy is to establish a triangle in which the male spiritual director turns back and forth between addressing the lady reader and an *ekphrasis* of the metaphorical battle of spears and shields, on the one hand, while on the other he offers a direct report of the battle of verbal argument between the vices and virtues. The literary function of the explicitly female addressee in this text recalls – and perhaps inverts – the gendered function assigned to Diotima in the *Symposium*.[24]

This text, too, takes up the theme of *consolatio*, but this time with repeated, almost driving reference to a host of Christian writers of previous

---

[22] On Julian the Apostate, see Markus (1990) 55–62.
[23] The text can be found in *Corpus Christianorum* 25A, although the editor's assignment of authorship is premature. For extended discussion of this text, with an English translation, see Cooper (2007).
[24] Recalling Halperin (1991).

generations, some of them cited *verbatim*. It is as if, while Boethius wished somehow to stand apart from the Christian literature with which he was almost certainly perfectly familiar, the author of *Ad Gregoriam* sought to consolidate an existing patrimony of Christian thinking for a new pastoral situation, and possibly to showcase his own command of a Christian literary inheritance. At the same time, *Ad Gregoriam* offers an exuberant exploration of the entertainment value of the travails of the Christian soul.

The linguistic register of *Ad Gregoriam* is closer than that of Boethius to the 'plain style' preferred by contemporary writers for works of spiritual instruction, but nonetheless, the author is able and willing to showcase a fully periodic style, by no means limiting himself to the repetitive parataxis of contemporary sermon literature. Where repetition is used, it is clearly used for effect, in accordance with the sensibilities of what Michael Roberts has called the 'jewelled style'.[25] Where philosophical ideas are concerned there is a similar sensibility at work: the writer seems both to want to show a full awareness of the Christian Stoic and neo-Platonic traditions, and at the same time to communicate with readers who are not *au courant* to the same degree. Thus the Christian Stoic vocabulary established by Tertullian and Cyprian is adopted, but the meaning of the text does not depend on a reader's ability to recognise the allusions. Neo-Platonic ideas appear in an easily accessible guise, with the ability to show forth virtue understood, for example, in mystical terms as a swelling of light through the body:

> For the Lord has shown his light in you for the good of many. And as that light spreads through your members He separates you from the shadows of this world, and makes you show forth varying powers (*virtutes*) to all.[26]

Similarly, the treatise ends with the theme of heavenly ascent, with the lady reader ascending the path toward heaven, looking neither to left nor right.

The metaphor of the viewing tower allows our author to invoke the ideal of the *miles Christi* while at the same time interposing an imaginary distance. The *domina* is asked to *view* the *altercatio* rather than fight – even though it is her own soul that must do battle with the forces of evil. It can be argued that she is assigned a passive role as a spectator, but the situation is more complex than this. In the main body of the text her own actions in daily life are viewed as a form of direct engagement in spiritual warfare, and this spills across to colour the interpretation of the sequences in which the

---

[25] Roberts (1989).   [26] *Ad Gregoriam in palatio* 25.

virtues – *her* virtues – are at war with the vices. Across the text as a whole Gregoria is both soldier and spectator.

GREGORY THE GREAT AND THE EVOLUTION OF CHRISTIAN DIALOGUE IN THE EARLY BYZANTINE MEDITERRANEAN DURING THE LATER SIXTH AND SEVENTH CENTURIES

The remainder of this paper will concentrate on aspects of the Christian search for orthodoxy, arguing that the clash of epistemologies expressed in Christian dialogue was crucial for the development of intellectual culture in the early Byzantine Mediterranean (*c.* 500–750) and for unravelling the meaning of the period's religious texts, including the ostensibly inexplicable 'revival' of Christian dialogue by Gregory the Great and other writers.[27] In other words, Christians did dialogue in the later sixth and seventh centuries as they had in earlier centuries; and the literary dialogues this created actually reflect a real socio-historical context of debate, dissent and disputation. The search for consensus and its opposite counterpart, the struggle to subvert it, could in fact be considered the characteristic dynamics of the intellectual culture of the period. It is up to the reader to decide how unique this was and how (if at all) the dialogic culture of the post-Justinianic Christian empire differed from that of Plato's (and Aristotle's) Athens.

In the second half of the ninth century Photius, the controversial patriarch of Constantinople, left a record of his reading for posterity.[28] Often Photius' notes are all that survive as evidence for the historian of otherwise unknown texts from classical and Christian antiquity. One text provides a priceless window for historians onto intellectual culture as it existed in the East Roman empire between the death of the emperor Justinian in 565 and the onslaught of first Persian and then Arab invasions that brought the empire to its knees.[29] Dating from the second half of the sixth century and attributed to a certain Stephen Gobar, the text constituted a series of propositions juxtaposed (in the majority of cases) with their exact counter-propositions. The first three may be taken as a case in point (note that the first contains Photius' own comments, indicated by square brackets):

(1) The 'idiom' and the 'character' and the 'form' are the 'hypostasis', but not so is the combination of 'being' and 'idiom', nor the 'authypostatic'. [The sayings first adduced by Gobarus maintain this; those next given,

---

[27] Dagron (1984).   [28] The text of Photius is to be found in Henry (1959–91).
[29] These probably began in 602 and 634 respectively. See among others Howard-Johnston (1999).

the opposite, namely that the 'idiom' and the 'form' and the 'character' are not the 'hypostasis' but the 'character' of the hypostasis.]

(2) John the Baptist was conceived in October – He was conceived in November.

(3) The conception of the Lord was announced to the Virgin in the first month, April, which the Hebrews call Nisan; she bore our Lord Jesus Christ after nine months, that is on 5th January, in the middle of the night of the eighth day before the ides of January – The Annunciation took place not in April but on 25th March, and our Saviour was born, not on 5th January but on the eighth day before the calends of January.[30]

At first sight this strange combination of Aristotelian philosophy of being and Christian festal speculation seems irreconcilable. In fact, however, Gobar's collection of opposing propositions illustrates the vital engagement with philosophy of the mid-sixth-century elite Christian culture associated with the empire's great cities. Justinian was, of course, the megalomaniac emperor who restored Roman rule to parts of the western Mediterranean where it had not been known directly for two generations, sometimes longer. But Justinian's reign was also synonymous with 'orthodoxy', or at least with the attempt to define and impose it.[31] To underline his commitment to orthodoxy – and to an orthodox Christian Empire in particular – Justinian proclaimed many of the 'Marian' feasts of the medieval Church calendar, including the Annunciation. Already one piece of the puzzle for piecing together the social reality which Gobar's curious text reflects has been provided. After all, what if the emperor was wrong in the date he ascribed to the Archangel's visit?

Whether despite or because of this emphasis on Christian orthodoxy, Justinian's reign also witnessed the continued revival of Aristotelianism – especially commentaries on Aristotle's logical works, the *Organon*, usually preceded in late antiquity by Porphyry's *Isagoge*, intended to reconcile Aristotelian logic with the Neo-Platonic metaphysics that had dominated intellectual life in the Mediterranean since Plotinus. This is the other half of Gobar's puzzle. While Justinian is usually best remembered for his closure of the Athenian Academy in 529 (apparently on account of the philosophers' loyalty to paganism), recent studies have emphasised the surviving strength of the philosophical tradition in other centres, especially Alexandria whose schools, so far as it is possible to tell, remained open throughout this

---

[30] Harnack (1923); further, Bardy (1947), (1949); and Wolska-Conus (1989).
[31] This can be seen especially in the convocation of the Second Council of Constantinople in 553.

period.[32] In Italy, of course, the early Byzantine renewal of interest in Aristotle was manifested in Boethius' works and translations. Frequent portrayals, therefore, of early Byzantium as a uniformly Christian and, therefore, 'dialogue-free' society are already misleading.

To realise the strength of the Christian dialogic tradition in this period, let us turn to one of the best known of these Christian texts, Gregory the Great's *Dialogues on the Miracles of the Italian Fathers*, written in Rome c.593. Traditionally, Gregory's *Dialogues* have rarely been considered worthy of the name and occasionally even as an embarrassment to the memory of an otherwise sensitive patristic moral and ethical teacher and skilled exegete.[33] Harnack famously dismissed them as the source of the *Vulgärkatholismus* of the middle ages,[34] and Francis Clark has argued since the 1980s that they were probably not by Gregory to begin with. The possibility of Gregory's text possessing real 'dialogic' quality was, however, underlined in an all too brief study by Marc van Uytfanghe during the 1980s.[35] To date, Uytfanghe's contention that the *Dialogues* reflect a setting of real doubt towards key aspects of Christian doctrine in the Rome 'ruled' by Gregory has provoked little comment from scholars.[36]

Matthew Dal Santo has already argued that intertextual criticism of the *Dialogues* reveals Gregory's awareness of, and engagement with, contemporary Aristotelian debates.[37] When considered alongside Eustratius of Constantinople's *On the State of Souls* (a spirited defence of the cult of the saints – and in particular the reality of the saints' post-mortem apparitions to supplicants at their shrines), Gregory's *Dialogues on the Miracles of the Italian Fathers* can be convincingly read as a defence of the sixth-century cult of the saints – or, at the very least, as a 'dialogic gloss' on the place of the saints in the Church and the validity of certain other (apparently connected) Christian doctrines, such as the afterlife of the soul and the

---

[32] Wildberg (2005). It was from Alexandria that Aristotelian texts were obtained for translation into Syriac by Stephen of Reš'aina and Paul the Persian – sixth-century translations of Aristotle that as sources for later Arabic translations directly influenced the thirteenth-century revival of Aristotelianism in the West: Gutas (1983); Hugonnard-Roche (1989), (2000). Most of the practitioners of Aristotelian philosophy known to us from the post-Justinianic period appear to have been Christian, the greatest student and critic of the age being John Philoponus: Sorabji (1990).

[33] Clark (1987), (2003).   [34] Harnack (1922).   [35] Van Uytfanghe (1986).

[36] Gregory's *Register* frequently gives the impression that the pope is responsible for the provisioning of Rome, the maintenance of civil order and external security from Lombard raids. But it is clear that the exarch in Ravenna retained ultimate authority over political life in Rome and Italy generally. Whether this is substantially different from the situation presented by Leontios in his description of the conflicts between the Augustal Prefect of Egypt and Alexandria's early seventh-century patriarchs in the *Life of John the Almsgiver* is open to question.

[37] Dal Santo (in press).

Church's ritual 'care for the dead' (i.e. offering of prayer and the Eucharist for the deceased).[38]

Indeed, to understand Gregory's *Dialogues*, it is important to understand his view, drawn from the epicurean tradition and explained most fully in his *Regula pastoralis*, that pyschagogy, or the enlightenment of souls, is a fine art, which must address each individual through the discourse that he is best able to apprehend.[39] His *Moralia* distils the idea into the well-known metaphor of scripture as a river that is deep enough for the elephant to bathe, while it is shallow enough for the lamb to find its footing.[40] Where *content* was concerned, for Gregory the most important message was the exclusive claims made by Christian 'orthodoxy' for the epistemological allegiance of practising Christians in the late sixth century – ahead of any rival intellectual commitments or traditions.

Gregory's *Dialogues* open with a *consolatio*: as the bishop expresses his sense of despair at his own inability to fulfil his mission to gather souls in the face of the coming *eschaton*, Peter begins to draw him out and eventually the bishop is re-energised by the momentum of his own response to artful questioning.[41] Across the text, it becomes evident that Gregory's intent is to elaborate a radical epicureanism, designed to develop among his close associates a band of orthodox eschatological missionaries trained in the art of psychagogy, whose mission it is to communicate the alarming fact of the impending end of the world to the wider community of the faithful in the starkest 'Catholic' terms.[42]

Telegraphing the discussion of the first three dialogues, Gregory's fourth dialogue is introduced by way of a shocking admission. At the end of the third dialogue,[43] the Deacon Peter (Gregory's interlocutor) requests that Gregory desist henceforth from telling the lives of the holy men because there were many in Rome who did not believe in the afterlife of the soul:

P: Considering how many there are within the fold of the Church who doubt the existence of the soul after death, I am urged to beg you for proofs from reason showing that the soul will continue to live on forever. And, if any examples from the lives of the saints come to your mind, use them to illustrate your explanations. Such a procedure will remove the doubt from the minds of many and will at the same time be a source of edification.[44]

---

[38] Eustratius of Constantinople: van Deun (2006); Constas (2002).
[39] Glad (1985); Leyser (2000) 160–77. On Gregory and the epicurean tradition, see Leyser (2000).
[40] Gregory, *Ad Leandrum* 4.   [41] *Dial.* Prol. 3.
[42] Leyser (2000) 134–5, a view adopted by Brown (2003).
[43] Pricoco now believes that the fourth dialogue was written at a later date than the first three: Pricoco and Simonetti (2006).
[44] *Dial.* 3.38.5.

What is, indeed, striking throughout Gregory's fourth dialogue is the strength of the questioning of eschatological orthodoxy that Gregory is forced to confront, based on an empiricism that is stringent in the demands it makes on Christian doctrine. The whole dialogue is carried out in terms of a broadly rationalistic distinction between the seen and unseen, the reasonable and that which can only be grasped by faith, with repeated appeals to what the 'eyes can see', 'objective proof' and reason. Peter's questions continually reveal a stridently materialist and rationalist position which the text makes plain the Deacon is serving as a literary device to rebut, even if his psychagogy requires that the 'weak' get a full run-through of disputed issues. Referring to the 'many' mentioned at the end of the third dialogue who doubted in the afterlife of the soul, Peter appeals to Gregory:

P: I beg you to bear patiently with me if I, too, like Ecclesiastes, impersonate the weak and continue the enquiry in their name in order to help them more directly.

G: Why should I be annoyed if you stoop to help a weak brother? Does not St Paul say, 'I have been everything by turns to everybody, to bring everybody to salvation?' In doing this out of charity, you deserve greater respect, because you are thereby imitating the practice of an outstanding preacher.[45]

Hence, in the setting created by the dialogue, the Deacon Peter is consciously styled as vicariously representing the doubts of the 'weak'. Gregory can be seen as attempting to bring elites (possibly influenced by the kind of philosophical speculation represented by Gobar) into full participation with the wider, non-intellectual church.

Gregory's urgency in this text should not be misunderstood. He means fundamentally to persuade his own circle not to be tempted by the complacency of the Roman clergy, men from established families who are hostile to his ascetic project and deaf to his warning of the impending *eschaton*. When he speaks of 'the weak' and 'the strong' he does not, however, mean his own circle against his enemies; rather, he is referring to two types of Christian within the polity of his own 'shock-troops'. The 'weak' are those for whom philosophical questions must be answered in a literate and logical way, while the 'strong' are those who are able to disregard their own habits as elite men of learning in the face of the coming eschaton. 'Blessed are they who have not seen and yet believe.'[46]

As such, the fourth dialogue, like the whole of Gregory's *Miracles of the Italian Fathers*, provides a unique source for the cultural and intellectual

---

[45] *Dial.* 4.4.9.   [46] John 20.29.

history of early Byzantine Rome – a city living in the decaying legacy of a glorious past, but nonetheless very much engaged in the intellectual debates and cultural permutations of contemporary East Roman society. Hence, the *Dialogues* belongs to a much larger body of literature that was concerned historically with making sense of the world created by Justinian, defined theologically by the Christological controversies set in motion by the Council of Chalcedon (451), and distinguished by the remarkable revival of commentaries on neo-Platonic and Aristotelian philosophy. In many ways, the early Byzantine Mediterranean and its hinterland during the sixth and seventh centuries probably witnessed the most protracted, detailed and fiercely contested debate on personhood and anthropology in human history – certainly, in the history of the ancient world – as Christian, Jewish and ultimately Muslim monotheisms fought to define the various 'orthodox' versions of their beliefs about God, man and the universe.

Averil Cameron has argued for a redefinition of knowledge in Byzantium between the end of the sixth and the beginning of the eighth centuries.[47] This 'redefinition' can broadly be defined as an attempt to create a coherent 'orthodox Christian' world view capable of articulating a new sense of Roman identity (of course, the Byzantines always called themselves 'Romans') and explaining the changing fortunes of the empire. The concerted effort to produce an authoritative systematisation of knowledge manifest in the birth of *florilegia* was undoubtedly crucial to this task. But as Gregory's text announces, so was Christian dialogue, complemented very often by narrative, especially hagiographies.

This perspective is confirmed not least because the questions from Gregory's *Dialogues* consistently resemble the paradigm provided by seventh-century Greek *erôtapokriseis*. The two most important texts are the *Questions and Responses* by Anastasius of Sinai († *c.* 700) and Pseudo-Athanasius' *Questions to the Duke Antiochus*. Anastasius' collection is usually dated to the later seventh century and its composition thought to have occurred in Egypt, Palestine or Mt Sinai.[48] Pseudo-Athanasius' collection probably dates from the first half of the eighth century and, again, most likely originated in Egypt.[49] Repeatedly, the same questions, or similar, are raised in both Gregory's fourth dialogue in Latin and the Greek question-and-answer literature. But Gregory, on the one hand, and Anastasius of Sinai and the Pseudo-Athanasius, on the other, often provide surprisingly different answers to what can appear basic elements of Christian doctrine. Unlike Gregory, for

[47] Cameron (1988), (1996); Fontaine and Hillgarth (1992).   [48] Text: Richard and Munitiz (2006).
[49] Thümmel (1992) 246–52, who considers the question at length; *pace* Dagron (1992) 63, col. 1.

example, neither Anastasius nor the Pseudo-Athanasius was prepared to believe in the post-mortem activity of souls – even those of the saints.[50] This is indicative rather of the space that existed for the creation of orthodoxy in the seventh century – a space that was very often colonised by dialogue. One may legitimately wonder what the later western medieval hagiographical tradition would have been like if the psychological and eschatological views of the Egyptian question-and-answer authors had prevailed rather than Gregory's.

But to gain the true measure of the role played by Christian dialogue throughout the formation of orthodoxy during the early Byzantine period, it is necessary to consider other writers and genres. The powerful liturgical hymns composed by Romanos the Melodist frequently achieve their goal of articulating Christian orthodoxy by creating a dialogue between biblical figures into which the 'audience' as singers was drawn as active participants in the search for true Christian understanding of biblical narratives and theological doctrine.[51] East of the empire's late antique frontiers, Christian dialogue flourished among Syriac-speaking authors, from Ephrem in the fourth century down to the dialogues composed by Christians at the Caliphs' court in Baghdad at the beginning of the ninth.[52]

As for Gregory's *Dialogues*, translated by Pope Zacharias (741–52) in the opening rounds of Byzantine iconoclasm, they were upheld as a model of orthodoxy by middle Byzantine spiritual writers and were praised by Photius as *biôphelestatous* ['most useful for life'], the well-read patriarch lamenting only that it had taken over one hundred and sixty-five years for them to be translated into Greek.[53] But iconoclasm – the crisis of the picture as the new 'word' (*logos*)[54] – can itself be seen as the fulfilment of this process of defining Christian belief through speech, both cataphatic (as in Christian dialogue and question-and-answer literature) and apophatic, as represented by the rise of Christian hagiographical tradition predicated upon the word as metaphor, the liturgy and the veneration of images.[55]

CONCLUSION

It is usually thought that dialogue petered out in the Mediterranean world in the aftermath of the triumph of Christianity. Yet, the tradition of dialogue

---

[50] Dagron (1992); cf. Krausmüller (1998/99).   [51] Krueger (2004).
[52] Brock (1982); Hunter (2002).
[53] For Gregory and middle Byzantine eschatology, Baun (2007); Photius in Henry (1959–91), vol. 7, cod. 252, 207–9.
[54] Brown (1999) 15–34.   [55] Averil Cameron (1991a).

continued throughout the late Roman and early Byzantine period, being adapted and moulded by a range of Christian authors to serve their own diverse needs. Did the rise of monotheism under the guise of Christianity (and especially the attempt to define Christian orthodoxy) 'shut down' debate and dialogue in the ancient world? The evidence for the liveliness and diversity of Christian dialogue as a literary genre presented by this contribution – from Boethius in Rome to question-and-answer authors in early Islamic Egypt – suggest that it could equally be asked whether Christianity presented dialogue with new subject matter and lent the genre new impetus.

PART V

Judaism and the limits of dialogue

No dialogue at the symposium?
Conviviality in Ben Sira and the Palestinian Talmud

Seth Schwartz

The symposium was one of those peculiarly Greek institutions that the Jews seem to have adopted early, broadly and with little ostensible cultural anxiety. Like many such institutions, it had significant congeners in the Near East and the eastern Mediterranean outside Greek lands, a fact which eased its later domestication there. The royal banquet/drinking bout was a significant theme in art and literature far back into the Near Eastern Bronze Age,[1] and the family or sacral feast – which might well include a party of what we could appropriately call *xenoi* and *philoi*, in addition to family members[2] – a common scene in the Hebrew Bible, and possibly not uncommon in the life of ancient Israel. As is also true of many such institutions, its embrace by the Jews was far more fraught than the surface of the evidence implies. Philo of Alexandria, for example, the most 'hellenised' of Jewish writers, devoted half of his essay 'on the contemplative life' (40–91) to an invidious comparison of the symposium, with its drunkenness, violence, gluttony, luxury, vapid *logoi* and pederasty, and the solemn, sober, orderly, profound and silent feasts of a Jewish monastic sect called the Therapeutae – a (not always intentionally) hilarious satirical *tour de force*.

Nevertheless, symposium-like parties are mentioned, described, prescribed for, in a great many ancient Jewish texts. One of them, *The Letter of Aristeas to Philokrates*, even provides an account of a peculiarly stilted and unsatisfying philosophical dialogue between a group of Jewish sages and Ptolemy Philadelphos, which mainly shows that some Alexandrian Jews' desire to tap into the prestige of the Platonic tradition was less conflicted, or nuanced, than Philo's. While this is not a trivial fact, I will examine two other texts in which the symposium figures importantly, which in my opinion are more interesting than *Aristeas*.[3] The first of these is the *Wisdom*

---

[1] See Ziffer (2005).
[2] 1 Samuel 20.5: David's attendance at his lord/patron Saul's New Moon feast is expected.
[3] See in general Honigman (2003).

of Jesus ben Sira (*Sirach; Ecclesiasticus*), an 'apocryphal' book (that is, one not included in the Jewish or Protestant biblical canons) composed at Jerusalem around 180 BCE. About three-fifths of the book survives in some approximation of the original Hebrew,[4] courtesy of six fragmentary high-medieval manuscripts discovered in the 1890s in the *genizah* (damaged book depository) of the Ben Ezra Synagogue in Fustat (Old Cairo), Egypt.[5] For the rest we rely on a Greek translation produced (according to its prologue) by the author's grandson, who can, however, be shown to have altered Ben Sira's Hebrew wisdom in ways great and small.[6] The state of the text of Ben Sira thus constitutes a central hermeneutical problem in an unusually basic and direct way.

The second text is the Palestinian Talmud, compiled and edited in some sense (not necessarily in written form) in Tiberias, Galilee, around 380 CE. Though the Palestinian Talmud is essentially a collection of legal statements, commentaries, arguments, etc., rather like a shaggier, more episodic and disorganised – often less readily comprehensible – version of the Digest, it also contains much narrative, some though not all of it used to establish legal precedent.[7]

Both texts exhibit surprisingly extensive and profound anxiety about the symposium, and especially about the status of speech, conversation, dialogue at the symposium, and it is these shifting anxieties that I wish to discuss in what follows. Both texts place the symposium at the nodal point in the cultural nexus of reciprocity, honour and hierarchy, notions which

---

[4] The qualification is necessary because, while there is now no doubt that the Genizah manuscripts reflect the original Hebrew, and are not a retranslation from later Greek or Syriac versions, as some once believed, the manuscripts, where they overlap, often preserve very different texts, all of them differ in significant ways from the Greek (which itself exhibits very wide divergences between manuscripts) and all of these differ in turn from the ancient fragments of the text discovered on Masada in 1964 (though the latter are close enough to the Genizah texts to demonstrate the latter's *fundamental* authenticity).
   Ben Sira is thus the only book of the 'apocrypha' demonstrably copied and read by Jews deep into the Middle Ages – the Genizah manuscripts were written in the twelfth century. In fact Ben Sira's status was anomalous: it is also the only non-biblical book to have been quoted approvingly in the Talmud (providing an additional collection of early textual witnesses).

[5] For an account see Reif (1997).

[6] Ben Sira's Hebrew is exceptionally difficult, both archaising and eccentric. Though there is uncertainty in many individual cases, it would be uncontroversial to say that frequently the author of the Greek text simply misunderstood his grandfather ('grandfather'?), and that in other cases the changes were conscious, leaving aside those cases where his Hebrew text differed. See in detail – with focus on the Greek translator's Hebrew *Vorlage* – Wright (1989).

[7] For the analogy to the Digest, see Hezser (1998). Here too the state of the text constitutes a core hermeneutical issue, for the opposite reason: there is only one tolerably complete manuscript of the PT, whose readings are often incomprehensible or manifestly mistaken. And here, too, some medieval fragments from the Cairo Genizah have survived, enough to warn us against the unchallenged authority of the Leiden manuscript, but not enough to give us a completely satisfying set of alternatives.

were peculiarly fraught for ancient Jewish sages, for reasons I will explain in the next section of this paper. Furthermore, and in a related way, in telling stories, composing rules and offering advice about the symposium, both Ben Sira and the rabbis were working out their relationship to the Greek culture with which they lived in an uneasy symbiosis. Thus, Ben Sira recommended silence at symposia in part, I will argue, because a certain compartmental *parrhêsia* was so characteristic of Greek sympotic practice, while the rabbis in general (but see below) embraced talk but insisted that it concern Torah, and nothing else.

RECIPROCITY, HONOUR, HIERARCHY VERSUS CORPORATE SOLIDARITY

I am suggesting then that we use the symposium to probe two important and related problems in the social and cultural history of the Jews in antiquity. The more familiar of the two is the problem of 'hellenisation', the extent and character of the Jews' struggles against/appropriation of the Greek culture normative in the Mediterranean world for the millennium after Alexander the Great. 'Hellenisation' has been overused hermeneutically, having been adduced to explain far too much of the Jews' social, cultural and political history. Even when used appropriately, it has become a shorthand for a process whose political and cultural complexities have too often been forgotten or ignored. Hence, the second problem, which has in my view been overlooked, but is one of the crucial issues in the social history of the Jews (and also of Christians and Muslims) down to about 1800. This problem requires more extended explanation.[8]

Let us begin by positing that there existed two ways of imagining societies. In the first conception, societies are bound together by densely overlapping networks of relationships of personal dependency constituted and sustained by reciprocal exchange, the sorts of relationships I will call institutionalised reciprocity. This may sound like modern social theory but in fact there is ample ancient attestation for it. Certainly it was shared by such diverse thinkers as Aristotle (*Eudemian Ethics* 7.1.2; 7.10.14ff.) and Seneca (it is at least implicit in *On Benefits*). In the second conception, societies are bound together not by personal relationships but by corporate solidarity based on shared ideals (piety, wisdom) or myths (for example

---

[8]　To which my forthcoming book, *Were the Ancient Jews a Mediterranean Society?* (Princeton University Press, 2008 or 2009, *insha'allah*) will be devoted. The next section of this paper adapts a brief part of the introduction to the book.

about common descent). This too resonates with modern social theory, for example the influential work of Benedict Anderson, but is very amply attested for antiquity. The Torah is one proponent of such a theory (see below). Plato was another. Both theories have emotional content – one is expected or even obligated to love, or at least have amicable or loyal feelings towards, those to whom one is connected. But this factor is responsible for a significant practical difference between the two, for the first theory requires you to love your patrons, clients, kinsmen and friends, but not all members of your nation, though it may be expected that your connections will love their connections and so on, so that everyone will ultimately be bound together in an indirectly solidary, segmented society. By contrast, the second theory requires you to love all members of the group whether or not they are personally connected to you. The Torah commanded all Israelites to love their fellows and Pericles urged his Athenian compatriots to be *erastai*, lovers, of their *polis* (so Thucydides wrote: II 43). In this scheme, kinsmen, patrons and friends enjoy no advantages.

Thus, although the two approaches are not irreconcilable, they are definitely in tension with each other. In fact, an Aristotle might assume a hierarchy of solidarities, and thereby reconcile loyalties to/affection towards household, patronage network and *polis*. Furthermore, all theorists, ancient and modern, recognised that states need laws and a sense of order, the effect of which is necessarily to restrain the untrammelled operation of institutionalised reciprocity; the latter is thus understood to be on some fundamental level antithetical to the interests of the state, even as it is thought to constitute an advance over the primordial or pre-social Hobbesian 'warre of all against all'.[9] But adherents of the second social theory might find it more challenging to incorporate local loyalties in their system without subverting it completely. In some sense the whole point of the theory is to overcome the clan-group and the patronage network:[10] it derives its emotional strength

---

[9] Contrast Gouldner (1960) 176. But he also characterises reciprocity as a 'starting mechanism' which logically/chronologically precedes the development of 'a differentiated and customary set of status duties'. In Gouldner's view, it is thus, I would infer, formative of society but prior to the state. More explicitly: Sahlins (1972) 168–71.

[10] See Leach (1954) 197–204, on the countercultural or revolutionary nature of the republican (*gumlao*) Burmese villagers, who, even according to their own corporate mythology, claimed to have rebelled against the hierarchical and exchange-oriented (the latter point noted by Leach in passing, but not emphasised) norms of general Kachin society. The obvious comparison here is with Athenian and Roman stories of the establishment of democratic or republican regimes following the expulsion, respectively, of the tyrannical Peisistratids and the monarchical Tarquinii. The Jews had no such myth (the story of the Exodus is hardly comparable) since the Babylonians had ended their monarchy for them. But they had stories opposing monarchy (e.g., 1 Sam 10.17–27) and laws restricting it (Deut 17. 14–20).

from its rejection of reciprocity-based loyalties and imagines that it is pursuing a 'higher' set of ideals. If, as I would argue, gift exchange has an inescapable tendency to be inegalitarian/competitive, the relationships created by it will slip inexorably into exploitation and injustice. The point of the second theory may thus be precisely to pursue equality and justice, and pure love of one's fellow, by rejecting reciprocity a priori. The not insignificant corollary of this is that the solidarity-based theory tends to construct the reciprocity-based theory as 'normal', and itself as revolutionary or countercultural. Adherents of solidarity-based systems, the Jews, for example, should have strong motivation to reject the trappings of institutionalised reciprocity.

Yet this expectation is not invariably met: this is because, notwithstanding the tension between them, I would argue that neither theory is entirely self-sufficient: they need each other. This implies that in their real-life manifestations, and even in their most highly elaborated theoretical expositions, the two positions are not always far apart.[11] The reciprocity-based theory needs the solidarity-based theory since reciprocity works best for small, localised, 'face-to-face' societies; it is unclear why, if it is to be based on reciprocity alone, anything larger than the local network should cohere. Or, to put it differently, a complex society which possesses no ideological foundation beyond gratitude and loyalty to benefactors and kinspeople will in short order dissolve into its segments.

Indeed, solidarity based on ideals rather than exchange was an important feature even of states which embraced reciprocity as a fundamental value. For example, though benefaction and gratitude were crucial components of the Roman system, the success of the Roman state lay precisely in its ability to organise this sense of personal loyalty pyramidally – to ideologise it: modest subjects were expected to feel gratitude to benefactors (governors, senators, emperors) who had given them nothing, whom they had never even seen. And this success was bolstered by a flow of propaganda from the centre that presented the Roman state and the emperor as embodiments of ethical and cultural values. A state which allowed reciprocity free rein could never survive.

Like the reciprocity-based theory, the solidarity-based theory works best, in its purest form, in small groups. These can easily attain through

---

[11] Cf. Leach (1970) 197. In general, my argument here is structurally indebted to Leach's discussion (on pages 197–212) of the analytic antinomy between hierarchically organised (*gumsa*) and republican or egalitarian (*gumlao*) Kachin (Burmese hill-country people), and its tension with the practical tendency of the two systems to merge into each other.

self-selection a sense of solidarity derived from shared purpose, and an equitable distribution of resources, without needing to rely on relationships of personal dependency. In larger entities, the only way at least to partially enable a more or less reciprocity-free society might be by assuring that the need rarely arises for people to rely on the personal generosity of their neighbours.[12] This is the purpose of much pentateuchal legislation. All Israelites are required to support all their fellows by leaving behind parts of their harvest, by periodically handing over to the poor 10 per cent of their agricultural production, by the obligatory provision of interest-free loans to those who have become impoverished, and most radical of all, by the septennial cancellation of debts and manumission of debt-bondsmen and, twice a century, by the redistribution of landholding. The Bible's elaborate rules are meant to ensure that the charitable donation (and likewise the donations which are meant to form the livelihood of the priestly and levitical temple staff) never degenerates into the dependency-generating gift. The pauper (like the priest) is meant to feel no gratitude – at least not toward the donor. Rather, charity is a prime expression of Israelite corporate solidarity, of the obligation of all Israelites to love one another regardless of familial or other connection.

But here, too, there are problems. First, given the ostensible naturalness of *ethical* reciprocity – the sense that 'one good turn deserves another' – or at least the fact that even small, hyper-egalitarian societies have trouble eradicating it, there is an inexorable tendency for charitable donation to turn into gift. In other words, the donors might expect the poor to show gratitude, and the poor might comply, because 'common sense' tells them, or because they feel constrained, to do so. James Laidlaw's analysis of the priestly *dan* (a charitable gift closely comparable to the biblical *terumah* – 'heave offering' – given to priests) among the Jains is important for demonstrating how much work it takes to ensure that charitable donation retains its 'purity'.[13] Historically, among Jews and Christians, there has almost always been slippage between charity and gift. On the one hand, the sense persists in both communities that the best, purest, donation is one which cannot be reciprocated, or ideally is even anonymous. At the same time, Jewish and Christian charity adopted features of Greco-Roman

---

[12] See Sahlins (1972) 188–91, on the distinction between reciprocity and 'pooling', and for a fundamental account of the social and symbolic aspects of the latter. My discussion here is anticipated by Sahlins's account of the 'sociology of primitive exchange' (185–275).

[13] Laidlaw (2002) 45–66.

patronage and euergetism[14] at a very early date; since then (if not even before), Jewish communal life has never lacked reciprocal elements.[15]

A second problem with ideologies of non-reciprocal solidarity is that in large-scale societies the only way to impose truly effective, as opposed to mainly symbolic, non-reciprocal redistributive systems like charity is through the functioning of a powerful state, or something similar. The Pentateuch's redistributive laws may or may not have been sufficient in principle to reduce the roles of clans or patronage networks. But without a strong state administering the rules, that is, with the rules being practised on what amounted to a voluntary basis, reciprocity could certainly not be eliminated. Indeed, the Pentateuch itself makes allowances for institutions which it clearly opposes, like debt bondage, and it is not clear if the biblical legislators meant periodic redistribution of land as anything other than a utopian ideal.

I would argue that much extant post-biblical Jewish literary production is concerned with navigating the tension between the Torah's ideal of corporate solidarity, and the more generally diffused cultural validation of institutionalised reciprocity. This is demonstrably true of both Ben Sira and the Talmud, and their appropriation of the symposium, which may be said to embody this tension, bears significant traces of the texts' accommodative struggles.

In what way did the symposium embody the tension between solidarity and reciprocity? On the one hand, one might have supposed that the Jews would happily have adopted the symposium, with its focus on fellowship, and on what we may follow Sahlins in calling the egalitarian 'pooling' of cognitive or conversational resources, as an ideal symbolic expression of their ideology of corporate solidarity. We may therefore expect the Jews to have embraced especially the Greek-style public banquet, which celebrated the ideals of the *polis*.[16] Indeed, there is excellent evidence that feasting functioned in precisely this way, in sectarian communities like those responsible for the Dead Sea scrolls, or among the early Christians, or in certain local Jewish communities in the Roman imperial diaspora.[17] Though such meals, as Philo emphatically claimed,[18] often had a very different feeling from the symposium, the rabbis, at least, imagined private

---

[14] See Schwartz (2001).
[15] For an account of a Christian society that convincingly treats charitable donation under the rubric of gift exchange, while noting the ways in which it does not fit, see Davis (2000).
[16] See in general Schmitt-Pantel (1992).
[17] See Davies (1999); on the diaspora communities see White (1998) 185–9.
[18] *De vita contemplativa* 40–91. See p. 193 above.

ritual feasts, like the Passover *seder*, not to mention the standard banquet, as an amalgam of liturgical and unambiguously sympotic elements, not excluding drinking (which was in fact often obligatory), singing and recitations.[19]

On the other hand, the symposium in its more private, 'secular' form – by which I mean not that it lacked religious elements, but only that the meal was not primarily in explicit commemoration of a religious festival, or an accompaniment to sacrifice – *should have been* problematic for those with a strong commitment to the ideology of Judaism. This is because it was a celebration, a fundamental ritual enactment, of the reciprocal relationship: it was where family ties, friendship both domestic and foreign, and clientele, were dramatically performed. Such relationships, even familial ones, were in the best cases ignored or limited and in some cases even prohibited by the Torah, and so, while it is not hard to see how or why the rabbis might have incorporated sympotic elements in liturgical or quasi-sacrificial feasts like the Passover *seder*, the embrace of the secular symposium, with or without the addition of some specifically Jewish liturgical elements, is more surprising and so more revealing.

BEN SIRA

Ben Sira devoted two poems in his Wisdom to correct sympotic behaviour. The first warns against greedy behaviour and overeating, and acknowledges the importance of a good vomit in case the latter nevertheless occurs (34[31].12–22).[20] The second, longer, poem is more relevant to my concern (34[31].22–35[32].13):[21]

(34.22) Hear, son, and do not despise me, and in the end you will grasp my speech; Hear, son, and receive instruction; do not mock me and in the end you will find my words. (23) Lips will bless one generous with food, the testimony of his goodness is

[19] On the Passover *seder* and other liturgical meals see Bokser (1986), especially 50–66, on the *seder*'s relation to the symposium; cf. Brumberg-Kraus (1999) (by ritualisation Brumberg-Kraus means transformation into religious ritual). For the rabbinic amalgamation of sympotic and liturgical elements in non-festival feasts, see Tosefta Berakhot 4.8–10, 5.5–10. I have not seen an adequate modern treatment of this issue, except in the antiquarian compendium of Krauss (1912) 26–63; Noy (1998) is a derivative and uncritical listing of evidence.

[20] A practice mocked by Philo, *De vita contemplativa* 45. In a general way the extremely basic etiquette promoted by Ben Sira bears comparison with some of the texts, especially the earlier ones, analysed by Elias (1994) 47–135. Ancient Jewish etiquette – which is quite amply attested – has yet to receive adequate non-antiquarian attention.

[21] My translation is based on the Hebrew text of Segal (1953), corrected against and supplemented by Beentjes (1997b) 57–9; and the Greek text of Ziegler (1965). The best commentaries by far remain those of Segal and of Smend (1906).

reliable. (24) One stingy with food will cause wrath at the gate, the knowledge of his wickedness is reliable. (25) And likewise [? Omitted in Gk] in wine [*yayin*] do not play the hero, for new wine [*tirosh*, surely meaning simply wine] has caused many to stumble. (26) A smelting pot wrought by a smith, so is wine for the character of scoffers.[22] (27) For which man is wine life [*vel sim.*; difficult]? For the one who drinks it in proper measure. What is life without wine, which from the start was created for rejoicing? (28) Rejoicing of the heart and happiness of the soul[23] is sufficient wine drunk opportunely. (29) A headache, wormwood [=bitterness] and humiliation, is wine drunk in emulation and anger. (30) Much wine is a trap for the fool, a diminisher of strength and provider of injury. (31) At a drinking-bout do not rebuke your neighbour, and do not embarrass him in his rejoicing. An insulting thing do not say to him, and do not sadden him before men. (35.1) If they have appointed you leader [i.e. symposiarch], do not exalt yourself over them, [and do not recline as head of a party of rich men][24] rather, be like one of them: care for them and then recline. (2) Provide for their needs and then lie down, so that you rejoice in their honour, and in return for your refinement you will receive consideration [*vel sim.* Gk: garlands]. (3) Speak, Old Man, for it is your due; but limit your wise words and do not withhold song.[25] (4) In the place of wine do not pour out conversation, and without music, why pour out conversation? Do not wax wise in an untimely way.[26] (5) An ornament of carnelian on a golden fruit [?], so is the custom of song at the drinking-bout. (6) Settings of pure gold and a seal of emerald, is the sound of music with the sweetness of new wine. (7) Speak, Youth, if you must, if they ask you forcefully two or three times.[27] (8) Refrain from talking, be very sparing, and resemble one who knows and is silent simultaneously. (9) Do not rise up among the elders, and do not pursue great men excessively. (10) Lightning will flash before hail, charm will shine before the modest man. (11) At the time of the conclusion (of the party) do not tarry, but depart to your house [,at the time of the meal do not speak much, but speak if something comes to mind].[28] (12) Depart to your house and bring your desire (to eat) to an end, in fear of God and not in absence of all [? Gk: do not sin through arrogant speech]. (13) And for all these things bless your Maker, Who sates you through His generosity.

Let us begin with some contextualisation. Ben Sira wrote 'wisdom' in the Israelite vein. The preserved examples of Israelite wisdom tend to combine

---

[22] The text is difficult but the meaning appears straightforward: just as smelting exposes the impurities of metal, so wine exposes the faults of the wicked.

[23] Following the Greek over the incomprehensible Hebrew.

[24] Hebrew lacks the first three clauses of this verse, the first two of which are supplied from the Greek, the third, which seems to me more problematic, from the Syriac.

[25] I follow the Hebrew; the Greek for the second clause says nothing about limiting speech, but rather encourages the elder to speak *en akribei epistêmei*.

[26] While the Hebrew suggests that talk be limited at the symposium in favour of music, the Greek seems simply to advise remaining silent during the musical performance (*hopou akroama mê ekkheeis lalian kai akairos mê sophizou*) – in my opinion an intentional alteration; see below.

[27] So Hebrew; Gk: Speak, Youth, if you must, no more than twice if you are asked.

[28] Absent in Greek, clearly transferred from above.

practical advice and pious exhortation, offered in a strongly personified, sometimes explicitly fictional, authorial voice, and written in rhetorically heightened style, featuring the *parallelismus membrorum* characteristic of all Semitic poetry before late antiquity.[29] Though Ben Sira shares certain formal features with archaic Greek lyric, and a surprising amount of content with the Theognidea in particular, it has never been suggested, as far as I am aware, that his poems were composed for or set at the banquet or symposium, as opposed to the school.[30] Most wisdom texts express a well-defined world view, usually pessimistic, though situated along a spectrum ranging from the very mild wariness about the world expressed by the author of Proverbs, through the scepticism and *aporia* of Job, to the piercing nihilism of Ecclesiastes. Some biblical scholars regard wisdom literature as unusually 'universalistic', in that its Israelite concerns appear rather de-emphasised, and its 'wisdom' is often surprisingly neutral, religiously/culturally speaking. I would argue, by contrast, that all extant Israelite/Jewish wisdom texts in fact are profoundly engaged with the core philosophical problem generated by Israelite monotheism: how to make sense of an unjust world allegedly created by a powerful and benevolent divine individual – that is, the problem of evil. What distinguished the authors of the wisdom books from the prophets and priests who wrote the other biblical books is that they viewed this issue through conceptual lenses shaped by the speculations and observations of Egyptian, Mesopotamian and, later, Greek scribes and sages.

Ben Sira was a rather late representative of the high tradition of Israelite wisdom. But (*contra* A. di Lella)[31] he did not simply recapitulate the relatively eirenic theologies of Proverbs or Deuteronomy – eirenic in that they suppose that God reliably rewards the righteous and punishes the wicked and therefore that the world is governed by an orderly moral economy. Ben Sira had distinctive concerns. He professed untrammelled commitment to the Torah and its laws, and throughout his book identified Jewish piety and wisdom (thereby, surely self-consciously, 'one-upping' Proverbs, which had regarded 'fear of the Lord' as merely the beginning of wisdom). At the same time his sociology and anthropology were far darker than those of Proverbs, in fact quite close to Ecclesiastes. Ben Sira's world was not a tidy place.

---

[29] See Kugel (1981).
[30] On Ben Sira and Greek lyric, especially the Theognidea, see the balanced discussion of Sanders (1983) 29–38.
[31] di Lella (1966).

Unlike either of his great predecessors, Ben Sira devoted sustained attention to social relations. As already suggested, the Hebrew Bible had generally ignored or even rejected relationships of social dependency, because they tended to exploitativeness and injustice, and interfered with the unconditional sense of solidarity all Israelites were meant to feel toward one another. When it did describe such relationships – as in the David cycle in the book of Samuel – it is easy to show that it did so to condemn them. Ben Sira, though, did not condemn such relationships: he asserted their inevitability – which at times he celebrated and at other times lamented – and advised his readers/listeners how to cope. Here is where the darkness enters the picture because Ben Sira believed that people tended to wish to deceive and exploit one another, and one needed caution and competence – 'wisdom' – in order to survive. This notion fits poorly with Ben Sira's repeatedly expressed belief that wisdom is equivalent to Torah-based piety, but I would argue that his insistence, his constant juxtaposition of these two ill-matched ideological systems, is precisely the point of his book. Ben Sira was trying to make a case for 'judaising' friendship and patronage, for declaring reciprocity compatible with the (anti-reciprocal) Torah.[32]

There is much in the second poem about correct sympotic behaviour that is familiar from the general tendency of Ben Sira's advice about social relations: the address to the apparently inexperienced youth who is instructed on how to behave toward/manipulate his elders and social superiors; the constant harping on the need for caution and the corollary sense that navigation through the shoals of social interaction in a hierarchical and hostile world is mortally dangerous; the counsel of moderation combined with what some may not wholly accurately regard as the non-biblical or non-Jewish celebration of material abundance; the consequent praise of generosity; and the exhortation to piety/fear of the Lord that incongruously concludes the poem. Ben Sira is, as usual, offering advice on how to avoid being crushed, on how to avoid being dominated, or at any rate how to cope safely with the inevitability of domination in an inegalitarian social situation: he advises caution and solicitousness – avoid greed and drunkenness, tend to your neighbours' needs, defer to your superiors and elders, enjoy the wine and music, and leave when your time is up. The *mishteh ha-yayin* (literally, wine-drinking (party); in the Greek (34.31): *sumposion oinou*) described is in almost all ways indistinguishable from a standard Greek symposium: it is apparently an all-male affair, it emphasises alcohol over

---

[32] For this argument see Schwartz (2005) 3–35.

food, the participants drink while reclining on couches, Ben Sira assumes that the drinking will be accompanied by sophisticated conversation and music or singing.[33]

But Ben Sira rejected the standard literary image of the symposium as a setting where the social solidarity of the democratic citizen body, or the egalitarian amity of the aristocratic *hetaireia*, is rehearsed. (He also says nothing about the sex or sexual play with boys and *hetairai* allegedly typical of at least the archaic and possibly the later symposium, though youths were in attendance, or about the domestication of these practices in the form of the erotic dialogue characteristic of the *logos sympotikos* starting in the classical period).[34] Instead, the symposium simply replicates the inequality of general social life in concentrated form, with the same potentially crushing results. Shorn of its aspirational elements, of its status as microcosmic distillation of democratic (or indeed oligarchic) ideals, Ben Sira's symposium is more Petronian than Platonic or Plutarchan:– a way to display – but also enjoy – wealth, perform one's dominance over clients;[35] one could say that it is rather a microcosmic distillation of the theodicy of good fortune, in which wealth and social clout are, if successfully achieved, regarded as a demonstration of wisdom and so by definition (in Ben Sira's terms) a gift of God. Likewise, Ben Sira advocates not conversational free exchange, but extreme caution and reticence. In fact, he advocates an ideal symposium in which people hardly converse at all but only sing or listen to music. Not insignificantly this theme is much more prominent in the Hebrew than in the Greek version of the book. One could say that from the Greek perspective, Ben Sira's *mishteh ha-yayin*, like the Roman *convivium*, was recognisably sympotic, but that, a part-barbarian who lived on the peripheries of the Hellenic world, he nevertheless got it slightly wrong; the Romans did, too, and in similar ways.[36]

---

[33] For the characteristics of the Greek symposium, see Murray (1990b) 3–13, especially 6–7, and König in this volume.

[34] See Murray (1983); Bremmer (1990); and Pellizer (1990) 177–84.

[35] Cf. Bradley (1998) 36–55. See also Lucian's account of the social perils of a grand Roman *convivium* for a poor though well-born young Greek: *De mercede conductis potentium familiaribus* 14–17.

[36] Some Roman aristocrats expected humble symposiasts to keep quiet; in D'Arms's account, the elite metropolitan Roman *convivium* featured an exquisite tension between an ideology of egalitarian conversational freedom and openness derived from Greek tradition and a peculiarly Roman set of anxieties about rank, social dependency, hierarchy; this bears comparison with the representation of the symposium in both Ben Sira and rabbinic texts: D'Arms (1990) 308–20. Philo's Therapeutae are also silent at their feasts, as they listen to their *proedros* deliver a discourse on the sacred scriptures, and then recite a hymn (*De vita contemplativa* 75–80).

  Greeks thinking the Romans were getting the symposium wrong: Cicero, *Verr.* 2.1.26.66, with Dunbabin (1998) 81–101.

There are several possible ways of understanding Ben Sira's promotion of sympotic silence. M. Z. Segal noted that the Babylonian Talmud also advocated silence during meals (Ta'anit 5b), or at least, in some passages, expressed admiration for the Persians who kept largely silent at feasts, apparently implying that silence at meals was somehow a specifically Jewish/'oriental' practice (see especially B. Berakhot 46b). But the Talmudic parallels to Ben Sira seem on closer examination to be less meaningful:[37] the Babylonian Talmud is filled with stories of mealtime conversations and arguments, which it reports without a hint of disapproval. It also quotes the view of one rabbi that it is unwise to talk while eating (not at a feast in general) for medical reasons: fear of choking. The Babylonian rabbis were acquainted with the Zoroastrian practice of refraining from conversation during feasts, especially in vernacular Middle Persian, because meals were sacred rites which began and ended with prayers in Avestan, and the intrusion of secular conversation was regarded as polluting; they were also familiar with the practice of whispering through closed lips, called *mahwag*, used to facilitate unavoidable communication ('pass the salt') during meals and other religious rituals. These practices resonated for the rabbis because they too believed that even secular meals had ritual or sacral elements, they too flanked their meals with prayers in a sacred language, and they shared the common Near Eastern view that rituals should be performed in silence. But they were ambivalent about the Zoroastrian practice, in some passages recommending its emulation and in others rejecting it. In all cases, the concerns of the Babylonian rabbis seem very remote from those of Ben Sira – not surprisingly since, among other things, Ben Sira lived probably some seven centuries before the redaction of the Babylonian Talmud, and in a very different sort of cultural environment. Remarkably, though the rabbis knew Ben Sira and frequently quoted his Wisdom, those rabbis who advised silence did not quote him for support.

Related to Segal's suggestion is the hypothesis that Ben Sira advocated avoiding speech at symposia precisely because the symposium he described was nearly identical to the Greek style of symposium. In this case, he was suggesting that the Jews might appropriately enjoy a good drinking bout – a product of divine bounty after all – but they should avoid the practice which most strongly marked the symposium as Greek – *parrhêsia*. I would not dismiss this view; if nothing else the Greek translator's systematic de-emphasis

---

[37] I am indebted to Geoffrey Herman for his advice on Babylonian rabbinic and Zoroastrian matters. What follows relies on his PhD dissertation (Herman 2005) 241–8, supplemented by email notes and conversation. Ben Sira's resemblance to the Babylonian Talmud was brought to my attention by Richard Kalmin.

of his 'grandfather's' exhortation to silence shows that some Jews in Ben Sira's environment were conscious of the oddity of his advice. That Ben Sira in general preferred reticence to *parrhêsia* (see below) does not mean that his rejection of speech at the symposium was not pointed, culturally speaking, even if Ben Sira never said so explicitly.[38]

Ben Sira's approach to the symposium is, as suggested above, consistent with his approach to social relations in general. His view of the human world was extremely pessimistic, but (and in this way he differs from the even darker Hellenistic-era Jewish sage who wrote the biblical book of Ecclesiastes) not so pessimistic that people are unable to master it. The wise can, and the wise are those who have understood how the fundamental rules of human interaction operate, who have fully come to understand the importance of reciprocity and domination in society. But such mastery is difficult: friends betray, patrons oppress and exploit, clients and slaves plot and deceive. Every interaction contains the potential for life-threatening disaster.

Speech plays an extremely potent role in Ben Sira's social doctrine, repeatedly emphasised.[39] Ben Sira was, to be sure, aware of the fundamental role of the gift in establishing and maintaining enduring relationships of social dependency, but saw speech as playing at least as important a role.[40] One of the chief characteristics of friendship for Ben Sira – though not of course for Ben Sira alone – is that it entails the exchange and preservation of information. No act destroys friendship as decisively as betrayal of confidences.[41] Speech reveals wisdom and conveys it to others (4.23–4; 8.8–9), but it is also highly dangerous, in that it can subvert the normal functioning of systems of exchange (5.13): the word is more powerful than the gift, as Ben Sira says in another passage (18.16). Speech can bring honour, but also disgrace (5.14). This is the main reason why Ben Sira regarded speech at the symposium, one of the settings in which the components of the social relationship are displayed with particular prominence, as peculiarly fraught:

---

[38] There is a large bibliography on Ben Sira and 'hellenism', some of which is rather uncritically surveyed in Reiterer (1997) 40–7. Ben Sira never mentioned the Greeks or their culture but the fact that he wrote very shortly before the Maccabean Revolt, when Judaeans are thought to have been very concerned with the problem, has made it attractive to read much of his wisdom as implicitly addressing it. The symposium is merely a specific case of the general hermeneutical problem, which I do not know how to resolve. One of the most sensible recent treatments is Collins (1997) 23–111.

[39] According to di Lella (1996) 33–48, Ben Sira has more to say about speech than any (other) biblical book. The fullest account of the issue is in Okoye (1995).

[40] See 3.17; 18.15–18; 20.13–16. See Schwartz (2005) 12–18.

[41] 22.19–26; 27.16–21; 37.1–6, with comments of Corley (2002) ad locc.

people in vulnerable positions, like young sages-to-be, had to be especially careful not to speak, and even for elders the symposium was a sufficiently sensitive situation that music was considered a better, safer, more enjoyable pastime than conversation. The result was that Ben Sira's symposium was not a celebration of wisdom, cultivation, amity or fellowship, but mainly of abundance. Otherwise it was, like most other intensely social situations, an ordeal that the wise knew how to endure and even enjoy, but only provided that the inevitable and unending human zeal for dominance was repressed through the maintenance of silence. That Ben Sira's symposium therefore would, if enacted, have had a different feel and effect from a Platonic, Xenophontic or indeed Plutarchan or Athenaean symposium may have been one of its creator's intentions, or it may have been an unintended consequence of the grimness of Ben Sira's anthropology and sociology.

THE TALMUDIC SYMPOSIUM

The meal is one of the central concerns of the Talmud. The first of the six orders of the Mishnah (the earliest rabbinic text – a topically arranged legal handbook – published around 200 CE, which serves as the basis for both the Palestinian (*c.* 380 CE) and Babylonian (500–650 CE) Talmuds) largely consists of laws about growing food, the ritual legal obligations associated with it, its susceptibility to impurity, its donation to priests, levites, the poor and the (long ruined) temple of Jerusalem. The fifth order concerns sacrificial meat but also contains a tractate which provides the exceedingly detailed and complicated laws (paradoxically so in light of the Pentateuch's neglect of the matter) on the slaughter of non-sacrificial animals. The second order concerns festivals and so contains the laws of the special festal sacrifices, as well as laws – by 200 CE far more relevant – concerning the preparation and consumption of non-sacrificial food on festivals, including the order and special rituals of Sabbath and holiday feasts.

The Mishnah has much to say about the ritual and liturgical aspects of commensality, but it contains little that is not strictly legal (in the Jewish sense), and so neglects the social aspects of the feast. But the later rabbinic collections all treat the issue abundantly, and in their account, the Jewish feast is even more obviously a Greco-Roman artefact than in Ben Sira's. For example, no Palestinian, as opposed to Babylonian, rabbinic compilation follows Ben Sira in advocating silence at symposia, or in emphasising the value of music or singing. If anything, the rabbis, for whom all feasts had a faintly sacrificial character, thought that frivolity, drunkenness and celebration were inappropriate as accompaniments to non-festival banquets, all the more so since the Jerusalem temple had been destroyed, but even so, they made exceptions, for example for wedding and holiday feasts.[42]

Indeed, on the whole, the symposium/convivium seems largely to have been naturalised by the rabbis. The case most frequently adduced probably also constitutes the least compelling demonstration of this proposition: the rabbinic Passover feast following the destruction of the Jerusalem temple no longer involved the consumption of the paschal lamb in or near the temple-precinct, but was a home-based feast featuring highly elaborate ritual consumption of food and wine, embedded in the recitation of a narrative, all performed while reclining. This feast (called *seder*, literally 'order') indubitably draws on the forms of the symposium or convivium; it has been thought to do so quite self-consciously, as if the point of the meal was to imitate the symposium.[43] But the alternative possibility is at least as likely: the rabbinic *seder* features sympotic elements because for the rabbis such elements were simply the normal way of conducting a festive meal: what is in this case distinctive about the *seder* is not its sympotic form but rather the distinctively Jewish content of the *logos sympotikos*, exegesis of the story of the Exodus.[44]

Be this as it may, the rabbinic adoption of the sympotic style went far beyond the ritual of the *seder*. The following passage from the Tosefta (Berakhot 5.5ff.) – a legal text compiled in Palestine probably in the middle or later third century CE – may serve to illustrate the point:

What is the order of reclining? When there are two couches, the leader reclines at the head of the first, the one second to him below him (etc.). When there are three couches, the leader reclines at the head of the middle one, the one second to him reclines above him and the third below him, and so on. (6) What is the order of handwashing? If there are up to five guests they begin with the greatest, five or more, with the least. What is the order of the mixing of the cups? During the meal, they begin with the greatest, after the meal they begin with the leader of the blessing.[45] If he [the host] wished to show honour to his master [i.e. teacher] or to one greater than he [by serving him first even after the meal], he is permitted to do so…

There is nothing, or almost nothing, in this passage which would not have been familiar to the elder Pliny, Plutarch or Athenaeus, except that standard procedure is presented as law, rather than as advice or instruction

---

[42] Krauss (1912) 2.39–42; 3.35–40. Philo felt similarly even before the Destruction.
[43] See Stein (1957).   [44] This is the view of Bokser (1986) 50–66.
[45] This manifestly reflects Roman practice according to which drinking both accompanied the meal and might continue after its conclusion, as opposed to Greek practice, which largely separated the two. See Roller (2006) 181–8.

or description. This fact is sufficiently odd – since these 'laws' have no scriptural source, or any other Jewish legal justification; they are not anticipated in the Mishnah or provided with any legal elaboration in the Talmuds – that some modern commentators have denied the prescriptive character of the passage, with a revealing adamance, arguing that it is descriptive/nostalgic.[46] Admittedly, rabbinic texts of the sixth century fantasised/speculated about the 'refined' (that is, Romanising) dining habits of the grandees of first-century Jerusalem, described in terms similar to the Tosefta's here, but for the authors/editors of these late texts the classical-style convivium may have been a thing of the past, especially for middling householders, as the rabbis mostly were; it had probably begun its retreat to the highest reaches of the aristocracy.[47] There is no reason to think that the much earlier rabbis of the Tosefta did not mean precisely what they said: any meal with more than two couches' worth of people present had to be conducted as a proper convivium, as a matter of Jewish law.

Indeed, one enigmatic Talmudic text seems to say that the practices of conviviality were so habitual among the rabbis' main adherents and supporters, the pious Jewish landowners of Palestine, that they acquired a quasi-legal force and came to trump the laws pertaining to the ritual purity of foodstuffs and the obligation to offer the priestly food donations even in the absence of a temple and a functioning priesthood. Let me explain: the Mishnah (Demai 2.2) had required anyone who wished to be a *ne'eman* (literally trustworthy, probably meaning someone who was determined to follow rabbinic laws without necessarily being a rabbi himself) to offer the priestly tithes from his agricultural production, and not to eat in the house of any Jew who did not follow this practice (called by the rabbis the *'am ha'aretz* – 'people of the land' (cf. Ezra 9.1), i.e. Jews who did not follow the rabbinic laws of ritual purity and priestly gifts). Yet both the Tosefta and the Palestinian Talmud (Demai 2.2, 22d) claim that 'landowners [who were *ne'emanim*] did not refrain from being entertained by their fellow [*'am ha'aretz*] landowners, while continuing to offer tithes from their own produce'.[48]

---

[46] Saul Lieberman, the most important commentator on the Tosefta, wrote (my translation): 'This passage describes the customary conduct of feasts in antiquity among the Jewish elites. It includes several details from which no legal conclusions should be drawn, because they originate in the local customs, and not in Jewish law. Generally, the order of the feast conforms with Roman and late Greek practice; there is no *law* of the feast here.' Lieberman (1955) 62.

[47] See *Midrash Ekhah Rabbah*, ed. S. Buber, pp. 141–3, and the rather different version of the same text preserved in a fragmentary Genizah manuscript of perhaps the tenth century, in Rabinovitz (1979) 151–4. On the retreat of the convivium, see Dunbabin (2003) 175–202.

[48] Lieberman (1955) 211, attempts to explain this away, but the texts seem quite unambiguous.

For the purposes of social and cultural analysis laws are a resource of real though limited value. Notwithstanding the passage from the Tosefta cited above, rabbinic laws generally were based however remotely on scriptural exegesis, and were elaborated through application of a set of formal principles. It is possible to speculate – sometimes convincingly or interestingly – about the social and cultural assumptions which contributed to the formation of rabbinic laws, but on the whole not every aspect of quotidian social and cultural praxis fell to the province of rabbinic legislation. If we wish to tease out the social and cultural tensions which were of particular concern to the rabbis, we must supplement analysis of law with analysis of narrative.

We may adopt the following generalisation: the later the rabbinic text, the more narrative it contains (why this should be true we need not consider here). Thus the Mishnah (*c.* 200 CE) contains almost none, the Tosefta (*c.* 250) contains little; it has been estimated that one-sixth of the Palestinian Talmud (*c.* 380) consists of narrative, and one-third of the Babylonian Talmud (*c.* 600). A similar pattern obtains in the *midrash* (exegetical/homiletical) collections: the earliest ones are rigorously exegetical, and the later ones (starting in the sixth and seventh centuries) tend to treat biblical verses as pegs on which to hang stories which had manifestly been formulated originally for non-exegetical purposes. In the following section I will discuss stories from the Palestinian Talmud, mainly because it provides the largest block of material whose provenance is culturally still markedly High and Later Roman Imperial. In many cases these stories in the Palestinian Talmud are pressed into practical use, either as legal precedents, or to support a piece of (non-legal) biblical exegesis. In the Palestinian Talmud, whose compilers – unlike those of the Babylonian Talmud – did not always explain why they arranged pericopae as they did, and why they incorporated the sources they did, stories are sometimes told for reasons which are not obvious; but even where their formal function is easily determined, it can often be shown that, as in the *midrash* collections, the stories were formulated and circulated independently of the literary context in which they are preserved.

TWO SYMPOTIC STORIES
IN THE PALESTINIAN TALMUD

For the rabbis as for Ben Sira the function of the secular feast was far less to express symbolically feelings of solidarity and amity than to perform social dependency in a ritualised way. Like Ben Sira, the rabbis were concerned with social hierarchy. There is a subtle difference, though: the rabbis were far more interested in honour, precedence and deference. One senses that for the rabbis, the social rules of the symposium were much more clearly defined: for Ben Sira they were implicit in the symposium as in any highly concentrated social situation, while for the rabbis they have been reified. This is because unlike Ben Sira, the rabbis were manifestly telling stories not about the classical (or relatively poorly attested early Hellenistic) symposium, but about the Romanised convivium, in which honour and precedence competed as explicit ideals with amity and free speech. At least some rabbinic stories are interested in exploring the subversion or manipulation of these rules, and its impact on the honour of the participants. Many rabbinic stories actually use the setting of the convivium to criticise the value of honour altogether, and to overturn ostensibly natural social hierarchies. The following brief but complex story illustrates the point:[49]

The tutor of the son of Rabbi Hoshayya Rabba was a blind man,[50] and he was accustomed to dine with his master daily. One time Rabbi Hoshayya had guests and did not ask the tutor to eat with him. That evening Rabbi Hoshayya went to the tutor and said, 'Let my lord not be angry at me; I had guests and did not wish to injure my lord's honour. For this reason I did not dine with you today.' The tutor responded, 'You have apologised to the one who is seen but does not see; may the One Who sees but is not seen accept your apology.' Rabbi Hoshayya asked, 'Where did you learn this expression?' The tutor responded, 'From Rabbi Eliezer ben Jacob, for once upon a time a blind man came to Rabbi Eliezer ben Jacob's village, and the rabbi sat below the man (on the couch at dinner), so that the guests said, 'if he were not a great man Rabbi Eliezer ben Jacob would not have sat below him', and so they provided for the blind man an honourable maintenance. The blind man said to them, 'Why have you done this for me?' They responded, 'Rabbi Eliezer ben Jacob sat below you.' And so the man offered the following prayer on the rabbi's behalf: 'You have performed a deed of mercy for one who is seen but does not see; may the One Who sees but is not seen perform a deed of mercy for you!''

This is a story which clearly juxtaposes and contrasts the two value systems discussed earlier in this paper: Rabbi Hoshayya Rabba seems at first to act as if he thinks that Torah is the only real value, that it overcomes the normative rules of precedence and honour, and so he happily dines daily with the blind man who teaches his son Torah. But this turns out to be true only when the rabbi is dining in private. When he has guests, the blind tutor

---

[49] The story appears in the Palestinian Talmud in two slightly different versions, one in Peah 8.9, 21b, the other in Sheqalim 5.5, 49b. I follow the former here. The differences are inconsequential.
[50] *Sagya nehora*, literally 'filled with light', a familiar euphemism for blindness in rabbinic Aramaic.

reverts to his servile or subordinate status: he is not invited. The rabbi then tries to appease the tutor with words which crudely (so I believe we are meant to read it) invert the correct rank of the protagonists. Hence the rabbi addresses the tutor repeatedly as 'my lord' and insists that by not inviting him he was preserving rather than wounding his honour. The tutor's response I take as a clever variant of 'go to hell'; it can also be read as an implicit critique of the view of Ben Sira that words can subvert the social impact of material exchange. Not only is Rabbi Hoshayya's declaration that the tutor outranks him, and is honourable, appearances to the contrary, sternly rejected, but the tutor takes the opportunity to extend the reproach by telling the rabbi a story which illustrates true generosity.

The story's setting, the vulnerability of the tutor to insult – exacerbated or indeed generated by the fact that he is not usually treated like a slave, the very ambiguity of his position in the story, in broad terms is reminiscent of the scene in Lucian's essay, *De mercede conductis potentium familiaribus*, mentioned above; there too, a hired (non-servile) tutor is warned about the social complexities of his position in a great house. In both cases, banquets are regarded as occasions when social unease is particularly heightened. Both cases reflect the 'status dissonance' of figures like tutors – servile even if not actually slaves, but by definition well-educated, possibly more so than their employers, and so bearing at least one diagnostic marker of social distinction. Both cases also reflect the importance of the convivium as an arena for social competition, not only in the metropolitan centre of the Roman Empire, but among the grandees – even the relatively modest ones, like the rabbis – of its eastern peripheries.[51]

If Rabbi Hoshayya pretends to consider the anti-reciprocal values of the Torah supreme but in reality values honour more, Rabbi Eliezer ben Jacob engages in the inverse dissimulation. He pretends to value the rules of hierarchy and precedence – this is why his guests interpret his seating plan as they do: the rabbi's decision to sit below the blind guest would not have been meaningful if he were not thought normally to respect social convention. In fact, though, Rabbi Eliezer only conforms with conventions, exploiting them in order to accomplish his true goal, which is the bestowal of a favour on a needy man in a way actually meant to preclude reciprocation. He tricks his friends into providing benefits for the blind wanderer, rather than offering a gift himself, hoping in this way to avoid embroiling the man in a relationship of social dependency with an individual patron. So Rabbi Eliezer plays along with socially competitive conviviality, but truly

[51] See Dunbabin (2003) 68–71.

embraces the values of the Torah. The blind man reciprocates anyway, with a prayer to God to bestow benefits on Rabbi Eliezer. The words of his prayer, used to express gratitude to a righteous benefactor, the blind tutor of Rabbi Hoshayya uses to shame his false benefactor.

I conclude with a second story which uses the setting of the convivium to dramatise the conflict between reciprocity/social hierarchy and *mitzvah*, while recapitulating the message that rabbis were willing to exploit the former to achieve the latter.

Teni:[52] Three hundred nazirites came up to Jerusalem in the days of Shimon ben Shetah [early first century BCE], one hundred and fifty found (with Shimon's help) a legal way of being released from their naziriteship without having to offer the required sacrifices, and one hundred and fifty did not. Shimon went to King Yannai [a historical figure who ruled Palestine 103–76 BCE] and said to him, 'There are three hundred nazirites who need nine hundred sacrifices. You pay for half of them from your money, I'll pay for half from mine.' So the king sent him four hundred and fifty sacrificial victims. An evil [though true!] rumour reached the king that Shimon had not paid for any sacrifices, and King Yannai heard this and was enraged. When Shimon learned of this he fled. Some days later some dignitaries from the kingdom of Persia [sic][53] visited and said to the king, 'We remember that there used to be a certain old man here who said before us words of wisdom. Let him teach us something; please send for him.' The king sent, gave Shimon his word [that he would not harm him][54] and had him brought. When Shimon arrived, he sat between the king and the queen.[55] The king asked him, 'Why did you deceive me?' He responded, 'I did not deceive you – you gave from your money, I gave from my Torah, as it is written, "for in the shadow of wisdom, in the shadow of silver" [Eccl 7.12]'.[56] The king said, 'In that case why did you flee?' He said, 'I heard that my lord was angry at me, and I fulfilled the verse, "hide for a brief moment until anger passes" [Is 26.20]'. And he applied to himself [or, the king

---

[52] Nazirites have taken a vow to refrain from drinking wine, cutting their hair or coming into contact with a corpse, usually for a limited period. The conclusion of a period of naziriteship is marked by the offering of three animals as sacrifices (Numbers 6.1–21). This was of course a prohibitive expense for most people so the charitable practice – reflected in this much later story – developed of providing nazirites with victims, or the money to pay for them. The word *teni* in the Palestinian Talmud normally marks what follows it as tannaitic – that is, formulated in the earliest period of rabbinic activity, before about 200 CE. However, if there is anything here tannaitic at all it is limited to the first sentence, which is in Hebrew. The point of the *baraita* would then be the desirability of finding legal ways to extricate nazirites from their vows – in addition to the fact that this is the functional equivalent of helping nazirites pay for their sacrifices, rabbinic ambivalence/hostility toward vows of all sorts is an important theme of several tractates. The continuation is in Aramaic.

[53] A slight anachronism: Parthians, not Persians, ruled in the days of Alexander Yannai.

[54] For this sense of the idiom *yahab leh milah*, see Sokoloff (2002), sub v. *yhb*, #6.

[55] The queen's presence marks the feast as specifically Roman in style (respectable women did not normally attend Greek symposia), anachronistically, since Yannai's reign predated the arrival of the Romans in Palestine.

[56] A notoriously difficult, probably corrupt verse, here taken simply to equate wisdom and money.

applied to him] the verse, 'And the advantage of the knowledge of wisdom will give life to its possessor' [Eccl 7.12]. And the king said to him, 'Why did you seat yourself between the king and the queen?' He responded, 'In the book of Ben Sira it is written, "Esteem her (wisdom) and she will exalt you, and cause you to sit among the mighty" [Ben Sira 11.1]'.[57] The king said, 'Take a cup and make the blessing.' They gave Shimon the cup and he said, 'Let us bless God for the food that Yannai and his friends have eaten![58] Or should I rather say, "Let us bless God for the food we did not eat"?' So the king commanded food to be brought for Shimon, he ate and said, 'Let us bless God for the food we have eaten.' (Y Nazir 5.4, 54b (=Y Berakhot 7.2, 11d))

This story, too, thematises a conflict of values, though in a more complex way than the previous one: Shimon represents the values of Torah, of the pure, unreciprocated gift, and the king implicitly embodies the 'Mediterranean' values of honour and reciprocity. This is because Shimon bestows a favour on the nazirites – using legal ingenuity to free them from the obligation to offer sacrifices – which almost by definition resists reciprocation; and for the remainder, he benefits them by convincing the king to offer them gifts: like Rabbi Eliezer ben Jacob in the previous story, he thus fulfils the values of the Torah by manipulating others who do not share those values, and so maintains the 'purity' of his gift, while also performing the *mitzvah* (scripturally prescribed obligation) of supporting the poor. The nazirites he could not free from their vows will be inclined to reciprocate the king, not Shimon. For his part, the king seems happy enough to offer benefits to the nazirites, but does not understand the nature of Shimon's benefaction, and so feels cheated by him. The king does not know what the Torah wants, only what Marcel Mauss wants.

The James Scott-like quality of the story, with Shimon playing the role of the conformist, but in reality resistant, dominand, is accentuated in the second half of the narrative, which also continues the theme already encountered of the social ambiguity of the sage. The king does not regard Shimon as his equal, and when he summons him back to his court it is to serve as the dinner entertainment for his guests. Shimon's job is, and apparently has been, to say 'wise things' at state dinners. He does not fail to do so when he returns to Yannai's court. But the wise things all turn out to be paradoxical actions which serve the dual function of provoking witty exegeses of biblical verses, and of humiliating the king. In terms of the story I believe Yannai

---

[57] On the text here see Labendz (2006) 371–3. Oddly, the first hemistich is not from Ben Sira, but from Proverbs 4.8.

[58] Y Berakhot adds here: 'The king said to him, "Must you be so difficult?"' (*amar leh, 'ad kedon beqashiutak)'.

deserves humiliation for two reasons: the explicit reason for his culminating humiliation (Shimon's blessings over the wine) is his failure to feed Shimon – in sum, his failure as a host, but also his failure to recognise Shimon as a proper guest, as opposed to a member of the staff. Under the surface, the point clearly seems to be that the king misprises the value system that Shimon represents: for him a sage, an expert in Torah, is not a peer, but merely a kind of entertainer, useful because he keeps the real guests entertained. Shimon by contrast constantly subverts the proceedings, mocking the king, belittling his generosity, and the rituals of the banquet, as a way of insisting, I would argue, on his true honorableness, as a representative of the Torah. Shimon is thus proposing an alternative system, in which honour is still the paramount attainment, but in which it is achieved not through social dominance, but through Torah.

CONCLUSION

Advice and stories about symposia and convivia, and their attendant rituals, were densely packed conveyers of social ideology. Jewish writers tended not to present them as generators of egalitarian amity. Instead, they used them – because they were scenes of intense but regulated social interchange – to explore the pervasive and formative tensions between the two competing value systems in which they lived, the one based on unconditional solidarity, the other on institutionalised reciprocity. Both Ben Sira and the rabbis saw the need to accommodate to both systems but they went about this project somewhat differently. Ben Sira idealised the practical wit needed to cope with a hierarchical social system and identified it with Jewish piety. In the case of the symposium he counselled caution and self-control: no compartmentalised openness of speech, but extreme reticence, even silence. The rabbis in their narratives counselled conformity and subversion but in their laws appeared to have internalised the values of honour, hierarchy and deference, though on closer examination they turn out not to mean by this to enable their audience to participate in the Roman system. Rather, they imagine an alternative social system which structurally resembles the Roman one, but where the currency whose exchange generates and sustains the system is not wealth and social clout, but Torah. So, both Ben Sira and the rabbis believed that honour inhered in Torah-based piety, but the rabbis saw themselves as outsiders in the larger social world and saw Torah-based honour as directly competitive with standard honour, which they wished to see subverted. Ben Sira was more integrationist, seeing Torah-based honour and social honour as generally (though not always) mutually confirmatory.

What about the cultural implications of the symposium? This seems to me more speculative, since neither Ben Sira nor the rabbis tended to be explicit about their attitudes to the Greeks and their cultural practices. (The rabbis were very explicitly hostile to Roman rule, but there were elements of Roman culture which they embraced, and about the rest were only rarely polemical even in their stories, let alone their laws). The banquet was an element of the ambient culture that the Jews, including highly traditionalistic figures like both Ben Sira and the rabbis, accepted, though not without qualifications. It is at least possible that some of these are due to anxiety about the status of a cultural practice so strongly marked as Greek (or Greco-Roman). The argument could be made that in the story of Rabbi Hoshayya Rabba and the blind tutor, the convivium serves as a kind of synecdoche for the Roman system as a whole – but the rabbis do not reject it for this reason, but regard it as a practice to be exploited for holier ends: reciprocal exchange can be diverted and turned into proper charity.

Dialectic and divination in the Talmud

Daniel Boyarin

It is a key feature of the Babylonian Talmud that its dialectic seems most often to be there for its own sake, that even the attempt to achieve truth through logical procedure has been abandoned (or transcended) in favour of the pure spiritual activity of the discussion itself.[1] Moreover, as has been frequently noted, anything that would suggest the arrival at a conclusion in the Babylonian Talmud is most often refuted and rejected and the dialectics almost always end up unresolved, while in the Palestinian Talmud such resolution is the order of the day. I would place the two Talmuds clearly in diachronic relation. The Palestinian Talmud was redacted, on all accounts, in the third quarter of the fourth century or so, the Babylonian Talmud at least two centuries later. It makes sense, at least heuristically, to regard the Palestinian Talmud as something like what the Babylonian Talmud looked like in the fourth century as well and to isolate the work of the *stammaim* through this comparison.[2] I mean to carry out comparative work of this sort elsewhere, especially insofar as it is crucial for understanding the place of dialogue in the Talmud, the main focus of the project as a whole. For the

I would like to thank Richard Kalmin and Virginia Burrus for reading and generously commenting on a draft of this paper. While the paper began its life at a conference in honour of the contribution of Prof. Froma Zeitlin to Jewish studies (and to whom it is dedicated), the paper benefited highly as well from the comments of the respondents and participants at the conference in Cambridge of which this volume is a souvenir. I would like, therefore, especially to thank Simon Goldhill for making it possible and for contributing his own intellectual spirit, elan and graciousness. This article is doomed to form a chapter (or perhaps two, or perhaps parts of two, or to have its disjecta membra used in several chapters) of my book in progress: *Socrates and the Fat Rabbis*.

[1] This characteristic has been known historically on more than one occasion to deteriorate into a logic-chopping empty even of spiritual passion and devotion and to become the virtual equivalent of a chess match. This is less often so, however, than enlightened enemies of the Talmud would have us believe.

[2] See too Halivni (2005) 108 on the Palestinian Talmud as precursor to the Babylonian in the work of dialectic. Halivni there seems to regard the change as largely a quantitative one ('light and simple dialectic' vs. that of the Bavli), whereas I detect here a major epistemological shift correspondent with other epistemological shifts within rabbinic Judaism and in the circumambient intellectual world as well.

meantime, the work of Christine Hayes is very instructive in helping us to understand this dissimilarity between the Talmuds.

Hayes articulates the distinction between two modes of understanding the differences between the Talmuds as an 'external' approach which sees these differences as being the product of 'cultural, regional, historical factors', versus an 'internal' approach that sees the differences as 'textual, exegetical/ hermeneutical, dialectical, redactorial', but also then as 'the natural evolution of a complex and fertile core tradition'. I am exploring here a third option, one that deconstructs the very opposition between 'external' and 'internal' approaches, namely positing that precisely the textual, exegetical/ hermeneutical, dialectical, redactorial factors are themselves bound up with complex historical, cultural interactions between the Rabbis respectively of Palestine and Mesopotamia and the other communities in which they were embedded. To put this another way, Hayes considers that a 'reductive historical approach' 'posits historical and contextual reasons for halakhic differences between the two Talmuds ... that ignore the textual, hermeneutical, and dialectical characteristics of the sources in question', but she does not seem to inquire into the historical and extratextual reasons for precisely those different 'textual, hermeneutical, and dialectical characteristics of the sources in question', which is the project of this current work of mine.[3] Hayes explicitly allows us to see 'historical' factors only when the respective exegetical methodologies of the two Talmuds are 'muted, compromised, or distorted', whereas I am seeking the history made precisely in and by the formation of those distinct exegetical methodologies and discursive practices more generally.[4]

In brief, I wish to suggest here that discursive developments that took place within the Christian world (including the Syriac-speaking Christian world) in the wake of Nicaea occasioned an epistemic shift that produced major effects on rabbinic Judaism as well. Aspects of the shift itself having

---

[3] Hayes (1997) 3–4.

[4] Hayes (1997) 8. It goes almost without saying that I am in fundamental agreement with Hayes's critique of a reductionist historicism, reductionist in its reduction of all culture to socioeconomic factors, but such vulgar Marxist historicism (such as was found indeed in the work of Louis Ginzberg a half-century ago) is surely a dead horse by now even among Marxists, let alone non-Marxisant historicists. The very positing of the alternatives as between 'external' and 'internal' factors is the problem, in my view, and not the solution. Hayes is, I think, mistaken when she refers to 'dialectical and redactional factors' as 'culturally neutral' and merely chronological in import, as if the Palestinian Talmud would look like the Babylonian Talmud if only the editors in fourth-century Palestine had had more time to work on their book. I have no wish to caricature her truly important work, but putting it in these terms suggests how implausible the terms of the discussion have been (before Hayes but not fundamentally shifted in her work).

been explored in previous work,[5] the task of the present writing is to further specify how these have impact on our question of the cultural meaning of dialogue and dialectic in rabbinic Judaism. More historical precision than I was in a position to mobilise previously will aid this endeavour. The differences between the 'textual, hermeneutical, and dialectical characteristics' of the Palestinian Talmud and the Babylonian one correspond roughly but tellingly, I would suggest, to differences that obtain within the larger cultural frame between discursive communities for whom rational inquiry and dialogical persuasion are useful and those for whom these and the notions of truth that subtend them have been discredited.

For Richard Lim, the fate of dialectic (although he seems not to clearly distinguish this from the fate of debate = rhetoric) in later antiquity represents a diachronic shift. Lim suggests two causal explanations for the turn within the Theodosian era (Theodosius II 408–50) from a culture in which dialectic and debate, more or less 'genuine' and open, prevailed to one in which even such public debates as did take place were entirely fixed games. One of these explanations involves the external historical condition of the orthodoxification of the Roman Empire with the concomitant declaration (notorious in the Theodosian Code) that certain religious positions other than Orthodoxy were now illegal, sometimes on pain of death.[6] Understandably enough, such a legal situation issued in major adjustments in the nature of discourse as well:

The ideological shift brought about by the outlawing of Manichaeism was decisive. With the rise of catholic and orthodox Christianities to a central position in the Roman Empire, increased social closure was needed to reflect the new imperial identity. In Max Weber's view, such social closure was achieved by increasing rigidity in group boundaries, curbing freewheeling competition, and preventing individual movement across boundaries. Public debates became no more than show cases exhibiting, for the edification of all Christian subjects as well as the marginalized Other, the wide gulf between sanctioned and illegitimate religious self-identifications.[7]

Were this the only explanation available, it would have little explanatory force for the Jewish suspicion of dialectic and debate, even in the Roman Empire, let alone outside of it, as these did not participate, one would assume, in such projects for securing a social closure that excluded them. This point should not be taken too far, however, as we cannot exclude

---

[5] Boyarin (2004) 159–60, 188–92. I am hoping to be able to use this occasion to modify, correct, make more coherent some of the arguments of the earlier work as well.
[6] Lim (1995), 104–5.   [7] Lim (1995) 106.

mimicry within such situations. Particularly since, as I have shown in earlier work, the Theodosian Code was not directed against rabbinic Jews so much as against those entities that more 'dangerously' threatened the borders of Christianity, such as Jewish-Christians, Manichees and other 'hybrids', one could imagine that rabbinic Jews, as well, would have an interest in stifling any real debate that would threaten their borders.[8]

A more compelling explanation, however, is provided by Lim's other (supplementing, not supplanting) hypothesis. According to this view, it was not so much the needs of an empire and a new imperial identity that drove the hierarchisation of discourse and the increased reliance on inarguable authority and traditionalism, so much as developments internal, as it were, to discourse itself, developments that, as he shows, challenged the emperor as well.[9] These developments were occasioned by a perceived failure throughout the Mediterranean *Kulturgebiet* (specifically including in this case at least the western reaches of the Sasanian world, as well) of reasoned argument to secure consensus. On this account the breakdown of attempts to achieve consensus through such argument in such grand councils as Nicaea led to more ponderous attempts to achieve agreement. Writing after Lim, but apparently not referring to him, Richard Vaggione has quite brilliantly characterised this dilemma:

> What this meant in historical terms was that when, after the breakdown of effective dialogue in 341, the two sides began to contemplate the positions of their adversaries, they found that what needed addressing was not the propositions themselves (which were often identical), but the place they occupied within an alien framework. In effect, context was now almost as important as content. The result was (in a situation where neither exegesis *nor* argument would convince) that the perceived source of error had to be systemic: 'heresy' could only be a defective orientation or *habitus* working itself out in doctrinal terms. Participants on both sides thus found themselves staring at one another across a cognitive gulf whose increasing width made communication all but impossible ...The result was a cognitive dissonance of major proportions, one which was in the end to prove insurmountable.[10]

My argument is, then, that given such an environment, a loss of faith in rational discourse (not entirely unlike our own) makes a great deal of sense, that the mood of disappointment with rhetoric and argumentation would spread far beyond the particular theological controversy and groups (central as they were) in which it originally took root, not implausibly affecting other groups in close intellectual – if not confessional – communion with each other. Such intellectual conflicts are, however, not only the product of

---

[8] Boyarin (2004) 214–20.   [9] Lim (1995) 152.   [10] Vaggione (2000) 97.

historical changes and epistemic shifts. In some sense, the problematic was always there, at least as far back as Gorgias, who, in his brilliant parody of Parmenides, already laid the groundwork for deep scepticism, even nihilism.

Gorgias' title, *On What is Not or On Nature*, is already parodic of Parmenides' title. Nature was generally considered as that which is. Parmenides' pupil Melissus wrote a book called *On Nature or On What is*. Gorgias sets out, it seems, to overturn Parmenides. And he does so on the grounds of something that we might call common sense. In the Peripatetic work *About Melissus, Xenophanes and Gorgias*, which is one of our main primary sources for Gorgias, we read the following justification for his shocking opinions to the effect that:

Gorgias declares that nothing exists; and if anything exists it is unknowable; and if it exists and is knowable, yet it cannot be indicated to others. To prove that nothing exists he collects the statements of others, who in speaking about what is seem to assert contrary opinions (some trying to prove that what is, is one and not many, others that it is many and not one; and some that existents are ungenerated, others that they have come to be), and he argues against both sides. For he says that if anything exists, it must be either one or many, and either be ungenerated or have come to be. If therefore, it cannot be either one or many, ungenerated or having come to be, it would be nothing at all. For if anything were, it would be one of these alternatives, and since it is not, then nothing is.

In other words, what Gorgias is doing is to deconstruct logical reason (the *logos*) by showing that it contradicts itself, in the sense that the perfectly constructed logical arguments of different thinkers can lead to opposite and mutually cancelling results. He then bids us to rely on our senses and our common sense and come to the conclusion that horses running on land, for instance, do exist, while horses running on the sea do not (*contra* Parmenides): 'for the objects of sight and hearing are for the reason that they are in each case cognized. But if this not the reason – if just as what we see is not the more because we see it, so also what we think is not the more for that.' 'If both thinkers [Parmenides and Gorgias] marshal deductions to reach contradictory but equally incredible conclusions, what becomes of Parmenides's theme that conviction unfailingly accompanies truth?'[11] In short, it would seem that Gorgias' aim is not only to argue that there is no knowledge but to demonstrate that this is so by performing an act of formal deduction that contradicts Parmenides and thus to discredit 'logic' – from *logos* – as a means to truth. The conflict is thus one that is age-old,

---

[11] Wardy (1996) 17.

going back to the very foundations of Greek intellectual life, although to be sure at different times and places one or another of these traditions might dominate. Plato, of course, is the great perpetuator of Parmenides.

Lim himself does not only argue chronologically. He argues that the so-called Anomoean controversy (the later stages of what has been called the Arian controversy) turned on ongoing distinctions of habitus, 'for also at issue were the definition and validation of competing habitus among late antique Christians'.[12] Crucial distinctions between the Palestinian and Babylonian Talmuds turn also on similar (not by any means identical) competing habitus. The battle between the Homoousians and the Anomoeans are portrayed in a fashion (by Nicene writers, of course) that renders them homologous, in my view, to the Platonic distinction between philosophy and sophistry. Basil the Great thus cites theologia vs. technologia (logic-chopping, sophistry) as the great divide within the Christian community: τεχνολογοῦσι λοιπόν, οὐ θεολογοῦσιν οἱ ἄνθρωποι.[13] As Lim persuasively shows, this cannot be a reference to the Anomoeans' alleged use of Aristotelian dialectic, since the 'orthodox' were no less partial to this form of argumentation. Although Lim cites at least one authority who argued that the term *technologos* as used here by Basil is 'tantamount to labeling him' a sophist, Lim himself rejects that argument, 'because the term "sophist" was mostly used as a slight devoid of specific content'.[14] Lim himself concludes that the distinction that Basil is making is between 'approved Christians' who 'employed dialectic as a tool to wage war for a just cause' and 'their opponents [who] did so out of single-minded ambition'.[15] What Lim seems to miss (as well he might given his generally positive remarks about Socrates) is that this is precisely the sort of polemic that Plato waged against his sophistic opponents; thus *theologia* becomes equivalent (socially, axiologically) to dialectic (true philosophy/theology), while *technologia* is the functional equivalent of rhetoric (falsehood) in Plato's terms.[16] It is just as difficult, frequently enough, to distinguish between approved philosophical dialectic and condemned sophistical eristic in Plato as well. The Anomoeans are, *pace* Lim, being portrayed as sophists by Basil. However, given their own understanding of truth and its susceptibility to proof via dialectical investigation and argument, the Anomoeans themselves have as much claim to the name theology, just as the ancient sophists do to philosophy (not necessarily a term of endearment for me), as

---

[12] Lim (1995) 111. Again the work of Vaggione (2000) 78–98 should be seen as supplementing Lim.
[13] Cited Lim (1995) 123.   [14] Lim (1995) 124–5.   [15] Lim (1995) 126–7.
[16] See too Vaggione (2000) 93 anticipating this point.

do their opponents, the 'orthodox', likely as not to be appealing to authority and mystical enlightenment as to anything rational in support of their position. Genuine sophism may have been the greatest victim of late antiquity. Sophistry, however, abided: 'In one letter, the Caesarean wrote eloquently of the perceived threat of dialectical questions, citing the celebrated question Anomoean sympathizers were prone to ask: "do you worship what you know or what you do not know?" Basil wisely declined to answer this question in an ad hoc manner, as he often did elsewhere; instead, he objected to the sophistry of dialectical questioning *sui generis*.' But of course the reader will quickly note how close the technique of the 'carefully crafted "yes or no" proposition', to which 'either response would provide the other side with a dialectical premise to refute',[17] is to the methods that Plato's Socrates employed in his *elenchus*.[18]

The diachronic difference between the two Talmuds (actually between the amoraic layer in both Talmuds and the stammaitic layer of the Babylonian) adds up to as significant a conflict of 'systems of social dispositions and cognitive structures' as the Arian controversy in its various stages within the development of Christianity, although carried out almost incognito.[19] Indeed, I would suggest, the various anxieties raised by conflict precluded for the *stammaim* openly acknowledging the difference in the understanding of difference between them and the early Babylonians or Palestinians. The Palestinian Talmud seems to consider determination of the correctness of one of the views of paramount importance, whereas for the Babylonian Talmud in its latest redaction it is most often the case that such an apparent proof of one view is considered a difficulty (*qushia*) requiring a resolution which, in fact, shows that there is no resolution, for 'These and these are the words of the Living God.' David Kraemer writes that 'This contrast in overall compositional preferences may be the most important difference

---

[17] Lim (1995) 136–7.   [18] I have looked at this in Boyarin (2007b).

[19] For extensive argument that there is, indeed, a shift within the history of rabbinic Judaism and that it takes place around the later redactional levels of the Babylonian Talmud, see Boyarin (2004) 159–63, 190–2, making use, *inter alia*, of the work of Shlomo Naeh and of my own student, Azzan Yadin. Cf. the explanations offered by Kraemer (1990) 114–20. Cf. also Kraemer (1990) 121 where we find a curious denial of history and change within rabbinism, substituting instead a sort of gradual revelation of a truth always known and held by the Rabbis: 'It is radical to deny that a single divine truth is available. This fact, at the earliest stages, had to be spoken softly. It could be fully realized only slowly and cautiously, and its comprehensive application had to wait much later.' To his credit, it must be said that Kraemer has at least recognised the diachronic dimension here in some wise even if I find his explanatory model less than compelling. See Neusner (1995) 103–6 for a rich characterisation of the Bavli that I believe is compatible with the aspect that I am exploring here, as well. Much of the rest of this paper is, in fact, a development, expansion and correction of the hypotheses of the portions of Boyarin (2004) referred to above in this note. For an explanation of the success of the Nicene movement as, itself, a kind of change incognito, see Vaggione (2000) 105.

between the Bavli [Babylonian Talmud] and the Yerushalmi [Palestinian Talmud].[20] When seen, as it traditionally is, from the point of view of the Bavli – after all, the hegemonic work for rabbinic Judaism – the practice of the Yerushalmi can seem as strange and even defective, but for that Talmud coming to conclusions is the very point of the dialectic while the practice of the Bavli resisting with all its power any such conclusivity is the stranger, the historical problem requiring solution. I suggest (as I have in *Border Lines* (2004) as well) that the important context for understanding this development is the transformations described by Lim, in which 'the attested growth of philosophical traditionalism in late antiquity' is connected to

the devaluation of dialectical dispute as a technique of social competition. As the philosopher-teacher evolved into a privileged figure of authority seated above those less established, philosophical disputation became an exercise in futility: if truth resided not in the dialectic of inquiry but in the very person of the philosopher (now appeared as a pagan holy man), dialectic was robbed of its ultimate legitimacy as a method for arriving at truth.[21]

Although I am less certain than Lim that there ever was truly a culture in which 'truth resided in the dialectic of inquiry' at least on the literary level, I am compelled by and large by his arguments that in the fifth-century dialogical discourse was in a crisis. This crucial, determinative, epistemic shift within Babylonian rabbinism that comes, on my hypothesis, fairly late in the day should be, I now suggest, read in the context of a late ancient Mediterranean culture in general and an emergency in discourse. This Talmud too, on my view, manifests a robbing of dialectic of its ultimate legitimacy *as a method for arriving at truth.*

There is more evidence from quite a different direction for a broad shift in discursive patterning during the crucial time for the formation of the Babylonian Talmud. For nearly a century scholars have been discussing the fact that 'in the fifth century there was an immense change of style',[22] that is in the writing of Byzantine documents. As Kovelman characterises this scholarship:

The rhetoric of Early Byzantine documents (fifth to seventh centuries) has usually been considered a manifestation of eastern servility and Christian humility. Features of this style, like verbosity, poeticisms, and archaisms, have been seen to testify to a drop in the value of the word in an atmosphere where legality and order failed to guarantee every letter of a document. Scholars thus saw the substantivized forms of Byzantine Greek as designed to reduce responsibility either for the word or for the deed. All this reputedly stemmed from a decrease in civic

[20] Kraemer (1990) 95.   [21] Lim (1995) 33.   [22] Kovelman (2005) 19.

spirit and self-respect, from the influence of Egyptian, Persian, and Babylonian traditions, and from the victory of 'Byzantinism.'[23]

Kovelman himself makes an elegant argument for quite a different interpretation of this situation, suggesting rather that the rise of a certain kind of rhetoric is a product of a certain economic and social situation in the late empire in which individual misery rather than being portrayed as 'extraordinary violations of the norm' was expressed as symptomatic of a situation of 'wretchedness', and 'What was needed was a way of expressing a situation that would not offend the feelings of high authorities. This is where rhetoric with its rationalism came into play.'[24] Studying petitionary papyri from Egypt, Kovelman provides quite a fascinating demonstration of a striking shift between the second–fourth centuries and the centuries that followed. While in the former, the rhetoric was one of fixed places in society (the arrogant rich man; the honest poor man), the latter petitions are based on dynamic narratives, structured either like the Passion or alternatively following the conventions of romance.[25] Strikingly comparing two petitions for similar cause, one from the early fourth century and one from the sixth, he writes, 'Serenilla's petition is reminiscent of a philosophical treatise, Sophia's of a novel.'[26] He concludes from his rich examples that 'The flourishing of poetry replaced the flourishing of philosophical and theological prose... . So it is not by chance that Roman petitions mostly resemble treatises, while Byzantine petitions resemble novels or poems. It was not only in Egypt that the flourishing of poetry replaced the flourishing of philosophical and theological prose. At the same time in Jewish Palestine, sermons [midrashic homilies] developed greatly and liturgical poetry (*piyyut*) was born. Poetical-mythical-historical sensitivity replaced the abstract moral stance of the previous age.'[27] Even more strikingly and in contrast to generally held prejudice of scholars and layfolk, 'With Christianization of the Empire and the fall of Rome the age of stagnation was over. History proved to be alive.'[28]

Kovelman writes further, 'an associative way of thinking was substituted for strict logic and was accompanied by a sober rationalism'.[29] As we see from this citation, for Kovelman 'strict logic' and 'rationalism' are not consistent with each other (or not necessarily so in any case). What he

[23] Kovelman (2005) 19. For the previous scholarship referred to, see Kovelman's note 81, ad loc.
[24] Kovelman (2005) 22. By 'rationalism' Kovelman means what we would call calculation, a certain calculatedness or design in the writing, and not logicality, as we will see just below.
[25] Kovelman (2005) 24–6.   [26] Kovelman (2005) 27.   [27] Kovelman (2005) 30–1.
[28] Kovelman (2005) 38.   [29] Kovelman (2005) 33.

means by this is that the rhetoric that is employed (including the senti-mental, or especially the sentimental) is calculated to be compelling, but in this very calculatedness reveals a breakdown in trust in logic as persuasive, hence the new forms. 'Rationalism', for Kovelman, means accordingly something like realism, the realism of Realpolitik. With this conclusion, based on well-established scholarly analyses of shifts in rhetorical style and strategy (albeit being explained in an entirely different fashion) between the third–fourth and the later centuries, Kovelman asserts that the Mishna with its passion for taxonomies and relative absence of narrative is similar to the literature of the Second Sophistic while the later midrashic texts are closer in spirit to the literature of early Byzance. In my terms (not only in mine), this represents the shift away from the passion for philosophy of the earlier period to the rejection of philosophy in the latter. Kovelman's results thus match Lim's coming from an entirely different scholarly and evidential base and, as Kovelman does not fail to point out, support Jacob Neusner's descriptions of a major shift in style of thinking between the Mishna's third century and the later time of the redaction of the midrashim and the Babylonian Talmud.

In other words, I am suggesting that the momentous mutation in rabbinic textuality that gave rise finally to the Babylonian Talmud is best understood as part of shockwaves running throughout the cultural area on both sides of the Mediterranean and both sides of the Roman *limes* as well. In what follows I shall try at least to expose this thesis without claiming at all to be able to demonstrate it. The Talmud represents, I suggest, the same move away from logic and rational thinking (in our terms) that we find in both Christian apologetic and the language of the legal petitions.

SILENCING THE *LOGOS*

Normally the Babylonian Talmud, however, is characterised by both tradi-tional and critical scholars as the very epitome of rational, dialectical discourse.[30] My thesis seems, then, to produce a paradox, arguing for an undoing of dialectic precisely at a moment of its apparently most vigorous development. This is an especially sharp paradox, since I claim, as does Halivni, that 'the *stammaim* of the Talmud were the first who saw an independent value to the dialectic and preserved it'.[31] The paradox is less of a paradox, however, when we pay attention to the fact that while dialectic

---

[30] See notably Fisch (1997), an important work on which I have commented extensively elsewhere.
[31] Halivni (2005) 107. For 'preserved', I would write, 'produced'. See too Rubenstein (2002).

is seemingly, of course, the very stuff of the Babylonian Talmud, it almost never issues in a resolution of the *dissensus*. The Babylonian talmudic text elaborates a third term in the paradigm, neither dialectic towards agreement nor the total rejection of dialectic, as the Christians and late antique philosophers had, but rather dialectic without *telos*: without ever reaching agreement or even seeking to do so, dispute that cannot ever be resolved as both Holy Rabbis are always already right even when they directly contradict each other. The practice of dialectic is, then, a pseudo-dialectical practice, a devotional – or even liturgical[32] – act (known as 'enlarging the Torah and making it wonderful') and not truly an intellectual one.[33] Better put, perhaps, it is a devotional (as opposed to teleological) use of the intellect. In the earlier Palestinian rabbinic imagination, presumably sufficient investigation could discover the original truth, whether Hillel's or Shammai's, much as for a third-century Origen truth would be discovered by 'man who is capable of being taught [and who] might by "searching out" and devoting himself to "deep things" revealed in the spiritual meaning of the words become partaker of all the doctrines of the Spirit's counsel'.[34] By the latter stratum, the contradictory views of the disciples of both of these Sages are being declared equally the words of the Living God. The (hypothesised) *stammaim* have moved beyond a notion of rational discovery of truth (or even the securing of agreement) through debate into a realm in which the words of the Living God are paradoxical, self-contradictory, undecidable and undiscoverable and talk goes on forever. The talk, however, is holy talk and therefore continues even without *telos*. In this Mesopotamian milieu, disputational learning is so central to piety that it cannot be forsaken even when its ostensible purpose no longer obtains.[35] In other words, what I propose (and shall develop in a future book

---

[32] My evidence for this would be moments in the Babylonian Talmud in which we find Rabbis refraining from communal prayer, arguing essentially: 'They do their thing and we do ours' (Becker (2006) 14).

[33] Many scholars, since at least the Middle Ages, have noted that much of the talmudic dialectic is epideictic and pedagogic but not actual inquiry. I am suggesting that this is the case for all of the dialectic, that it is all 'to enlarge the Torah and make it great'.

[34] Origen (1973) 282.

[35] For the centrality of study and learning in the circumambient Christianity, see Becker (2006) 34–5 and throughout. Of course, this claim is not to be taken to mean that study was not absolutely central to rabbinic piety before the *stammaim* but that that form of devotion took on special form at the time of the redaction of the Talmud. The claim thus parallels that of Becker, writing, 'Christianity has derived from scripture and tradition clusters of metaphors which have allowed Christians at different times and in different places to define for themselves the essence of Christianity and herald it to others. This panoply of images, metaphors, and expressions was continually adapted to fit the needs and circumstances of any particular locale. The pedagogical model of Christianity … is one of these clusters. Furthermore, … this cluster of pedagogical metaphors was reduced and lost its metaphorical

project) is that the controlled pseudo-*dissensus* of the stammaitic level of
the Talmud was as effective a method for securing a hierarchical ordering of
society as any other.[36] As Gerald Bruns has written, 'From a transcendental
standpoint, this [rabbinic] theory of authority is paradoxical because it is
seen to hang on the heteroglossia of dialogue, on speaking with many voices,
rather than on the logical principle of univocity, or speaking with one mind.
Instead, the idea of speaking with one mind ... is explicitly rejected; single-
mindedness produces factionalism.'[37] But multi-mindedness, *within the
confines of the rabbinic system and the rabbinic institution*, produces absolute
authority, an authority which leaves nowhere (or so it seems) from whence
to challenge it.

For Lim the distinction for Christian society is between deference as a
system, 'an unspoken rule of conduct enmeshed in a complex system of
social exchange', and the case where 'simplicity is a vocal ideology promoted
by interested parties to mimic the former'. Lim refers as well to 'many
individuals and groups [who] sought to domesticate the perceived threat of
dissensus in public disputing, choosing from various ideological strategies
and cultural values to mobilize hierarchical forms of authority against a
culture that validated individualistic claims and rational argumentation'.[38]
My proposal is that for the Babylonian Rabbis, debate without end was
equally a vocal ideology to effectively monovocalise the dialogue, and I shall
try to show this in some detail elsewhere. In this sense, their habitus is
perhaps most easily comparable to that of the Anomoeans, especially
Eunomius as characterised by Lim himself. In a conclusion that will provide
some significant illumination for our study of the talmudic habitus, Lim
writes, 'For the most part, Aetius and Eunomius presided over a broad
confederation of likeminded people rather than a discrete organization
or community ... . I suggest that the solidarity of such groups came from
disputing and questioning rather than adherence to set beliefs. These groups
could flourish only at the margins of more stable communities, with which
they shared a symbiotic relationship.'[39] The same could be said I warrant for
the kind of scholastic debating that was carried on in the East Syrian schools

---

valence with the development of the East-Syrian school movement; Christianity for certain East-
Syrian elite males was literally a form of pedagogy with its own institutions and way of life. This led to
the development of a whole social group who could be imagined as such' (Becker (2006) 39–40).

[36] But not, of course, entirely successful. At the very least, the Karaite schism which took place during
the centuries of formation of the stamma needs to be studied carefully from this perspective. We need
a revolution in the historiography of rabbinic Judaism on the order of the revolution in the study of
the Nicene controversy that has taken place in the last decades, since, at least arguably, the work of
Gregg and Groh (1981).

[37] Bruns (1990) 199.   [38] Lim (1995) 30.   [39] Lim (1995) 130.

as well. The point is that such *internal* disputing and questioning in which there was little at stake in the conflict, arguing distinctions that made virtually no difference, is a practice that effectively eliminates the kind of genuine debate that might be threatening to the group. David Stern has already articulated this point: 'The conclusion of such a discourse is, of course, a powerful and tendentious support for rabbinic hegemony ... [T]he citation of multiple interpretations in midrash is an attempt to represent in textual terms an idealized academy of Rabbinic tradition where all the opinions of the sages are recorded equally as part of a single divine conversation. Opinions that in human discourse may appear as contradictory or mutually exclusive are raised to the state of paradox once traced to their common source in the speech of the divine author.'[40] It is this practice, I suggest, that issued in the famous dialectic, the endless debate that is said to characterise the Rabbis but is better understood as the product of a certain defining historical moment in the history of that movement and its texts. Lim has called at the end of his book for further research on 'the growth and articulation of the consensual tradition both within and outside of the Christian church, and the mechanisms that contributed to the sanctification of both synchronic and diachronic consensus', suggesting that the doctrine of *homonoia* ought 'to be viewed in the context of its dialectical relationship with competing modes of social order'.[41] It seems not unfair to see the highly controlled dissensus promulgated by the late framers of rabbinic texts and especially the *stammaim* as such a competing mode, one, however, strikingly alike in its effects both social and religious.[42]

This turn had for the Rabbis, I suggest, no less than for the Church, effects on the level of theological practice, with at least some texts narrating a turn from rational exegesis of the Torah to a traditionalist and revelationist account of the Oral Torah itself, paralleling Lim's shift of 'the source of philosophical authority' away from 'rational discourse to divine revelation'.[43] A remarkable story in the Talmud is a product, I reckon, of this cultural nexus and demonstrates both its antirationalism as well as the power effects of the turn to fideism, traditionality and virtual divination for rabbinic authority:

---

[40] Stern (1996) 37.   [41] Lim (1995) 234.

[42] A further fascinating point of comparison here would be the actual practice of disputation/dialectic/debate as found in East Syrian religious texts and that of the Talmud. In Boyarin (2007a), I undertake such a comparison, having been afforded an opportunity through the publication of Walker (2006) esp. 166–80.

[43] Lim (1995) 46. It should be noted that this formulation is quite different (nearly opposite) from the way I described the situation in Boyarin (2004) in which the theology (the rejection of Logos theology) drives the other cultural shifts.

Rabbi Yehudah said that Rav said: In the hour that Moses ascended on high, he found the Holy Blessed One sitting and tying crowns for the letters. He said before him: 'Master of the Universe, What [lit. who] holds you back?' He said, 'There is one man who will be after several generations, and Akiva the son of Joseph is his name, who will derive from each and every stroke hills and hills of *halakhot*.' He said before him: 'Master of the Universe, show him to me.' He said to him: 'Turn around!' He went and sat at the back of eight rows [in the study house of Rabbi Akiva], and he didn't understand what they were saying. His strength became weak. When they reached a certain issue, the disciples said to him [to Akiva], 'From whence do you know this?' He said to them: 'It is a *halakha* given to Moses at Sinai.' [Moses'] spirit became settled. He returned and came before the Holy Blessed One. He said to him: 'Master of the Universe, You have such a one and yet You give the Torah by my hand?!' He [God] said to him: 'Be silent! That is what has transpired in My thought.' (Babylonian Talmud Menahot 29b)

It is, to be sure, difficult to assert positively a late date for this narrative, given its attribution to Rav Yehuda in the name of Rav, but, in any case, it is clearly of Babylonian provenience and at the earliest a product of the fourth century, a generation or so after its named speakers. Thus the following argument will work even on the most radical dating assumptions one could make about the Talmud, namely assuming both the reliability of attributions as well as the substantial literal identity of the cited utterance and its 'original', and is only rendered stronger on the more conservative (and to my mind more plausible) assumption that traditions take their form within the context of their emplacement in the whole text.

In this talmudic story, knowledge is thoroughly opaque in its form; no one, not even Moses himself, could possibly know what Rabbi Akiva knows nor contest rationally his interpretive assertions. The latter's mode of interpretation of the Torah could be fairly characterised as divination clothed in the language of tradition.[44] Rabbi Akiva's 'divination' – if I may call it that – seems to involve something like contemplation of the serifs of the letters to divine their meanings. Rabbi Akiva seems to be dangerously innovating using virtually divinatory methods, but the tradition (Moses) is mollified (at least somewhat) when he describes the contents of his divination as having been transmitted (only to him?) from Moses at Sinai. How different, after all, is Rabbi Akiva's (imputed) claim to be able

---

[44] 'A third class of critic consists of those who either interpret the divine scriptures quite correctly or think they do. Because they see, or at least believe, that they have gained their ability to expound the holy books without recourse to any rules of the kind that I have now undertaken to give, they will clamour that these rules are not needed by anybody, and that all worthwhile illumination of the difficulties of these texts can come by a special gift of God' (Aug. *De doctr.*, cited Becker (2006) 15).

to divine the meaning of the text from linguistically meaningless marks from the Syriac Stephen of Sadaili, who was characterised as 'ascribing to himself "revelations and visions" and saying "that to him alone is it given to understand the Scriptures correctly"'?[45] Unless one is prepared to believe literally that Rabbi Akiva's interpretation was handed down to Akiva from Moses at Sinai – and the text itself denies this ironically – who but an 'Akiva' could know what is meant by jots, tittles and decorations on letters? And how could we know other than by being his disciples? It will be seen that something like apostolic authority is being promulgated here. The only way that such knowledge could be garnered is via access to the teaching of a particular institution, the Yeshiva. 'Moses' would represent on this account a more rational, logically based reading of the Torah, while Rabbi Akiva represents almost a post-rational (near-Evagrian/Pseudo-Dionysian?[46]) account. I would like to suggest that this story represents a conflictual moment in the historical development of Babylonian rabbinism, one in which earlier dialectical methods for discovering truth were beginning to be replaced by divinatory and traditionalist ones, while at the same time the act of study was made an end in itself, not requiring any results to achieve its religious purpose, the notion that becomes, incidentally, determinative within later rabbinic Judaism as the concept of Torah for its own sake. This is, itself, strikingly akin to the place of dialectic and study within the East Syrian school of Nisibis as described by Adam Becker and bespeaks some kind of cultural interaction between the two communities, without asking for or even imagining the validity of inquiry into or a model of a specific historical account of influence in one direction or the other.[47] Indeed, the time has come, I think, to cease thinking in terms of influence and think rather of shared and overlapping cultures imbricated on each other and partly simply just the same culture in different variants.[48]

In the face of Moses' demand, as it were, for rational understanding of Rabbi Akiva's discourse, he is told in effect to be silent and have faith. Moses' faith is, however, to be tested even more severely, for:

---

[45] On him, Becker (2006) 266, n. 63 and literature cited there.

[46] Becker (2006) 178. Notice too the mystical role of the letters for Evagrius (Becker (2006) 132–3).

[47] This is a moment to illustrate the compatibilities and differences between my approach and that of Hayes (1997) 18–19. Thus while elegantly (and convincingly) interpreting the passage as being about rabbinic anxiety and also self-confidence in respect of their hermeneutic positions vis-à-vis the Bible, she does not even consider the question of why this particular narrative was told when and where it was told and what may have generated this particular reflection at that time.

[48] 'In contrast to most prior research I advise against the positivistic search for "influences" when dealing with similarities', Hezser (2000) 162. I couldn't agree more.

He said to Him: 'Master of the Universe: You have shown me his Torah, show me his reward.' He said to him: 'Turn around!' He turned around and saw that they were weighing the flesh of Rabbi Akiva in the market [after his martyrdom]. He said to Him: 'Master of the Universe, This is the Torah and this is its reward?!' He said to him: 'Be silent! That is what has transpired in My thought.'

This silence is redolent of the silence of the apophatic moment in Christian theology, as well. Lim argues that the exigency of articulating an opposition to debate in Christian theology comes, in a sense, in the wake of the success of that very debating discourse. He describes a situation in which: 'In a language game that allowed for the clear articulation of nuances, people pressured each other to profess their beliefs in the middle of a controversial minefield, the features and contours of which were just beginning to be mapped.'[49] This pressure led to the conclusion that the endemic dissension of the Christian church had arisen precisely because of 'vain disputes and questionings',[50] even among some who had been trained as highly skilled practitioners of this discursive modality. One solution to this problem was the turn to a mystical and apophatic theology, as most fully expressed in the writings of Evagrius of Pontus and Pseudo-Dionysius, the former of whom had, as suggested above, a major impact precisely on the propensity towards the apophatic (and subordination of the cataphatic to it) in the East Syrian church.[51] Related to this was the demand, on the part of such a centrally located theological authority as Gregory Nazianzus, to avoid debate and engage in Christian practice.[52] One of the responses that the Cappadocian Fathers articulated to Christian theological argumentativeness was the catechism,[53] from one perspective at least not at all different from God's reported command to Moses himself to shut up and accept God's will without question. But differences remain. A typical bit of paideutic advice from one of the most important thinkers of the fourth-century Church and architect of the Christian monastic habitus, Basil of Caesarea, will help clarify this. As cited by Lim, Basil expects the Christian ascetic, that ideal Christian figure of the fourth century, to be: 'quiet of demeanour, not hasty in speech, nor contentious (μὴ ἐριστικός), quarrelsome (μὴ φιλόνεικος), vainglorious, nor given to interpreting of texts

---

[49] Lim (1995) 153–4.
[50] The *Vita Danielis* 90, cited Lim (1995) 156, n. 35. See also McLynn (1992) 15–44. Particularly striking and amusing in our present socio-cultural context is the description by Gregory Nazianzen of dialecticians as being analogous to the wrestlers of the WWF and not even genuine athletes, *apud* Lim (1995) 162.
[51] For the extraordinary impact of Evagrius on the church of the East, see Becker (2006) 178.
[52] Lim (1995) 158–64.   [53] Lim (1995) 165–7.

(μὴ ἐξηγητικός)'.[54] We find these recommendations repeated, moreover, in the writing of an important East Syrian monastic writer, a certain Dadiso of Bet Qatraye, who complains of the schoolmen that owing to demonic influences, they engage in 'constant and disordered meditation on scripture, a disparate wandering after seeking its meanings', which 'leads Christians to engage in intellectual disputes'. Because they attempt to interpret scripture like schoolmen, 'when they come together they end up falling into disputes'.[55] From a talmudic perspective, these lists of negative behaviours and traits are remarkable, if not stunning. Perhaps a rabbinical mentor in Basil's position would recommend that his disciple be quiet in demeanour and not hasty in speech, but contention, quarrel and the interpreting of texts are the very *habitus* of the Babylonian rabbinic Study House, the House of Midrash.[56] So it would seem at first glance that the Talmud is on the side, as it were, of the Syriac schoolmen, but it's more complicated than that given the antischolastic turn of our story about Rabbi Akiva. Turning one way and another, now seeming to agree with the monastics, now with the scholastics of the Syrian church, in both instances (I would suggest) it is the same crisis to which the *stammaim* are responding in their various ways.

Without determining lines or directions of influence, indeed denying, as I do, the significance and even possibility of such determination, I would, nevertheless, submit that such comparisons bespeak a common intellectual, discursive, spiritual milieu between patristic Christianity and Babylonian rabbinic Judaism.[57] I think we are witness in this text to a distinctive turn to both fideism and apophaticism in Babylonian rabbinic circles that answers to similar developments within patristic Christianity both western and eastern. To be sure, such developments were sharply contested both within Christian circles and, as the multiple ironies and double-voicing of the Akiva legend attest, among the rabbis, as well. It is the contest that I claim

---

[54] Cited in Lim (1995) 144, n. 190. Of course, ideas such as this circulated in Christian hands before Basil, notably in Tertullian (noted as well by Lim), who also advises his charges to avoid interpreting texts (*Prescriptions Against Heretics* 17–19), to seek 'simplicity of heart' and avoid speculation and dialectic (*Prescriptions Against Heretics* 7), and see discussion in King (2003) chapter 2.

[55] Cited Becker (2006) 189–90.

[56] As Origen had already put it: 'Moreover, there was in Judaism a factor which caused sects to begin, which was the variety of the interpretations of the writings of Moses and the sayings of the prophets.' (Chadwick (1953) 135.)

[57] See too Richard Kalmin, who in the introduction to his *Jewish Babylonia between Persian and Roman Palestine* (2006) writes: 'Rather, it is my contention that the Jewish and Christian developments in the region during the fourth century, continuing until the advent of Islam in the seventh century, may be closely related, and that processes accelerated by Shapur's dramatic conquests of the third century may have had pronounced literary and practical consequences in Babylonia and surrounding territories.'

as significant evidence for converging discursive cultures, not necessarily its particular resolution.

In earlier work, I made extensive reference to the contribution of David Stern in demonstrating the amount of anxiety produced among the Babylonian Rabbis owing to their constant debating.[58] By insisting that all sides in the debate are correct, all are the words of the Living God, all were given by one shepherd, the power of debate and dissent is completely vitiated. I would suggest that this anxiety is very much on the order of that which, according to Lim and Vaggione, led to the discrediting of dispute and debate themselves among fourth-century and later Christian circles. The argument of Celsus against the Christians that their disputes discredit the truth of the Gospels and Christianity is not different in content from the despair of the hypothesised auditor of the rabbinic disputes who is led to scepticism – How can one learn Torah? – owing to their constant disagreements. Even closer, it would seem, is the despair of the Bishop at the Council of Seleucia who declared, 'If to proclaim personal opinions day after day is to confess the faith, we will never express the truth with accuracy',[59] and this council, in 410, when Nicaea became the orthodoxy of the church in Sasanian realms, brings us nearer and nearer to our rabbinic world of Babylonia, held as it were in the very epicentre of Babylonian rabbinic authority. The grounds of contention for the Babylonian Rabbis can be illustrated from the following quotation from the antirabbinite Qara'ite text:

I have set the six divisions of the Mishna before me. And I looked at them carefully with mine eyes. And I saw that they are very contradictory in content. This one mishnaic scholar declares a thing to be forbidden to the people of Israel, while that one declares it to be permitted. My thoughts therefore answer me, and most of my reflections declare unto me, that there is in it no Law of logic nor the Law of Moses the Wise.[60]

Now where once, very recently indeed, I would have thought of the Qara'ite text as being later than the Talmud, even in its latest significant redactorial activity, this no longer seems quite as clearly the case to me. Without claiming (although just about imagining with great fear and love) that the work of the *Stamma* is a response to the proto-Qara'ite challenge, I would, nonetheless, argue that a charge such as this one well illustrates the climate in which the work of the *Stamma* took place, and it is remarkably like the intellectual climate in which Lim argues that the work of shutting

---

[58] Boyarin (2004) 62, 311 n. 47.
[59] Socrates, *H.E.* 2.40.20, cited in Vaggione (2000) 222.   [60] Nemoy (1969) 71.

down of debate took place among Christians as well.[61] In a world in which, as Lim shows, there were diverse and converging reasons for 'the quelling of *dissensus*', explicitly proposing that dissensus isn't dissensus at all would provide another solution to the same problems. What I am suggesting is that just as for Christians 'the practice of disputing among Christians was an obvious concern for those who prized hierarchical authority',[62] so too for Jews. One doesn't need to posit influence in either direction but merely a recognition of shared discursive space (analogous to something like modernism, if you will) to explain the similarities of response that issue with all their differences, as well[63]. Lim suggests that 'the mystification of the divine essence (οὐσία)) and a concomitant insistence on communal prayer' were efforts to curb rampant disputing[64], while I, in turn, suggest that the mystification of interpretation (together with halakhic decision-making) and the turn to an apophatic hermeneutics manifested by our talmudic text of Rabbi Akiva support the same ends.

Becker himself reveals the two types of divine epistemology as subsisting together in the East Syrian world: 'These two types of institution [monastery and school] differed in their intellectual positions, especially in their notions of epistemology and their understanding of the accessibility of the divine.'[65] He suggests that the intellectual differences can be accounted for by means of a material homology, intellectual difference responding to the differences between the two institutions:

Social tension and intellectual difference could exist between those who devoted themselves to a more solitary monastic lifestyle and those who remained within the

---

[61] Some colour may be lent to this suggestion by the following:

> According to the Chronicle of Siirt, the School of Seleucia was founded by Mar Aba(Catholicos 540–52), after he bested a Zoroastrian in a public debate in the same location. The tale that the Chronicle presents is a miraculous one; the lack of any earlier attestation and the use of a stereotypical conversion motif suggests that it is not reliable. To be sure, Aba's importance in the sixth-century school tradition is beyond doubt, as is easily demonstrated by the number of figures in the school movement associated with him by the sources. Yet the bulk of this fascinating story of miraculous one upmanship seems to be a fictional foundation myth for the School of Seleucia. For example, however much Mar Aba's Life describes him as a teacher, it nowhere mentions him founding a school. That this mythic founding of the school begins with a dispute with a Zoroastrian is appropriate: theological controversy was a major impetus to the development of the school tradition. (Becker (2006) 157–8)

> Is it possible – just – that the ferment that presumably led to the formal Qara'ite schism had an impact on the forming of the postamoraic Yeshivot as well?

[62] Lim (1995) 29.
[63] Lim is surely to be commended for moving us beyond notions of 'a spirit of irrationalism' infecting the age, which are, indeed, 'at once unhelpfully tautological and mystifying' (Lim (1995) 24).
[64] Lim (1995) 150–1.   [65] Becker (2006) 171.

school as teachers in its hierarchy of offices. Beyond this, a homologous relationship existed between the intellectual and social life that each of these institutions, the monastery and the school, advocated. Thus, it is not a coincidence that an institution advocating group study put more emphasis on the notion that the divine was completely inaccessible without instruments such as language and pedagogy, while an institution that promoted private meditation allowed for the divine to enter into the consciousness of the pure without mediation.[66]

While Becker's explanation is certainly cogent, the analysis I have undertaken of talmudic text suggests, perhaps, that the conflicts run much deeper than a distinction of institutional settings, which, after all, does not obtain for the Rabbis, there being no monasteries among them. It may be, rather, that instead of the institutional setting producing, as it were, the theory, the theoretical conflict may have had an impact on the institutional formations. What I learn, however, from Becker here is that what I have narrated in my previous work as a diachronic shift might be reconsidered as synchronic tensions and discord,[67] or at any rate, that the shifts, not – never – being complete, may have left such synchronic discord in their wake and it is this that is being reflected in the texts, as well as the diachronic movements themselves. This approach would make the stories less allegorical records of historical events so much as narrations of 'social tensions and intellectual difference' in the present of the narrators. Note, however, that I am *not* mapping the particular breaks and faultlines in the Syriac tradition onto those of the Babylonian Rabbis; they won't map neatly. The lack of fit can be partly accounted for by the fact that we have only the records of one institution, the rabbinic Yeshiva, for the Jews and not two separate ones as for the Christians.[68] The two 'sides' thus interact quite differently in the two corpora as they may have in the two communities, as well; we just don't and, for my money, *can't* know.[69] The issues, however, of truth and logic, adequacy of language or not, cataphatic and apophatic theologies, seem close enough to consider these two textual communities as working within the same milieu of problematics.

The significance of the argument does not rest, therefore, on the theorisation of a particular Christian/Jewish milieu within which the institutions of rabbinic Judaism and the Church of the East developed together.

---

[66] Becker (2006) 172.   [67] Becker (2006) 16.

[68] Although I am led to wonder anew about the provenience of the mystical texts of those who descend to the Merkabah, so near and yet so far in ethos from the nearly contemporaneous – if not fully contemporaneous – Babylonian Talmud. For the nonce, at least, see Davila (2001).

[69] Although it might prove useful to think of the relation of the Talmud to the nearly contemporaneous mystic literature in terms of separate institutions, partially overlapping and partially conflicting, much as the schools and monasteries of the East Syrian tradition. Another vision for the future.

I am suggesting that we look in general at the Greek intellectual culture of late antiquity in its various manifestations as an important aspect of the context within which Babylonian rabbinic Judaism developed even in its phases that are independent of further Palestinian input, subsequent, that is, to the end of vigorous literary creativity in Palestine.[70] The Church of the East (and other Syriac-speaking Christians) provide, then, a pendant on which to hang – by analogy – the plausibility of claims for Hellenism in Jewish Babylonia as much, or more, than as a vehicle for transmission. The extent to which the postamoraic rabbinic community in Babylonia seems to have been open to scholasticism like that of the Nisibene foundation renders the notion of a hermetically sealed, exclusively inner-directed community less and less convincing.[71] In addition to the Persian connections discovered by such scholars as E. S. Rosenthal and Shaul Shaked and increasingly being exposed by Ya'akov Elman,[72] we certainly need, I would suggest, to be looking to the West and the Greco-Roman Christian world as well in order to understand the culture of the Babylonian Talmud.

We can use the evidence of such specific connections to reconstruct a shared cultural milieu, one indeed that is not specifically Christian or rabbinic, indeed not necessarily 'Judaeo-Christian' at all. Once again, the sophistical doxographers have something to contribute here, for I think that the Kulturkampf being dramatised in the narrative about Rabbi Akiva above manifests itself as well in a story that we find in Eunapius. This legend manifests the rivalry between reasoned debate and dialectic, on the one hand, and thaumaturgy and divination, on the other, in the latter part of the fourth century (during Julian's reign, the same Julian whom the Christians call 'the apostate' and Eunapius 'the holy').

In this narrative we are told that Aedesius, a great sophist, had two pupils in the latter fourth century, Chrysanthius and Eusebius. Eusebius remained entirely loyal to the old rule of dialectic and logic, while Chrysanthius became particularly attached to the new-fangled doctrines of Maximus: 'Now Chrysanthius had a soul akin to that of Maximus, and like him was

---

[70] As Hayes (1997) informs us, the doyen of Palestinian Talmud studies in our time, Prof. Y. Sussman of the Hebrew University, regards the end of Palestinian amoraic activity to have been in the third quarter of the fourth century, while the Babylonians went on for centuries more elaborating and producing their Talmud.

[71] Although, to be sure, as Richard Kalmin has shown, precisely this openness to cultural impact from the surrounding Sasanian world promoted another kind of insularity among the Babylonian Rabbis, insulation from contact with or power over and among their fellow, non-rabbinic Jews: Kalmin (1994a). This very insularity can be read also as part and parcel of the scholasticism of the Babylonian Rabbis and thus not unlike, once again, their Syriac compatriots.

[72] Elman (2006).

passionately absorbed in working marvels, and he withdrew himself in the study of the science of divination.' Eusebius, it seems, was somewhat in awe of this Maximus, for 'when Maximus was present, [he] used to avoid precise and exact divisions of a disputation and dialectical devices and subtleties; though when Maximus was not there he would shine out like a bright star, with a light like the sun's; such was the facility and charm that flowered in his discourses ... Julian actually reverenced Eusebius. At the close of his exposition Eusebius would add that these [dialectical discussions] are the only true realities, whereas the impostures of witchcraft and magic that cheat the senses are the works of conjurors who are insane men led astray into the exercise of earthly and material powers.' 'The sainted Julian' was puzzled by this peroration that he regularly heard and asked Eusebius what he meant, whereupon the latter said: 'Maximus is one of the older and more learned students, who, because of his lofty genius and superabundant eloquence scored all logical proof in these subjects and impetuously resorted to the acts of a madman ... But you must not marvel at any of these things, even as I marvel not, but rather believe that the thing of the highest importance is that purification of the soul which is attained by reason.' Eusebius receives something of a surprise, for 'when the sainted Julian heard this, he said: "Nay, farewell and devote yourself to your books. You have shown me the man I was in search of"'[73] (much like, even verbally, the 'You have shown me his Torah' of the talmudic text).[74] The earlier, traditional commitment to dialectical investigation and surety that logic would provide answers has been rejected, and by no less, it seems, than the sainted Julian, in favour of thaumaturgy and divination but not without conflict, a conflict, I think, demonstrated also in the narrative about Rabbi Akiva. Lim's inquiry into the downfall of debate can be extended both further east and outside of Christian circles as well (not, I hasten to add, that Lim had ever said or implied that it was a singularly Christian, or western, phenomenon).[75] Looked at from one point of view, our narrative about Rabbi Akiva and

---

[73] Texts taken from Wright (1998) 433–5. My own interpretation here follows Wright's construal of the text here and not that of Lim (1995) 50–3, which I rediscovered after writing these paragraphs upon rereading Lim after a decade. The lack of an adversative in a sentence is not outweighed by the clear narrative logic; it must be Eusebius whom Julian now abandons and not Chrysanthius or the story hardly makes sense in my humble opinion.

[74] I wish to thank Dr. Ronald Reissberg for pointing this out to me.

[75] 'Indeed, a sequel to Lim's work, which would include the Sasanian world, might well begin at the court of Justinian and Theodora. As Antoine Guillaumont emphasized twenty-five years ago, teachers and clergy from the Sasanian world repeatedly participated in theological debates at the early Byzantine court', Walker (2006) 173. Walker emphasises there as well that Lim's description fits the Theodosian era much more than the later time when debate and dialectic had become again favoured, at least in certain churchly quarters, and remained so in the east, in any case.

Moses could provide one station on a route that, as Kovelman has put it, leads from *logos* to *mythos*[76] (while at the same time conceding, cheerfully, that this was not the only journey available).[77]

What could possibly be the cause of such cultural transformations as I am hypothesising around the Mediterranean from west to east? Paul Veyne has wisely written (about a quite different topic): 'What can be said about this moral transformation is approximately the same that can be said of an "event" in the history of ideas. After a century of historical sociology, many historians frankly admit that they are incapable of explaining cultural mutations and, even more, that they haven't the slightest idea what form a causal explanation might take.'[78] Lim himself offered a connection with an 'attested growth of philosophical traditionalism in late antiquity', arguing that, 'as the philosopher-teacher evolved into a privileged figure of authority seated above those less established, philosophical disputation became an exercise in futility: if truth resided not in the dialectic of inquiry but in the very person of the philosopher (now appearing as a pagan holy man), dialectic was robbed of its ultimate legitimacy as a method for arriving at truth'.[79] Although precisely on Veyne's terms this hardly counts as a 'causal explanation', it does suggest that a similar turn to traditionalism and to the Rabbi as holy man (Rabbi Akiva) might similarly be connected with a similar enervation of dialectic as a method for arriving at truth. Just as for late antique philosophers, according to Lim (or at any rate *some* late antique philosophers), prestige and power shifted from the quality of one's logic to 'privileged access to the divine world', so too for Rabbi Akiva according to this Babylonian legend.[80] If we are not to speak, however, of a mystifying *Zeitgeist*, some way of getting from the West (Cappadocia!) to the East (Mesopotamia) and from Hellenistic philosophers and Christians to Rabbis needs to be hypothesised.

The East Syrian connection provides the historical scene upon which a drama can be played with characters as seemingly incongruous as Cappadocian Fathers and Babylonian Rabbis. As Becker has shown, all of the intellectual developments that took place among Nicene Christians and in their world became transferred to the Syriac realm as well and then translated further east with the founding of the school in Nisibis. Shouldn't

---

[76] Kovelman (1991) 135–52.

[77] It could be said, for example, that one route leads to Kabbala and the other to Judaeoscholasticism.

[78] Veyne (1997) 43.   [79] Lim (1995) 33 referring to Armstrong (1984) and Fowden (1982).

[80] 'Thus, the true worth of a philosopher depended not on his skill in philosophical discourse but on the nature and power of his daimon', Lim (1995) 59. Of course, I am not claiming this for the 'real' Rabbi Akiva nor yet for the Rabbi Akiva of the tradition in general but for this specific tradition, which is, of course, my precise point.

we consider, at least as a possibility, the notion that increased interaction between Aramaic-speaking Rabbis and Aramaic-speaking Christians, interaction that has been shown to have had enormous institutional impact on the Rabbis and the East Syrian Church in the very founding of their most characteristic institutions, the postamoraic Yeshiva and the school at Nisibis, also makes plausible significant imbrication in the ways that these two scholastic communities thought and spoke? Becker has pointed out that public dispute with those of other 'creeds' was a particular and self-conscious practice of the East Syrian scholastics.[81] As he has argued as well with respect to other similar interactions: 'In the process [of polemicising], these intellectuals ironically developed a common ground in which their disputation could occur. The fact that teachers and students could come from different religious backgrounds and even engage in polemic with each others' faiths, yet could still maintain their academic relationships, demonstrates the proximate intellectual space that they shared.'[82] Could we not say the same for our Rabbis and East Syrian schoolmen?

Richard Kalmin has demonstrated that contrary to what might be expected from the Talmud's own self-representation, it is in the Babylonian Talmud that we find a much greater instance of confrontations with early Christians narrated.[83] Although to be sure, most of these narratives are about Palestinian Sages, this phenomenon of much more prevalent narration of such confrontations can best be explained in my view by assuming that Christians and Christianity were important dialogue partners (or polemic partners) in fourth-century and later Mesopotamia.[84] The Talmud itself would seem to want to suppress such a connection:

Rabbi Abbahu used to praise Rav Safra [a Babylonian immigrant to Caesarea Maritima] to the minim that he was a great man [i.e. a great scholar]. They released him from excise taxes for thirteen years. One day they met him. They said to him: 'It is written: Only you have I known from all of the families of the earth; therefore I will tax you with all of your sins' [Amos 3:2]. One who is enraged,[85] does he punish his lover? He was silent, and didn't say anything to them. They threw a scarf on him and were mocking him. Rabbi Abbahu came and found them. He said to them: 'Why are you mocking him?' They said to him: 'Didn't you say that he is a great man, and he could not even tell us the interpretation of this verse!' He said to them: 'That which I said to you has to do with Mishna, but with respect to the Scripture, I didn't say

[81] Becker (2006) 14.
[82] Becker (2003) 390. This formulation is quite similar to my own notion of smuggled 'wheelbarrows' as developed in Boyarin (2004) 1–5.
[83] Kalmin (1994b) 155–69.   [84] For a related point, Becker (2006) 382, n. 39.
[85] Trans. following Rashi ad loc.

anything.' They said to him: 'What is it different with respect to you that you know [Scripture also]?' He said to them: 'We who are located in your midst, take it upon ourselves and we study, but they do not study.' (TB Avoda Zara 4a)

We find the Talmud here explicitly denying that in Babylonia the Rabbis were 'located in the midst' of Christians. In general, in the scholarly tradition this has been taken as evidence that the Rabbis of Babylonia had no Christians with which to contend,[86] but given the historical conditions exposed here, I would see its rhetorical function as quite different from that straightforward reading, indeed almost as evidence for the opposite conclusion. Just as, as S. Cohen has shown, the sites in which the most avid disavowal of Hellenism is found are very Hellenistic sites,[87] so we might argue vis-à-vis the Babylonians and Christianity. The very overstatement and vehemence of that denial, the palpably false claim that there are no Christians in the midst of the Babylonian Rabbis, can (at least) be defensibly read in the wake of Cohen's work as manifesting the effort of the Babylonian Talmud to disavow any connection, intercourse with and influence of Christians, just as the Qumran-folk and the Hasmoneans wish to present themselves as the very opposite of Hellenised Jews. It seems hardly implausible to consider even the Rabbis of the Sasanian empire, even as late as the end of late antiquity, as part and parcel of the Hellenistic world. As Becker, once again, sharply put it, 'Our assumptions about the lack of any interrelationship between the Jewish and Christian communities in late antique Mesopotamia have too often limited our capability of imagining how to use our wealth of textual evidence in new ways.'[88] The transition into a Gaonic period (eighth to eleventh centuries) in which Babylonian rabbinism was deeply and explicitly involved in Greek thought will seem much less abrupt and sudden on this account, and it would be the overall developments of thought in late ancient eastern Hellenism, including Syriac Christianity, and not only the Muslim conquest that would have brought about such transitions. While nothing, of course, can be proven, it seems more and more plausible to see the characteristics that are considered most distinctive, differentiating and indeed exemplary of rabbinic Judaism – the seeming resistance to truth claims, the turn to traditionalism, endless dialectic that has no *telos* and the multiplicity of interpretation – as being part and parcel of an epistemological shift that took place all over the Mediterranean world of late antiquity, reaching, moreover, across the borders of Rome and deep into the east as well.

---

[86] See now too Schremer (2005) 223–4 critiquing the usual position.
[87] Cohen (2000) 216–43.   [88] Becker (2006) 392.

Bibliography

Achard, G. (1991) *La Communication à Rome*. Paris.

Adamson, P., Baltussen, H. and Stone, M. eds. (2004) *Philosophy, Science and Exegesis in Greek, Arabic and Latin Commentaries*. London.

Alker, H. R., Jr (1988) 'The dialectical logic of Thucydides' Melian dialogue', *The American Political Science Review* 82.3: 805–20.

Allatius, L. (1655) *De Utriusque Ecclesiae Occidentalis atque Orientalis Perpetua in Dogmate de Purgatorio Consensu*. Rome.

Allison, J. W. (1997) *Word and Concept in Thucydides*. Atlanta.

Altman, J. G. (1986) 'The letter book as a literary institution 1539–1789: toward a cultural history of published correspondences in France', *Yale French Studies* 71: 17–62.

Amato, E. (2005) '*Rhetorike deipnizousa*: il banchetto di Dione di Prusa, Favorino e Luciano', *Euphrosyne* 33: 341–53.

Anderson, G. (1997) 'Athenaeus: the sophistic environment', *Aufstieg und Niedergang der römischen Welt* 2.34.3: 2173–85.

André, J-M. (1966) *L'otium dans la vie morale et intellectuelle romaine des origines à l'époque augustéenne*. Paris.

Andrieu, J. (1954) *Le dialogue antique: Structure et présentation*. Paris.

Annas, J. ed. (2001). *Cicero: On Moral Ends*, trans. R. Woolf. Cambridge.

Annas, J. and Rowe, C. eds. (2002) *New Perspectives on Plato, Modern and Ancient*. Cambridge, Mass.

Armstrong, A. H. (1984) 'Pagan and Christian traditionalism in the first three centuries, A.D.', *Studia Patristica* 15: 414–31.

Athanassiadi, P. (2002) 'The creation of orthodoxy in Neoplatonism', in Clark and Rajak (eds.).

Aubert, J.-J., and Varhelyi, Z. eds. (2005) *A Tall Order: Writing the Social History of the Ancient World. Essays in Honor of W. V. Harris*. Munich/Leipzig.

Auerbach, E. (1965) *Latin Literary Language and its Public in Late Latin Antiquity and in the Middle Ages*. London.

Ausland, H. (1997) 'On reading Plato mimetically', *American Journal of Philology* 118: 371–416.

Bakhtin, M. (1984) *Problems of Dostoevsky's Poetics*, ed. and trans. C. Emerson. Manchester. [First published in Russian in 1963.]

(2006a) *Speech Genres & Other Late Essays*, ed. C. Emerson and M. Holquist, trans. V. W. McGee (10th paperback printing; orig. 1986). Austin, Tex.

(2006b) *The Dialogic Imagination: Four Essays*, ed. M. Holquist, trans. C. Emerson and M. Holquist (16th paperback printing; orig. 1981). Austin, Tex.

Barber, B. R. (1996) 'Misreading democracy: Peter Euben and the *Gorgias*', in Ober and Hedrick (eds.).

Bardy, G. (1947) 'Le florilège d'Étienne Gobar', *Revue des études byzantines* 5: 5–30.

(1949) 'Le florilège d'Étienne Gobar', *Revue des études byzantines* 7: 51–2.

Barigazzi, A. (1966) *Favorino di Arelate. Opere.* Florence.

Barnish, S. J. (1990) 'Maximian, Cassiodorus, Boethius, Theodahad: Poetry, philosophy and politics in Ostrogothic Italy', *Nottingham Medieval Studies* 34: 16–32.

Baun, J. (2007) *Tales from Another Byzantium: Celestial Journey and Local Community in the Middle Greek Apocrypha.* Cambridge.

Beaujeu, J. ed. (1964) *Minucius Felix: Octavius.* Paris.

Becker, A. H. (2003) 'Beyond the spatial and temporal *limes*: Questioning the "parting of the ways" outside the Roman Empire', in Becker and Reed (eds.).

(2006) *The Fear of God and the Beginning of Wisdom: The School of Nisibis and Christian Scholastic Culture in Late Antique Mesopotamia.* Philadelphia, Pa.

Becker, A. H. and Reed, A. Y. eds. (2003) *The Ways That Never Parted: Jews and Christians in Late Antiquity and the Early Middle Ages.* Tübingen.

Beentjes, P. ed. (1997a) *The Book of Ben Sira in Modern Research: Proceedings of the First International Ben Sira Conference, July 1996, Soesterberg, Netherlands.* Berlin.

(1997b) *The Book of Ben Sira in Hebrew: A Text Edition of All Extant Hebrew Manuscripts and a Synopsis of All Parallel Hebrew Ben Sira Texts.* Leiden.

Behr, J. (2000) *Asceticism and Anthropology in Irenaeus and Clement.* Oxford.

Benson, H. H. ed. (2006) *A Companion to Plato.* Oxford.

Berchman, R. (1984) *From Philo to Origen: Middle Platonism in Transition*, Brown Judaic Studies 69. Chico, Calif.

Bialostosky, D. (1992) *Wordsworth, Dialogics, and the Practice of Criticism.* Cambridge.

Bigelmair, A. (1902) *Die Beteiligung der Christen am öffentlichen Leben in vorkonstantinischer Zeit: ein Beitrag zur ältesten Kirchengeschichte.* Munich.

Billault, A. ed. (1994) *Lucien de Samosate.* Lyon.

Blank, D. (1988) 'Socratics vs sophists on payment for teaching', *Classical Antiquity* 4: 1–49.

Blondell, R. (2002) *The Play of Character in Plato's Dialogues.* Cambridge.

Boedeker, D. and Rauflaub, K. eds. (1998) *Democracy, Empire, and the Arts in Fifth-Century Athens.* Cambridge.

Bokser, B. (1986) *The Origin of the Seder: The Passover Rite and Early Rabbinic Judaism.* Berkeley.

Bonner, G. (1986) *St Augustine of Hippo: Life and Controversies*, rev. edn. Norwich.

Bosworth, A. B. (1993) 'The humanitarian aspect of the Melian dialogue', *Journal of Hellenic Studies* 113: 30–44.

Bowersock, G. (1978) *Julian the Apostate.* London.

Bowie, A. M. (1997) 'Thinking with drinking: wine and the symposium in Aristophanes', *Journal of Hellenic Studies* 117: 1–21.

Boyarin, D. (1990) *Intertextuality and the Reading of Midrash*. Bloomington.

(2004) *Border Lines: The Partition of Judaeo-Christianity*. Philadelphia.

(2007a) 'The agon and the ecstasy: Platonic love and social conflict in the Talmud', unpublished ms.

(2007b) '"The Measure of All Things": Protagoras's Politics', unpublished ms.

Bradley, K. (1998) 'The Roman family at dinner', in Nielsen and Nielsen (eds.).

Branham, R. B. (1989) *Unruly Eloquence: Lucian and the Comedy of Traditions*. Cambridge, Mass.

ed. (2002) *Bakhtin and the Classics*. Evanston, Ill.

Braun, W. (1995) *Feasting and Social Rhetoric in Luke 14*. Cambridge.

Braund, D. and Wilkins, J. eds. (2000) *Athenaeus and his World. Reading Greek Culture in the Roman Empire*. Exeter.

Bremmer, J. (1990) 'Adolescents, symposion, and pederasty', in Murray (ed.).

Brittain, C. (2001) *Philo of Larissa: The Last of the Academic Sceptics*. Oxford.

Brock, S. (1982) 'From antagonism to assimilation: Syriac attitudes to Greek learning', in Garsoian, Matthews and Thomson (eds.). [Repr. in S. Brock (1984) *Syriac Perspectives on Late Antiquity*. London.]

Brooke G. J. and Kaestli, D. eds. (2000) *Narrativity in Biblical Studies*. Leuven.

Brown, P. (1968) 'Pelagius and his supporters: Aims and environment', *Journal of Theological Studies* 19.1: 83–114.

(1970) 'The patrons of Pelagius: The Roman aristocracy between East and West', *Journal of Theological Studies*, 21.1: 56–72.

(1971) 'The rise and function of the holy man in late antiquity', *Journal of Roman Studies* 61: 80–101.

(1988) *The Body and Society: Men, Women, and Sexual Renunciation in Early Christianity*. New York.

(1992) *Power and Persuasion in Late Antiquity: Towards a Christian Empire*. Madison, Wis.

(1998) 'The rise and function of the holy man in late antiquity, 1971–1997', *Journal of Early Christian Studies* 6: 353–76.

(1999) 'Images as a substitute for writing', in Chrysos and Wood (eds.).

(2000) *Augustine of Hippo: A Biography*. rev. ed. Berkeley. [Orig. ed. London 1967.]

(2003) *The Rise of Western Christendom: Triumph and Diversity, AD 200–1000*. Oxford.

Brumberg-Kraus, J. (1999) '"Not by bread alone…" The ritualization of food and table talk in the Passover Seder and in the Last Supper', *Semeia* 86: 165–91.

Bruns, G. (1990) 'The hermeneutics of midrash', in R. Schwartz (ed.) *The Book and the Text: The Bible and Literary Theory*. Oxford.

Buber, S. ed. (1899) *Midrash Ekhah Rabbah*. Vilna.

Buell, D. K. (1999) *Making Christians: Clement of Alexandria and the Rhetoric of Legitimacy*. Princeton.

Buonaiuti, E. (1921) 'The ethics and eschatology of Methodius of Olympus', *Harvard Theological Review* 14: 255–66.

Burnaby, J. (1954) 'The Retractions of St Augustine: Self-criticism or apologia?', *Augustinus Magister* 1: 85–92.

Burns, P. C. (2001) 'Augustine's use of Varro's *Antiquitates rerum divinarum* in his *De Civitate Dei*', *Augustinian Studies* 32.1: 37–64.

Burnyeat, M. F. (1990) *The Theaetetus of Plato*. Indianapolis.

Burton, P. (2005) 'The vocabulary of the liberal arts in Augustine's *Confessions*', in Pollmann and Vessey (eds.).

(2007) *Language in the Confessions of Augustine*. Oxford.

Calame, C. and Chartier, R. eds. (2004) *Identités de l'auteur*. Grenoble.

Cameron, Alan (1966) 'Date and identity of Macrobius', *JRS* 56: 25–38.

(1995) *Callimachus and his Critics*. Princeton.

Cameron, Averil (1988) 'Byzantium and the past in the seventh century: the search for redefinition', in *Proceedings of a Joint French and British Colloquium at the Warburg Institute, 8–9 July 1988*.

(1991a) *Christianity and the Rhetoric of Empire: The Development of Christian Discourse*. Berkeley.

(1991b) 'Disputations, polemical literature and the formation of opinion in the early Byzantine period', in Reinink and Vanstiphout (eds.).

(1992a) 'New themes and styles in Greek literature: seventh to eighth centuries', in Cameron and Conrad (eds.).

(1992b) 'Byzantium and the past in the seventh century: the search for redefinition', in Fontaine and Hillgarth eds. (1992).

(1996) *Changing Cultures in Early Byzantium*. London.

(2007) 'Enforcing Orthodoxy in Byzantium', in Cooper and Gregory (eds.).

Cameron, A. and Conrad, L. I. eds. (1992) *The Byzantine and Early Islamic Near East*, vol. I: *Problems in the Literary Source Material*. Princeton.

Cameron, A. and Garnsey, P. eds. (1998) *Cambridge Ancient History*, vol. XIII: *The Late Empire, AD 337–42*. Cambridge.

Cardauns, B. (1976) *M. Terentius Varro, Antiquitates rerum divinarum*, 2 vols. Wiesbaden.

Carlos, H. de (2001) 'Poetry and parody: Boethius, dreams, and gestures in the letters of Godfrey of Rheims', *Essays in Medieval Studies* 18: 18–30.

Cary, P. (1988) 'What Licentius learned: A narrative reading of the Cassiciacum dialogues', *Augustinian Studies* 29: 141–63.

(2000) *Augustine's Invention of the Inner Self: The Legacy of a Christian Platonist*. Oxford.

Ceccarelli, P. (2000) 'Dance and desserts: an analysis of Book fourteen', in Braund and Wilkins (eds.).

Chadwick, H. (1953) *Origen: Contra Celsum*. Cambridge.

(1981) *Boethius: The Consolations of Music, Logic, Theology and Philosophy*. Oxford.

Chartier, R. (1990) *Les origines culturelles de la Révolution française*. Paris.

Chroust, A.-H. (1977) *Socrates, Man and Myth: The two Socratic Apologies of Xenophon*. London.

Chrysos, E. K., and Wood, I. N. eds. (1999) *East and West: Modes of Communication*, vol. 5: *Transformation of the Roman world*. Leiden.

Ciccarese, M. P. (1971) 'La Tipologia delle lettere di S. Agostino', *Augustinianum* 11: 471–503.

Clark, F. (1987) *The Pseudo-Gregorian Dialogues*. Leiden.

(2003) *The 'Gregorian' Dialogues and the Origins of Benedictine Monasticism*. Leiden.

Clark, G. (2004) *Christianity and Roman Society*. Cambridge.

(2007a) 'City of Books: Augustine and the world as text', in Klingshirn and Safran (eds.).

(2007b) 'Augustine's Porphyry and the way of universal salvation', in Sheppard and Karamanolis (eds.).

Clark, G. and Rajak, T. eds. (2002) *Philosophy and Power in the Graeco-Roman World*. Oxford.

Clay, D. (1994) 'The origins of the Socratic dialogue', in Vander Waerdt, (ed.).

(2000) *Platonic Questions: Dialogues with the Silent Philosopher*. University Park, Pa.

Cohen, S. J. D. (2000) 'Hellenism in Unexpected Places', in Collins and Sterling (eds.).

Cole, T. (1991) *Origins of Rhetoric*. Baltimore.

Collins, D. (2005) *Master of the Game: Competition and Performance in Greek Poetry*. Cambridge, Mass.

Collins, J. J. (1997) *Jewish Wisdom in the Hellenistic Age*. Louisville, Ky.

Collins, J. J., and Sterling, G. eds. (2000) *Hellenism in the Land of Israel*. Notre Dame.

Connor, W. R. (1984) *Thucydides*. Princeton.

Constas, N. (2002) 'An apology for the cult of saints in late antiquity: Eustratius Presbyter of Constantinople, *On the State of Souls after Death*', *Journal of Early Christian Studies* 10: 267–80.

Conybeare, C. (2000) *Paulinus noster: Self and Symbols in the Letters of Paulinus of Nola*. Oxford.

(2005) 'The duty of a teacher', in Pollmann and Vessey (eds.).

(2006) *The Irrational Augustine*. Oxford.

Cooper, K. (2000) 'Matthidia's Wish: Division, reunion, and the early Christian family in the pseudo-Clementine *Recognitions*', in Brooke and Kaestli (eds.).

(2005) 'Ventriloquism and the miraculous: Conversion, preaching, and the martyr exemplum in late antiquity', in Cooper and Gregory (eds.).

(2007) *The Fall of the Roman Household*. Cambridge.

Cooper, K. and Gregory, J. eds. (2005) *Signs, Wonders, and Miracles*, Studies in Church History 41. Woodbridge.

eds. (2007) *Discipline and Diversity*, Studies in Church History 43. Woodbridge.

Copeland, R. ed. (1996) *Criticism and Dissent in the Middle Ages*. Cambridge.

Corley, J. (2002) *Ben Sira's Teaching on Friendship*. Providence, R.I.

Cox, V. (1992) *The Renaissance Dialogue: Literary Dialogue in its Social and Political Contexts, Castiglione to Galileo*. Cambridge.

Crabbe, A. (1981) 'Literary design in the *De Consolatione Philosophiae*', in Gibson (ed).

Crane, G. (1996) *The Blinded Eye: Thucydides and the New Written Word*. Lanham, Md.

(1998) *Thucydides and the Ancient Simplicity: The Limits of Political Realism.* Berkeley.

Crepsin, R. (1965) *Ministère et sainteté: Pastorale du clergé et solution de la crise Donatiste dans la vie et la doctrine de Saint Augustin.* Paris.

Crossley, N. and Roberts, K. M. (2004) *After Habermas: New Perspectives on the Public Sphere.* Oxford.

Dagron, G. (1981) 'Quand la terre tremble…', *Travaux et Mémoires* 8 *(Hommage à M. Paul Lemerle)*: 87–103.

(1984) *La romanité chrétienne en Orient: Héritages et mutations.* London.

(1992) 'L'ombre d'un doute: l'hagiographie en question, VIe–XIe siècles', *Dumbarton Oaks Papers* 46: 59–68.

Dal Santo, M. (in press) 'Gregory the Great and Eustratius of Constantinople on the miracles of the saints', *Journal of Early Christian Studies.*

Daly, L. W. and Suchier, W. (1939) *Altercatio Hadriani Augusti et Epicteti philosophi.* Urbana, Ill.

Dancy, J. (1995). '"For here the author is annihilated": reflections on philosophical aspects of the use of the dialogue form in Hume's *Dialogues concerning Natural Religion*', in *Philosophical Dialogues: Plato, Hume, Wittgenstein. Proceedings of the British Academy* 85: 29–60.

Danzig, G. (2003) 'Apologizing for Socrates', *Transactions and Proceedings of the American Philological Society* 133: 281–321.

D'Arms, J. (1990) 'The Roman Convivium and the Idea of Equality', in Murray (ed.).

Davies, P. R. (1999) 'Food, drink and sects: The question of ingestion in the Qumran texts', *Semeia* 86: 151–64.

Davila, J. R. (2001) *Descenders to the Chariot: The People Behind the Hekhalot Literature.* Leiden.

Davis, N. Z. (2000) *The Gift in Sixteenth-Century France.* Madison, Wis.

Dawson, D. (1992) *Allegorical Readers and Cultural Revision in Ancient Alexandria.* Berkeley.

Denning-Bolle, S. (1987) 'Wisdom and dialogue in the ancient Near East', *Numen* 34: 214–34.

(1992) *Wisdom in Akkadian Literature: Expression, Instruction, Dialogue.* Leiden.

Deun, P. van ed. (2006) *Eustratii Presbyteri Constantinopolitani De statu animarum post mortem*, Corpus Christianorum Series Graeca 60. Leuven.

Dewald, C. (2005) *Thucydides' War Narrative: A Structural Study.* Berkeley.

Diepen, H.-M. (1959) 'La pensée christologique d'Arnobe le Jeune: Théologie de l'Assumptus Homo ou de l'Emmanuel?', *Revue Thomiste* 59: 535–64.

Diesel, A. A. et al. eds. (1996) *'Jedes Ding hat seine Zeit…' Studien zur israelitischen und altorientalischen Weisheit. Diethelm Michel zum 65. Geburtstag*, Beihefte zur *Zeitschrift für die Alttestamentliche Wissenschaft* 241. Berlin.

Dieterle, R. (1966) 'Platons Laches und Charmides. Untersuchungen zur elenktisch-aporetischen Struktur der platonischen Frühdialoge. Dissertation, Freiburg.

Döpp, S. (1978) 'Zur Datierung von Macrobius' *Saturnalia*', *Hermes* 106: 619–32.

Doty, W. (1973) *Letters in Primitive Christianity.* Minneapolis.

Dougherty, C. and Kurke, L. eds. (1998) *Cultural Poetics in Archaic Greece.* Cambridge.

Dufour. R. (2005) 'Review of M. Fattal, *La philosphie du platon. Tome 2*', *Bryn Mawr Classical Review* 2005.10.35. [online journal]

Dunbabin, K. (1998) ' *"Ut Graeco more biberetur": Greeks and Romans on the dining couch*' in Nielsen and Nielsen (eds.).

   (2003) *The Roman Banquet: Images of Conviviality.* Cambridge.

Dupont, F. (1977) *Le plaisir et la loi: du 'Banquet' de Platon au 'Satiricon'.* Paris.

Düring, I. (1957) *Aristotle in the Ancient Biographical Tradition.* Göteborg.

Edwards, M., Goodman, M. and Price, S. eds. (1999) *Apologetics in the Roman Empire: Pagans, Jews and Christians.* Oxford.

Elias, N. (1994) *The Civilizing Process: Sociogenetic and Psychogenetic Investigations,* rev. ed. Oxford.

Elman, Y. (2006) 'Middle Persian culture and Babylonian sages: Accommodation and resistance in the shaping of rabbinic legal traditions' in Fonrobert and Jaffee (eds.).

Emerson, C. (1997) *The First Hundred Years of Mikhail Bakhtin.* Princeton.

Enders, J. (1996) 'Rhetoric, Coercion, and the Memory of Violence', in Copeland (ed.).

Eno, R. B. (1981) 'Doctrinal authority in Saint Augustine', in *Augustinian Studies* 12: 133–172.

Euben, J. P. (1996) 'Reading democracy: Socratic dialogues and the political education of democratic citizens', in Ober and Hedrick (eds.).

Evans, R. (1968) *Pelagius: Inquiries and Reappraisals.* New York.

Fattal, M. ed. (2005) *La philosophie de Platon,* vol. 2. Paris.

Ferrary, J.-L. (1988). *Philhellénisme et impérialisme: Aspects idéologiques de la conquête romaine du monde hellénistique.* Rome.

Fisch, M. (1997) *Rational Rabbis: Science and Talmudic Culture.* Jewish Literature and Culture. Bloomington.

Flacelière, R. and Irigoin, J. eds. (1987) *Plutarque: Oeuvres Morales,* Vol.I.1 (Budé). Paris.

Flamant, J. (1968) 'La technique du banquet dans les *Saturnales* de Macrobe', *Revue des études latines* 46: 303–19.

   (1977) *Macrobe et le néo-platonisme latin à la fin du IVe siècle.* Leiden.

Foley, M. P. (1999) 'Cicero, Augustine, and the philosophical roots of the Cassiciacum dialogues', *Revue des études augustiniennes* 45: 51–77.

Fonrobert, C. and Jaffee, M. eds. (2006) *Cambridge Companion to Rabbinic Literature.* Cambridge.

Fontaine, J., Gillet, R. and Pellistrandi, S. eds. (1986) *Grégoire le Grand: Actes du colloque de Chantilly 15–19 sept. 1982.* Paris.

Fontaine, J. and Hillgarth, J. N. eds. (1992) *Septième siecle: Changements et continuités.* London.

Ford, A. (2001) 'Sophists without rhetoric: the Arts of Speech in Fifth-century Athens', in Too, Y.L. (ed.).

   (2005) 'From Letters to Literature: Reading the "Song Culture" of Classical Greece', in Yunis (ed.).

Fowden, G. (1982) 'The pagan holy man in late antique society', *Journal of Hellenic Studies* 102: 33–59.

(1998) 'Polytheist religion and philosophy', in Cameron and Garnsey (eds.).

Frazier, F. (1994) 'Deux images des banquets de letters: les *Propos de Table* de Plutarque et le *Banquet* de Lucien', in Billault (ed.).

Frazier, F. and Sirinelli, J. eds. (1996) *Plutarque – Oeuvres Morales*, vol. IX.3 (Budé). Paris.

Frede, M. (1992) 'Plato's arguments and the dialogue form', *Oxford Studies in Ancient Philosophy*, suppl. vol.: 201–19.

Fredriksen, P. (1999) '*Secundum carnem*: history and Israel in the theology of St Augustine', in Klingshirn and Vessey (eds.).

(2006) *Augustine and the Jews*. New York.

Frend, W. H. C. (2003) *The Donatist Church: A Movement of Protest in Roman North Africa*. Oxford.

Fuhrmann, F. ed. (1972) *Plutarque – Oeuvres Morales*, Vol. IX.1 (Budé) Paris.

Gabba, E. ed. (1983) *Tria Corda: Scritti in onore di Arnaldo Momigliano*. Como.

Gaiser, K. (1959) *Protreptik und Pärenese bei Platon: Untersuchungen zur Form des Platonischen Dialogs*. Stuttgart.

Garsoian, N., Mathews, T. and Thomson, R. eds. (1982) *East of Byzantium: Syria and Armenia in the Formative Period*. Washington, DC.

Giangrande, G. (1967) 'Sympotic literature and epigram', in *L'Epigramme grecque. Entretiens Hardt* 14: 93–177.

Giannantoni, G. (1990) *Socratis et Socraticorum Reliquiae*, 2nd edn. Naples.

Gibson, M. ed. (1981) *Boethius: His Life, Thought and Influence*. London.

Gildenhard, I. (2007). *Paideia Romana: Cicero's Tusculan Disputations. Cambridge Classical Journal*, Suppl. Vol. 30. Cambridge.

Gill, C. (2002) 'Dialectic and the dialogue form', in Annas and Rowe (eds.).

Gill, C. and McCabe, M. M. eds. (1996) *Form and Argument in Late Plato*. Oxford.

Gilliard, F. D. (1984) 'Senatorial bishops in the fourth century', *Harvard Theological Review* 77: 153–75.

Glad, C. (1985) *Paul and Philodomeus: Adaptability in Epicurean and Early Christian Psychagogy*. Leiden.

Glucker, J. (1995) '*Probabile, veri simile*, and related terms', in Powell (ed.).

Goldhill, S. (1986) *Reading Greek Tragedy*. Cambridge.

(1995) *Foucault's Virginity: Ancient Erotic Fiction and the History of Sexuality*. Cambridge.

ed. (2001) *Being Greek Under Rome: Cultural Identity, the Second Sophistic and the Development of Empire*. Cambridge.

(2002) *The Invention of Prose*. Oxford.

Goldhill, S. and Osborne, R. eds. (1998) *Performance Culture and Athenian Democracy*. Cambridge.

Goldschmidt, V. (1963) *Les dialogues de Platon: Structure et méthode dialectique*, 2nd edn. Paris.

Goldstein, J. (1968) *The Letters of Demosthenes*. New York.

Görgemans, H. (2002) 'Dialogue', in *Brill's New Pauly*, Vol. III: 351–52. Leiden.

Gouldner, A. (1960) 'The norm of reciprocity: A preliminary statement', *American Sociological Review* 25: 161–78.

Gowers, E. (1993) *The Loaded Table: Representations of Food in Roman Literature.* Oxford.

Graumann, T. (2007) 'Council proceedings and juridical process: The cases of Aquileia (AD 381) and Ephesus', in Cooper and Gregory (eds.).

Greenwood, E. (2004) 'Making words count: Freedom of speech and narrative in Thucydides', in I. Sluiter and R. Rosen (eds.) *Free Speech in Antiquity.* Leiden and Boston.

(2006) *Thucydides and the Shaping of History.* London.

Gregg, R. C. and Groh, D. (1981) *Early Arianism: A View of Salvation.* Philadelphia.

Griffin, M. T. (1997) 'The composition of the Academica: motives and versions', in Inwood and Mansfeld (eds.).

Grimm, V. (1996) *From Feasting to Fasting, the Evolution of a Sin: Attitudes to Food in Late Antiquity.* London and New York.

Griswold, C. ed. (1988) *Platonic Writings, Platonic Readings.* New York.

Gundert, H. (1971) *Dialog und Dialektik.* Amsterdam.

Gutas, D. (1983) 'Paul the Persian on the classification of the parts of Aristotle's philosophy: A milestone between Alexandria and Baghdad', *Der Islam* 60: 231–67.

Habermas, J. (1989) *Structural Transformation of the Public Sphere.* Cambridge, Mass.

Habinek, T. (2005) *The World of Roman Song: From Ritualized Speech to Social Order.* Baltimore.

Halivni, D. (2005) 'Aspects of the formation of the Talmud' [in Hebrew], *Sidra* 20: 68–116.

Halperin, D. (1991) 'Why is Diotima a woman?', in Zeitlin, Halperin and Winkler (eds.).

1992 'Plato and the erotics of narrativity', in Hexter and Selden (eds.).

Halperin, D., Winkler, J. and Zeitlin, F. eds. (1990) *Nothing To Do With Dionysus?* Princeton.

Handelman, S. (1982) *The Slayers of Moses: The Emergence of Rabbinic Interpretation in Modern Literary Theory.* Albany.

Hardie, P. R. (1992) 'Plutarch and the interpretation of myth', *Aufstieg und Niedergang der römischen Welt* 2.33.6: 4743–87.

Harmless, W. (1995) *Augustine and the Catechumenate.* Collegeville, Minn.

Harnack, A. von (1922) *Dogmengeschichte*, 6th edn, Tübingen.

(1923) 'The "Sic et Non" of Stephen Gobarus', *Harvard Theological Review* 16: 205–34.

Harran, D. (1970) 'Towards a definition of the early secular dialogue', *Music & Letters* 51: 37–50.

Harris, W. V. (1989) *Ancient Literacy.* Cambridge, Mass.

Harrison, C. (2000) *Augustine: Christian Truth and Fractured Humanity.* Cambridge.

(2006) *Rethinking Augustine's Early Theology: An Argument for Continuity.* Oxford.

Harrison, S. (2006) *Augustine's Way into the Will.* Oxford.

Hart, R. and Tejera, V. eds. (1997) *Plato's Dialogues – The Dialogical Approach*. New York.

Haslam, M. W. (1972) 'Plato, Sophron and the Dramatic Dialogue', *Bulletin of the Institute of Classical Studies* 19: 17–38.

Hayes, C. (1997) *Between the Babylonian and Palestinian Talmuds*. Oxford.

Henderson, J. G. W. (2000) 'The life and soul of the party: Plato's Symposium', in Sharrock and Morales (eds.).

Henry, R. (1959–91) *Photius. Bibliothèque*. Paris.

Herman, G. (2005) 'The Exilarchate in the Sasanian era', PhD dissertation, Hebrew University.

Hermann, A. (1950) 'Dialog', in *Reallexikon für Antike und Christentum*, vol. III: cols. 928–55.

Hermanowicz, E. (2004) 'Book Six and Augustine's *De Musica* and the Episcopal Embassies of 408', *Augustinian Studies* 35: 165–98.

    (2008) *Possidius of Calama: a study of the North African Episcopate*. Oxford.

Hesk, J. (2000) *Deception and Democracy in Classical Athens*, Cambridge.

Hexter, R. and Selden, D. eds. (1992) *Innovations of Antiquity*. New York.

Hezser, C. (1998) 'The Codification of Legal Knowledge in Late Antiquity: The Talmud Yerushalmi and Roman Law Codes', in Schäfer (ed.).

    (2000) 'Interfaces between rabbinic literature and Graeco-Roman philosophy', in Schäfer and Hezser (eds.).

Hillard, T. W., Kearsley, R. A., Nixon, C. E. and Nobbs, A. M. eds. (1998) *Ancient History in a Modern University*, vol. II. *Early Christianity, Late Antiquity and Beyond*. Grand Rapids, Mich.

Hirzel, R. (1895) *Der Dialog*, 2 vols. Hildesheim.

Hoffmann, M. (1966) *Der dialog bei den christlichen Schriftstellern der ersten vier Jahrhunderte*. Berlin.

Holmes, C. and Waring, J. eds. (2002) *Literacy, Education and Manuscript Transmission in Byzantium and Beyond*. Leiden.

Holquist, M. (1990) *Dialogism: Bakhtin and his World*. London.

Honigman, S. (2003) *The Septuagint and Homeric Scholarship in Alexandria: A Study in the Narrative of the Letter of Aristeas*. London.

Hopkins, K. (1998) 'Christian number and its implication', *Journal of Early Christian Studies* 6: 185–226.

    (1999) *A World Full of Gods*. London.

Horden, J. (2004) *Sophron's Mimes*. Oxford.

Hornblower, S. (1994) *Thucydides*, 2nd rev. edn. London.

Horsfall, N. (2003) *The Culture of the Roman Plebs*. London.

Howard-Johnston, J. (1999) 'Heraclius' Persian campaigns and the revival of the East Roman Empire, 622–630', *War in History* 6: 1–44.

Hudson-Williams, H. (1950) 'Conventional forms of debate and the Melian dialogue', *American Journal of Philology* 71.2: 156–69.

Hugonnard-Roche, H. (1989) 'Aux origines de l'exégèse orientale de la logique d'Aristote: Sergius de Reš'aina († 536), médecin et philosophe', *Journal Asiatique* 277: 1–17.

(2000) 'Le traité de logique de Paul le Perse: une interprétation tardo-antique de la logique aristotélicienne en syriaque', *Documenti e Studi sulla Tradizione Filosofica* 11: 59–82.

Humfress, C. (2007) *Orthodoxy and the Courts in Late Antiquity*. Oxford.

Hunter, E. C. D. (2002) 'The transmission of Greek philosophy via the school of Edessa', in Holmes and Waring (eds.).

Hunter, R. (2004) *Plato's Symposium*. Oxford.

Hutchinson, G. O. (1998) *Cicero's Correspondence: A Literary Study*. Oxford.

Inwood, B. and Mansfeld, J. eds. (1997) *Assent and Argument: Studies in Cicero's Academic Books*. Leiden/New York/Cologne.

Irwin, E. and Greenwood, E. eds. (2007) *Reading Herodotus: A Study of the Logoi in Book 5 of Herodotus' Histories*. Cambridge.

Irwin, T. H. (1979) *Plato: Gorgias*. Oxford.

(1986) 'Coercion and objectivity in Plato's dialectic', *Revue Internationale de Philosophie* 156–7: 49–74.

Jacob, C. (2001) 'Ateneo, o il dedalo delle parole', in A. Canfora (ed.) *Ateneo. I deipnosofisti. I dotti a banchetto*. Rome: xi–cxxi.

Jeanneret, M. (1991) *A Feast of Words: Banquets and Table-Talk in the Renaissance*, trans. J. Whiteley and E. Hughes. Cambridge. [First published in French in 1987.]

Joël, K. (1894–95) 'Der λόγος Σωχρατικός', *Archiv für d. Geschichte. d. Philos.* 8: 466–83.

Jordan, M. D. (1981) 'A preface to the study of philosophic genres', *Philosophy and Rhetoric* 14: 199–211.

Kahn, C. (1996) *Plato and the Socratic Dialogue: The Philosophical Use of a Literary Form*. Cambridge.

Kalmin, R. (1994a) 'Christians and Heretics in Rabbinic Literature of Late Antiquity', *Harvard Theological Review* 87: 155–69.

(1994b) *Sages, Stories, Authors, and Editors in Rabbinic Babylonia*. Brown Judaica Studies 300. Atlanta.

(2006) *Jewish Babylonia Between Persia and Roman Palestine*. Oxford.

Kaster, R. (1980) 'Macrobius and Servius', *Harvard Studies in Classical Philology* 84: 219–62.

Katos, D. (2007) 'Socratic dialogue or courtroom debate? Judicial rhetoric and stasis theory in the *Dialogue on the Life of St. John Chrysostom*', *Vigiliae Christianae* 61: 42–69.

Kelly, J. N. D. (1975) *Jerome, His Life, Writings and Controversies*. London.

Kemp Smith, N. ed. (1935) *Hume's Dialogues concerning Natural Religion*. Oxford.

King, K. L. (2003) *Making Heresy: Gnosticism in Twentieth-Century Historiography*. Cambridge, Mass.

Kirkby, H. (1981) 'The scholar and his public', in Gibson (ed.).

Klagge, J. C. and Smith N. D. eds. (1992) *Methods of Interpreting Plato and his Dialogues*, Oxford Studies in Ancient Philosophy, Suppl. Oxford.

Klingshirn, W. (1994) *Caesarius of Arles: The Making of a Christian Community in Late Antique Gaul*. Cambridge.

Klingshirn, W. and Safran, L. eds. (2007) *The Early Christian Book*. Washington, D.C.

Klingshirn, W. and Vessey, M. eds. (1999) *The Limits of Ancient Christianity: Essays on Late Antique Thought and Culture in Honor of R. A. Markus.* Michigan.

König, J. (2007) 'Fragmentation and coherence in Plutarch's *Quaestiones Convivales*', in König and Whitmarsh (eds.).

(forthcoming) 'Athenaeus and the voices of the library', in Wilkins (ed.).

König, J. and Whitmarsh, T. eds. (2007) *Ordering Knowledge in the Roman Empire.* Cambridge.

Konstan, D. (1997) *Friendship in the Classical World.* Cambridge.

Kovocs, J. (2001) 'Divine Pedagogy and the gnostic teacher according to Clement of Alexandria', *Journal of Early Christian Studies* 9: 3–25.

Kovelman, A. B. (2005) *Between Alexandria and Jerusalem: The Dynamic of Jewish and Hellenistic Culture.* Leiden.

(1991) 'From logos to myth: Egyptian petitions of the fifth to seventh centuries', *Bulletin of the American Society of Papyrologists* 28, 3–4: 135–52.

Kraemer, D. C. (1990) *The Mind of the Talmud: An Intellectual History of the Bavli.* New York.

Krausmüller, D. (1998/99) 'God or angels as impersonators of saints: a belief in its context in the *Refutation* of Eustratius of Constantinople and the writings of Anastasius of Sinai', *Gouden Hoorn* 6 [electronic journal].

Krauss, S. (1912) *Talmudische Archaeologie*, volume III. Leipzig. [Repr. New York, 1979.]

Kraut, R. (1988) 'Reply to Clifford Orwin', in Griswold (ed.).

(n.d.) 'Why Dialogues?' in *Stanford Encyclopedia of Philosophy.* http://plato.stanford.edu/entries/plato/.

Krueger, D. (2004) *Writing and Holiness: The Practice of Authorship in the Early Christian East.* Philadelphia.

Kugel, J. (1981) *The Idea of Biblical Poetry.* New Haven.

Labendz, J. (2006) 'The Book of Ben Sira in Rabbinic Literature', *Association of Jewish Studies Review* 30: 347–92.

Laborderie, J. (1978) *Le dialogue platonicien de la maturité.* Paris.

Laidlaw, J. (2002) 'A free gift makes no friends', in Osteen (ed.).

Laidlaw, W. A. (1968) 'Otium', *Greece and Rome* 15: 42–6.

Laird, A. (1999) *Powers of Expression, Expressions of Power: Speech Presentation and Latin Literature.* Oxford and New York.

Laks, A. (2004) 'Sur l'anonymat Platonicien et ses antecedents', in Calame and Chartier eds. (2004).

Lancel, S. (1972) *Actes de la Conférence de Carthage en 411*, vol I. Sources chrétiennes 194. Paris.

(2000) *St Augustine.* London.

Lane, M. (2001) *Plato's Progeny: How Plato and Socrates Still Captivate the Modern Mind.* London.

Lasserre, F. (1944) 'Erôtikoi logoi', *Museum Helveticum* 1: 169–78.

Leach, E. (1954) *The Political System of Highland Burma: A Study of Kachin Social Structure.* Reprinted in 1970: LSE Monographs on Social Anthropology 44. London.

Leclercq, J. (1982) *Love of Learning and the Desire for God: A Study of Monastic Culture*, trans. C. Misrahi. New York.

Lella, A. di (1966) 'Conservative and progressive theology: Sirach and wisdom', *Catholic Biblical Quarterly* 38: 139–54.

(1996) 'Use and abuse of the tongue: Ben Sira 5.9–6.1', in Diesel et al. (eds.).

Lerer, S. (1985) *Boethius and Dialogue: Literary Method in the Consolation of Philosophy*. Princeton.

Letrouit, J. (1991) 'A propos de la tradition manuscrite d'Athénée: une mise au point', *Maia* 43: 33–40.

Levine, P. (1958) 'Cicero and the literary dialogue', *Classical Journal* 53: 146–51.

Leyser, C. (2000) *Authority and Asceticism from Augustine to Gregory the Great*. Oxford.

Lieberman, S. (1955) *Tosefta Kifshutah*, vol. I. New York.

Liebeschuetz, W. (1968) 'The structure and function of the Melian dialogue', *Journal of Hellenic Studies* 88: 73–7.

Lieu, J. M. (2004) *Christian Identity in the Jewish and Graeco-Roman World*. Oxford.

Lilla, S. R. C. (1971) *Clement of Alexandria: A Study in Christian Platonism and Gnosticism*. Oxford.

Lim, R. (1991) 'Theodoret of Cyrus and the speakers in Greek dialogues', *Journal of Hellenic Studies* III: 181–2.

(1995) *Public Disputation, Power, and Social Order in Late Antiquity*. Berkeley, Calif.

(2004) 'Augustine, the grammarians and the cultural authority of Vergil', in Rees (ed.).

Lissarague, F. (1990) *The Aesthetics of the Greek Banquet*. Princeton.

Livingstone, N. (2001) *A Commentary on Isocrates' Busiris*. Leiden.

Llewelyn, S. R. (1995) 'Sending letters in the ancient world: Paul and the Philippians', *Tyndale Bulletin* 46: 339–49.

Lloyd, G. E. R. (1987) *The Revolutions of Wisdom: Studies in the Claims and Practice of Greek Science*. Berkeley.

Lodge, D. (1990) *After Bakhtin. Essays on Fiction and Criticism*. London.

Löhr, W. (2000) 'The theft of the Greeks: Christian self-definition in the age of the schools', *Rev. Hist. Eccl.* 95: 403–26.

Long, A. A. (1995) 'Cicero's Plato and Aristotle', in Powell (ed.).

Long, A. G. (2005) 'Character and consensus in Plato's *Protagoras*', *The Cambridge Classical Journal* 51: 1–20.

Loraux, N. (1986a) *The Invention of Athens. The Funeral Oration in the Classical City*, trans. A. Sheridan. Cambridge, Mass.

Loraux, N. (1986b) 'Thucydide a écrit la Guerre du Péloponnèse', *Métis* I: 139–61.

Lossky, V. (1957) *The Mystical Theology of the Eastern Church*. London.

Louth, A. (1981) *The Origins of the Christian Mystical Tradition from Plato to Denys*. Oxford.

Lunn-Rockliffe, S. (2007) *Ambrosiaster's Political Theology*. Oxford.

Maas, M. ed. (2005) *Cambridge Companion to the Age of Justinian*. Cambridge.

McCabe, M. M. (2000) *Plato and his Predecessors: The Dramatisation of Reason*. Cambridge.

(2006) 'Form and the Platonic dialogues', in Benson (ed.).

MacCormack, S. (1998) *The Shadows of Poetry: Vergil in the Mind of Augustine.* Berkeley, Calif.

MacGeorge, P. (2002) *Late Roman Warlords.* Oxford.

MacKendrick, P. (1989) *The Philosophical Books of Cicero.* London.

Macleod, C. (1983) 'Form and meaning in the Melian dialogue', in C. Macleod *Collected Essays*, ed. O. Taplin. Oxford.

McLynn, N. (1992) 'Christian controversy and violence in the fourth century', *Kodai* 3: 15–44.

(1999) 'Augustine's Roman Empire', in Vessey, Pollmann and Fitzgerald (eds.).

MacMullen, R. (1989) 'The preacher's audience (AD 350–400)', *Journal of Theological Studies* 40: 503–11.

Magalhães-Vilhena, V. de (1952) *Socrate et la légende platonicienne.* Paris.

Maier, H. B. (1913) *Sokrates: Sein Werk und seine geschichtliche Stellung.* Tübingen.

Maier, H. O. (1994) 'Clement of Alexandria and care of the self', *Journal of the American Academy of Religion* 62: 719–45.

Männlein, I. (2000) 'What can go wrong at a dinner-party. The unmasking of false philosophers in Lucian's *Symposium* or *Lapiths*', in Pollmann (ed.).

Mariani, G. (1982) *Sant'Agostino guida spirituale: Lettere del vescovo di Ippona a Proba, Giuliana e Demetriade.* Rome.

Markus, R. (1990) *The End of Ancient Christianity.* Cambridge.

(1994) *Sacred and Secular: Essays on Augustine and Latin Christianity.* Aldershot.

(2002) 'The Legacy of Pelagius, orthodoxy, heresy and conciliation', in Williams (ed.).

Marrou, H.-I. (1960) 'Introduction générale', in H.-I. Marrou and M. Harl (eds.) *Clément d'Aléxandrie*, Le Pédagogue, *Livre 1.* Paris.

Martin, J. (1931) *Symposion: die Geschichte einer literarischen Form.* Paderborn.

Martin, R. (1998) 'The seven sages as performers of wisdom', in Dougherty and Kurke (eds.).

Martindale, C. and Thomas, R. eds. (2006) *Classics and the Uses of Reception.* Oxford.

Martinetto, G. (1971) 'Les premières réactions antiaugustiniennes de Pélage', *Revue des études augustiniennes* xvii: 83–117.

Matthews, J. (1981) 'Anicius Manlius Severinus Boethius' in Gibson (ed.).

Mauss, M. (1966) *The Gift*, trans. I. Cuisson. London. [Orig. *Sur le don*, Paris 1925].

Maxwell, J. (2006) *Christianization and Communication in Late Antiquity: John Chrysostom and his Congregation in Antioch.* Cambridge.

Mayor, J. B. ed. (1880–5) *M. Tulli Ciceronis De natura deorum libri tres.* Cambridge.

Mendels, D. (1999) *The Media Revolution of Early Christianity.* Grand Rapids, Mich.

Meyendorff, J. (1975) *Byzantine Theology: Historical Trends and Doctrinal Themes.* London.

Meyer, M. (1980) 'Dialectic and questioning: Socrates and Plato', *American Philosophical Quarterly* 17: 281–9.

Möllendorf, P. von (1995) *Grundlagen einer Ästhetik der Alten Komödie: Untersuchungen zu Aristophanes und Michail Bachtin.* Tübingen.

Momigliano, A. (1971/1993) *The Development of Greek Biography*, expanded edn. Cambridge, Mass.

(1984) 'The theological efforts of the Roman upper classes in the first century B.C.', *Classical Philology* 79: 199–211.

Monceaux, P. (1901–23) *Histoire littéraire de l'Afrique Chrétienne*. Paris.

Morgan, K. (2000) *Myth and Philosophy from the Presocratics to Plato*. Cambridge.

Morrison, J. V. (2000) 'Historical lessons in the Melian episode', *Transations and Proceedings of the American Philological Society* 130: 119–48.

Mourant, J. (1970) 'The emergence of a Christian philosophy in the dialogues of Augustine', *Augustinian Studies* 1: 69–88.

Müri, W. (1944) 'Das Wort Dialektik bei Platon', *Museum Helveticum* 1: 152–68.

Murray, O. (1983) 'The Greek symposium in history', in Gabba (ed.).

(1985) 'Symposium and genre in the poetry of Horace', *Journal of Roman Studies* 75: 39–50.

ed. (1990a) *Sympotica: A Symposium on the Symposium*. Oxford.

(1990b) 'Sympotic History' in Murray (ed.).

(2003) 'Sympotica – twenty years on', *Pallas* 61: 13–21.

Murray, O. and Tecuşan, M. eds. (1995) *In Vino Veritas*. London.

Musurillo, H. ed. (1958) *St Methodius, The Symposium: A Treatise on Chastity*, Ancient Christian Writers 27. Westminster, Md.

ed. (1963) *Méthode d'Olympe: Le Banquet*. Sources Chrétiennes 95. Paris.

Nehamas, A. (1999) *Virtues of Authenticity*. Princeton.

Nemoy, L. (1969) *Karaite Anthology, Excerpts from the Early Literature*, Yale Judaica Series 7. New Haven.

Neusner, J. (1995) *The Documentary Foundation of Rabbinic Culture: Mopping up After Debates with Gerald L. Bruns, S. J. D. Cohen, Arnold Maria Goldberg, Susan Handelman, Christine Hayes, James Kugel, Peter Schaefer, Eliezer Segal, E. P. Sanders, and Lawrence H. Schiffman*. Atlanta.

Nielsen, I. and Nielsen, H. eds. (1998) *Meals in a Social Context: Aspects of the Communal Meal in the Hellenistic and Roman World*. Aarhus.

Nightingale, A. W. (1993) 'The folly of praise: Plato's critique of encomiastic discourse in the *Lysis* and *Symposium*', *Classical Quarterly* 43: 112–30.

(1995) *Genres in Dialogue: Plato and the Construct of Philosophy*. Cambridge.

Noy, D. (1998) 'The sixth hour is the mealtime for scholars: Jewish meals in the Roman world', in Nielsen and Nielsen (eds.).

Nuffelen, P. van and Mitchell, S. eds. (forthcoming) Monotheism between Pagans and Christians in Late Antiquity. Amsterdam.

Ober, J. (1989) *Mass and Elite in Democratic Athens: Rhetoric, Ideology and the Power of the People*. Princeton.

(1998) *Political Dissent in Democratic Athens: Intellectual Critics of Popular Rule*. Princeton.

Ober, J. and Hedrick, C. eds. (1996) *Dēmokratia: A Conversation on Democracies, Ancient and Modern*. Princeton.

O'Daly, G. (1999) *Augustine's City of God: A Reader's Guide*. Oxford.

O'Donnell, J. J. (1992) *Augustine: Confessions*. Oxford.

(2005) *Augustine: Sinner and Saint*. London.

Okoye, J. (1995) *Speech in Ben Sira with Special Reference to 5.9–6.1*. Frankfurt am Main.

O'Meara, J. J. (1951) 'The historicity of the early dialogues of Saint Augustine', *Vigiliae Christianae* 5: 150–78.

Orfanos, C. and Carrière, J.-C. eds. (2003) *Symposium. Banquet et représentations en Grèce et à Rome, Pallas* 61.

Origen (1973) *On First Principles*, trans. and introd. G. W. Butterworth, with an introduction by Henri de Lubac. Gloucester, Mass.

Orwin, C. (1994) *The Humanity of Thucydides*. Princeton.

Osteen, M. ed. (2002) *The Question of the Gift: Essays Across Disciplines*. London.

O'Sullivan, N. (1992) *Alcidamas, Aristophanes and the Beginnings of Greek Stylistic Theory*. Stuttgart.

Owen, G. E. ed. (1968) *Aristotle on Dialectic: The Topics*. Oxford.

Patterson, L. G. (1993) 'Methodius' millenarianism', *Studia Patristica* 24: 306–15.
   (1997) *Methodius of Olympus: Divine Sovereignty, Human Freedom, and Life in Christ*. Washington, D.C.

Pease, A. S. (1926) 'Things without honor', *Classical Philosophy* 21: 27–42.
   ed. (1955) *M. Tulli Ciceronis De natura deorum libri tres*. Cambridge, Mass.

Pellizer, E. (1990) 'Outlines of a morphology of sympotic entertainment', in Murray (ed.).

Perler, O. (1969) *Les Voyages de Saint Augustin*. Paris.

Perrin, M. Y. (1992) '"Ad Implendum caritatis ministerium". La place des couriers dans la correspondance de Paulin de Nole', *Mélange d'école française de Rome* 104: 1025–68.

Pollmann, K. ed. (2000) *Double Standards in the Ancient and Medieval World*. Göttingen.

Pollmann, K. and Vessey, M. eds. (2005) *Augustine and the Disciplines*. Oxford.

Popper, K. (1945) *The Open Society and Its Enemies*, 2 vols. London.

Poster, C. (1998) 'The idea(s) or order of platonic dialogues and their hermeneutical consequences', *Phoenix* 52: 282–98.

Powell, J. G. F ed. (1995) *Cicero the Philosopher*. Oxford.

Preston, R. (2001) 'Roman questions, Greek answers: Plutarch and the construction of identity', in Goldhill (ed.).

Price, J. J. (2001) *Thucydides and Internal War*. Cambridge.

Pricoco, S. and Simonetti, M. (2006) *Storie di santi e diavoli: Dialoghi*, 2 vols. Milan.

Prince, M. (1996) *Philosophical Dialogue in the British Enlightenment*. Cambridge.

Purcell, N. (1995) 'Literate games: Roman urban society and the game of *alea*', *Past and Present* 147: 3–37.

Quesnel, M., Blanchard, Y-M., and Tassin, C. eds. (1999) *Nourriture et repas dans les milieux juifs et chrétiens de l'antiquité. Mélanges offerts au Professeur Charles Perrot*, Paris.

Rabinovitz, Z. M. (1979) *Ginze Midrash: The Oldest Forms of Rabbinic Midrashim According to Genizah Manuscripts*. Tel Aviv.

Race, W. H. (1987) 'Pindaric encomium and Isocrates' *Evagoras*', *Transactions and Proceedings of the American Philological Society* 117: 131–55.

Rajak, T. (1999) 'Talking at Trypho: Christian apologetic as anti-Judaism in Justin's *Dialogue with Trypho the Jew*', in Edwards, Goodman and Price (eds.).

Ramage, E. S. (1961) 'An early trace of Socratic dialogue', *American Journal of Philology* 82: 418–24.

Rapp, C. (2005) *Holy Bishops in Late Antiquity: The Nature of Christian Leadership in an Age of Transition*. Berkeley and Los Angeles.

Rawson, E. (1975) *Cicero: A Portrait*. London.

Rebillard, E. (1998) 'Augustin et le rituel épistolaire de l'élite sociale et culturelle de son temps: Élements pour une analyse processuelle des relations de l'évêque et de la cité dans l'antiquité tardive' in Rebillard and Sotinel (eds.).

Rebillard, E, and Sotinel, C. eds. (1998) *L'Évêque dans la cité du IVe au Ve siècle: Image et autorité*. Rome.

von Reden, S., and Goldhill, S. (1998) 'Plato and the performance of dialogue', in Goldhill and Osborne (eds.).

Rees, R. ed. (2004) *Romane memento: Vergil in the Fourth Century*. London.

Reif, S. (1997) 'The discovery of the Cambridge Genizah fragments of Ben Sira: Scholars and texts', in Beentjes (ed.).

Reinhardt, T. (2000) 'Rhetoric in the Fourth Academy', *Classical Quarterly* 50: 531–47.

Reinhardt, T., ed. (2003) *Tullius Cicero: Topica*. Oxford.

Reinink, G. J. and Vanstiphout, H. L. J. eds. (1991) *Dispute Poems and Dialogues in the Ancient and Medieval Near East: Forms and Types of Literary Debates in Semitic and Related Sources*. Leuven.

Reiterer, F. V. (1997) 'Review of recent research on the Book of Ben Sira (1980–1996)', in Beentjes (ed.).

Relihan, J. (1992) 'Rethinking the history of the literary symposium', *Illinois Classical Studies* 17: 213–44.

   (1993) *Ancient Menippean Satire*. Baltimore.

Reynolds, S. (1996) *Medieval Reading: Grammar, Rhetoric and the Classical Text*, Cambridge Studies in Medieval Literature 27. Cambridge.

Richard, M. and Munitiz, J. A. eds. (2006) *Anastasii Sinaitae Quaestiones et responsiones*, Corpus Christianorum Series Graeca 59. Leuven.

Ridings, D. (1995) *The Attic Moses: The Dependency Theme in some Early Christian Writers*. Göteborg.

Roberts, M. (1989) *The Jeweled Style: Poetry and Poetics in Late Antiquity*. Ithaca.

Roller, M. (2006) *Dining Posture in Ancient Rome: Bodies, Values, and Status*. Princeton.

Romeri, L. (2002) *Philosophes entre mets et mots: Plutarque, Lucien et Athénée autour de la table de Platon*. Grenoble.

Rosen, R. (2003) 'The death of Thersites and the sympotic performance of Iambic mockery', in Orfanos and Carrière (eds.).

Rossetti, L. (1975) 'Alla ricerca dei logoi Sokratikoi perduti (II)', *Rivista di Studi Classici* 23: 87–99.

   (1997) 'Arguing and suggesting within a Platonic dialogue: towards a typology', in Hart and Tejera (eds.).

   (2005) 'Logoi Sokratikoi: Le contexte littéraire dans lequel Platon a écrit', in Fattal (ed.).

Rousseau, P. (1998) '"The preacher's audience": a more optimistic view', in Hillard, Kearsley, Nixon and Nobbs (eds.).

Rowe, C. J. (1993) *Plato: Phaedo*. Cambridge.

Rubenstein, J. L. (2002) 'The thematization of dialectics in *Bavli Aggada*', *Journal of Jewish Studies* 53.2: 1–14.

Rubenstein, J. L. ed. (2005) *Creation and Composition: The Contribution of the Bavli Redactors (Stammaim) to the Aggada*. Tübingen.

Russell, D. A. and Wilson, N. G. (1981) *Menander Rhetor*. Oxford.

Rutherford, R. B. (1995) *The Art of Plato*. London.

Ryle, G. (1968) 'Dialectic in the Academy', in Owen (ed.).
  (1979) *On Thinking*, ed. K. Kolenda. Oxford.

Rynearson, N. (2006) 'Socrates' Erotic Expertise: From Socrates' erôtikê tekhnê to Plato's Textual Seduction', PhD dissertation, Princeton University.

Sahlins, M. (1972) *Stone Age Economics*. New York.

Sanders, J. T. (1983) *Ben Sira and Demotic Wisdom*. Chico, Calif.

Sayre, K. M. (1995) *Plato's Literary Garden*. Notre Dame and London.

Schäfer, A. (1997) *Unterhaltung beim griechischen Symposion: Darbietungen, Spiele und Wettekämpfe von homerischer bis in spätklassische Zeit*. Mainz.

Schäfer, P. ed. (1998) *The Talmud Yerushalmi and Graeco-Roman Culture*, vol. I. Texts and Studies in Ancient Judaism 71. Tübingen.

Schäfer, P. and Hezser, C. eds. (2000) *The Talmud Yerushalmi and Graeco-Roman Culture*, vol. II. Texts and Studies in Ancient Judaism 79. Tübingen.

Schmitt-Pantel, P. (1992) *La cité au banquet. Histoire des repas publics dans les cités grecques*. Paris.

Schmitz, T. (1997) *Bildung und Macht. Zur sozialen und politischen Funktion der zweiten Sophistik in der griechischen Welt der Kaiserzeit*. Munich.

Schofield, M. (1986) 'Cicero for and against divination', *Journal of Roman Studies* 76: 47–65.

Schremer, A. (2005) 'Stammaitic Historiography', in Rubenstein (ed.).

Schubert, H. von (1903) *Der sogennante Praedestinatus: Ein Beitrag zur Geschichte des Pelagianismus*. Leipzig.

Schwartz, S. (2001) *Imperialism and Jewish Society 200 BCE to 640 CE*. Princeton.
  (2005) 'A God of reciprocity: Torah and social relations in an ancient Mediterranean society', in Aubert and Varhelyi (eds.).

Scott, D. (1999) 'Plato's pessimism and moral education', *Oxford Studies in Ancient Philosophy* 17: 15–36.

Sedley, D. N. (1995) 'The dramatis personae of Plato's *Phaedo*', in *Philosophical Dialogues: Plato, Hume, Wittgenstein. Proceedings of the British Academy* 85: 3–26.
  (2003) *Plato's Cratylus*. Cambridge.

Seeskin, K. (1987) *Dialogue and Discovery*. Albany, N.Y.

Segal, M. Z. (1953) *Sefer Ben Sira Ha-Shalem*, Jerusalem. [Reprinted in 1972.]

Sharrock, A. and Morales, H. eds. (2000) *Intratextuality: Greek and Roman Textual Traditions*. Oxford.

Sheppard, A. and Karamanolis, G. eds. (2007) *Studies in Porphyry*, BICS Supplement.

Simmel, G. (1949) 'The sociology of sociability', *American Journal of Sociology* 55: 254–61.

Simon, M. (1964) *Verus Israel*, 2nd ed. Paris. [English trans.: Oxford, 1986].

Slater, W. J. (1982) 'Aristophanes of Byzantium and problem-solving in the Museum', *Classical Quarterly* 32: 336–49.

ed. (1991) *Dining in a Classical Context*: Ann Arbor.

Smend, R. (1906) *Die Weisheit des Jesus Sirach, hebraeisch und deutsch*. Berlin.

Smith, D. (2003) *From Symposium to Eucharist: The Banquet in the Early Christian World*. Minneapolis.

Smith, N. D. (1998) *Plato: Critical Assessments*. London.

Smith, P. R. (1995) '"A self-indulgent misuse of leisure and writing"? How not to write philosophy: did Cicero get it right?', in Powell (ed.).

Snell, B. (1971) *Leben und Meinungen der Sieben Weisen*, 4th edn. Berlin.

Sokoloff, M. (2002) *A Dictionary of Jewish Babylonian Aramaic of the Talmudic and Geonic Periods*. Baltimore.

Sommerstein, A. ed. (1994) *Religion and Superstition in Latin Literature*. Bari.

Sorabji, R. ed. (1987) *Philoponus and the Rejection of Aristotelian Science*. London.

Sorabji, R. ed. (1990) *Aristotle Transformed: The Ancient Commentators and their Influence*. London.

Steel, C. (2005) *Reading Cicero: Genre and Performance in Late Republican Rome*. London.

Stegemann, E. W. and Stegemann, W. (1999) *The Jesus Movement: A Social History of its First Century*, trans. O. C. Dean. Minneapolis. [First published in German in 1995.]

Stein, S. (1957) 'The influence of symposia literature on the literary form of the *Pesah Haggadah*', *Journal of Jewish Studies* 8: 13–44.

Stern, D. (1996) *Midrash and Theory: Ancient Jewish Exegesis and Contemporary Literary Studies. Rethinking Theory*. Evanston.

Stock, B. (1996) *Augustine and the Reader: Meditation, Self-Knowledge, and the Ethics of Interpretation*. Cambridge, Mass.

Stowers, S. K. (1984) 'Social status, public speaking and private teaching: The circumstances of Paul's preaching activity', *Novum Testamentum* 26: 59–82.

(1986) *Letter Writing in Greco-Roman Antiquity*. Philadelphia.

Suchier, W. (1910) *L'Enfant sage: Das Gespräch des Kaisers Hadrian mit dem klugen Kinde Epitus*. Dresden.

Swain, S. (1996) *Hellenism and Empire: Language, Classicism, and Power in the Greek World AD 50–250*. Oxford.

Swain, S. ed. (2000) *Dio Chrysostom: Politics, Letters, and Philosophy*. Oxford.

Szlezák, T. (1999) *Reading Plato*. London.

Tarver, T. (1994) 'Varro, Caesar and the Roman calendar', in Sommerstein (ed.)

Teixeira, E. (1992) 'Remarques sur l'esprit scientifique de Plutarque d'après quelques passages des *Propos de Table*', in I. Gallo (ed.) *Plutarco e le scienze*. Genoa.

Thomas, R. (2000) *Herodotus in Context*. Cambridge.

Thümmel, G. (1992) *Die Frühgeschichte der ostkirchlichen Bilderlehre: Texte und Untersuchungen zur Zeit vor dem Bilderstreit*. Berlin.

Tilley, M. A. (1997a) 'Sustaining Donatist self-identity: from the Church of the Martyrs to the Collecta of the Desert', *Journal of Early Christian Studies* 5.1: 21–35.

(1997b) *The Bible in Christian North Africa: The Donatist World*. Minneapolis.

Todd, F. A. (1943) 'Some *cucurbitaceae* in Latin literature', *Classical Quarterly* 37: 101–11.

Too, Y. L. (1995) *The Rhetoric of Identity in Isocrates*. Cambridge.

(2000) 'The walking library: the performance of cultural memories', in Braund and Wilkins (eds.).

ed. (2001) *Education in Greek and Roman Antiquity*. Leiden.

Tornau, C. (2006) *Zwischen Rhetorik und Philosophie: Augustins Argumentationstechnik in* De Civitate Dei *und ihr bildungsgeschichtlicher Hintergrund*. Berlin.

Trapp, M. (2000) 'Plato in Dio', in Swain (ed.).

Trout, D. E. (1988) 'Augustine at Cassiciacum: *otium honestum* and the social dimensions of conversion', *Vigiliae Christianae* 42: 132–46.

Ullrich, F. (1908–9) *Entstehung und Entwicklung der Litteraturgattung des Symposion*, 2 vols. Würzburg.

Unterseher, L. A. (2002) 'The mark of Cain and the Jews: Augustine's theology of Judaism', *Augustinian Studies* 33.1: 99–121.

Urbaincyzk, T. (2002) *Theodoret of Cyrus: The Bishop and the Holy Man*. Ann Arbor, Mich.

Usener, H. ed. (1887) *Epicurea*. Leipzig.

Uytfanghe, M. van (1986) 'Scepticisme doctrinal au seuil du Moyen Age? : les objections du diacre Pierre dans les Dialogues de Grégoire le Grand', in Fontaine, Gillet and Pellistrandi (eds.).

Vaggione, R. P. (2000) *Eunomius of Cyzicus and the Nicene Revolution*. Oxford.

Vander Waerdt, P. ed. (1994) *The Socratic Movement*. Ithaca.

Veer, A. de (1968) *Oeuvres de Saint Augustin Traites Anti-Donatistes*, vol. IV. Paris.

Vernant, J.-P. and Vidal-Naquet, P. (1988) *Myth and Tragedy in Ancient Greece*, trans. J. Lloyd. Brighton.

Vessey, M., Pollmann, K. and Fitzgerald, A. eds. (1999) *History, Apocalypse and the Secular Imagination: New Essays on Augustine's City of God*. Bowling Green, Ohio.

Veyne, P. (1997) *The Roman Empire*. Cambridge, Mass.

Vlastos, G. (1991) *Socrates, Ironist and Moral Philosopher*. Ithaca.

Voss, B. (1970) *Der Dialog in der frühchristlichen Literatur*. Munich.

Walker, J. T. (2006) *The Legend of Mar Qardagh: Narrative and Christian Heroism in Late Antique Iraq*. Berkeley.

Wardy, R. (1996) *The Birth of Rhetoric: Gorgias, Plato and their Successors*. London and New York.

Wassermann, F. M. (1947) 'The Melian dialogue', *Transactions and Proceedings of the American Philological Society* 78: 18–36.

Watts, E. (2006) *City and School in Late Antique Athens and Alexandria*. Berkeley.

White, C. (1992) *Early Christian Friendship in the Fourth Century*. Cambridge.

White, J. L. (1986) *Light From Ancient Letters*. Minneapolis.

White, L. M. (1998) 'Regulating fellowship in the communal meal: Early Jewish and Christian evidence', in Nielsen and Nielsen (eds.).

Whitmarsh, T. (1999) 'Greek and Roman in dialogue: The pseudo-Lucianic Nero', *Journal of Hellenic Studies* 119: 142–60.

(2000) 'The politics and poetics of parasitism: Athenaeus on parasites and flatterers', in Braund and Wilkins (eds.).

(2004) *Ancient Greek Literature.* London.

(2006) 'True Histories: Lucian, Bakhtin, and the pragmatics of reception', in Martindale and Thomas (eds.).

Wickham, L. (2002) 'Pelagianism in the East' in R. Williams (ed.).

Wilamowitz-Moellendorff, U. von (1920) *Platon*, 2 vols. Berlin.

Wildberg, C. (2005) 'Philosophy in the age of Justinian', in Maas (ed.).

Wilken, R. (1986) *The Christians as the Romans Saw Them.* New Haven.

Wilkins, J. ed. (forthcoming) *Athenaeus and his Philosophers at Dinner.* Exeter.

Williams, B. (2002) *Truth and Truthfulness: An Essay in Genealogy.* Princeton and Oxford.

Williams, H. (2007) 'Taming the muse: Monastic discipline and Christian poetry in Hermann of Reichenau's *On the Eight Principal Vices*', in Cooper and Gregory, (eds.).

Williams, R. ed (2002) *The Making of Orthodoxy: Essays in Honour of Henry Chadwick.* Cambridge.

Wilson, N. G. (1970) 'Indications of speaker in Greek dialogue texts', *Classical Quarterly* 20: 305.

Witt, R. E. (1937) *Albinus and the History of Middle Platonism.* Cambridge.

Wollheim, R. ed. (1963) *Hume on Religion.* London and Glasgow.

Wolska-Conus, W. (1989) 'Stéphanos d'Athènes et Stéphanos d'Alexandrie: essai d'identification', *Revue des études byzantines* 47: 5–89.

Woods, M. C. (2001) 'Boys will be women: Musings on classroom nostalgia and the Chaucerian audience(s)', in Yeager and Morse (eds.).

Wright, B. (1989) *No Small Difference: Sirach's Relation to its Hebrew Parent Text.* Atlanta.

Wright, W. C. F. (1998) *Philostratus and Eunapius: The Lives of the Sophists.* Text with translation. Cambridge, Mass.

Yeager, R. F. and Morse, C. C. eds. (2001) *Speaking Images: Essays in Honor of V. A. Kolve.* Asheville, N.C.

Yunis, H. (1998) 'The constraints of democracy and the rise of rhetoric', in Boedeker and Raaflaub (eds.).

ed. (2005) *Written Texts and the Rise of Literate Culture in Ancient Greece.* Cambridge.

Zeitlin, F. I., Halperin, D. and Winkler, J. J. eds. (1991) *Before Sexuality: The Construction of Erotic Experience in the Greek World.* Princeton.

Zetzel, J. ed. (1995) *Cicero: De Re Publica. Selections.* Cambridge.

ed. (1999) *Cicero: On the Commonwealth and On the Laws.* Cambridge.

Ziegler, J. (1965) *Sapientia Iesu Filii Sirach.* Göttingen.

Ziffer, I. (2005) 'From Acemhoeyuek to Megiddo: The banquet scene in the art of the Levant in the second millenium BCE', *Tel Aviv* 32: 133–67.

Zorzi, M. B. (2003) 'La reinterpretazione dell' eros platonico nel "Simposio" di Metodio d'Olimpio', *Adamantius* 9: 102–27.

Index

Academy 64, 65, 68–9, 70, 73, 76, 81–2, 121, 123, 168, 183
ad Gregoriam in palatio 175, 180–2
Adeimantus 53–5, 58, 64
Aedesius 237
Aeschines 38, 42
Agathon 53
Akiva, Rabbi 230–2, 233, 235, 238, 239
Albinus 34, 35, 36, 38, 42
Alcibiades 5, 42, 44, 95
Alexemanus 29, 33
Alker, H. 22
Alypius 120–1
Ambrose 143
Anastasius of Sinai 187–8
Anderson, B. 196
Anicii 143–7
Annas, J. 72
Anomaeans 222–3, 228
Antiphon 39, 42
Antisthenes 44
Aristeas 193
Aristocracy, Christian 161–2, 166, 175
Aristophanes 53
Aristotle 29, 33, 35, 39, 65, 68, 82, 121, 164, 174, 182, 183, 195, 196
Arnobius 175–6
Athenaeus 4, 85, 87, 88, 89, 90–1, 92–4, 98, 101, 107, 159, 207, 208
Athens 19–28, 30, 39, 151, 168, 182
Augustine 5, 7, 96–8, 118–48, 160, 168, 169, 179, 180
  Cassiacum Dialogues 160–1
  City of God 119–20, 122, 127, 129–32
  Confessions 118, 120, 122, 127, 161
  contra Academicos 118, 122–3, 160
  contra Gaudentium 137
  contra Petilium 136
  de baptismo 138–9
  de bono viduitatis 144
  de Genesi contra academicos 125

de utilitate credendi 123, 126
  epistulae 138, 145, 146
  retractiones 138, 140–1
Authorial presence 2, 24–7, 32, 64, 70–3, 74–5

Bakhtin, Mikhail 1, 8–9, 16–7, 25, 91–4
Basil of Caesarea 169, 222–3, 232–3
Becker, A. H. 231, 235–6, 239, 241
Ben Sira 194, 200–7
Berkeley, Bishop 65
Biography, as origin of dialogue 31–3
Bishop, curial 166, 167
Bishop, role of, 124, 126–7, 133–4, 146, 154
Boethius 174–89
  Consolation 179–80
Bosworth, B. 19, 24
Brown, P. 133
Bruns, G. 228
Burnyeat, M. 57
Busiris 43

Callicles 51, 53
Cameron, Alan 112
Cameron, Averil 187
Carneades 69
Celsus 157, 167, 234
Chadwick, H. 177, 178
Character, in dialogue 42–3, 47–8
Chariton 6
Chartier, R. 170
Chreiai 5–6
Christ *see* Jesus
Christianity 5–8, 45–6, 73, 94–113, 117–89, 219–20, 222–3, 228–9, 232–3, 237
Chrysanthius 237
Cicero 5, 63–84, 108, 118, 120, 121, 123, 129–32, 155, 169–70, 179
  Academica 81–2
  de amicitia 77

263

Cicero (cont.)
  de diuinatione 63, 71, 77, 79–80, 81, 82
  de fato 66, 76, 77, 83
  de finibus 63, 66, 69, 70–4, 77, 78, 79,
    82, 83
  de legibus 65, 66, 76
  de natura deorum 63, 65, 67, 72–3, 77, 79, 82, 123
  de oratore 68, 70, 75, 76, 77, 80
  de republica 75, 76, 78
  de senectute 77
  epistulae ad Atticum 75, 76–7, 80–1
  epistulae ad familiares 76
  Tusculans 68, 69, 76, 77, 78, 79, 81, 82–3
Clark, F. 184
Clement 99–102
Cohen, S. 241
Conversion 48–51
Cooper, K. 176
Cotta 72–3, 80
Crane, G. 26–7
Cresconius 136–7
Crito 32
Cyprian 179, 181

Dadiso of Bet Qatraye 233
Dal Santo, M. 184
Demetrias 143–6
Demetrius of Phalerum 32
Democracy 1, 23, 24, 28
Demosthenes 39
Dewald, C. 24–5, 26
Dialectic 35, 47–8, 54–5, 117–18
Dialegesthai 35–9
Dialogic/Dialogism 9, 17–18, 19, 24–7, 91,
    104–6, 117–18, 152, 184
Dialogos 35–9
Dialogue,
  Academic 63, 71
  Christian 85–7, 94–8, 112–13, 117–34, 135–55,
    156–66, 167, 174, 184–9
  dictionary definition of, 15–16, 17, 18
  form of 23, 24–7, 45, 87–90, 93, 128,
    152, 171
  interfaith 128
  internal 6, 55–8
  Jewish-Christian 158
  as literary genre 2–8, 16, 31, 39–44, 45–6,
    67, 70, 87–90, 153, 171
  origins of form 29–31
  Platonic 3, 4, 33, 37, 46–59, 95, 123, 152–3
  Socratic 29–44, 46–59, 66, 73, 91–2
  Sympotic 4, 5, 85–113, 153–4, 208
Dice game, Pompeian 163–4
Dionysius of Halicarnasus 24, 25–6
Disputation 42, 119, 131

Donatists 126, 127, 133, 134, 135–41, 147
Dramatic elements of dialogue 22, 25–6, 64–9,
    75, 173

Eliezer ben Jacob, Rabbi 211–13, 215
Elite, Greco-Roman 78, 87, 140, 142, 154,
    155, 170
Elman, Y. 237
Epictetus 100
Epicureanism 66, 71, 123
Euclides 38
Eunomius 228
Eusebius 237
Eustratius of Constantinople 184
Evagrius 230, 231

Festival culture 88–9
Fictionality 32, 44, 91
Fredriksen, P. 6

Gaiser, K. 39
Galen 100
Gaudentius 137
Glaucon 53–5, 58, 63
Gluttony 100–2
Gobar, S. 182–3
Goldhill, S. 27
Gorgias 37–8, 43, 221–2
Gregorius 174–5, 182–9
Gregory Nazianzus 232

Habermas, J. 170
Halivini, D. 226
Halperin, D. 96
Harnack, A. von 184
Harris, W. 156
Hayes, C. 218
Hellenisation 195
Heraclitus 56
Hippocrates 52
Hirzel, R. 147
Hitler, A. 9
Hobbes, T. 196
Holquist, M. 17
Homer 34, 100
Homoiousians 222–3
Hopkins, K. 86, 156
Hoshayya, Rabbi 211–13, 216
Hume, D. 63, 64–6, 74
hupakouein 19–23

Identity, Hellenic 87–9
Interference, and dialogue 15–19, 28
Interlocutors 21–2, 51–3, 53–5, 67, 82–3,
    101, 128–9

isegoria 23, 27
Islam 10, 188, 189
Isocrates 41, 43

Jacob, C. 88
Jerome 123–4, 139, 141, 144–5, 159
Jesus 117–18, 121–2, 137, 183
John Cassian 175
John Chrysostom 143
Judaism 10, 218–19
Julian 237–8
Justin Martyr 6, 86, 158
Justinian 182–3, 187

Kalmin, R. 240
Kaster, R. 107–8, 110
Kovelman, A. 224–6, 238
Kraemer, D. 223–4

Lactantius 113
Laidlaw, J. 198
Laird, A. 26
Letters, Christian 139–41, 142–3, 169–70
Liebeschutz, W. 22
Lim, R. 139, 176, 219–20, 222–4, 228–9,
    232, 234, 235, 238
Listening 19–23
Literacy 156–7
Lloyd, G. E. R. 2–3
Logos 39–44, 99, 100, 102
Lucian 87–8, 96, 156, 212
Lucius 71–2
Luke 113, 117
Lysias 32, 39, 40, 42, 49

MacCormack, S. 94
MacKendrick, P. 67
Macrobius 4, 94–5, 107–13, 155
Manichaeans 125, 126, 135, 161, 162, 219, 220
Marcellinus 128
Mark the Hermit 6–7
Maximus the Confessor 178
Maximus of Ephesus 237–8
Melian Dialogue 2, 15, 18, 19–28
Menander 5
Mendels, D. 176–7
Methodius 5, 85–6, 98, 102–6, 112–13, 158–9
Minucius Felix 73
Mishnah 207, 209, 226
Momigliano, A. 32
Monastic rules 175
Morrison, J. 22
Moses 230–1, 238
Musonius Rufus 156
Musurillo, H. 103, 104

Neusner, J. 226
New Testament 100, 118
Nightingale, A. 40

Ober, Josiah 3
Octavius 73–4
O'Donnell, J. 133
Origen 157, 167, 227
Otium 118–19, 155, 161

Paideia 158, 168, 169, 170, 171
Parmenides 221–2
Paul 157
Paulinus of Nola 133, 143, 144, 147
Pelagius, Pelagians 141–8, 162, 180
Pericles 21, 40, 42, 44, 196
Peter, Deacon 185–6
Petilian 136–7
Phaedo 38
Philo 178, 193, 199
Philosophy, as motive for dialogue 30–3, 46–7,
    64, 67–9, 120, 153, 179–80
Photius 182
Pinianus 142
Piso 71–2
Plato 3, 4, 9, 16, 23, 27, 30, 33, 34, 36, 39, 40,
    46–59, 63, 76, 78, 93, 100, 105, 112, 123, 124,
    151, 152, 168, 182, 207, 222
    Apology 34, 35, 42, 43, 46
    Cratylus 47–8
    Gorgias 51, 53, 55, 58, 69
    Menexenus 40
    Phaedo 73
    Phaedrus 49–51
    Philebus 57, 58
    Protagoras 36–7, 51–2, 53, 55, 58, 69
    Republic 53–5, 58, 63
    Symposium 4, 53, 85, 96, 102, 159, 180
    Theatetus 55–8
Platonism 122–3
Playfulness 90, 97, 154, 164
Pleasure 66, 101, 154
Pliny 208
Plotinus 124, 133, 179, 183
Plutarch 85, 87, 88, 89, 90, 96, 97, 100, 106, 107,
    108, 109–11, 207, 208
Polycrates 32, 33
Popper, K. 9
Porphyry 124, 131, 133, 183
Prefaces 76–9
Prince, M. 95, 96
Protagoras 52, 53, 56
Proverbs 202
Prudentius 6, 175
Pseudo-Athanasius 187–8

Pseudo-Dionysius the Areopagite 178, 231, 232
Psychomachia 6, 175, 180

Qara'ites 234–5

Reader engagement 50, 89–90, 142–3
Rebillard, E. 144
Recognitions, Pseudo-Clementine 176
Reden, S. von 27
Roberts, M. 181
Rome, as model 129–30
Roman religion 130–2
Romanos the Melodist 188
Rosenthal, E. S. 237
Rossetti, L. 30

Safra, Rabbi 240–1
Sahlins, M. 199
Scipio 78
Segal, M. Z. 205
Self-presentation 7–80
    See also authorial presence
Semonides 100
Seneca 100, 179, 195
Sermo 118
sermo humilis 166–8
Shaked, S. 237
Shimon ben Shetah 213–15
Simmel, G. 154–5
Socrates 3, 7, 9, 29–44, 47–8, 53, 57, 63, 151, 152,
    168, 222
Song 162–3
Sophists 37–8
Steel, C. 67, 79
Stephen of Sadaili 231
Stern, D. 229
Stoicism 65, 69, 71, 72, 73, 82, 179, 181
Sydenham, F. 95
Symposium as institution 32–3, 85–7, 90, 153–5,
    193–4, 199–200
Szlezák, T. 96

Talmud, Babylonian 205, 207, 210,
    217–41
Talmud, Palestinian 8, 194, 207–16, 217–18,
    222, 223
Teaching 48–51, 117–18, 124
Tertullian 179, 181
Theodectes 32
Theodoret 165–6
Thrasymachus 53, 56, 63
Tosefta 208, 209, 210
Tragedy 3
Thucydides 2, 15, 18, 22, 23, 24, 25, 196

Urbaincyzk, T. 166
Uytfanghe, M. van 184

Vaggione, R. 220, 234
Vander Waerdt, P. 29–30
Varro 75, 81, 129–32
Veyne, P. 239

Yehudah, Rabbi 230

Vernant, J.-P. 3
Vidal-Naquet, P. 3
Virgil 94, 120, 123, 125, 129
Voices 23, 26, 73, 91, 92, 101, 102,
    104, 107

Wardy, R. 221
Wasserman, F. 21, 22
Weberian analysis 151
Whitmarsh, T. 18
Wilamowitz, U. 42
Wollheim, R. 64–5

Xenophon 29, 30, 31–2, 36, 37, 42, 43, 85,
    89, 152, 207

Zacharias, Pope 188
Zeno 41